Allied Encounters

WORLD WAR II: THE GLOBAL, HUMAN, AND ETHICAL DIMENSION
G. Kurt Piehler, series editor

Allied Encounters

The Gendered Redemption of World War II Italy

Marisa Escolar

Fordham University Press | New York 2019

Copyright © 2019 Fordham University Press

All rights reserved. No part of this publication may be reproduced, stored in a retrieval system, or transmitted in any form or by any means—electronic, mechanical, photocopy, recording, or any other—except for brief quotations in printed reviews, without the prior permission of the publisher.

Fordham University Press has no responsibility for the persistence or accuracy of URLs for external or third-party Internet websites referred to in this publication and does not guarantee that any content on such websites is, or will remain, accurate or appropriate.

Fordham University Press also publishes its books in a variety of electronic formats. Some content that appears in print may not be available in electronic books.

Visit us online at www.fordhampress.com.

Library of Congress Cataloging-in-Publication Data available online at https://catalog.loc.gov.

Printed in the United States of America
21 20 19   5 4 3 2 1
First edition

for Sylvia and Aaron

Contents

Preface		ix
	Introduction	1
1	**Redeeming Destination Italy:** *A Guide to the Occupation of Enemy Territory*	17
2	**"Liberated" Rome beyond Redemption:** Roberto Rossellini's *Paisà* and Alfred Hayes's *All Thy Conquests* and *The Girl on the Via Flaminia*	42
3	**Happily Ever after Redemption:** Luciana Peverelli's "True" Romance Novels of Occupied Rome	66
4	**A Queer Redemption:** John Horne Burns's *The Gallery*	91
5	**Sleights of Hand, Black Skin, and the Redemption of Curzio Malaparte's *La pelle***	111
6	**The Redemption of Saint Paul:** Norman Lewis's *Naples '44*	132
	Epilogue	153
Acknowledgments		163
Notes		167
Works Cited		213
Index		231

Preface

In September 2001, my newfound passion for Italian brought me two books, an encounter that would determine my choice to become an Italianist: Dante Alighieri's *Divina Commedia* and Curzio Malaparte's *La pelle* (*The Skin*). Medieval and modern, poetry and prose, canonical and little known, these texts spoke to me with a power amplified by the tragedy that had just hit my city. Images of smoldering towers conjured infernal references in the press, but what reached me from across seven centuries was Dante's testimonial drive. His commitment to tell the souls' stories resonated deeply, as I stutter-stepped between makeshift memorials on daily walks to the subway.

As hellish as anything Dante had imagined, Malaparte's Allied-occupied Italy affected me viscerally. In narrating the encounter of the victorious Americans and the defeated Italians, populations that had long mythologized one another, Malaparte marshals the Western literary tradition to render the violence of their reciprocal myths crashing into devastating reality. As the long-awaited liberators transformed into occupiers, *La pelle* created an uncanny echo of the rhetoric we began to hear on the news, in Afghanistan and Iraq. Positioning the Allied encounter within a cultural genealogy—Virgil, Dante, Boccaccio, Tasso—it also made a case for the power of literature as a site through which to explore contemporary struggles.

Caught by the narrator's provocation that the horrors he witnessed in Allied-occupied Italy were beyond belief, I sought other cultural representations to flesh out Malaparte's *Skin*: in Italian, Roberto Rossellini's film *Paisà* (1946; *Paisan*), Luciana Peverelli's romance novels *La lunga notte* (1944; *The Long Night*) and *Sposare lo straniero* (1946; *Marry the Foreigner*), and Maria Luisa D'Aquino's diary *Quel giorno trent'anni fa* (1975; *That Day Thirty Years Ago*); in English, the Allied military guidebooks for invasion and occupation (1943–87); Alfred Hayes's novels *All Thy Conquests* (1946) and *The Girl on the Via Flaminia* (1949), John Horne Burns's novel *The Gallery* (1947), and Norman Lewis's diary *Naples '44* (1978). Like *La pelle*, these texts scrutinize the Allies' promise to redeem the "fallen" Italian nation. Like *La pelle*, these texts make Dante a touchstone, but ready-made analogies between war and hell are only the tip of the iceberg. Recounting bombed-out, crime-ridden cityscapes, populated by starving civilians and debauched Allies, their premise is: Italy has fallen—has she been redeemed? In asking the question as such, these texts make the feminine pronoun more than symbolic, foregrounding the sexual encounter between servicemen and civilians in their exploration of the "contact zone"[1] of Allied-occupied Italy: a fleeting love affair, a happy marriage, a simultaneous orgasm, a brutal rape, or, most emblematically, a financial transaction. From screaming throngs to melodramatic heroines to matter-of-fact sex workers, in Allied-occupied Italy the prostitute appears ubiquitous. In their representation of street prostitution, these texts evoke the historical encounter of the Allied-occupied cities of Naples and Rome; concomitantly, they belong to a Dantean tradition of feminizing the Italian body politic in order to critique "Italy who has compromised her political integrity and allowed herself to be seduced by foreign powers."[2]

Not simply a salacious backdrop, the gendered encounter becomes a key to these texts' narrative agenda, whether they claim to reflect the truth of Allied-occupied Italy, to use the historic moment as an allegory, or to position themselves at the intersection of historical event and literary invention. *Allied Encounters* traces how these cultural representations constitute the gendered redemption of World War II Italy, in this constant slippage between history and allegory, Italian whores and Italy-as-whore; but it considers just as central to understand what the paradigm has obscured. To this end, I take a lesson from the Dantean inheritance of many of these texts, as they draw on the *Comedy*'s conversion narrative structure and related rhetorical strategies. In creating the fiction of his eyewitness testimony, Dante tells the story of how the pilgrim undertakes an unbelievable but true journey that transforms him into the poet who writes it, all while making us forget that the pilgrim is the poet's creation. Leading us through Allied-occupied Italy, we have no shortage of Dantes who insist on the veracity of their visions, as they use gendered, sexualized and—as is less often recognized—racialized figures to tell us whether the encounter was a love affair, a rape, a marriage, a financial transaction, or some combination thereof. Instead of reading the texts according to their self-imposed parameters, by emphasizing their formal dimensions—generally overlooked in favor of their harrowing content—I consider how they manipulate generic expectations on their way to affirming their authority to represent Allied-occupied Italy, whether they assert realist or allegorical intent. In this, my reading is informed by my first Dantean encounter and the example of Teodolinda Barolini, who argues that by "standing resolutely outside of the fiction's mirror games, we can begin to examine the formal structures that manipulate the reader so successfully that even now we are blinded, prevented by the text's fulfillment of its self-imposed goals from fully appreciating its achievements as artifact."[3]

Working at the intersection of historical context and literary tradition, *Allied Encounters* examines the historical and rhetorical figures used to flesh out redemption in order to ask: What effects does the gendering produce, and who or what does it exclude and why? In this truly global encounter, how does the racialization of certain groups reinforce or trouble this gendered, sexualized narrative? Asking these questions about individual texts and the larger corpus I have assembled, I also interrogate these dynamics within their transatlantic reception by literary and film scholars, historians, cultural critics, and others. Thus, I trace the ways in which readers across disciplines and national traditions reinforce these mirror games, ratifying selective interpretations of an already narrow canon, a sign of how "academic criticism conditions the very norms of 'legibility.'"[4] In response, I ask: Where is textual authority located, and why do we collectively believe some (parts of) texts at the expense of others? By reading these texts in dialogue with one another, with the literary tradition they evoke and the historical moment they represent, *Allied Encounters* seeks to redress these blind spots and, in the process, change our understanding of the Allied-Italian encounter and the rich cultural production it inspired.

Introduction

World War II Italy eludes easy definition. After fighting on the side of the Axis for over three years, the birthplace of European fascism experienced a series of watershed events whose political and cultural legacy is still being debated.[1] On July 10, 1943, "Operation Husky" brought Anglo-American troops to Sicily's shores, making Italy the site of the Allies' first European occupation. In Sicily, the Allies were unquestionably occupiers; the name Allied Military Government of Occupied Territory spells out as much. Yet Italy's status started shifting after Mussolini was deposed on July 25, a shift that accelerated following the unconditional surrender to the Allies with the September 8 armistice.[2] In response to this perceived betrayal, the German army began occupying the territory of its onetime ally. Thus, as the Allies inched northward, many Italians in "German-enslaved" cities celebrated their arrival.[3] On October 1, 1943, Naples, the first liberated European city, went "mad with joy" at the sight of Allied troops;[4] on June 4, 1944, Rome, the first liberated European capital, cheered American General Mark Clark and his troops.[5] However, "liberation" did not bring the promised "image of finality" but only further hardship.[6] As disease, starvation, prostitution, and the black market fed into one another, relations between Allies and Italians fell into precipitous decline.

Liberation or occupation? The seminal work of David Ellwood sheds light on the difficulty of defining the Allied-Italian wartime encounter, stemming from the ambiguity of the terms: "liberation," in fact, has no formal military definition.[7] Compounding the difficulty, the British and U.S. governments were in conflict over how to handle their former enemy, respectively embracing a punitive and redemptive approach—a theoretical disagreement that had far-reaching practical consequences.[8] Susan Carruthers nuances the question by demonstrating that the United States strived toward a "'good' occupation," a concept that suggests the strategic interdependence of the blurred boundaries between liberation and occupation.[9] The *New York Times* coverage of the liberation of Rome makes that blurring plain—and unproblematic: Declaring the occupation of the city,

General Mark Clark was "cheered" as a "liberator," suggesting occupation to be a military fact, liberation, a state of mind.[10] Compounding these tensions, the Allied-Italian encounter becomes more fraught thanks to its extended timeframe, the diverse spaces in which it unfolded, and the populations it united, many of which held mythic status in the other's cultural imaginary. Set on such shaky foundations, World War II Italy can rightly be called "one of the war's more unstable, indeterminate political spaces."[11]

Working at the nexus between liberation and occupation, I read Anglo-American and Italian cultural representations of Allied-occupied Italy—military guidebooks, novels, and films—through a term related to both but reducible to neither, redemption. In the Hebrew Bible, redemption has two meanings: "to recover a man or thing that had once belonged to you and your family but had got lost" and "the deliverance of men or things from their doom."[12] This first meaning of economic restitution is carried forward in the Latin, *redimere*, to buy back, while the second becomes a central tenet of Christianity,[13] insofar as "God's sacrifice of his Son inaugurates Christian history, rescues humanity from paganism, and sets it on its path toward redemption at the end of time."[14] Religious and secular meanings intertwined, this trope is widespread in American and Italian political discourse, particularly in terms of national self-identity in relation to foreign powers. As Sam B. Girgus notes, "since the Puritans, the idea of redemption has been connected to the meaning of America in the world. Individual redemption became inescapably involved with the national mission as a beacon to the world."[15] As Franco Baldasso argues, "Every war undertaken by the Italian state since the Risorgimento was promoted as redemption from past sins and errors."[16] In the wake of the armistice, the national discourses ran headlong into one another: The United States eagerly fashioned itself as Italy's redeemer, promising to restore what had been morally lost when the birthplace of Western democracy "fell" into the sin of fascism; in Italy, a discourse of self-redemption arose alongside antifascist resistance movements (*Resistenza*).

On September 9, the *New York Times* dedicated articles, cartoons, and celebratory advertisements to one of the most significant markers of progress in the war to date, effusing, "Americans hailed yesterday the unconditional surrender of Italy as a triumph for the arms of the United Nations and a deliverance for the Italian people." Still, amid the celebratory rhetoric, former President Herbert Hoover worried that the armistice might yield opposite results, "We have now quickly to show the Italian people that this is their redemption from oppression: that it is resurrection, not the destruction of their national life."[17] Hoover's discourse fits within the "benevolent" wartime policy of the United States, in contrast with the British government's punitive stance;[18] belonging on the liberation side of the binary, redemption "aimed at helping Italy to 'reconstitute herself.'"[19] However, such positive associations are attenuated once this political usage is informed by redemption's religious valence. In her study of post–Civil War America, historian Carole Emberton articulates redemption's "deep ambivalence," insofar as it "signified both the promise of deliverance from suffering and violence as well as the wrath of God's punishment for sin and corruption." In this sense, a violent occupation *is* redemptive, insofar as the history of domestic conflict in the United States shows that "redemption *from* violence" also entails "redemption *through* violence."[20] Thus, in order to propagate this paradoxical logic in the context of World War II, a rhetorical doublespeak is required to distinguish the capricious violence of the Germans and fascists from the "good" violence of the Allies.[21] Yet official words did not hold water in the face of the Allies' administration of their occupied territories, as Baldasso notes: "Allied bombings did not stop after the armistice. The new air warfare aimed at exporting freedom to Fascist countries through massive bombings of civilian targets. With a self-indulgent rhetorical abuse, the Allies named the new strategy 'wings of democracy.'"[22] As the cultural representations largely maintain, this ambivalence disrupted the mythology of the Allies as benevolent liberators.

Alongside and in competition with the United States, Italy voiced a discourse of self-redemption that gained traction during the occupation and blossomed afterwards. Declaring war on Germany on October 13, 1943, gave Italy the chance to redeem itself "in the eyes of the world" by "cut[ting] all fascist ties" and fighting alongside Allied troops.[23] The following day, a *New York Times* article quotes the new Italian prime minister, Pietro Badoglio, as saying, "Italy has chosen the hard road to redemption."[24] Nonetheless, the Allies did not welcome Italy on equal footing but only as a cobelligerent, a sign that all was not forgiven—especially by the British, who had endured Italian bombardments. Thus, the article continues, Italy's road was to be mapped out by the "three great Powers" who determine "what national redemption means."[25] By the summer of 1944, the U.S. State Department believed that Italy had been redeemed and made provisions to transition back to self-governance.[26] At the same time, independent from (and often thwarted by) governmental machinations, Italian partisans made significant contributions to the country's final liberation in the spring of 1945, laying the groundwork for "the founding narrative of post-fascist and postwar Italy."[27] Similarly dependent on "good" and "bad" violence, this narrative locates redemption in the *Resistenza* and the partisan fighters of central and northern Italy, leaving southern Italians and women to mark the nation's fall.[28]

Gendering Redemption: Between Italian Whores and Italy-as-Whore

In this feminization of fallen Italy, Italian and Anglo-American texts converge; after all, to gender and sexualize a nation is a common patriarchal discursive strategy whose effect is to exclude women from national agency. As Anne McClintock argues, "Excluded from direct action as national citizens, women are subsumed symbolically into the national body politic as its boundary and metaphoric limit.... Women are typically construed as the symbolic bearers of the nation, but are denied any direct relation to national agency."[29] So, too, do outside travelers feminize and exoticize the land they visit, whether motivated by leisure, warfare or what Vernadette Gonzalez has described as a "strategic and symbiotic convergence" of both.[30] Long before the wartime encounter, the gendering Italy's body politic entered Italian and then Anglo-American literary currents through Dante, whose preoccupation with the redemption of individual souls is inseparable from the collective. In *Purgatorio*, he laments: "Ah, slavish Italy, dwelling of grief, ship without a pilot in a great storm, not a ruler of provinces, but a whore!"[31] Perpetuated over centuries by Italian poets from Petrarch to Leopardi to D'Annunzio, this topos spread to Anglo-American writers familiar with Italian poetry whose dualistic vision of Italy was similarly gendered and sexualized.[32] On the romantic side, Italy is a seductive, mysterious place of ancient ruins and timeless nature; on the negative underbelly, her degraded urban spaces and fragmented body politic attest to a premodern "backwardness," embodied by the "particularly 'primitive'" southern Italians.[33] Following a downward trajectory from illustrious past to decayed present, the personification of this dualism lends itself to a "fall" narrative with contemporary Italy as a whore whose Roman or Renaissance glory underwrites the promise of redemption.[34] Thanks to this "backward" state, however, Italy could offer redemption to its visitors; as John Russo argues, for the Anglo-American traveler to Italy, Italy's failure to fulfill the promise of modernity offered by the Renaissance nonetheless "furnished them with experience on the pulse by which they could examine, condemn and resist what they regarded as the evils in modernity."[35] Italy—mediated through careful readings of Dante—offered a space of "death-and-renewal to 19th-century American writers such as Charles Eliot Norton and Margaret Fuller."[36]

The power of this topos intensifies when it dovetails with the historical circumstances of post-armistice Italy. Many saw Italy's signing the September 8, 1943, armistice as a "whorish" betrayal of their former German allies.

As Ellwood writes, "To most outsiders, this looked like a people which, when things started going wrong, had dumped the leader they had worshipped for 20 years—Mussolini—and apparently without a moment's hesitation had sought to join the Anglo-American camp."[37] This symbolism appeared all the more apt when thousands of desperate Italians were seen prostituting themselves to the Allies, in cities like Naples and Rome where the Allies' presence was lengthy and the living conditions dire. In representations of these cities, the metonymic relationship between "fallen" women and the feminized nation becomes commonplace; as if verified by the widespread literal phenomenon, Italy-as-whore becomes the emblem for the encounter, the literal and the figurative reinforcing one another tautologically. This symbolism is further strengthened by the U.S. military's self-representation as liberators prepared to redeem the Italian people; when the soldiers arrived flush with cash, the irony of redemption—a financial transaction that resulted in moral decay—provided a ready-made critique of the official rhetoric. However, if this devastated landscape weakened the soldier-redeemer, it made fertile ground for the Grand Tour paradigm to reemerge in the soldier redeemed from his consumerist modern life by the authenticity of backward Italy—often facilitated by a beautiful (fallen) woman.

Born of a confluence of the historical events surrounding the armistice, together with the transnational Dantean rhetorical tradition, the gendered redemption of World War II Italy depends upon and feeds longstanding assumptions about Italian "character" that both kinds of "prostitution" seemed to verify.[38] Was the women's behavior a response to economic desperation or a symptom of intrinsic Italian corruption?[39] Both, concludes a U.S. military study on communicable diseases in World War II, citing a 1944 report issued by the Fifth Army Surgeon that claimed that "only the prostitute earned an income which could pay the inflationary black market price for the available food." The official extrapolated, "It was not lust, but necessity, not depravity of the soul but the surge of instinct to survive which led numerous women into the ranks of amateur prostitutes on whom regulatory legislation had little or no effect." This exculpation only comes grudgingly, however, after qualifying that the Allies did not cause the situation in Naples, which had "long been notorious for its widespread prostitution."[40] No sooner does he (partially) absolve the women, then the author blames *all* of Italy for the "tremendous problem" of "clandestine prostitution": "While some of this was undoubtedly due to the existing adverse economic conditions, *a great amount was also due to the moral standards of the Italian people.* There was an almost complete breakdown in civilian law enforcement with failure to enforce existing laws against soliciting, which had been carried on flagrantly by men, women, and children."⁴¹ Projecting guilt onto the entire nation, the report makes the prostitute a symptom of Italy's low moral standards—a prostituted nation full of prostitutes.

This attitude is also visible in popular texts, such as CBS correspondent Eric Sevareid's account of postliberation Rome in his memoir, *Not so Wild a Dream* (1946). Feminizing the country, Sevareid notes, "Italy was either in its death throes or in the labor pains of rebirth, and no two Italians agreed which it was," before segueing into a critique of rampant prostitution: "the Eternal City became the unholiest of pleasure palace in Europe. It is not likely that this war had seen anything to compare with the Hotel Excelsior, once the smartest in Rome, which developed into such a roaring, nightlong brothel that decent girls were forbidden by their mothers even to be seen in the vicinity." From Eternal City to pleasure palace, from elite hotel to shady brothel—even "the quality of the girls frequenting the place gradually went down until they were almost exclusively common whores from the slummier districts." In his bluntness, Sevareid crystalizes the patriarchal logic of prostitution: "It was hard for anyone to blame the young officers, who had come back from the miserable front lines and wanted to make the most of their precious three days of liberty. There was something deeply disturbing about the behavior of the women." Condemning their "biological instinct," he laments that the women "gave themselves to the victors, whatever their nationality, no matter what they had done to the Italian men or the Italian land. Everywhere in Europe one saw this expression of women's need to attach themselves to the stronger party."⁴² Although this gendered asymmetry is widespread in the context of World War II and beyond,⁴³ Sevareid's focus on the *Italian* prostitute as a symbol for Europe's degradation is not incidental but evokes and reinforces Italy's status as Europe's feminized, internal other.⁴⁴

During the war, the symbolic elision between Italian women, prostitutes, and the fallen nation had a concrete impact on women living in cities like Naples and Rome who were caught in dragnets, submitted to humiliating medical exams and, in the case of infection, given substandard treatment compared to soldiers.⁴⁵ After the war, the effects may still be felt insofar as the ubiquitous sexualization of Italian women continues to obscure a multitude of female wartime experiences. Writes Ellwood, "the women of the Resistance, of the families who sheltered Allied soldiers and airmen, the mothers, wives or girlfriends of the Italian soldiers working as prisoners-of-war for the Allies even after the 8th of September, or fighting alongside them, get no mention at all."⁴⁶ To this end, recent historiography serves as a corrective. From the 1970s onward, the Italian feminist movement has brought to light a range of female experiences, including women's contributions to the *Resistenza*.⁴⁷ Today, historians like Silvia Cassamagnaghi, Stephanie Depaola, Michela Ponzani, and Maria Porzio shed light on experiences of female partisans, war brides, rape victims, and others. Scholars have also turned a critical eye to the often-invisible Allied soldier; in addition to Depaola, who focuses on the understudied Italian context, Susan Carruthers, Cynthia Enloe, Marilyn Hegarty, Robert Lilly, and Mary Louise Roberts examine the contradictory attitudes that informed the U.S. and British military's ambivalent policies about soldier-civilian sexual encounters from rape and prostitution to marriage. Crucially, they signal the systemic inequities in the institutional disciplinary response, determined by the soldier's race and class, with African American soldiers disproportionately punished according to all available measures. Those inequities are exponentially magnified in the case of the colonial soldier, according to Moshe Gershovich and Driss Maghraoui who critique the widespread use of the Franco-Moroccan *goumier* as shorthand for indiscriminate violence—rape, sodomy, mutilation.⁴⁸

With all the renewed historical interest in race and gender dynamics in World War II, incomparably rich sources remain as yet untapped. Studying World War II Italy through cultural representations that foreground the gendering of redemption, *Allied Encounters* argues for the unique understanding they afford by opening the encounter beyond the United States and Italy, beyond occupation and liberation. In these texts, Allied-occupied Italy is not a space of fallen women and literal or symbolic soldier-redeemers, nor a gauge of U.S.-Italian relations. Instead, it is constituted by a multiplicity of encounters that renegotiate conventional rhetorical alignments of gender, sexuality, and nationality as they intersect with, and are troubled by, race. In a first instance, the racializing dynamics between the United States and (particularly southern) Italy, appear to align with the gendering of the nations to produce a conventional imperialist narrative: white, masculine United States redeeming black, feminized Italy. This facile alignment is disturbed, however, by the racial makeup of the Allied forces. Not only did the U.S. military include African American "buffalo soldiers" and Italian American GIs, populations that faced similar prejudices in the United States, but the British and French armies also relied on colonial troops (including the infamous *goumiers*) from across their empires.⁴⁹

Cultural representations underscore how racialized national boundaries crack under the strain of the Allied-Italian encounter. Moreover, they undercut the christological echoes of the Allies' redeemer guise by evoking racial turmoil vis-à-vis the legacy of slavery or colonialism. Here, the original meaning of *redemptio*, "to purchase a slave out of bondage," becomes all the more relevant, as it "reminds us of the centrality of slavery to America's redemption stories."[50] According to Carruthers, the unhealed trauma of slavery and internal occupation troubles the redeemer construction that the United States sought to project in World War II Italy; in crafting its policy, "the history and memory of military government over the Confederate South presented the greatest challenge to those reinventing occupation as a source of national pride and positive instructional lessons."[51] Thus, the promise of the United States to redeem Italy cannot be disentangled from its racialized ideas of Italians nor from its domestic race relations; at the same time, the focus on U.S. slavery and British or French colonialism becomes a means to deflect attention away from Italy's violent past, foremost its responsibility for the crimes of fascism—including colonialism and the Holocaust.

Reading Redemption

In the chapters that follow, *Allied Encounters* shows how cultural representations of Allied-occupied Italy are informed by, consolidate, and critique the dominant gendered redemption narratives. Chapter 1 provides the first-ever transhistorical reading of U.S. military guidebooks to Italy over four decades, starting from the 1943 *Guide to the Occupation of Enemy Territory— Italy* (*GOETI*), written in preparation for "Operation Husky." In painting the wartime landscape for U.S. soldiers who would have been more familiar with Italy as a land of leisure, the *GOETI* claims Sicily's most dangerous inhabitants are the "warm-looking, attractive women," who are actually diseased fascist spies.[52] Reading the prostitute as the *GOETI*'s paradigm for false, beautiful Italy, I show how redemption is not understood in terms of communication with the Italians, but a consumption of the people and the country. As the *GOETI* plans for war but looks forward to peace, redemption appears as a dialectic between Americanization (that is, democratization and modernization), and the restoration of "destination Italy," an idealized land of leisure.[53] Continuing to the post-armistice *Soldier's Guide to Italy* and the postwar *Pocket Guide to Italy* (*PGI*, 1952–87), I use them as an example of the long-standing gendering of redemption, regardless of Italy's shifting status from enemy to cobelligerent to friend. In successive revisions of the *PGIs*, I show how the *GOETI*'s contradictory goals play out and to what end. As each guide brags of Italy's increasing Americanization, it reasserts Italy's difference, maintaining a similar discourse as during wartime; instead of singling out women, the *PGI* foregrounds the feminized Italian—friendly and entertaining, but not a valid interlocutor.[54] This continuity suggests an American notion of Italianness that is as durable as it is contradictory: While Italy is attractive as a space that requires and provides redemption, its people are at once always redeemable and beyond redemption. Concomitantly, however, the guidebooks display a significant transhistorical shift as they cast the soldiers as evermore welcome tourists and, simultaneously, their "History" sections report ever-briefer accounts of fascism, colonialism, and war. Erasing the violent traces of the wartime redemption, the postwar guidebooks rewrite the Allied-Italian encounter and restore a mythic past.

After tracing the paradigm of Italy-as-whore in U.S. military guidebooks from the invasion of Sicily through the Cold War, the balance of the book focuses on literary and cinematic representations of the Allied-Italian encounter: in Chapter 2, Roberto Rossellini's film *Paisà* (1946; *Paisan*) and Alfred Hayes's novels *All Thy Conquests* (1946) and *The Girl on the Via Flaminia* (1949); in Chapter 3, Luciana Peverelli's novels *La lunga notte* (1944; *The Long Night*) and *Sposare lo straniero* (1946; *Marry the Foreigner*); in Chapter 4, John Horne Burns's novel *The Gallery* (1947); in Chapter 5, Curzio Malaparte's novel *La pelle* (1949; *The Skin*); in Chapter 6, Norman Lewis's diary *Naples '44* (1978); and in the Epilogue, Maria Luisa D'Aquino's diary *Quel giorno trent'anni fa* (1975; *That Day Thirty Years Ago*).[55] With this selection, I focus on texts produced (or purportedly written) during and immediately after the war. While representations from subsequent decades certainly need to be studied, I choose these early texts for their powerful, transnational cultural influence;[56] many of these representations are regularly cited as historical sources thanks to their authors' proximity to the events they describe.

While I have selected these early postwar representations in order to understand their outsized cultural authority, I also am interested in the simultaneous negotiation of two political redemption narratives that occurs in this immediate postwar period: the recent memory of wartime encounter and the Allies' promise to redeem the Italians from fascism, as it intersects with the American postwar promise to rebuild Italy, formalized through the Marshall Plan—the economic happy ending to the wartime pledge.[57] In these texts, reconciling the memory of the encounter goes hand in hand with envisioning—even influencing—the unfolding relationship. Reading these texts, I ask, what parts of the wartime encounter must be repressed in service of the postwar relationship? Just as the U.S. military guidebooks contribute to the myth of the American redeemers and the "good" Italians (*italiani brava gente*) by erasing the violence of fascism and World War II, these texts have an ambivalent relationship to traumas such as the war's largest urban massacre at the Fosse Ardeatine outside of Rome (Chapters 2 and 3), the deportation of Rome's Jews and the Holocaust (Chapters 3 and 4), the legacy of slavery and colonialism (Chapters 4 and 5), and mass rape perpetrated by Allied colonial soldiers on Italian civilians (Chapters 5 and 6). According to current cultural history, traumatic events that contradicted the redemptive paradigm were repressed by writers and filmmakers in early postwar Italy. Instead, *Allied Encounters* shows that these events function as sites of conflict within—and between—texts that enjoyed widespread popularity; yet decades of scholarly analysis have glossed over—or censored outright—these earliest efforts to represent the traumas of World War II Italy, a testament to the paradigm's continued dominance.

The problem of representing Rome's occupation is the focus of Chapters 2 and 3, a story that does not start with the June 4 liberation, as Allied soldiers' memoirs have it, but instead stretches back to the armistice and the nine months under the Germans. Robert Gordon reflects on Rome's representational richness during this fraught historical moment: "Something in the very tangled and complex stories of Rome in 1943 and 1944 contains a strange fascination and emblematic power, something of the shape and resonance of myth, which gives shape to large collective experiences and legacies of the entire era."[58] While the Allies sought to represent their arrival as a new beginning for the city—and a turning point in the war—the link between the two occupations is undeniable; the Allies and the Germans made Rome a cultural battleground as each side "claimed a particular entitlement to these stones," as Mussolini himself had done.[59] Aside from their shared rhetoric, German- and Allied-occupied Rome were linked by a traumatic event: the German's March 24, 1944, massacre of 335 victims at the Fosse Ardeatine in retaliation for a partisan attack the day before. One of the first challenges facing postliberation Rome was the trial of Pietro Caruso, Rome's police chief under the Nazis, an event that only generated further trauma when it was overrun by a mob of the victims' families that lynched a witness for the prosecution. As scholars concur, the dominant representation of German-occupied Rome and seminal neorealist film, Rossellini's *Roma città aperta* (1945; *Rome Open City*), represses the events surrounding the Fosse Ardeatine, in order to preserve the film's redemptive function.[60] Revisiting the neorealism debate in the context of *Paisà*, Chapter 2 argues that the melodramatic prostitution narrative in the "Rome" episode continues in this vein by eliding the botched Caruso trial. This traumatic event is foregrounded, on the contrary, by Rossellini's collaborator, Hayes, in *All Thy Conquests*. Using Hayes's largely forgotten novel as an intertext, I bring the marginalized "Rome" episode into the conversation on the construction of the redemptive myth of neorealism and show the prostitute's crucial function in preserving it.

The exclusion of "Rome" from critical interpretations of *Paisà* rehearses in miniature the problem in Chapter 3 that analyzes two *romanzi rosa* (romance novels) by Luciana Peverelli. Published while the events were still unfolding, *La lunga notte* and its sequel *Sposare lo straniero* represent those traumas, but in a form disparaged as deleterious to its (female) readers' sense of reality and linked to the gender myths of fascism.[61] As feminist scholars have shown, the *rosa*—characterized as the "careless," feminine counterpart to redemptive, male-centric neorealism—becomes a cultural scapegoat to be expelled as part of the postwar return to "reality."[62] Read in dialogue with canonical, male-authored texts, Peverelli's novels offer a rejoinder to the Italian neorealist paradigm and popular American representations of the "fallen" Italian woman. Recognizing Italian women to be actors in and transmitters of collective trauma, the novels refuse to limit them as metonyms for the nation but instead position them as "borderline" spaces in which to negotiate postwar Italian identity.[63] In parallel, these *rosa*, with their self-conscious embrace and rejection of many of romance's tenets, may be considered "borderline."[64] Self-consciously affirming their unique ability to represent the absurd realities of the historical moment, these *rosa* embody the hybridity disavowed by the post-facto construction of neorealism. Taking seriously their historical engagement as they revisit the *rosa*'s conventions, I read them for what they say about the period they represent together with the context in which they were produced and received: Forgotten in Italy and never translated into English, *La lunga notte* has produced no critical readings, leaving unexplored its blind spot with regard to Italian anti-Semitism and the Holocaust; interrogating it, I show how *La lunga notte* dispels the myth of the "good Italians" by condemning Italian involvement in the Holocaust, even as it falls prey to anti-Semitic logic. Then, as *Sposare lo straniero* shifts away from the Holocaust to deliver the *rosa*'s requisite happy ending, it seems to exhibit "the indifference shown for the tragedies experienced by the Jews after the liberation" that *La lunga notte* critiques.[65] Nonetheless, the traumas of the German and Allied occupation do, in fact, resurface. As the gendered violence of the encounter persists within the putatively happy ending, *Sposare lo straniero* locates redemption outside of the patriarchal institution of marriage and within the transnational bounds of friendship between Italian war brides, who become one another's readers.

In renegotiating the symbolic meaning of the capital after its fascist, German and Allied appropriations, the representations of occupied Rome explored in Chapters 2 and 3 use gendered redemption plots to critique official rhetoric, illustrating the tragic disjuncture from individual experience for the women who coexist as symbol and subject. Yet within these texts, the relationships are whitewashed and heteronormative: Insofar as these texts acknowledge the possibility of an interracial, sexual encounter, it is limited to the "buffalo soldier," who appears in a choral context;[66] insofar as they include references to nonnormative sexuality, they are pathologized.[67] After these chapters, which consider the construction of the encounter as it converges around Anglo-Italian, male-female relations set in Rome, the latter half of the book looks to the transnational dimension of Allied-occupied Italy in representations of Naples, "Italy's 'problem city,' *par excellence.*"[68]

When a flood of people from all over the world began to enter Naples after the October 1 liberation, according to historian Sergio Lambiase, they would have found it without electricity, gas, and water, its interrupted sewers regurgitating vile liquids, one-third of its buildings destroyed, the port bombed beyond recognition. They would have found corpses littering the streets, swollen by the rain, stripped of their clothes by desperate passersby.[69] In Malaparte's description, they also would have found it crowded with soldiers, "shouting in a hundred strange, unfamiliar tongues,"[70] with "races from every country rub[bing] elbows," D'Aquino observes, "giving it the feel of a colony."[71] In cultural representations of Allied-occupied Naples, this "contact zone" inspires contradictory impulses.[72] On the one hand, texts convey a palpable sense of the unbelievable nature of the situation and, with it, a need to affirm the narrator's authority in guiding readers through it. Descending into the hell of Naples, these narrators emerge—not unlike Dante's pilgrim—to testify to what they saw. As part of this witnessing, these narrators inevitably confront the "colonial" aspect of Naples, in particular the interracial, sexual encounters between "black" Allies and "white" Italians, a troubling of the traditional colonizer/colonized power dynamics that also carried a threat of miscegenation. On the other hand, the global makeup of the city lends itself to an allegorical reading where, for instance, the hundred unfamiliar tongues of the soldiers are not the languages of the Allies but symptoms of a present-day Babel. Here, Naples is not Naples, but Italy, Europe, the entire universe; nor are prostitutes and soldiers individuals but symbols for their respective nations.

The texts in Chapters 4, 5, and 6 play with this dynamic in different ways. Deceptively plotless, all three texts are intricate autofictional narratives that perform a sleight of hand on readers, directing them to one desired interpretive approach: while the narrators of *The Gallery* and *La pelle* suggest an allegorical reading, the narrator of *Naples '44* hotly affirms its nonfictional status. Critics, as we will see, tend to accept the parameters dictated by each: Universalizing the two novels at the expense of their historical engagement, they accept the diary as an historic document at the expense of its highly crafted rhetorical strategy, which, in part, depends on its relationship to Burns's and Malaparte's novels. However, these narratives provide keen insight when read in terms of how they interweave the historical and literary threads: Critiquing the representational parameters of Allied-occupied Italy, they move beyond the U.S.-Italy dynamic, evincing its transnational dimension.

Chapter 4 examines how *The Gallery* revises the Anglo-American vision of Italy as a site of redemption into a queer, transnational space of encounter.[73] Praised as a unique example of American war fiction that "affirm[s] . . . the humanizing effects of the view of life as tragedy," *The Gallery* tells the story of John, who, over the course of his military journey through North Africa and Naples, "dies" as an American, only to be reborn outside the nation's bounds as a contemporary Dante.[74] At the same time, it alternates these first-person chapters (called promenades) with third-person short stories (called portraits), that converge around the city's famous arcade, the Galleria Umberto I, in August 1944. By reading these promenades in dialogue with the portraits, I show how the novel rejects the heteronormative gendering of the encounter and its future-looking temporality. Whereas Rossellini, Hayes, and Peverelli envision marriage as the redemptive (if often elusive) ending for their heroines, Burns dismisses it as the basis of a nationalistic, egotistic conception of the self that catalyzes war. Instead, the novel favors a momentary communion that erases *all* difference, most overtly nationality but no less crucially, gender, as the narrator's rebirth culminates in an orgasmic encounter with a genderless Italian. Tracing the narrator's personal redemption, I show how it depends on a transnational dimension that crisscrosses the Mediterranean in time and space, moving between the United States, North Africa, and Naples while performing a constant metonymic slippage between the Galleria Umberto I, Naples, Italy, and the Universe. As it affords dehistoricized Italy a privileged position between colonized North Africa and imperialist United States, *The Gallery* participates in a literary erasure of the local identities that lead to his rebirth. Thus, the novel narrates how we forget history, specifically the queer spaces and bodies that preface his personal redemption: ambiguously gendered North Africans, a Neapolitan virgin, and a Jewish soldier killed by a German.

In Chapter 5, I turn to Curzio Malaparte's *La pelle*, the emblematic Italian narrative of Allied-occupied Naples, and the long-reviled counterpart to the beloved *Gallery*.[75] Captain Malaparte, liaison officer to the Allies, is the heavy-handed, first-person narrator who recounts grotesque spectacles only to suggest that they be read as a metaphor for the horrors of war.

While early Italian scholarship focused on the novel's autobiographical dimension to condemn it as a false representation of a self-serving narcissist, recently critics outside of Italy have embraced its allegorical directive in an effort to disentangle it from the author's fascist past. However necessary a corrective, this latter approach nonetheless obscures how *La pelle* uses the gendered, racialized bodies of Neapolitan women, "Negro" soldiers, and Franco-Moroccan *goumiers* to intertwine historical referent and allegory. Thus, the novel's redemption comes at the expense of its astute critique of the racist, misogynist topoi commonplace in cultural representations of the occupation, *La pelle* included. Taking a twofold approach similar to my analysis of *The Gallery*, I read in terms of historical context and allegorical significance. In so doing, I show how these novels insert the Allies and Italians into a transnational network where the gendering and racialization of redemption signals unresolved traumas surrounding slavery, colonialism, and mass rape.

In Chapter 6, I jump thirty years ahead to *Naples '44*, a text that not only embodies the redemption paradigm but, to a large extent, is responsible for having perpetuated it. As a British "wedding officer" in Naples, Lewis distinguishes Italian war brides and rape victims among a sea of prostitutes, a task whose ultimate end is not to determine their status but to stage his own redemption. Starting as a hardnosed intelligence officer who does more harm than good, Lewis's character "dies" and is reborn as the authoritative narrator, making his diary a Dantean conversion narrative much like *The Gallery*. After I chart Lewis's conversion, I put his diary-novel in dialogue with Malaparte's *La pelle*, whose grotesque spectacles *Naples '44* rewrites in order to assert its own "matter-of-fact precision."[76] The consequences of this intertextual power play are significant: Published thirty-plus years after the events it describes but nonetheless treated as a nonfictional diary, *Naples '44* arbitrates the sexuality of Neapolitan women and the men who love, purchase, or violate them. Lewis represents all women in Naples as whores and all Moroccans, "sexual psychopaths,"[77] and yet still emerges as a "clear-eyed" narrator in the eyes of critics.[78] Thus, this final chapter takes a cue from Dantistas as they work to "dispel the unexamined assumption, encouraged by the fiction, of an innocent author describing an infernal reality rather than constructing it."[79] To do so, it is essential to understand the grounds on which Lewis's unparalleled authority is based; here, the praise of Neapolitan writer and critic Raffaele La Capria is suggestive, singling out the text for its generic purity: "In so many books, comedies, films, the story of Naples of those crucial years became a mixture of folkloric legend and melodrama. . . . Not in this book, where the precision of writing is accompanied by the sobriety of a gaze, 'blue like the color of truth.'"[80] *Allied Encounters*, instead, argues that it is precisely the texts' hybridity, when valorized rather than disciplined, that opens up the Allied-Italian encounter beyond the conventional paradigms.

One of the animating impulses of *Allied Encounters* is to critique and redress the way in which the gendered redemption of Allied-occupied Italy obscures the figures on which it depends: As Ruth Glynn argues, the cultural fixation on understanding national pride "in terms of male heterosexuality ensures that attention is directed away from women's experiences and subjectivity in favor of the objectification of women through the conventional alignment of female bodies and national territory."[81] In response, the Epilogue offers a revision of redemption through a reading of an unknown diary by Neapolitan aristocrat and poet Maria Luisa D'Aquino. Published in the same years as *Naples '44* and similarly set in the Campanian countryside, *Quel giorno trent'anni fa* makes a proleptic rejoinder to *Naples '44* as a rare glimpse into the daily struggles of a widowed mother of five and as a literary artifact. Like *Naples '44*, *Quel giorno* is a conversion narrative that tracks the narrator from her descent into hell to her rebirth as writer. However, whereas Lewis constructs his diary with an eye to establishing his authority over the events, D'Aquino does so in order to inscribe herself within them, making herself a gendered, sexualized symbol for the Italian nation and the author of her own redemption.

Analyzing texts in which the gendering of redemption goes hand in hand with a self-conscious narrative hybridity, *Allied Encounters* traces their negotiation of the porous boundaries between fiction and history, between sexualized bodies and national territory, between gender, sexuality, and race. Engaging these narratives with transhistorical, transnational intertexts, it shows them to be neither a gauge of, nor wholly distinct from, U.S.-Italian relations. Instead, these texts, and the Allied-Italian encounter, become a site through which to explore gender, sexual and racial dynamics as they reinforce and trouble national discourses.

1

Redeeming Destination Italy
A Guide to the Occupation of Enemy Territory

"YOU and your outfit have been ordered to invade and conquer an enemy country—Italy." The U.S. Army's *Guide to Occupation of Enemy Territory—Italy* (*GOETI*) opens with a simple order.[1] However, as they prepared for the July 9, 1943, invasion of Sicily, the Allies had to confront the daunting prospect of waging war in a mythic space, produced through centuries of travel and travel writing.[2] "First and foremost an idealized land of leisure," destination Italy made for an unlikely warzone, inhabited by an unwarlike enemy—friendly, hospitable, feminine.[3] The power of destination Italy is felt throughout the *GOETI*: Admonishing GI readers to avoid sightseeing or buying souvenirs, the *GOETI* uses tourism as a point of reference in its instructions: "toward the historical monuments of Italy, the art museums and the palaces, take the same careful attitude you would do if you were a tourist"; if billeted in an Italian home, "your attitude should be that of the lodger in a strange hotel where he is not particularly welcome."[4] For Allied soldiers in Italy, these analogies suggest, the tourist is the more familiar role than the invader.

In order to encourage a shift in mindset, the *GOETI* aims to discredit Italy's cultural past and the people's "natural" hospitality in contrast with the present-day violence of fascism. With rhetorical flourish, the *GOETI* admonishes:

> No matter what one may think of the Italian people, no matter how great have been their contributions to art, literature, discovery, science, politics and the cause of human freedom, no matter how much civilization owes to the moderating influences of the ancient Roman Empire, it is futile to look for any aspects of nobility in the recent military undertakings of the Italian people when it is clear that the military policy of their government has been from first to last worthy of a jackal.[5]

However, the *GOETI*'s picture of the modern Italian warzone was based on little concrete information: operating in almost total ignorance, military intelligence perpetuated stereotypes that "seem to be drawn more from literature than from any social scientifically informed approach."[6] Preparations for the invasion, in fact, appear conditioned by the tourist experience of individual officers. One member of the Italian Office of Strategic Services (OSS) laments that they had "meager information about both the planning and the execution of the invasion of Sicily," while another gives his "vacations in Italy" as a credential.[7] Not even the (probable) author of the *GOETI*, military journalist Samuel Lyman Atwood Marshall, felt prepared to "inform [soldiers] about the terrain, the customs of the countryside, and the habits, ceremonies, taboos, and so forth of the people." When commissioned by the American Special Service Division (SSD) in early 1943, Marshall claims he was not even told which Mediterranean island would be the site of the invasion: "The extent of my briefing on the plan to invade Sicily ... was an exercise in mental telepathy. Since I put little stock in ESP, during the weeks that followed, while I toiled at the project, one thought plagued me. 'What if the guy was thinking about Corsica?'"[8] Whether or not Marshall's tale is apocryphal, accounts of the soldiers' preinvasion briefings depict a similarly slipshod enterprise. A bridge announcer preparing an American ship with three hundred officers and twelve hundred men for Operation Husky remarks on the dearth of books about Sicily on board.[9] To cobble together a description, he cites an intelligence report that cautions soldiers against "close contact" with the "excitable and suspicious" Sicilians. Supplementing it with the British-issued *Soldier's Guide to Sicily*, he adds primitivizing details such as this: "The modern Sicilian is said to be a mixture of all the people who have abused his land. He is reported to be violent, with a violence born of the accumulation of their conflicts."[10] No wonder one serviceman recalls that reading this guide led him to expect "a land of opera singers, saints, violent menfolk and gangsters living in a land plentiful with food, wine and ruins of antiquity."[11]

The pull of destination Italy is palpable throughout the *GOETI*. In fact, more than debunking the myth, the *GOETI* only seeks to stave it off, promising the soldiers they will soon partake in its pleasures:

> In time to come it is expected that the conditions within the occupied country will become sufficiently stabilized that you will have great relief from your strictly military duties and will be able to devote a reasonable portion of your time to recreation of various kinds. There will be a season for sightseeing and for the hunting of souvenirs. When that time comes, you will be provided with a second *Guide to Italy* which will inform you about the history and the romance of the country and will make it possible for you to get full

information, the better to enjoy the scenic beauties and the historic places and monuments of one of the most fascinating and interesting countries on earth. That time has not yet arrived. What is foremost now is that you do your duty as a soldier.[12]

Nonetheless, despite its assertion that tourism has no place in the invasion, the *GOETI* links the two. Indeed, even as the *GOETI* uses the war to insist on a *break* with the past, it underscores that Italy's position in the Anglo-American wartime imaginary is inextricable from a multifaceted discursive tradition that depends upon a notion of a "backward" Italy,[13] racialized and feminized as "'the subaltern within' due to its position on the interior borders of an Orientalizing European space."[14] Closely tied to the Grand Tour tradition, America's earliest literary pilgrims looked to "backward" Italy as an ideal setting for their personal rebirth, whereas U.S. foreign policy in World War II sought to *offer* redemption to the fallen country;[15] yet as oppositional as they seem, during this interstitial moment captured in the *GOETI*, these objectives commingle, suggesting their profound and profoundly ambivalent interrelation.

To this end, the pages of the *GOETI* are rife with instructive contradiction; while it contains seeds of America's future role in helping Italy modernize, it also envisions its restoration as a premodern tourist destination, as it looks beyond the invasion and promises to transform the soldiers into tourists.[16] This fashioning of the soldier-tourist—an ongoing practice celebrated throughout the Cold War editions of the military's *Pocket Guide to Italy*—was not seen as a distraction; as Andrew Buchanan argues, "Military planners saw [tourism] as a way to relieve both boredom and the stresses of combat, but they also viewed it as a vehicle for the projection of the engaged benevolence that they believed to be critical to the remaking of Italy along liberal and pro-American lines."[17] Indeed, despite the "commonsense" incompatibility between militarism and tourism, World War II Italy attests to their "strategic and symbiotic convergence," an assertion developed by scholars of militarism and travel/tourism alike.[18] Building on work by Cynthia Enloe, Vernadette Gonzalez argues that tourism's naturalized opposition to militarism allows it to appear "softer" even while "its extractive logics and damaging epistemologies are no less hard edged than the kind militarism puts into play."[19] Claiming to restore destination Italy, in fact, has a powerful ideological function, insofar as the tourist guidebook coats its colonialist attitude in a "patina of leisure" that obfuscates the asymmetrical power relations on which it depends.[20]

Within this dynamic interrelationship between tourism and militarism, the ambivalence of Italy's rhetorical gendering becomes visible. Delineating the parameters of invasion *and* anticipating a return to destination Italy before the war's end, the *GOETI* virilizes and feminizes the Italians, casting them as colonialist aggressors and primitive victims.[21] Yet, for all the emphasis on virile aggressions, the *GOETI*'s strongest warnings are against Italy's "warm-looking" women, likely to be diseased fascist spies whom the soldiers—the guide acknowledges—will inevitably enjoy.[22] The "false" Italian woman is more than a singular threat; she is emblematic of the Italian people whose "friendly" demeanor conceals "their outrageous acts,"[23] and Sicily, whose superlative tourist status conceals its dangerous reality. After examining how the preinvasion *GOETI* entangles invasion and destination Italy as it lays the groundwork for the GIs to redeem the Italians, I move to the September 1943 *Soldier's Guide to Italy* (*SGTI*), published as Italy began its shift from enemy to cobelligerent, and then to the postwar *Pocket Guide to Italy*, revised from the 1950s to the 1980s, as Italy became one of the most strategically important friends of the United States.[24] This transhistorical reading shows an ongoing ambivalence in the foreign policy narrative that traps the country between past and present, awaiting a redemption that never comes. At the same time, a shift emerges across the successive revisions of the guidebooks: As they increasingly emphasize the soldiers' status as welcome tourists, their accounts of fascism, colonialism, and war become ever weaker. Rewriting the Allied-Italian encounter, the postwar guidebooks erase the violence of the wartime redemption and restore a mythic past.

A Guide to Occupation of Enemy Territory—Italy (July 1943)

From its title to its contents, the *GOETI* is no conventional guidebook. While its touristic counterpart embraces monuments and eschews discussions of politics and daily life, the *GOETI* forbids sightseeing and devotes sections to Italian politics and customs.[25] However, in its attempt to serve the guidebook's didactic function, the spaces of invasion and destination Italy coalesce. For instance, in preparing the GIs for their landing in Sicily, the *GOETI* acknowledges that its natural beauty and archeological monuments make it "one of the top experiences of world travel."[26] Yet it insists that this merely amounts to a "superficial appearance of wellbeing," turning from tourist delights of "times past," to negative descriptions of the present: Sicily's beautiful coast conceals "primitive conditions"—disease, famine. Laying the blame on Mussolini, who broke his promise to make Sicily "one of the most fertile countries on earth," the *GOETI* calls it the most "shabbily treated" part of Italy, cautioning: "But when you leave the coast, this beauty and interest quickly vanish," giving way to "inferior wheat country," "sparse grain fields," and a "desolate forest of stunted trees."[27] This disavowal of Sicily's superlative tourist status layers a contemporary agenda onto the discourse of the beautiful, false Italy, in this case hiding the ills of fascism.

This dynamic plays out in the instructions for dealing with each of the groups of Italians the *GOETI* envisions GIs will meet: shopkeepers, prostitutes, and "friendly" Italians, who all hide a threat beneath their attractive exterior. Despite a blanket ban on fraternization, the *GOETI* suggests that soldiers use members of the tourist industry as a social interface. Excusing soldiers from learning Italian, the *GOETI* writes: "Many Italians speak English in one degree or another. The waiters, hotel clerks, porters, shine boys, barbers and shop keepers can usually make a pretty good pass at our language." Yet this suggestion is immediately qualified: "They acquired it during the years when Fascist Italy was making a great play for our tourists, thereby harvesting our dollars and using them to build up Italian armament." After blaming the shopkeepers and Anglo-American tourists for financing the war, it reframes their language skills in positive terms: "These people usually enjoy speaking English and they will probably be happy to assist you in getting about the country."[28] Thus, even as the *GOETI* insists on the Italians' enemy status, it sends the soldier to engage with these pleasure-seeking Anglophiles. Ricocheting between depictions of Italian vendors as welcoming and devious, in a section on "Financial Wisdom," the *GOETI* again questions the advisability of speaking English to members of the tourist industry:

> Some Italian vendors have long regarded American tourists as easy marks. The shops are loaded with fake antiques and imitation art goods—stuff little better than is to be won on a wheel at a county fair in America. If you waste your money on any of this junk, the chances are ten to one you'll never take it home because you'll quickly realize how thoroughly bad it is. True, you will want to buy souvenirs. The thing to do is buy moderately, examine the merchandise critically and make sure you are getting a good value. Despite the rather general use of English, you will be well advised to study Italian.[29]

As the soldier walks the path trodden by the tourist with the same advantages and drawbacks, fascism becomes the scapegoat for a guidebook precaution so commonplace as to have inspired its own coinage: paying *alla inglese*.[30] In response to the similar threat posed by souvenirs, the *GOETI* offers contradictory advice: As soldiers, they are not to "win" souvenirs but as tourists, they may "hunt" them (although the guide waivers on whether it would be best to avoid, defer or limit purchases).[31]

The allure of false Italy is amplified in the section "Contacts with Women," which portrays Italy's "many warm-looking, attractive women" as the most eminent threat: "all that has been said about the dangers of fraternization applies with special emphasis to consorting with a 'pick-up' anywhere in Italy." Much as the GI must avoid the temptation to purchase what *look* like antiques, he must steel himself against the woman whose request for a cigarette inevitably hides something sinister:

> The type of woman who approaches you on the street in Italy and says: "Please give me a cigarette!" isn't looking for a smoke. Yet that first touch may lead to major indiscretions that will endanger many of your comrades and bring a final disgrace upon your own head. Venereal disease is not the only danger arising from such associations in enemy country. Relaxed morals breed loose talk.[32]

To interpret Italy's most menacing and enticing of beauties, the *GOETI* evokes Hollywood: "It is notorious that women of the type discussed in this paragraph are in better position to work themselves into a soldier's confidence, ply him with liquor and drain him of valuable information than any other kind of enemy agent. This kind of thing happens not only on the Hollywood screen but in real warfare."[33] In her 1944 memoir, *Life* photojournalist Margaret Bourke-White echoes the *GOETI*'s warning that prostitutes are disease-carrying spies, but she goes one step further in degrading them into "sordid imitations" of Hollywood spies: "inevitably, by the very nature of the work, many prostitutes were in the pay of enemy agents. Although the glamorous spy of fiction is conspicuously lacking from the war, thousands of more significant and sordid imitations exist."[34] In light of the Allies' belief in the apolitical nature of the Italians, this politicization of the prostitute reads as fanciful, all the more so because it was not standard-issue across wartime guidebooks.[35] Indeed, as the *GOETI* pits Italy's "false" women against Hollywood's "true" representation, the specificity of the Italian context cannot be overstated: although the 1944 *Soldier's Guide to France* (*SGF*) also expresses concern about prostitution, it tries to *dispel* fantastical representations such as "Mata Hari."[36] Moreover, while the *GOETI* only discusses prostitutes, the *SGF* also addresses "decent" women, telling soldiers to *forget* familiar stereotypes in their interactions: "France has been represented too often in fiction as a frivolous nation where sly winks and coy pats on the rear are the accepted form of address. You'd better get rid of such notions right now if you are going to keep out of trouble."[37] The *GOETI*'s and the *SGF*'s respective treatments of women extend to the people as a whole: While the Italians are masters of artifice, the French are "realistic."[38]

In much the same way as the *GOETI* uncovers the threat presented by Sicily, antiques, and warm-looking women, it exposes the crimes of fascism concealed by Italian friendliness. Here, it sets up an opposition between Italian falsity and American transparency. Although Italians may appear hospitable, unspeakable acts lurk behind their "natural" kindness:

> The Italians are a naturally hospitable people. But hospitality is a large word and it means chiefly "kindness to strangers." Before you become over impressed with the kind of hospitality which persuades an Italian to invite you into his home, you might weigh it against the brand of "kindness" which permitted the Fascist armies to spray mustard gas on the naked warriors of Ethiopia and bring on Greece a situation which has resulted in death by starvation for thousands of women and children.[39]

Providing a crash course in contemporary Italian politics, the *GOETI* mixes condescension with horror in recounting the rise to power of Mussolini, a "smalltime political racketeer" who "chang[ed] sides when it suited his pocketbook." Through brainwashing, coercion, and brutal force, fascism "convert[ed]" the Italians, "[taking] hold of these naturally friendly and unwarlike people and turn[ing] them against us."[40] Throughout these descriptions, the *GOETI* depicts fascists' use of language as deceptive—propaganda for the GI to debunk. However, while initially the *GOETI* instructs soldiers to do so with words and actions, later it suggests they "convert enemies into friends" solely with actions.[41] This latter guideline, indeed, is more consonant with the *GOETI* as a whole that discourages linguistic exchange.[42] Rather than speak to the Italians, the *GOETI* tells GIs to avoid "oratory" or a "barrage of propaganda" and to embody the values of the U.S. flag, "a symbol of freedom on the one hand [and] of overwhelming power on the other."[43] Hence, the *GOETI* places tantamount importance on outward appearance:

> Be more painstaking about keeping your appearance smart and about conducting yourself in a military manner than at any time in your military service. Untidiness, sloppiness of carriage, carelessness of habits, and laxness of discipline will do more to promote the contempt of the Italians for our arms and for the American nation than all other factors combined.[44]

Unlike the duplicitous Italians whose beauty hides fascist lies, the American soldiers' meticulous outside corresponds to their democratic inside, shaped by the "Four Freedoms."[45] If they follow the guide's instructions, soldiers will need no words to be understood, and the Italians will need only to "awaken to reality."[46] Here, then, in the contrast between the *GOETI*'s expectations for intercultural communication, the structuring asymmetry becomes plain. The *GOETI* acknowledges that the encounter between soldiers and civilians starts from reciprocal misunderstanding; yet whereas the GIs' stems from the Italians' duplicity, the Italians' grows out of fascist brainwashing. As such, whereas the GIs must look beneath the beautiful surface presented by Sicily, antique souvenirs, warm-looking women, or friendly Italians in order to uncover the truth of fascism, Italians must only awaken in order to read the truth of democracy transparently embodied by the GI.

This attitude cannot be attributed exclusively to Italy's enemy status. To wit, despite the fact that the GIs were forbidden to fraternize with the Germans, an entire section of the 1944 *Pocket Guide to Germany* called "Alibis" formulates hypothetical, elaborate responses for soldiers to give to Germans who might defend the Nazis.[47] While Germans are envisioned as participating in a rational discussion, Italians' use of language is associated with ease and pleasure, if not "bunk."[48] Where Italy is concerned, the redemptive encounter is not grounded in linguistic exchange; even as "General Administrative Instruction No. 1" dictates that soldiers "should make it clear to the local population whenever opportunity presents itself that military occupation is intended a) to deliver the people from the Fascist regime which led them into the war and, b) to restore Italy as a free nation," so too does it prohibit them "to discuss political matters with Local Italians."[49] Instead of opening a dialogue, the soldier-redeemer is encouraged to decode and consume, an attitude that intensifies in the post-armistice *SGTI*, even as Italy inches toward ally status.

The Soldier's Guide to Italy (September 1943)

The weeks between the distribution of the *GOETI* and the *SGTI* were some of the most dramatic of the Italian campaign: after the successful invasion of Sicily and the fall of Mussolini, negotiations for the armistice began. Differences in the new guidebook, distributed just ahead of the Allies' September 3 landing at Salerno, reflect these watershed events.[50] For instance, the *GOETI*'s statement that "Italy is an Axis country but its people are not all pro-Axis nor are they all profascist," is revised in the *SGTI* to put fascism in the past: "its people are not all pro-Axis nor *were* they all profascist."[51] Less sweeping in assigning culpability, the *SGTI* absolves most citizens with invented statistics: "It is probably true that over 90 per cent of the Italian people, after the wars in Abyssinia and Spain, didn't want another war at all, and even less with America than with Britain."⁵² Whereas the *GOETI* implicates all Italians with harsh rhetoric, the *SGTI* attributes fascism to the "folly" of the leader and the people, describing them as "somewhat easily led into mass enthusiasm and obedience" only to qualify that by saying, "although these are often merely superficial. They are good judges of character and can size up men quickly as to their worth."⁵³ In a further explanation, the guide offers more magnanimous justifications for fascism's rise: After the party grew in size, bolstered by a majority of members who "were blackmailed or bullied into submission and gradually cut off from the outside world," eventually, "the more simple people and much of the youth of the country came to accept blindly all they were told and do as they were directed for fear of worse."⁵⁴ Zigzagging back in the direction of mockery, the *SGTI* states soon after, "Their minds have become so deformed by the stream of Fascist propaganda that they will not see things the way you see them. They will appear to you amazingly misinformed about conditions in other countries, and maybe even their own."⁵⁵

Alongside a less aggressive condemnation of fascism and a more ambivalent assessment of the Italians' acquiescence to it, the *SGTI* demonstrates a slight opening toward Italian friendliness and Italy's cultural patrimony. While friendliness is viewed as a potential threat in the *GOETI*, the *SGTI* suggests the soldiers use that trait to their advantage during the shift to cobelligerency: "In the mass the Italians are by nature friendly and courteous. They instinctively resent a haughty and arrogant attitude."⁵⁶ Whereas the *GOETI* tells the GIs to avoid the "intimacy of friendship" and only to exhibit "mild friendly interest," in the *SGTI*, friendliness becomes a tool: "Italians are very susceptible to a civil manner of approach. You will, therefore, generally obtain more with a smile. We learnt this in Sicily."⁵⁷ At the same time, the *SGTI* recognizes Italy's artistic patrimony: "If you are interested in art, you will have a wonderful chance for study; if you are not, there will still be plenty to look at and enjoy. Italy is so rich in art treasures that she is herself like a huge art gallery. In any case, you will have a great opportunity to learn something about Italians at their best."⁵⁸ Offering a brief description of the main cities and pictures of iconic sights, it gestures toward potential sites of interest: With pride of place given to Florence, "one of the most interesting and attractive places in the world," it also signals the modern art museums of Milan, Venice and Rome, the "matchless situation, splendid harbours and glorious past" of Genoa, the archeological museums of Naples, an ample compensation for the unattractive city.⁵⁹

Despite this overt shift, however, the preinvasion and post-armistice guides demonstrate continuity in two key ways: the treatment of language, and the threat posed by the deceptive land and women. Even with the impending announcement of the armistice, the *SGTI*'s tepid encouragement of collaboration suggests a dismissive attitude, visible in the *SGTI*'s page-long list of "useful words and phrases" that comes verbatim from the preinvasion British *Soldier's Guide to Sicily*. Although the *SGTI*'s attitude toward the difficulty of learning the Italian language "really well" pivots one-hundred-eighty degrees from the *GOETI*'s claim that "Italian is not a difficult language to master," the guides are uniform in their low expectations of the role of verbal communication.[60] Aside from pleasantries, the *SGTI*'s phrases enable soldiers to express a desire, to verify whether they have been understood and answer in the negative ("Capisci?" "Non capisco.") The verbs make a series of demands—give me, bring me, I wish to eat, to drink, to buy, to pay, to go.[61] Eight nouns are foodstuffs—tea, coffee, water, wine, bread, egg, meat, and fish—and the only other is "woman." Facilitating little beyond a negotiation for comestibles or women, this vocabulary suggests that more than redeeming Italy through any substantive conversion, Allied soldiers were expected to consume Italian "goods."[62]

Another source of continuity is to be found in precautions against disease, seen in passages copied from the British *SGTS*'s detailed preventive measures and remedies for potential diseases including malaria, typhoid and V.D.—including the monition to "avoid contact with civilians as much as possible."[63] The *SGTS* writes: "The native, living as he does in primitive conditions, has become immune from many diseases which British soldiers are likely to contract. The insanitary condition of the Island is one of its best defences against an invader, and casualties from disease could well be higher than those caused in the field," an observation the *SGTI* extends to Italians in general.[64] In this wholesale transposition of the description of Sicily into the context of the entire peninsula, Sicily moves from "a poor but vicious Cinderella," exemplary in her backwardness, to a paradigm for Italy.[65]

On the subject of venereal disease, the *SGTI* instead follows the *GOETI*, replicating verbatim, "Contacts with Women." However, post-armistice, the *SGTI* acknowledges the possibility for other kinds of encounters in a section on "The Family and Women." Nonetheless, after making an overture to the common ground between Allied soldiers and Italians through a generic reference to their shared appreciation of "family life," the *SGTI* stresses Italy's difference through its treatment of women: "Like ourselves, to the ordinary Italian, family life means everything. Families are large and united, and divorce is rare. The men are by nature jealous and, particularly in the south, keep a close check on their women." Initially relegating these behaviors to the South, the *SGTI* extends them into "a general rule": "It is true that in the north the younger generation of women, at least in cities, has recently acquired more liberty in their movements and activities, but as a general rule Italian women and girls are everywhere allowed less freedom in their conduct than would be thought normal in America or Great Britain."[66] Thus, despite entertaining the possibility of intercultural romance, the *SGTI*'s treatment of "respectable unmarried girl[s]" and "strange women" differs only by degree.[67] While prostitutes threaten venereal disease, even a romantic relationship poses eminent danger: "Don't therefore think that you are going to find it easy to pick up a respectable girl in Italy without running the risk of a first-rate row, and remember that a number of Germans came to an untimely end through trying."[68]

In *SGTI*, both "respectable girl[s]" and "strange women" embody the threat of Italy's "backwardness": with the latter, the soldier risks infection or fascist infiltration but even with the former, he risks an honor killing. In the more explicit words of the *SGTS*, "The Sicilian is still . . . well known for his extreme jealousy in so far as his womenfolk are concerned, and in a crisis still resorts to the dagger."[69] As seen in the *SGTI*, Italy's transformation from enemy to cobelligerent only serves to spread the threat from the prostitute to respectable southern women to Italian women in general. The preinvasion *GOETI* contemplates only prostitution among possible sexual encounters; as Italian-Allied relations improve, the *SGTI* recognizes the possibility of romance, yet at no point do the Italian guides raise the possibility of marriage. Here, as we will continue to see in the postwar, the Italian guide makes a powerful contrast with France's and even Germany's, where marriage is discouraged but plausible.[70]

The Pocket Guide to Italy (1952–87)

From wartime enemies to Cold War allies, the history of U.S.-Italian relations forms a trajectory of progress, most apparent in the postwar Marshall Plan, whose goal was to help Italy transform from a "pre-capitalist state or at most a developing democracy" to the rightful heirs of "the ideals of democracy and republican government of Ancient Rome."[71] Successive revisions of the Cold War military guidebooks suggest that despite the ostensible progress, Italy-as-whore has not been redeemed. As the *GOETI* works to define the space of invasion, it predicts with prophetic accuracy what will be required to "restore" destination Italy. To dampen the allure of Italian hospitality, the *GOETI* evokes the horrors of fascism; as an antidote, the

Pocket Guide to Italy (*PGI*) censors the warzone evoked by the *GOETI* over the course of its postwar editions, until the final 1980s guide makes hospitality synonymous with Italianness, and their friendliness, the number-one tourist experience: "You will share their foods, the tourist sights that most Americans see only in travel books, and, most of all, the people's friendliness."[72] However, this shift masks a fundamental continuity: the paradigm of Italy-as-whore cannot be dismissed as a product of the hostilities of war, insofar as it is perpetuated throughout the postwar guidebooks that trumpet U.S.-Italian friendship; to wit, even as the *PGI*s no longer acknowledge prostitution, they nonetheless represent (southern) Italian women as the symbol of Italian backwardness and use conventionally feminized traits such as deception and a lack of control of language in their characterization of the Italian people.

In the wartime guidebooks, as in the cultural texts that I analyze in subsequent chapters, the prostitute (both the literal women and the personification of the country) offers an interpretive key. A reading of the postwar *PGI*s shows that Italy the "whore" has not been redeemed, and destination Italy has not been restored. As such, the revisions of the *PGI*s challenge the postwar paradigm of "Americanization" insofar as Italy remains "a ponderous mystery [that] we have yet to unravel," even after the country has been subsumed into America's orbit.[73] Nonetheless, successive editions of the *PGI*s do make a significant change, increasingly abbreviating any reference to the "virile" incursions of fascism that the *GOETI* foregrounds: No longer marred by war, "she" returns to her "destination" status even while inching toward an unobtainable modernity that would confer parity with the United States. The guidebooks' repression of militarism is not, however, simply an act of goodwill toward the Italians but concretely beneficial for the United States: Italy's "return" to a feminized, mythic destination, visited by tourists not soldiers, erases *all* traces of warfare, extending the "patina of leisure" to the Americans' ongoing military presence.[74]

Starting from the removal of the word "soldier" from the title, the postwar *PGI*s trace a path back to destination Italy. In the 1952 guide, GIs appear on the whimsical, line-drawn cover that depicts them strolling among iconic Italian spaces, making the book more visually appropriate for general audiences (Figure 1).[75] Recognizing the countries' improving relations, the 1952 *PGI* negotiates the soldier's relationship to the Italians: "The ties between the United States and Italy become stronger and more friendly as time goes on. By your conduct and attitude as an American serviceman you can help make those ties even stronger and more friendly." Emphasizing that democracy has not fully defeated communism, it warns soldiers that their

Figure 1. Cover, *A Pocket Guide to Italy*, 1956 (Office of Armed Forces Information and Education, Department of Defense).

uniforms may be misinterpreted.[76] However, if some Italians are unable to forget war, the 1952 *PGI* helps the soldier start on that path by revising Italian history far beyond localizing blame on Mussolini.[77]

One of the *GOETI*'s core accusations against fascism is its colonialist aggressions. The *PGI*'s account of colonialism is comparatively toothless: "as dictator, Mussolini abolished all political parties except his own and set out to build a new Italian empire which would extend into Africa, control the Mediterranean, and furnish an outlet for Italy's increasing population."[78] Here Mussolini's war on Ethiopia is a tentative, well-mannered effort, as he *sets out to build*, *extend*, and *control* in order to *furnish* space for his people. Fascism's agenda is not a mindless militarization nor a greedy conquest, nor is colonialism *the* catalyst for the war, as it is in the *GOETI*. Skipping an explanation for the Nazi-Fascist alliance altogether, the *PGI* speeds from the Allied victories in Sicily to the end of Italy's empire:

> In the ninth month of World War II, Italy under Mussolini entered the conflict on the side of the Nazis. But a little more than three years later, when Allied victories in Sicily and Northern Africa turned the tide of war against Italy, Mussolini was forced to resign and a new Italian government signed an armistice with the Allies. (Mussolini was put to death, by a group of antifascist partisans in 1945.) In the final peace treaty between the Allies and

Italy, signed in 1947, Italy gave up its African empire and most of the other possessions that it had acquired before and during Mussolini's dictatorship.[79]

In this first postwar guide, the implied reader is a hybrid soldier-sightseer. The 1952 *PGI* praises (and takes much credit for) Italy's progress yet, at the same time, showcases the picturesque in photographs of iconic tourist panoramas such as the Ponte Vecchio and the bay of Naples. In fact, even the photos meant to provide evidence of "progress" are undermined: An aerial shot of a train underscores crowding; photos of rebounding Italian "industry" show simple handicrafts and a basic factory. These photos are paired with line drawings whose whimsical style highlights the "quaint" elements of Italian culture. For instance, the photo of Italian industry appears on a facing page with a line drawing of a mule cart carrying bottles of wine, with lazy smiles on the face of the driver, the mule and the boy hitching a ride (Figure 2). Many of the cartoons trumpet stereotypes like the penchant of Italians for opera that, during the war, was used to emphasize their uncontrollable passion and question their capacity for self-governance.[80] Drawings meant to help the GIs adjust to cultural differences are similarly condescending: one that shows a GI and a live octopus frightening each other, explains, "Fish served in Italy may differ from what you're accustomed to" (Figure 3).

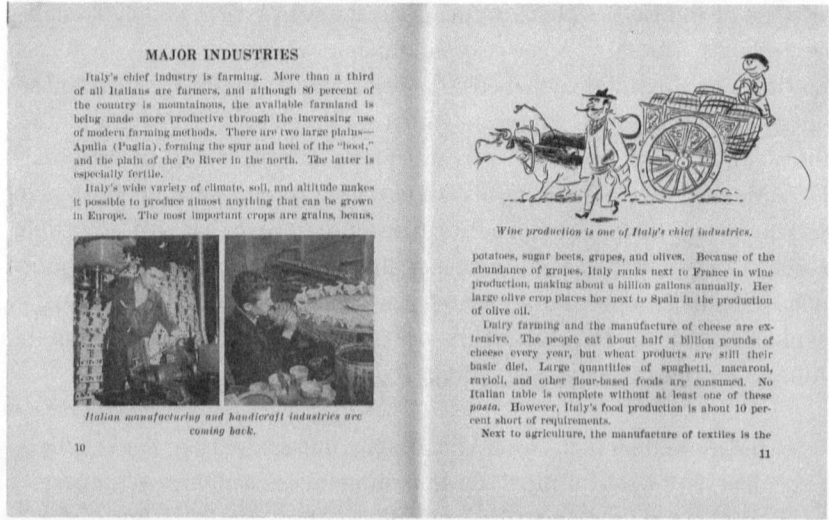

Figure 2. Italy's major industries are depicted as quaint, *A Pocket Guide to Italy*, 1956 (Office of Armed Forces Information and Education, Department of Defense).

peaches, apricots, grapes, pears, apples, bananas, etc. The coffee is strong and black and is drunk with plenty of sugar. The good restaurants have excellent ice cream.

Fish served in Italy are quite different from those of the Atlantic seaboard. Tuna fish, *polpi*, *calamaretti* (octopuses), and squids are on many menus. Venice and Genoa are famous for *zuppa di pesce* (ZOOP-ah dee PESH-shay), a fish soup. *Capretto* (kid) and *abacchio* (lambkin) are well known Italian meat dishes. Italians

Fish served in Italy may differ from what you're accustomed to.

25

Figure 3. A cultural lesson in cartoon form, *A Pocket Guide to Italy*, 1956 (Office of Armed Forces Information and Education, Department of Defense).

If Italian food is strange and threatening, the women are familiar—and they are there to be ogled: although this guidebook has no section devoted to "women," the drawings hint at its attitude: in a warning about traffic conditions, a soldier cranes to see a female passerby amongst the lackadaisical peasants ignoring the military vehicle; in another, two soldiers in a gondola stare at a woman on the dock. The images in the contemporary

Figure 4. On the left, images from *A Pocket Guide to Italy*, 1956; on the right, images from *A Pocket Guide to Germany*, 1956 (both Office of Armed Forces Information and Education, Department of Defense).

Pocket Guide to Germany provide a telling juxtaposition—near identical drawings of the traffic and the gondola, minus the gawking, which suggests that this imagery is pertinent to soldiers stationed in Italy (Figure 4).⁸¹ The 1951 *Pocket Guide to France* also makes a useful contrast. Although it warns against the presence of "a special sort of hardboiled dame who, for obvious business reasons, is sitting alone at a café table," its description of French women runs the gamut from business women, to female farmers, to respectable French girls who date only after following requisite formalities.⁸² Most strikingly, the guidebook writes, "They helped keep the country going during the war, when so many of their men were prisoners in Germany. They educated their children at home when the schools were closed. An impressive number were active members of the Resistance. They deserve lasting admiration."⁸³ Comparatively, the recognition of Italy's contribution to the war in the 1952 *PGI* is mild—and silent on women: "Above all, Italians are typically a warmhearted and hospitable people, endowed with quick and curious minds and a deep feeling for humanity. They are willing to help others even at personal risk, as happened often during World War II, when many of them in the cities and in the countrysides risked their lives for Allied servicemen in distress."[84]

The 1964 *Pocket Guide to Italy*, instead, makes "women" an explicit topic, discussing them in terms of Italy's backwardness, showing how their symbolic value holds steady before and after the fall of fascism and, moreover, from invasion to occupation to peace: "In the south, where traces of the cloistering influence of Saracens and Spaniards linger, respectable Italian girls do not go about in public at night without an escort. They are closely chaperoned. Northern girls do not take a chaperone along when they go out in the evening." Then backwardness spreads northward, as the southern woman becomes exemplary of a national phenomenon: "A direct approach to an Italian girl would be a serious mistake. Even the most tolerant Italian men would resent it, to put it mildly, and some would go to any lengths to avenge an insult to their family honor." The passage ends by stressing that Italian women deserve the same respectful treatment as Americans, yet this affirmation must be read alongside the warning that Italians cannot withstand a direct approach to their women, entrapped, as they are, in past traditions.[85] Here, the 1965 *Pocket Guide to Germany* demonstrates that this attitude toward Italian women is neither a product of Italy's former enemy status nor representative of a general treatment of foreign women; introducing German women in the opening page, the *PGG* uses her as a point of connection with American society, noting, "A pretty Fraulein in Hamburg or Heidelberg may remind you of the girl next door at home. This isn't surprising when you consider how many Americans have a German ancestor or so on their family trees."[86] If Germany's women are familiar because of immigration, Italian women should be, too; yet, they require decoding as a result of their long history of racialization in the United States. Concluding that Italian women's independence is a work in progress, the 1964 *PGI* writes, "Long dominated by fathers, brothers, and husbands, Italian women have become much more independent since World War II," but this "domination" is not so long past if even the *most* tolerant Italian men would resent what the guide implies is the American norm. Moreover, the evidence of the progress, "They vote and work at all kinds of jobs, including acting in films, modeling, and fashion-designing" only strengthens their association with artifice as it condescendingly dispatches Italian women's postwar gains.[87]

In the 1964 *PGI*, the tension between modernity and backwardness—embodied in the representations of Italian women—is similarly visible in the evocation of ancient ruins alongside every mention of modern skyscrapers: "Italy abounds in historical ruins, but the Italians also take pride in their skyscrapers and the many other signs of modern progress"; "Steel and glass skyscrapers tower above ancient ruins."[88] Even as it starts with signs of Italy's hard-won modernity—Milan, Florence, Turin, and Rome have "smartly dressed people going to work in modern offices or going home to modern apartments"—it ends on the "quaint" and "picturesque" conical stone huts, or *trulli*, "in the heel of the Italian boot."[89] Countering descriptions of the "modern" north with the "picturesque" south, it maps a north-south divide only to collapse it:

> Italy in a sense is two countries—north and south. The bustling activity of the industrial and urban north contrasts sharply with the sleepy, rustic charm of the south. As a rule, the northern Italian is more prosperous and sophisticated than his cousins in the south. The southerner, however, prefers a slower pace and his picturesque rural surroundings. One thing Italians, north and south, have in common—their zest for life.[90]

This makes a striking contrast with the 1966 *Pocket Guide to Greece*, which similarly puts the country's glorious past in constant relief but nonetheless comes down on the side of modernity with statements such as, "The Greeks do not rest on the laurels of their glorious past. They are more concerned with today and the future," and photographs of modern architecture and industry captioned, "Some Greek architecture is as modern as tomorrow" and "Petroleum plant—an example of the modern industries."[91]

Still, despite the tension that emerges out of the guidebook's struggle to maintain Italy's contradictory position between incipient modernity and intractable backwardness, the 1964 *PGI* pushes the soldier more definitively toward the sightseer, a change apparent in the cover with its invitation to the reader to follow the gondolier down a canal bathed in sunlight (Figure 5), as a prelude to the opening: "So you are going to Italy. You'll enjoy your stay. Many an armchair traveler will envy you the opportunity to see some of the world's most famous sights and meet some of the world's most warm-hearted, colorful people."[92]

Now squarely in the realm of travel and pleasure, fascism is nearly gone from the "History" section. Mussolini simply "took control of the government"; there is no catalyst for the war, no mention of colonialism, and barely an allusion to Italy's former enemy status:

> Italy fought with the Allies in World War I. Soon afterward, in 1922, Benito Mussolini's Fascist Party took control of the government. Under the dictatorship of Mussolini, Italy entered World War II on the side of Germany and Japan. Italian defeats in North Africa and Sicily, however, caused the

Figure 5. Cover, *A Pocket Guide to Italy, 1964* (Armed Forces Information and Education, Department of Defense).

collapse of Mussolini's dictatorship in 1943, and Italy fought the rest of the war on the side of the Allies.

Italy abolished the monarchy in 1946 and became a democratic republic. It joined NATO in 1949 and the United Nations in 1955.[93]

By the 1981 guide, this transformation is complete; congratulating the GI for his good fortune, the guide promises "you will enjoy the Italians as personal friends, since the friendliness of the Italian people is legendary."[94] The sides of World War II are not drawn up as the twenty-six years between Mussolini's rise to power and the adoption of the Constitution pass in three (not fully accurate) sentences:

> In 1922, Benito Mussolini came to power and, in the course of the next few years, eliminated the old political parties, curtailed liberties, and installed a fascist dictatorship called the Corporate State.
> The King, with little power, remained titular head of state.
> After World War II, the Constitution of 1948 abolished the monarchy and set up a republic.[95]

The contrast with the 1943 *GOETI* could not be starker. It recounts:

> Mussolini soon became a dictator. His party took control of the life of the country. His secret police hounded the people. Opposition leaders were either exterminated, intimidated into silence or forced to flee the country. The Fascists tortured their victims by force-feeding them large doses of castor oil. That's the kind of people they are. No gang of hoodlums ever showed as little regard for common decency as did the Fascist leaders.[96]

From the 1943 *GOETI*, where Mussolini hounds, exterminates, intimidates, exiles, and tortures, to the 1981 *PGI*, where he generically curtails liberties, a wholesale erasure of fascism and colonialism has taken place. In 1981, the only—vague—allusion to Italy's relationship to its neighbors comes in a geography lesson, under "Your Host Nation": "Surrounded by five seas and with Sicily just 90 miles from mainland Africa, the Italian peninsula has been the jumping-off place to the African continent and to the far reaches of the Orient for centuries."[97] The subject-less "jumping-off place" may imply the voyages of Marco Polo, Mussolini's army—or the strategic position of the bases inhabited by the U.S. soldier. The implications of this geography lesson, however, are lost within the 1981 guide's exuberant embrace of the soldier as supertourist: "Your assignment to Italy is a good reason to start celebrating! During your tour of duty in Italy, you will have more pleasant and interesting experiences than any tourist could ever afford."[98] By restoring mythic destination Italy, the United States downplays its present-day military importance. Indeed, the very touristic conceptualization of Italy that the *GOETI* represents as a potential distraction *from* war is instead a distraction that *allows* war to be waged quietly, during the Cold War and beyond; David Vine writes about the contemporary situation: "Most tourists think of Italy as the land of Venetian canals, Roman ruins, Florentine Palaces, and, of course, pizza, pasta, and wine. . . . But Italy's fifty 'base sites' give it more American base locations than any country in the world except Japan, Germany, and South Korea."[99]

Destination Italy works to mask the violence of continued occupation yet the censoring effect is reciprocal. Even as the 1981 *PGI* promises *more pleasant and interesting experiences than any tourist could ever afford*, it contains less destination Italy than even the *GOETI*; the 1981 *PGI*'s tourist section is a four-item "must-see" list: ruins, opera, the Vatican and art.[100] Indeed, with each *PGI*, the touristic descriptions decrease as the soldier's identity is eclipsed by his role as super-tourist: a twenty-two page section in 1952 becomes single-sentence descriptions of major cities and a bibliography for future reading in 1964, while the 1981 *PGI* reveals a discourse that has reached exhaustion: "American armed forces have been in Italy for years. Every installation library has a special section set aside for books on Italy—things to see and do in the area of the installation as well as throughout the country."[101] Sending its readers to generic past publications because "there are too many places to visit and things to see to be covered in this small brochure,"[102] the 1981 *PGI*'s refusal to represent Italy suggests awareness that the "destination" is fossilized—a symptom of the relentless intertextuality of an "archeological attitude" that perpetuates a series of images, "virtually unchanged, over the centuries."[103] Soldiers are told, "take time to read about Italy's accomplishments, past and present, and let your Italian friends know that you appreciate their rich culture," yet they must go do their own research to do so.[104] Starting from the generic cover (Figure 6), the 1981 *PGI* has no photos, just icons that take for granted that the Coliseum, gondolas, and spaghetti are in the reader's referential frame. The Italian host is even more thoroughly effaced: other 1980s guides, such as to Greece and Turkey, use icons with specific cultural markers to depict their hosts, be it traditional garb or stereotypically racialized features (Figure 7). The illustration of Italy's opening section, "Welcome—Benvenuto," depicts two identical white bodies melding into one another in an embrace, delocalized and stripped of distinguishing features—a sign that the exhortation of the Marshall Plan, "you too can be like us," has come to pass.[105]

A happy conclusion to U.S.-Italian relations is also visible in the icon illustrating the 1981 language section: two identical openmouthed silhouettes saying "*buon giorno*" that resonate with this ethos of cultural reciprocity, again distinct from other country guides' language icons. Compared to the *GOETI*'s dismissal of the importance of learning Italian and *SGTI*'s list of useful words that include "*non capisco*" ("I don't understand"), the 1981

Figure 6. Cover *A Pocket Guide to Italy*, 1981 (Armed Forces Information Service, Department of Defense).

PGI's icon of communication is utopic. Yet this transformation once again distracts from an essential continuity. Although the *PGI*s encourage soldiers to learn Italian, the motive remains pleasure over communication: "Learn to speak some Italian, even if you speak it badly. The people will like it, and you'll get along better"; "Any attempt you make at speaking Italian will be warmly received."[106] Moreover, even when Italians are hosts and GIs guests, the guide expects no substantive communication: "The Italian prefers talking to listening and is not at all shy about expressing his views";

Figure 7. Top row, *A Pocket Guide to Italy*, 1981; middle row, *A Pocket Guide to Germany*, 1982; bottom row, *A Pocket Guide to Turkey*, 1981 (all Armed Forces Information Service, Department of Defense).

"There is more talking than there is listening, but all enjoy the sport of conversation."[107] In contrast with the menacing prohibition of fraternization, the postwar descriptions seem like an improvement, if the worst one might fear from a conversation with Italians is that it be unbalanced. But as the *PGI* praises Italians for having a "zest for life" and "sheer joy of living,"[108] in no case does it represent them as valid interlocutors, echoing "one of the primary features of [Italy's] female identity, as Northern men characterized it": "the Italians' inability consciously to express themselves, to control language and the *logos* that underlies it."[109] The 1981 guide's encouragement to "learn the language of your hosts" spells out its priorities for soldiers' intercultural communication: "Even if you learn only a few words a day, in a few months' time you will have a vocabulary for traveling, shopping, friendship."[110] Thus, the 1981 *PGI* fulfills the promises of the *GOETI*. Having redeemed the Italians from fascism, they can now enjoy and consume them.

Nonetheless, the *PGI*s evidence the asymmetries explicitly depicted during the open hostilities of invasion. For instance, the warning about fake souvenirs is reframed in terms of Italian craftsmanship that results in particularly "excellent imitations."[111] Moreover, whereas the wartime guides condemn southern indolence, the *PGI*s reposition it as a positive lifestyle choice, a la *dolce vita*: "The southerner . . . prefers a slower pace and his picturesque rural surroundings"; "Take time for the little courtesies that many of us overlook in the rapid pace of American life"; "Go a little slower though each day. When you can make the time to stop for a chat with your neighbors on the street, practice the little courtesies they enjoy, and share your food and drink with them, then you will be truly an ambassador."[112] Even as the *PGI*s stress U.S.-Italian friendship, they return to Italy's difference, demonstrating the continuity of the *GOETI*'s essentialized Italian—backward, deceptive, feminized. Indeed, the 1981 *PGI*'s icons of Anglo-Italian intercultural embrace obscure the overt violence as the asymmetries of the civilian-soldier encounter are covered by a "patina of leisure," in the transformation to guest/host and ultimately friend/friend.

Deceptive, feminized mysteries, Italians are always hiding something, good or bad: "The happy-go-lucky exterior of many Italians conceals a sensitive nature and a deep sense of pride in everything Italian"; "Even when times are not the best, they have a smile for the world."[113] This characterization is repeated by H. Stuart Hughes—one of America's foremost historians of Italy, who was appointed to the OSS as the director of its Italy Research and Analysis Department—in his seminal book *The United States and Italy* (1953).[114] Hughes chides Americans for their lack of true knowledge of Italy, building an analogy between postwar tourists who fall for "shiny" shop fronts and "delectable" food and their fathers who were tricked by Mussolini:

> One has the impression that Americans have been so busy enjoying the country that they have not had time to think about its problems. Italy is certainly to be enjoyed. But it is not to be enjoyed with the guilelessness of those tourists who assume that all is well just because the shop fronts are shiny and the food in the restaurants is delectable—as their fathers assumed that all was in order because Mussolini had cleaned up Naples and made the trains run on time. To enjoy Italy and to love it is not enough. One must also see, in the words of one of its greatest contemporary students, that it is a "tragic country—with a smiling face."[115]

Hidden beneath a smiling face, punctual trains or delicious food, Italy's "true" self can be found only with effort: mysterious yet accessible in Grand Tour writings; "a land that seems greatly familiar [but] . . . is inadequately known" in the immediate postwar; "a ponderous mystery . . . that we have yet to unravel," even when our nations are the best of friends.[116] Superlatively backward, Italy remains the fungible symbol for alterity it is in the *GOETI*: "Perhaps, when the last word is said, that is the most important point to remember in your relations with the Sicilians, the Sardinians, the people of the Italian mainland, or the men and women of any land to which your military duties may take you. They have had less opportunity than we of the United States."[117]

Having traced the gendering of redemption in U.S. military guidebooks from the invasion of Sicily through the Cold War, in the next chapter I turn to three postwar texts that revise and critique the paradigm: the canonical neorealist film *Paisà* (1946), directed by Roberto Rossellini, and the novels *All Thy Conquests* (1946) and *The Girl on the Via Flaminia* (1949) by Alfred Hayes, an intelligence officer who remained in Italy after the war and originated the "Rome" episode for *Paisà*. In representing the symbolically laden "liberation" of Rome, these texts use the sexual encounter between an Italian woman and an American soldier to echo the long-awaited but short-lived "honeymoon" between nations. In so doing, each text shapes redemption within its respective national context: While the American novels fantasize the restoration of destination Italy, the Italian film uses the fallen woman to repress the traumas of postliberation Rome, in service of the redemptive myth of neorealism.

2 "Liberated" Rome beyond Redemption
Roberto Rossellini's *Paisà* and Alfred Hayes's *All Thy Conquests* and *The Girl on the Via Flaminia*

The story is boy meets girl, the setting the Allied liberation of Rome. He is an American soldier who has endured a brutal nine-month journey up the peninsula, while she, an Italian civilian, has endured the brutal Nazi occupation of a city that was "open" only in name.[1] In the celebratory confusion, she leads him to her apartment to wash up. Limited in his knowledge of Italian, he learns only her name, Francesca. After this chaste flirtation, he rejoins the troops, promising to return. When he does, a happy reunion is impossible; by then, the American liberators are drunks, the Italian women whores. In the hell of postliberation Rome, Francesca's namesake can only be Dante's infernal heroine.

In two 1946 representations, this failed romance takes place amid an inexorable slide experienced by the entire city, as the liberation turns into an occupation. In Alfred Hayes's novel *All Thy Conquests* (1946), Harry gives up his three-month search for Francesca, realizing: "She went away with those four hours when we liberated this city. She belongs with those hours. I'll never see her again."[2] In the third episode of Roberto Rossellini's film *Paisà* (Italian release 1946; U.S. release 1948), Fred chances upon Francesca six months later but, failing to recognize her, condemns her as a symbol: "Rome's full of girls like you," he mutters, "Now you're all alike." As he tells his story, Francesca recognizes herself in the angelic heroine. She strategizes a daytime reunion—but his disillusionment is total. Standing in front of her door beneath a cloud that seems to only rain on her, Francesca dons her frilly dress, "awaiting an appointment with the soldier/redeemer who never shows up."[3]

Both novel and film were well received when they appeared in their respective countries in 1946. Today, however, the substantive connection of *All Thy Conquests* to "Rome"—neither coincidence nor plagiarism—has been relegated to a footnote in the voluminous scholarship devoted to Rossellini's canonical film: Hayes, a U.S. intelligence officer who got involved with the Italian film industry when he stayed in Rome after the war, is credited as the cooriginator of the subject of *Paisà*'s "Rome," along with Klaus Mann. Significantly revised by Rossellini and his collaborators into the final version, the story was also transformed by Hayes to become part of *All Thy Conquests*.[4] Beyond this plotline, novel and film received similar praise for their groundbreaking realism within their respective national traditions of Italian cinematic neorealism and the American war novel.[5] Their episodic structure engenders further comparison: *All Thy Conquests* traces the downfall of six protagonists (three Americans and three Italians) on a single day in September, 1944; *Paisà* travels through six locations northward up the peninsula over nearly the entire span of the Allies' wartime presence in Italy. Starting from the July invasion of Sicily, *Paisà* moves to postliberation Naples, postliberation Rome, the ongoing liberation of Florence, an Apennine monastery removed from the horrors of war and, finally, to the delta of the Po River in the winter of 1944–45, where Allies and Italian partisans die side by side.

Considering the stark asymmetry between scholarship on *All Thy Conquests* with respect to *Paisà*, I frame this chapter with a critical reading of the latter body, in particular the "Rome" "problem" that implicates both texts. Here, *Paisà*'s episodic structure becomes crucial insofar as it demands the viewer's involvement in the production of meaning, in terms of how to relate and weight the disjointed parts. In Millicent Marcus's words, "The Italy of *Paisà* is composed in the viewers' minds—the various fragments emerging from the six regional stories only assemble themselves into a national whole at the end of the film, and that whole becomes a creation of the audience, which actively integrates its disparate parts as the viewing experience draws to an end."[6] For decades, critics have, in rather coherent fashion, built a hierarchy: Systematically excluding "Rome," they privilege the first and last, Sicily and the Po, whose characters fall to their death: Carmela on the rocky Sicilian terrain, and the partisans into the murky river.[7] Today, thanks to compelling readings, the third episode is no longer reviled as a melodramatic "alien" that threatens to contaminate its neorealist host, yet critics interested in exploring Rossellini's postfascist renegotiation of the Eternal City, nonetheless look to his earlier film, *Roma città aperta*.[8] This preference may be due to the fact that *Roma città aperta* "resort[s] to a synecdochal relationship between Rome and Italy," whereas *Paisà*'s structure "enables Rossellini literally to encompass the entire nation in his film."[9] Nonetheless, despite the expanded geographical focus of *Paisà*, the same Rome/Italy relationship at the heart of *Roma città aperta* manifests itself in *Paisà* through Francesca, commonly read as an allegory for the fallen nation in need of redemption.¹⁰ As Danielle Hipkins has argued, the connection between *Roma città aperta* and *Paisà* is strengthened by the casting of Maria Michi to play the fallen woman in both.¹¹ Bringing together analyses of "Rome" such as Hipkins's, together with efforts in Italian cinema studies to problematize neorealism's construction of the myth of national redemption, this chapter redresses "Rome's" ongoing outsider status within *Paisà* scholarship.¹² Starting from Giuliana Minghelli's powerful assertion that *Paisà* be read, "Not [as] an epic of national liberation and rebirth, but a monument, even more so today, to the embattled character of Italian postwar memory," I engage *Paisà* and *All Thy Conquests* in an intertextual reading in order to argue that in its melodramatic rendering of the fallen woman, "Rome" lies at the heart of this monument for what it represents as much as for what it represses.¹³

Another structural similarity between the "Harry" of *All Thy Conquests* and the "Rome" of *Paisà* that informs my analysis is their use of the flashback to juxtapose the joyous day of liberation in June with a later moment that represents the city's fall, albeit with an important difference of three versus six months. While "Rome" begins, like all six of *Paisà*'s episodes, with newsreel footage and a voiceover signaling the Allies' progress, the jump-cut from June to December sets "Rome" apart.¹⁴ Amid drinking games, two fur-clad women provoke a fight that spirals into a full-blown brawl as the military police raid the locale. Rounding up the fleeing women, the MPs load them onto a truck (Figure 8). (Although the truck's destination is not specified, the historical response to the postliberation venereal disease epidemic tells us that they will be delivered to the Italian police, subjected to humiliating medical exams and given substandard treatment.)¹⁵ Caught by an MP, Francesca breaks free and escapes his pursuit by ducking into a movie theater. On her way out, she picks up a drunken GI and escorts him to a nearby apartment, where he sleepily resists her advances as he tells the story of a girl he met six months earlier. As the liberation returns in a flashback, Francesca is part of an ecstatic crowd welcoming Fred as he emerges from his tank. Wearing a frilly dress and a smile at turns inviting and shy, she brings him up to her apartment. As he washes off the filth of the campaign, they exchange awkward dialogue in broken Italian and guidebook English, talking briefly about the long-anticipated liberation. Six months later, as Fred lies in Francesca's bed, unaware of her identity, he laments the fall of Rome's women; so deeply disillusioned, Fred cannot follow her new script to reunite them.

Just as in "Rome," the "Harry" vignette of *All Thy Conquests* uses flashbacks in order to contrast the paradisiacal moment of the liberation with the

Figure 8. Women accused of prostitution are carted away for a medical exam in *Paisà* (1946), directed by Roberto Rossellini.

hell that unfolded. However, the novel's September setting is not arbitrary: *All Thy Conquests* takes place on a day that left a tragic mark on the city, September 18, 1944, the start of the first postliberation trial of Rome's High Court, part of an ill-conceived effort of public defascistization meant to demonstrate Italy's postwar redemption. The defendant was Pietro Caruso, Rome's police chief under the Nazis, "a fringe character in the Fascist hierarchy."[16] Charged for his role in the March 24, 1944, Fosse Ardeatine massacres, "the only coldblooded mass execution perpetrated in the space of a big city," Caruso was sentenced to death and executed by firing squad on September 22.[17] However, this grand piece of judiciary theater only concluded after an unscripted start when courtroom spectators seized Donato Carretta, former prison director and a witness for the prosecution. Dragging him outside, they brutalized and threw him into the Tiber. After drowning him, they carried his dead body through the streets of Rome and hung it up in front of the prison. Scandalizing the international community and eliciting a joint statement of condemnation from Roosevelt and Churchill, the lynching raised doubts about Italy's ability to self-govern.[18]

Strategically absent from *Paisà*, as I discuss, a fictionalized version of the Caruso-Carretta affair provides the frame for *All Thy Conquests*. On this charged backdrop, the protagonists experience a personal downfall, leaving Allies and Italians alike products of—and metonyms for—Rome beyond redemption.[19] Despite its promising early fortunes and ties to one of postwar Italy's most celebrated cinematic products, *All Thy Conquests* never obtained lasting recognition, a fate I believe is, in part, attributable to its fictionalization of the Caruso-Carretta affair and its relationship to "Rome." The treatment of Hayes by Tag Gallagher, one of "Rome's" loudest naysayers, is emblematic, as he reduces the biographical connection between Hayes and Rossellini to a footnote.[20] However, when he narrates how *Paisà* achieved the "aura of a national epic," Gallagher uses Hayes as a placeholder to represent the initially dominant "American" perspective, erased as Rossellini strived to capture an Italian point of view.[21] Observing that Hayes's draft focuses on the American GI while Rossellini's final version favors the Italian woman, Gallagher claims that this shift emblematizes a transformational process undergone by each of the episodes.

Contemporary reevaluations of the film amply demonstrate the artificiality of Gallagher's nationalistic lens and instead contextualize neorealism in a North Atlantic, Marshall Plan–era dynamic. Karl Schoonover suggests "an even more radical postnational redefinition of the neorealist aesthetic in which neorealism indexes the increasing role of U.S. interests in Italy as much as it showcases the peninsula's newfound independence."[22] However, by privileging the "Sicily" and the "Po Delta," episodes that frame the film with fallen corpses, Schoonover and others miss the way in which the melodramatic "Rome" narrative enables neorealism's "foundational national fantasy" by repressing the trauma that threatens "Italy's redemption."[23] In light of Lorenzo Fabbri's claim that "neorealism in fact supports the illusion ... of a nation pure at heart that, having left its past behind, is fully prepared to move forward and fully deserves the economic support coming in from the Marshal [sic] plan," it is essential to understand what is repressed by these redemption narratives, produced when Italy's economic fate was being negotiated.[24]

This intertextual dialogue with *All Thy Conquests* further contextualizes *Paisà* in a North Atlantic dynamic and contributes to readings of "Rome" that insist on its historical engagement through its gendered redemption narrative. Building on Hipkins's analysis of the prostitute in Italian cinema "as a 'lightning conductor' for a whole range of social anxieties and issues," I argue that *Paisà* uses Francesca to repress the trauma of the Fosse Ardeatine that *All Thy Conquests* instead foregrounds through the botched Caruso trial and the mob.[25] Pointing to unhealed wounds in Italy, the mob was a doubly problematic symbol insofar as it evoked the American context where regular lynchings questioned the civic health of the supposed redeemers (as Italian politicians were quick to point out). However, as we will see, when he revisits the setting in *The Girl on the Via Flaminia* (1949), Hayes comes closer into alignment with "Rome," effecting his critique by focusing exclusively on the "fallen" woman.[26] As *The Girl on the Via Flaminia* employs the symbolism of the liberation as drama, it sharply revises the celebratory tone of journalistic accounts that used "fallen" Italian women to right the redemptive arc of the Allied-Italian encounter threatened by the "hysterical" (always feminized) Roman mob.

The "Liberation" of Rome

Nine costly months after the armistice, on June 5, 1944, the Allied army attained "the goal of conquerors throughout the ages." Reaching the Eternal City through "the almost impossible north-south campaign" earned the U.S. Fifth Army a superlative place in history, Herbert Matthews wrote in that day's *New York Times*.[27] Celebrated as an unparalleled triumph, the liberation of Rome starred American General Mark W. Clark, "crowned not with the laurel leaves of the Caesars but with a simple overseas cap over a simple field uniform, and riding not in a chariot but in a jeep." Singular for his military achievement, "the victor of Rome" was also the first "conqueror" to be "cheered" as a "liberator."[28] In that same issue, Anne O'Hare McCormick underscores the symbolic dimension of Rome's liberation, as she envisions "the birthplace of fascism" as a global stage on which the Allies could "dramatiz[e] the part played by the New World in the deliverance of the Old."[29] *Life Magazine* chimed in: "Rome's fall, for the first time in its history to liberators, not conquerors, was an epic achievement."[30] Continuing their effusive coverage, the next day McCormick praised the "magnificent" timing of the event, "potent as a symbol of the conflict between civilization and the new barbarism," while Matthews elated, "Never has there been such a Roman triumph as was this day. Jeeps on the Campidoglio, tanks rolling past St. Peter's almost under the windows of the Pope's office, G.I.'s buying flowers for Roman lassies and excitement everywhere."[31] In similar tones to McCormick, Matthews's triumphant narrative continued throughout the summer, as he cast the June "deliverance" as a rebirth that revealed the true nature of the Roman people:

> Then we entered, first timidly in the dark of June 4, then openly on the morning of June 5, and Rome seemed to rise from the ashes. That attitude of indifference, cynicism and world-weariness proved to be only a mask after

all, even though it is a mask that almost never is taken off. Here was fervor, excitement, joy and friendliness that flowed like a river to welcome not conquerors, but deliverers.[32]

This changed abruptly on September 18, 1944, little more than one hundred days after the supposed turning point in the triumphant "drama of Liberation," as the trial of Rome's former police chief, Pietro Caruso, was about to begin in the High Court.[33] What was meant to be the start of Italy's defascistization, instead devolved into a harrowing event that Matthews relayed in graphic detail in the next day's *New York Times*: Donato Carretta, a witness for the prosecution, was "viciously beat[en] . . . over the head with the curved handle" of an old man's cane and "dragged out, thrown on the ground, jumped on and kicked until unconscious." Singling out "one young girl with black hair and sunglasses, dressed well in a white summer outfit and looking like a student," he also lambasts the onlookers for enjoying the gruesome spectacle: "Many laughed as two men next to me did gleefully when they realized that Caretta [*sic*] was going to be thrown into the river." As part of his emphatic condemnation of the Roman people, Matthews quotes one bystander: "'Poor Italians!' one Italian said. 'Unless the Americans come to defend us, they will kill us all.'" Here, in this tellingly unattributed remark, lies the symbolic importance Matthews ascribed to the event: Italy's provisional government "has proved unable to keep order" and "enough people have lost all sense of civic virtue to make an extremely ugly situation in Rome."[34] Amplifying this position, *Life Magazine* published a detailed photospread accompanied by dramatic headlines and captions that underscore the symbolism of the degradation of present-day Rome, "the city which gave justice its first strength and meaning in the Western World."[35] McCormick similarly ascribes broad significance to the mob; extrapolating to the entire city, she suggests that "If the route of the parade of hate had been longer it could easily, one felt, have drawn in the whole population of Rome." Going further, she interprets the mob as a symptom of a "disease latent and waiting to oversweep many countries besides Italy . . . anarchy." As observers rushed to diagnose the health of the Italian body politic, the Roman mob became a malleable symbol. Were its members thugs, aggrieved families, fascist or communist agitators? Was the lynching an aberrant event or a "manifestation" of the state of the Italian people?[36] The answers, proffered by Italian and Anglo-American newspapers alike, interpreted Carretta's death "depending on the editorial staff."[37]

Two days later, damage control was underway: Caruso's trial recommenced in a new venue, he was found guilty, sentenced to death and executed on September 22—an ending that afforded the debacle a patina of respectability and Caruso, a measure of dignity: "Upon hearing the verdict, those nearby reported that a tear came to Caruso's eye, and even *Avanti!* discerned, perhaps, some air of redemption in this touch of humanity."[38] Matthews lauded Caruso's bravery, concluding, "I only wish that when my time comes I can behave half as well as did that despicable brute, Pietro Caruso."[39] In response to the event, Roosevelt and Churchill decided to afford Italy *more* autonomy, and in appreciation the Italian government reaffirmed its commitment to the Allies by declaring war on Japan. At the same time, Italy moved forward with inquiries to bring closure. In November, Carretta was exonerated for his antifascist contributions and Maria Ricottini, a woman whose son was killed by the Nazis, was blamed for instigating the mob, not for any political motive but because she was crazy, a diagnosis supported by her sister's certified lunacy.[40]

These efforts notwithstanding, the Caruso-Carretta affair deflated the tone of Matthews's and McCormick's coverage: shortly after the trial Matthews wrote a long essay on defascistization, introducing the word as "not only hard to say," but also, "something that is terribly hard to do." Perpetuating McCormick's rhetoric, Matthews makes a grim prognosis: "Nor is fascism like an infected toe on the boot of Italy which can be amputated. It is a symptom of an organic sickness—an effect rather than a cause." Two years later in his memoir, Matthews validates his unfettered condemnation of the brutality. However, he revises what he understood to be the moment when liberation became conquest; rather than recognize the Carretta lynching as the turning-point in his own reporting, Matthews claims that it was the epidemic of prostitution that soured the Allied-Roman "romance," a belief asserted in other memoirs of postliberation Rome; he recalls:

> It was not long before I had to write that, as far as Rome and the Allies were concerned, "the honeymoon was over." Within ten days the wits were grumbling, "Rome was never like this," and asking when the soldiers were going to leave, why they were eating up Roman food, and whether Italians were supposed to enjoy the way Roman girls and women were throwing themselves into the arms of the American soldiers.[41]

Italian courts, too, replicated this tendency to blame women from Ricottini to Cornelia Tanzi, one of Mussolini's lovers sentenced to thirty years in prison, compared to two fascist generals sentenced only to twenty. In its coverage of the respective trials, the *New York Times* suggests that Tanzi's made for popular theater: "There often were only a few score spectators at the generals' trial but the Tanzi trial was packed and today many spectators were standing. They seemed to have a reasonably good time while the defendant did considerable weeping."[42]

In contrast to the gendered "vision of morally rotten Fascists and Nazis" that continues to inspire "comment in the popular press and on the screen," the Roman mob was a symbol of very short duration.[43] Despite initial fears that it signified the irreversible moral decay of Rome, Italy and all of Europe; despite photographic, filmic, and eyewitness testimony, the Caruso-Carretta affair left little trace in postwar cultural production, with *All Thy Conquests* a singular exception. Indeed, more than benign neglect, there appears to have been an explicit intent to repress its memory: Luchino Visconti, who captured live footage of the lynching for the resistance documentary *Giorni di gloria* (1945), included only the briefest clip of the courtroom chaos with "no suggestion of the fatal conclusion," precisely because—the filmmakers decided—such inclusion would give the episode a symbolic value they asserted it did not have.[44] In parallel with this work on *Giorni di gloria*, critics have shown how Rossellini's *Roma città aperta* goes further in repressing the Fosse Ardeatine in order to preserve the film's "redemptive and affirmative functions."[45] In Minghelli's sophisticated reading, this sublimated trauma makes its return in *Paisà*, as "Rossellini displaces his closest monument to the Fosse Ardeatine from the terrestrial to the aqueous environment of the Po."[46] Extending her claims, I argue that "Rome's" melodramatic mode works to repress the Caruso-Carretta episode, and that this repression is continued by the film's episodic structure that anchors its redemptive trajectory in the northern *Resistenza*. This tendency is furthered by critics who, as they leap over Francesca's fall to concentrate on the fallen partisans, help depict the Resistance "as a redemptive force that absolved Italy from the sins of the past."[47] For all their commonalities, *All Thy Conquests* shouts what *Paisà* and its critics repress, painting the mob as the symptom of a city crushed under the symbolic weight of its drama.

All Thy Conquests: The Drama of "Liberation"

From its title and epigraph—a citation from Shakespeare's *Julius Caesar*—*All Thy Conquests* foregrounds the motif of the "liberation" of Rome as drama whose climax is the trial of an unnamed fascist official.[48] Divided in three acts, it opens with a "Chorus" that describes the trial as a spectacle.[49] However, although the Palace of Justice has the requisite "Latin inscriptions" and "famous statues of famous lawgivers," the weather does not match the mood for "a day of judgment."[50] Nor does the main actor appear well cast, the narrator remarks when Caruso's literary doppelganger is introduced in the first of four vignettes: "He did not look, to those who did not know him, as they had expected him to look.... He did not look menacing, he did not look like a tiger."⁵¹ Observing his fellow actors—the journalists and lawyers—the defendant becomes insecure; despite having rehearsed, he imagines the frustrated expectations of the "ticket holders" who want to see someone who embodies the crime:

> It was because of this man, they were thinking to themselves, that in a sandpit, during a March afternoon, three hundred and fifty innocent men had been machinegunned to death, and their corpses dynamited and buried in the raw earth, and the crime was of such incredible proportions, the dead of so huge a number, they felt he must share some of the unhuman characteristics of the deed.⁵²

Instead of the Fosse Ardeatine massacre personified, the reader sees an imbecile, as a portrait emerges of a man who followed orders until the end, foolishly waiting in Rome on the eve of the Allies' arrival after his superiors had all fled.

The purpose of the performance is spelled out in the second vignette, as the prosecutor describes his haunting visit to the scene of the crime, dwelling on the "indescribable odor" that permeates the air: "The earth is damp, mottled, the roof scooped out and hollow, and here it seems as though everything gives off that sickening taint: rock, sand, clay, and dirt, so that one's whole world becomes foul, the infection personal, the decay intimate."⁵³ From his experience of the putrid smell, the prosecutor represents the trial as a start in Italy's task of "cleans[ing] our skies of this odor," which requires getting to the root of the country's fascist illness.⁵⁴ Here, Hayes's prosecutor takes a different approach from that of his historical counterpart, who attacked Caruso not "as a creature of fascism but as a thug, a mad dog ... not a career bureaucrat but rather a kind of mobster, an authentic hired assassin."⁵⁵ Instead, as Hayes's prosecutor elaborates on the defendant's life, he sketches this "primitive film" loosely enough for it to morph into the nation's. Taking on a series "of social disguises," the defendant plays the role of "the squadristo [sic], the fledgling blackshirt," until: "We see him everywhere now, multiplied."⁵⁶ Advancing a Crocean interpretation of fascism as a sickness of the national body, the prosecutor suggests that his conviction will be part of the cure; he asks rhetorically, "who knows what terrible surgery may be needed before we are healed?"⁵⁷ Yet what if the illness were not localizable and all of Italy were implicated? The defendant makes his case for absolution on this basis. Claiming to have assumed these roles out of duty to his father, his party and his *patria*, he argues that any person could have played the part. Stretched to its endpoint, this logic collapses perpetrator and victim, a point the text illustrates by veering into the fantastical, as a dead man appears as a witness; when the defendant asks, "what would you have done were you in my place on the night when the orders were given to me?" his victim stops the cross-examination with his emphatic assertion: "I am not you.... I could not have been you."

If the trial tries to maintain one boundary, the final vignette, "The Sentence," features a collapse of individual identity that derails the drama of defascistization, as the organizers "saw their effective scenery, so carefully erected, and before which they were to perform, torn apart, and the drama, so carefully rehearsed, come to another, and unforeseen, last act."[58] Here, the narrator is identified as one of the courtroom spectators who describes the experience of losing himself in the mob that carries out the death sentence that had yet to be pronounced.[59] Meditating on how his identity is subsumed within the collective, the narrator likens his acquiescence to this primal anger to "a volcano [that] began to erupt," a description that resonates with McCormick's account of "a wholly spontaneous flareup of animal rage that spread like wildfire from the few hundreds in the courtroom, mostly wives and mothers of the Ardeatine victims, to the crowds outside."[60] As the people coalesce, the narrator starts to feel "that slow enormous movement, the many bodies moving together, toward the long marble corridor and toward the oak doors of the chamber in which he was awaiting sentence, moving and moving."[61] Soon, he becomes a passionate, vocal member of the mob, unrecognizable even to himself: "I, myself, who had not shouted until then, was not conscious of my own voice, how harsh and how unlike my own it was, coming from my own throat."[62] By the end of his description, the ancient volcano has been transformed into the city of Rome, "All the city beat him: every alley, every palazzetta, every square and marketplace beat him," a personification that goes only one step further than McCormick's hyperbolic conjecture: "If the route of the parade of hate had been longer it could easily, one felt, have drawn in the whole population of Rome."[63] This is the tragic outcome of the drama of "liberation": not a deliverance but a tragedy that implicates every one of Rome's living residents.

For all its lyricism, the account in *All Thy Conquests* of the Roman mob corresponds in large part to Matthews's and McCormick's, including details about the mob's majority female makeup and its specific acts of violence: throwing its victim into the Tiber, "bloody, an eye almost gone, his broken arm, dragged down by his clothes," until men in a rowboat beat him with oars.[64] Nonetheless, Hayes stops when the defendant's body sinks beneath the surface of the Tiber, rather than continue on to its public exhibition in front of the Regina Coeli prison, a horrific visual that foreshadows Mussolini's end in Piazzale Loreto.[65] This omission allows Hayes to avoid the connection between this Italian tragedy and widespread lynching in the United States, a link that Italian politicians were quick to draw in an effort to deflect the harsh criticism heaped upon them.[66] In addition to this revision, Hayes goes so far as to change the mob's victim: rather than introduce the complication of the murder of Carretta, a witness for the prosecution, Hayes's crowd murders the unnamed defendant. Critics have read this substitution as a moral expedient, insofar as the extrajudicial murder of the putatively guilty Caruso represents enough of a gray area.[67] However, Hayes's exchange of victims might also be read within the structuring logic of the novel whose vignettes suggest that the postliberation "fall" of Rome is not caused by individual actors but instead is a function of the drama itself—indirectly laying blame on the politicians and, indeed, the journalists like McCormick and Matthew who collaborated on the script. If the drama of "liberation" reduces everyone to the most basic of roles (whore, drunk, fascist), it does not matter whom the crowd murders, as Matthews himself comments: "They did not get Caruso, but they got one who represented in their minds all that Caruso did."[68] Rossellini's Fred accuses Francesca, "Now you're all alike." This logic, extended to the entire population, is what leaves Rome beyond redemption.

All Thy Conquests assigns blame to each of its characters. However, it gives the starring role to the infinitely exchangeable soldiers and prostitutes.[69] Over three sections entitled "The Liberated City" that open each act, Rome's descent into a Dantean inferno (where copies of the *Divine Comedy* languish on booksellers' carts)[70] is mapped from a carefree affair to disinterested solicitation: the search for *a* girl, *any* girl. Following each "Liberated City," vignettes recount the miseries of three Italians: Giorgio, an unemployed barman who resorts to petty theft; Aldo Alzani, a marquis who blackmails his fascist father-in-law into committing suicide; Carla, a young woman who falls in love with a married GI who impregnates and abandons her. Two Americans also figure: John Pollard, an officer who falls into despair when his English lover goes back to her husband and ends up passed out drunk and naked in front of the Colosseum; and Harry, a GI who returns to Rome to find a girl he met on the day of the liberation. As *All Thy Conquests* explores the moral complexity of postliberation Rome, it foregrounds the gendered, sexualized intercultural encounter: Carla's loss of Greg and their unborn child; Captain Pollard's pathetic attempt to seduce a starving woman; Harry's failure to find Francesca.

The most extended meditation on the *soldati* and *signorine*—and the explicit point of overlap with Rossellini's *Paisà*—are the "Harry" vignettes. Relegated to a flashback, Harry's Francesca is linked to the fleeting romance of the first hours of the liberation—a time when "Americano!" was not an epithet, a time when Rome was, "the city, everybody cheering, flowers and wine, handshakes and vivas, speeches and sigaretti, and it was a city, a wonderful, a real city, clean, a city with streets wide and sunny and lined with streets, bars in it and shops with stuff in the windows and hotels with marquees, a city standing up all in one piece, smelling and looking like a city."[71] First introduced as "the girl hurrying on the street," Francesca is an elliptical presence: "She smiled. She had nice teeth. She was wearing a thin flowered dress, very short."[72] The two share a meal and a brief conversation that ends with: "A kiss and a flower and a goodbye. The flower you wore in your helmet marching out of town. And the look you remembered in her eyes."[73] Enraptured by her gaze, Harry mistakes this infernal Francesca for a divine Beatrice, but the paradise of liberation is forever lost in September 1944, from flowers and virgins for the heroic liberators to jeers and whores for the cowardly occupiers; for Harry, as for *Paisà*'s Fred, the tension lies in "the contrast between the memory of an enchanted world, of a lost romance, and the degradation of the current situation."[74] Three months after, *the* girl has now become *a* girl, and in the lexicon of postliberation of Rome, *a* girl means a prostitute. Telling a bartender her name gets him nowhere: the bartender replies, "How would I know? ... Fernanda, Francesca, they're all alike to me."[75] Drunk beyond rationality, Harry "finds" Francesca in a whorehouse, but this revelation—presaged by the sight of a framed picture of Jesus—proves false; she is a whore named Bianca. Giving up, Harry realizes Francesca belongs to a lost paradise where the heroic soldier gets *the* girl; after the "fall," Francesca, Fernanda, Bianca, Adriana are all the same, and they are all whores.

Nonetheless, even as Francesca remains a figment of Harry's imagination, *All Thy Conquests* does not lose sight of the inordinate burden borne by the Italian woman in this drama. In the final vignette preceding the "Sentence," Carla spells out the twofold consequences she suffers because of the gendering of redemption. When Carla falls on her way to entreat her lover to make a life with her and loses the baby, she seems to tumble headlong into cliché. However, her third act delves into the aftermath of the fall, in a symbolic but also literal manner, describing the physical sensation of losing the pregnancy: "She, lying there, still knew the secret going-away of her blood, and still felt ... that lifelessness that seemed to separate her from the world."[76] Beyond the facile metaphoric meaning for the aborted future of U.S.-Italian relations, the miscarriage is described in intimate detail; atop the physical loss, the novel dwells on Carla's psychological anguish of being made into a symbol, as the chapter ends with her hallucinating the condemnation of her fellow Romans and her own mother.[77] Inured to her mother's theatrics, Carla transforms into a disembodied spectator of her own tragedy: "It was true; she felt nothing. A deadness separated her from the world. The blood, secretly flowing, had emptied the world of what importance tears or hysterics or domestic shame might have. It was not as though her mother but a curiously unhappy marionette wept."[78] Thus, *All Thy Conquests* critiques the symbolism of the fallen woman that it employs: For all the insight afforded into the Americans' psychology, it is the Italian women who suffer disproportionately as their personal experience is appropriated to nationalistic ends.

In the attempt to understand the sickness of the Italian national body, *All Thy Conquests* relies on sexual encounters but foregrounds the mob as the symbol for Rome beyond redemption—a decision that no doubt hindered the afterlife of the novel, which was never translated into Italian, as were so many American postwar novels set in Allied-occupied Italy, such as Hayes's *The Girl on the Via Flaminia*. Reprinted for just a decade in the United States, when it was acquired by Lion Books in 1950, it was repackaged as a romance, its cover overstating its sexual content (Figure 9).[79] The 1956 edition continues in this vein: "You want Francesca ... ," the title page interpellates its readers. Conflating their identity with Harry's, it encourages their single-minded pursuit of the fantastical Italian woman. In overlooking the tragic historical narrative, the novel's packaging directs them to behave much like Harry who, in the single explicit connection between the vignettes and the frame, walks by the courthouse, blind to the unfolding drama in his search for Francesca: "On the Lungotevere there had been a big crowd of people outside the courthouse and it was a trial of some kind, some fascist, but he had not stayed except to look among the people for her."[80]

Furthermore, in focusing on Francesca, the publisher's marketing strategy recalls that of the North American distributors of *Paisà*, who believed American viewers would want "Francesca." Using scantily clad images of Maria Michi, movie posters took advantage of stereotypes of Italian sexual openness to downplay the political content that might have dampened ticket sales; *Life Magazine* put a bedroom scene, prominently featuring Francesca's legs, as the leading image of its review of the film.[81] Here, then, the fallen body of the Italian woman serves a double function: it confirms stereotypes about the feminized, sexually open Italian people *and* represses

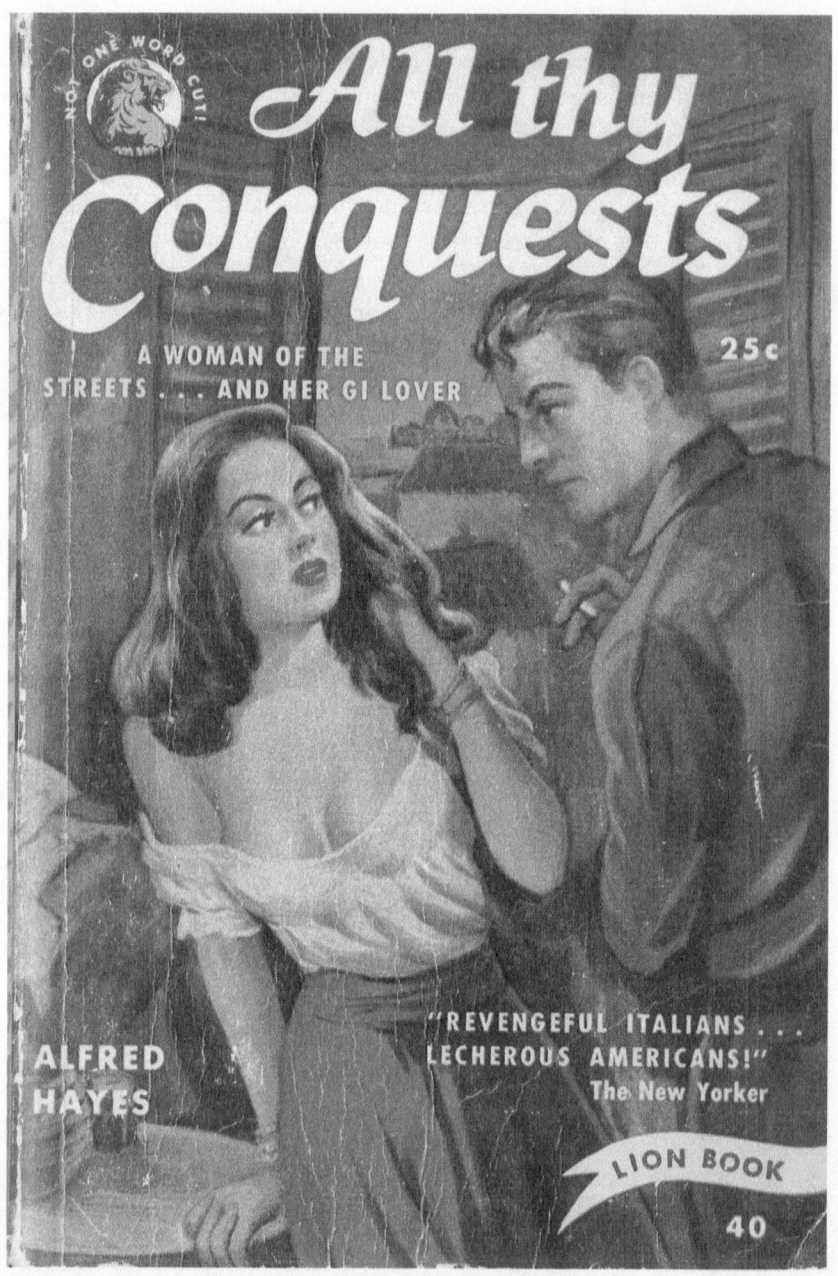

Figure 9. Cover of Alfred Hayes's *All Thy Conquests* (Lion Books, 1950).

Figure 10. A bar fight among prostitutes is easily contained in *Paisà* (1946), directed by Roberto Rossellini.

the symbol of the mob that pointed to dark spots in Italian and American culture.[82] Whereas Carretta's lynched corpse symptomized the tragic end to the drama of Rome's "liberation" and raised the specter of America's internal occupation of its own South, the fallen woman reassuringly set the stage for the unfolding tale of postwar U.S.-Italian relations that would end happily ever after thanks to the Marshall Plan.

From this perspective, the melodrama of *Paisà*'s "Rome" appears highly strategic—less a deviation from the film's staging of the neorealist rebirth of the nation than an essential step in that process, diverting attention from one of wartime Italy's most traumatic wounds. Thus, instead of an uncontrollable mob that symptomizes Italy's potentially fatal illness, "Rome" gives us a banal bar conflict, easily managed by the police (Figure 10). Instead of the lynched body of Carretta, with its inevitable evocation of Piazzale Loreto and the worst of the American south, "Rome" leaves behind forlorn Francesca, only to segue into the "Florence" episode where an American nurse searches for the mythical Italian partisan who has captured her heart. Speeding past Francesca's moral fall, *Paisà* travels northward to recount "a battle missing from war reports but perhaps even tougher and more desperate," as the newsreel announcer states at the start of the sixth episode, an act of commemoration that pushes other episodes (of the film, of history) offscreen.[83]

The Girl on the Via Flaminia: "A Grotesque and Obscene Play"

In many ways, *The Girl on the Via Flaminia* takes its cue from *Paisà's* "Rome," from its December 1944 setting to its thematic focus. Only pragmatism underwrites Lisa's "marriage" to Robert: He wants the comfort of a woman and a private room to help him escape the soldier's anonymity, while she wants food and shelter. As the two confront their relationship as intimate strangers, their arguments circle around the symbolic status each holds in the other's eyes. Robert sees Lisa and Italy as interchangeable in their shared beauty; when she rejects his kindness, he is quick to emphasize Italy's defeat.[84] For Lisa, Robert is the prosperity of the United States and its materialism, which she alternately devours and rejects. Although each critiques the other, the asymmetry is apparent, insofar as his privileged position allows him to fantasize its equitability. Insisting he does not want a *real* whore, he explains his logic in entering into this agreement with Lisa: "I thought I would just be exchanging something somebody needed for something I needed. Something somebody wanted for something I wanted."[85] However, she wants sustenance, while he wants a person—a structural imbalance that "provokes, for Lisa, a messy web of consequences."[86]

Despite Robert's recourse to the guise of marriage, the premise of their arrangement is the exchangeability of women in postliberation Rome: As Lisa angrily asks him, "Why should it matter . . . what mouth you kiss? Today a Lisa's . . . tomorrow a Maria's . . . they are all mouths . . . waiting for the soldier."[87] Here, the soldier, too, is fungible, but the patriarchy metes out different consequences for each. When another soldier barges into their apartment with a police officer to denounce Lisa's landlady, Adele, for procuring him a "sick" girl, Adele deflects the charge saying, "So? . . . It was probably another American who made [Maria] sick."[88] The officer chastens her with a reply that echoes with centuries of "science" that blamed women for the spread of venereal disease.[89] Maria is never found but Lisa, caught cohabitating without marriage papers, takes her place: registered as a prostitute, she is given a yellow card despite testing negative for VD. Recalling the exam, Lisa asks rhetorically, "There were so many girls. . . . But where were the soldiers? There must have been soldiers."[90] Yet, according to the patriarchal logic, the woman is the source of the disease, while the man who seeks her is fulfilling his natural role.

Revisiting Robert's version of the events, we can see this logic spelled out: the start of his story with Lisa coincides with his arrival as a soldier in Europe, where the threat of mortality made the pursuit of sexual pleasure seem inevitable.[91] However, Robert cannot bring himself to stand in line with the other men who wait to take their turn with the "real" whores.[92] Instead, in imagining a distinction between the anonymous women and Lisa, Robert seeks to recreate an authentic home where his identity, lost in the barracks, can be restored. Like a partaker of a Grand Tour looking beyond Italy's decayed present to its glorious past, Robert prides himself on doing just that with Lisa and, from there, extrapolates to all Italians as he perceives an intrinsic worth in girl and country, invisible to his fellow soldiers.[93] As Robert imagines Lisa's redemption, he intensifies her connection to Italy, weaving his fantasy out of her reminiscence of an innocent childhood in a pristine Ligurian town: "She'd been happy in Portofino, Robert thought: it was a white town, and the sea was blue. He wanted to see all of Italy: the quiet and undestroyed places, where the sea was blue. There must be many places like that, undestroyed. It was impossible to destroy everything. They never could destroy everything." Over the passage, Lisa slips out of view as Robert imagines restoring destination Italy; even as he acknowledges her trauma, he subsumes it in his redemptive project:

> It must have been bad in the *questura* for her. But now it would be different; the difference would be in how he felt. He could borrow the jeep again. They could ride out into the country, or when the summer came swim on the Lido, or visit the old castles. They would clear the mines out of the sea and the swimming would be good. It would be different in the sunlight on the sand and the mines cleared away.[94]

From her "fall" in the *questura*, he shifts to a landscape restored, parallel happy endings for country and girl that allow him to enjoy both. However, faced with a choice of being the destination of an American soldier-tourist or the whore of the Italian patriarchy, she embraces the latter.

The Girl on the Via Flaminia's critique is complicated by Adele's deserter son, Antonio, who is excluded from the U.S.-Italian, male-female relationship. Although he takes responsibility for Italy's state, he makes Lisa bear the collective shame, underscoring the asymmetries of their respective gender roles. Moreover, the Antonio/Lisa conflict suggests that the prostitute's symbolic status comes from outside Italy's borders but also from within. Just as Italy-as-whore does not implicate all Italians equally, neither is it a foreign imposition: The Italian rhetorical tradition gives Antonio an arsenal against Lisa, as he expresses his disdain by quoting verses of Giacomo

Leopardi's "O patria mia."[95] Lyric poetry soon devolves into a physical threat, as Antonio takes a knife to Lisa's hair and spells out the symbolic status of this common punishment of women accused of sleeping with foreign soldiers: "No signorina, it's not Antonio who will cut your hair. It is only your country, avenging itself a little."[96] Antonio, like the prosecutor of *All Thy Conquests*, envisions a metaphoric surgery that severs the metonymic connection between the "dishonourable" part of Italy and the body of the nation.

Caught between Antonio's and Robert's competing visions, Lisa reminds readers of the weight of the Anglo-American and Italian rhetorical traditions women unequally bear, which has the paradoxical effect of bringing them to the foreground and silencing them.[97] At the same time, she details the material consequences faced by Italian women; her self-conscious reflections evince the difficulty of narrating this status, most apparently as she privately recalls the trauma of her exam:

> She sat there, and piece by piece the involuntary images of her day would rise up into her mind, and she would look at them in their remembered light like the pieces of *some grotesque and obscene play into whose plot she had fallen*, and then she would, her whole mind shrinking, push them away again, thrust them back, and then they would return: the nakedness of the women in the big cold gray empty surgical room, waiting to be examined; the girl, shrieking, in the truck, as they drove through the streets, and the girl who spat at everything; and the hands emerging to touch her, the faces emerging, professional, official, dry, indifferent, disbelieving.[98]

With this theatrical metaphor, the narrative signals its critique of the Italy-as-whore topos and its impact on flesh-and-blood women. A source of information, Lisa is poked and prodded in order to determine Italy's moral worth; but the faces are "professional, official, dry, indifferent, disbelieving," uninterested in her story outside the scripted roles. As Hayes provides an uncommon window into these medical practices through Lisa's memory, he also gestures to the difficulty in narrating them to an audience; Lisa's account to her friend Nina is restrained compared to her self-recollection:

> "Then, afterwards ... they put all of us into a big truck. There were so many girls. ... When we drove through the streets ... everybody looked at us sitting there in the truck. Then some of the girls shouted and some even sang and some spat at the people in the street and some cried. There were so many girls ... Then in the hospital ... they put us into a big room, and they said

undress, and when we undressed they examined us. Have you ever seen, Nina, many women together naked in a big cold room?"[99]

Whereas her memory singles out individual women (the girl, shrieking; the girl who spat at everything; herself), Lisa's story to Nina stresses their sheer numbers, *there were so many girls*—at once an indication of the scope of the historical phenomenon and a sign of their loss of identity. Moreover, her testimony reveals the inequity she faces both in the physical consequences of the collective humiliation and her limited power of representation with respect to Antonio's and Roberto's: While Lisa's testimony is marked by ellipses, Antonio can hurl Leopardi against her, and Robert can turn her into "a very funny story."[100] In these contrasts, Lisa avoids being flattened into a symbol or a statistic but instead voices one of the lesser-known stories of occupied Italy, rarely made accessible to either an Italian or Anglo-American public. Lisa offers a further metatextual comment on the difficulties of finding an audience for such a story, as she remembers her "first time" with Robert: "She thought: we do finally what we thought we were incapable of doing, and it is less than we thought the doing would be, and at the same time more. And nobody listens, nobody cares, one is alone. There are no drums, no overture, no curtain rising. The audience is cold or asleep."[101] The leading lady stands at center stage, but all the audience wants to see is the Italian nation.

The Girl on the Via Flaminia, then, stresses the individual experience of one woman's fall. Looking back at "Rome," Francesca's "fall" is comparatively benign: In Lisa's description of her journey on the MP's truck, we can recall Francesca who escapes roundup by hiding in the movie theater, her story thus unfolding within a private room rather than at the truck's humiliating destination. However, unique as *The Girl on the Via Flaminia* is in representing the consequences faced by Italian women, the minute narration of Lisa's transformation from "pure" to "fallen" is also instrumental for Robert's development; no common soldier who waits on line for whores, Robert uses Lisa to cast himself as the authentic traveler capable of discerning true worth beneath Italy's crumbling facade. Despite the novel's overt sympathy for Lisa, the details serve to prove that she is, in fact, fallen. It may not be fair that Lisa is like all the others but ultimately, she is: "It will be so much easier now that I am what the others are," she says, embracing her assigned role.[102] *Paisà*, on the contrary, elides Francesca's transformation: Showing Francesca in discrete snapshots six months apart, it provides a beginning and an endpoint that leaves her transformation uncertain. Certainly, the language of melodrama and the rhetoric of Italy-as-whore imply a downward trajectory from "pure" to "fallen." Nonetheless, the film subtly undermines those signifiers, suggesting that "Francesca's lost self may be as much a fantasy as her present performance."[103] Thus, while we might say that "Rome" leaves barely visible the grotesque aspects of the story that *Girl on the Via Flaminia* brings to light, it also refuses to provide the basic premise of a redemption narrative on which *Girl on the Via Flaminia* depends: proof of intrinsic worth. Here, then, the elliptical style of Rossellini's "Rome" may also disrupt the Italy-as-whore narrative, dependent upon knowledge that it refuses to give the soldier and the viewer.

Robert's failed redemption has been read as the novel's condemnation of "the symbolic constraints of the American salvation myth, the false mutuality of the sexual contract, and the veneration of utopian marriage in idealizations of the nuclear family."[104] However, Hayes attenuates the force of Lisa's refusal in a *New York Times* article published at the same time as the book, "Italy—Enchantress of Writers," a reflection on the power World War II Italy holds for American authors such as John Hersey, John Horne Burns, and himself. Starting from an impersonal soldier's perspective, Hayes echoes Robert as he stresses the link between the beauty of Italy and its women, and describes how the war—temporarily—impeded enjoyment of both:

> One remembers how, even with the war on and all the enormous physical destruction, there were moments when the beauty that has always been Italy's would flash out and astonish even the dog-tired soldier marching on some sunken and dusty road between mountains pitted with old pillboxes and green lovely fields full of hidden and menacing bakelite mines.
>
> One could only go so far, during the war, in the direction of that physical loveliness—and that included the Italian women; but now obscure martyrs have sacrificed themselves in the small villages to decontaminate the fields. Industrious trowels, using the old painted bricks, have restored what the batteries of the Fifth Army and the German panzers demolished, and Italy is again the paradise (a limited one, still) of the *touristi*.[105]

As Hayes makes the beauty of the country and its women interchangeable, the connection to Robert—who imagines that his relationship with Lisa can be rebuilt—is explicit:

> He remembered suddenly one of the towns in the south. It was a summer afternoon. Bricklayers were rebuilding a wall of a shelled or bombed house. The war had been in the town only two months before. Now the *trowels* of the bricklayers made sharp distinct clinks as they knocked the bricks into place

and set them in the mortar. They were *the old bricks* on the house. They were putting up the wall with the same bricks and a fresh mortar.[106]

If Robert seems naïve to believe that redemption was possible in 1944, the article suggests that it was only a question of time. Now, five years later, in the Marshall Plan era, destination Italy's restoration is underway thanks to *industrious trowels* and *old painted bricks*. In this blithe cure, Hayes tightly circumscribes Lisa's trauma, blunting the force of the novel's critique. When Lisa rejects Robert and runs out into the night toward the notorious via Flaminia, the novel suggests that for the women, there can be no return to the world of metaphor: Robert cannot rebuild her like a house; she cannot be his home. Earlier she wonders, "Perhaps, in the morning, when she awoke, the war would be over, and then she could go back to Genoa, and see Portofino again, and everything would be in the past, a dream one had had during a very bad time, and in that dream she had done certain things, and waking she would forget them," but by the conclusion it becomes clear that she cannot awake from a dream: "The room came back, empty, cold, surgical, and the girls naked in the room. And the hands. They reached out to touch her. All her flesh crawled away with a soundless shriek from that touch."[107] Although Robert and Lisa cannot have a "home" together in 1944, in 1949, tourists and writers can.

In reading Hayes's account of the restoration of destination Italy, we also see an echo of the revision of Italian history performed by the postwar editions of the *Pocket Guide to Italy* discussed in Chapter 1, which required forgetting the acts the wartime guidebooks emphasized in order to cast Italy as a virile, bellicose nation: colonialism. Hayes, in fact, performs this erasure in a single clause: "But fortunately, despite Addis Ababa, the real Italy looked backward to the past, to the very opposite of empire: the marvelously developed city-states; and this reluctance to come all the way into the twentieth century saved her."[108] Reducing Italian colonialism to "Addis Ababa," Hayes embraces the "real," backward-looking Italy and erases the associations of modernity and virility that conflict with his enchantress figuration. In so doing, Hayes dehistoricizes Italy, an act of censorship played out in the myth of the "good Italians" (*italiani brava gente*) and in *The Gallery* by John Horne Burns, in whose name the article commissions Hayes to speak. With colonialism relegated to a grammatical aside, the American tourist can safely be driven to distraction by the Italian women; this transformation is so complete that, by the end of his essay, the soldier and the war that motivated the article have vanished. Whereas once the war distracted soldiers from the women, now the women distract the writer from Italy's "actual self":

> I, too, may be inventing my Italy as others, out of their own necessities, invented theirs; and her real face, her actual self may be equally as different. The sun was perhaps too bright for me also, there were too many flowers for sale at the foot of the Spanish Stairs; I liked the sandaled women walking in their bright print dresses in the Roman evening a little too much.[109]

However, the possibility of misconstruing Italy is but the briefest of worries, as Hayes reaffirms his gendered perception in the next sentence: "But there she lies: still wounded, a leg in a cavalryman's boot extended into the Mediterranean." Dismissing his potential misunderstanding, he assuages any self-doubt that Italian women distracted him from the true meaning of Italy: *they* are the true meaning of Italy. Insisting on Italy's grammatical feminization, Hayes dresses her up in a mismatched metaphor that makes her a wounded woman's leg in an American army boot, poorly dressed for her maritime location. The final sentences of the article double down on this gendered redemption, as he concludes: "and the writers and the other tourists, I am happy to know (since she is the kind of a country one wishes only the best for) pour into her historic gates, full of *cambio*, ready to be seduced. O, after all our big smoke-filled ugly unresponsive cities of the West, more than ever anxious to be seduced."[110] Coupling an economic reference with the promise of seduction, Hayes sexualizes tourism and alludes to sex tourism: On this "return" trip, Italy is an enchantress, a wife, a seductress, even a whore. And, were we to doubt what kind of ending this is, the parenthesis leaves no question.

In the happy ending of "Italy—Enchantress of Writers," Hayes blunts the critique *Girl on the Via Flaminia* levels against the "grotesque and obscene play" and the double burden it places on the Italian women conscripted as its star. Gone are the traumatized women who once furnished the soldiers a home, leaving only reconstructed brick buildings to shelter tourists who stream back inside this wounded "leg" with active libidos and piles of cash. The text has no interest in what *after* means for Italian women or for Italy, aside from providing pleasure and self-knowledge to the tourist, which is, instead, a question that will be central to Luciana Peverelli's romance novels analyzed in Chapter 3, where the liberation of Rome does not provide the genre's promised happy ending that must instead be negotiated by the Italian heroines.

Authored by an Italian woman, about Italian women, for Italian women, Peverelli's forgotten romance novels will add another voice to this analysis of the gendering of redemption in Rome; in this chapter, however, we see what is to be gained by reading an Italian film with American literary intertexts. In *All Thy Conquests* Hayes shows prostitution to be a symptom of Rome's fall that progresses into the incurable disease of the mob, a sign of a nation beyond redemption; in "Rome," the melodramatic woman provides a critique but also functions as a reassuring symbol to repress the mob and the trauma of the Caruso-Carretta affair. In *The Girl on the Via Flaminia*, Hayes, too, moves away from the mob to focus on the emblematic fallen woman, and the unequal burden it puts on flesh-and-blood women, evidencing the grotesque elements of his heroine's "fall" that "Rome" elides; but precisely in its elision, "Rome" undermines the misogynist logic on which Robert's redemptive agenda depends. Alongside these individual readings, tracing Hayes's journey from *All Thy Conquests* to *The Girl on the Via Flaminia* to "Italy—Enchantress of Writers," shows how the Roman woman's fall marks the start of a trajectory that makes redemption the purview of the American soldier-tourist who returns to postwar Italy to be seduced by the Marshall Plan's success. In contrast, *Paisà*, with its episodic structure, presents its own journey that critiques Italy-as-whore only to substitute one gendered nationalism for another: the northern, male partisans' bodies disappearing beneath the surface of the Po become synonymous with U.S.-Italian fraternity, Italy's postwar rebirth, and neorealism's "authentic" antirhetorical aesthetics.

It has taken decades to valorize the hybridity of texts such as *Paisà* that lie at the heart of postwar Italy's privileged representational mode, and this chapter contributes to such efforts by arguing that the melodramatic episode set in the capital facilitates Italy's redemption by repressing the mob with the prostitute. The hegemony of neorealism not only censors conflicting threads *within* texts like *Paisà* but, as I consider in the next chapter, also marginalizes cultural production from the same years that fall "outside the critical parameters that deemed (and still deem) neorealism to be the only cinematic style capable of adequately representing postwar society."[111] Exploring the avowed hybridity of Peverelli's "true" romance novels, I show them to be "inhabited" by melodrama insofar as they "understand events of public history and private emotions being equally significant."[112] Marginalized for their lack of realism yet engaged with the traumatic events neorealism represses, these novels tout their ability to represent occupied Rome and consider what *after* means for those implicated in its redemption—foremost, their contemporary female audience.

3

Happily Ever after Redemption
Luciana Peverelli's "True" Romance Novels of Occupied Rome

In 1953, novelist and critic Anna Banti wrote a brief history of a "fallen" genre: the romance novel (*romanzo rosa*, literally pink novel).[1] Starting from the *rosa*'s foreign origins, Banti discusses Mura and Liala, the two most prominent Italian romance authors of the early twentieth century whose aristocratic atmospheres evoke Gabriele D'Annunzio's decadent novels of the fin-de-siècle.[2] While Banti sees the *rosa* after D'Annunzio as damaging to their defenseless readers' taste, she also deems them so detached from reality as to have no impact on their behavior.[3] More worrisome is a trend that begins the 1930s: Influenced by American romance that features lower-class heroines and realistic settings, these *rosa* pose a grave social danger insofar as they might instill hopes of upward mobility in their readers. Rather than the pink of the *rosa*, Banti offers gray as the more apt descriptor: "the color of speed, of crowds and also of distraction: read, if statistics don't deceive, by three million people."[4] If these novels degrade further, Banti prophesies, even the least exigent of readers may find them beyond redemption.

As a singular exemplar of this infelicitous mixing, Banti points a finger at Milanese Luciana Peverelli, "industrious inventress of countless collisions between women who are lazy and rich, women who are poor and ambitious, and men with strong jawlines."[5] Without citing a single line or referring to a specific title, Banti dismisses Peverelli's sloppy prose and her New Yorkified Milanese setting before zeroing in on the danger of such work: "The typist soon to meet with great adventure, namely the love of the rich, married hero, will stop for a coffee, buy a three-ply skein of wool, and fry herself a couple of eggs, with the mannerisms and words of each of the readers who, moving from that controlled verisimilitude to the delicious risk of the novelesque, will emulate the heroine with an approximation full of hope."[6] For Banti, "the novel *alla Peverelli*, that is, the contemporary dime novel," threatens female readers by infusing romance with reality: "Despite the constant conformism and banality of the plot, needed to win over casual and impatient readers, the squalid page nonetheless hides many minute, true-to-life gestures, predictable but natural reactions, a reflection of real, lived experience."[7]

In this seminal essay, Banti's assumption that the *rosa* negatively influences the behavior of the "inexperienced" reader is consonant with attacks faced by popular literature across cultural contexts.[8] Within postwar Italy, moreover, it carries a political valence: Robin Pickering-Iazzi notes how, as a genre that flourished during the fascist period, the *romanzo rosa* was assumed "to be irreparably tainted."[9] As Banti "focuses particularly on the tendency among some women romance writers to show a faddish devotion to the male myths of virility, heroism and aggression, and to female myths of 'admiration for the male warrior,' willing submission, and the importance of motherhood," she claims that by tricking its susceptible readers with a blend of fantasy and reality, the *romanzo alla Peverelli* helped produce fascist women.[10] Careless and corrupting, within this schema the *rosa* becomes an ideal cultural scapegoat, the exact opposite of "engaged," "redemptive" neorealism; and their respective gendering cannot be incidental.[11] More than *symbolizing* the nation's fall, the *rosa* is seen as helping to precipitate it by indoctrinating the female masses into believing that adherence to "fascist" myths of gender would pave the way to their own redemptive ending. For intellectuals such as Banti, expiating the *rosa* from Italian cultural production belongs to a larger postwar process, traced by Ruth Ben-Ghiat, whereby Italian leftist intellectuals rewrote the history of realism as an antifascist mode to efface its close association with fascism. Bracketing off fascism as a period of "unreality" and casting the *Resistenza* a "return to history," this cultural redemption privileges texts that claim (however fallaciously) a "stylistic rupture" with fascist cultural production;[12] it also favors those that repress the traumatic events of fascism and its fall, such as the massacre of the Fosse Ardeatine discussed in Chapter 2.

La lunga notte and *Sposare lo straniero*

Characterized as an ideological tool for the regime, Banti's Peverelli bears no resemblance to the "antifascist intellectual, partisan, and emancipated woman" who translated John Steinbeck's antifascist missive *The Moon Is Down* (1944) and wrote two novels of Rome's German and Allied occupation, *La lunga notte* (1944; *The Long Night*) and *Sposare lo straniero* (1946; *Marry the Foreigner*).[13] Today, even as scholars take issue with assumptions about the *romanzo rosa* (and popular literature more generally), embodied by Banti's "involuntarily cruel classicism," Peverelli's more than four hundred romances, mysteries, photonovels, and editorial work on the popular magazines *Stelle*, *Bella*, and *Stop* remain unstudied.[14] Continuing in the vein of scholars who revisit the cultural products marginalized by this redemptive "return to history," in this chapter I offer the first sustained analysis of Peverelli's *La lunga notte* (set during the German occupation of Rome), together with *Sposare lo straniero* (set during the Allied occupation).[15] Written and published while the events they describe were unfolding and still in print thirty years later, *La lunga notte* and *Sposare lo straniero* affirm realist pretensions, claiming to document "only real episodes and characters who actually existed,"[16] in contrast to other *rosa* of the period that had "a strong propensity for bucolic backdrops—simple and pure."[17] Based on Peverelli's partisan experiences, *La lunga notte* recounts a love triangle whose members are affected by the traumatic events of German occupied Rome. Describing the deportation of the Jews and the massacre of the Fosse Ardeatine, it joins only Giacomo Debenedetti's *Eight Jews* and *16 October 1943* among Italian Holocaust narratives published at that early date, and stands—despite its exclusion from recent studies—as the earliest known Italian novel on the subject.[18]

For its part, *Sposare lo straniero*, a unique representation of the war bride phenomenon from the perspective of Italian women, receives little more consideration.[19] As Ilaria Serra notes, the war bride was a popular figure in *Life Magazine* in the 1950s, which published reportage on weddings between Italian women and American GIs and reviewed fictionalizations such as Fred Zinnemann's movie *Teresa* and the stage version of Alfred Hayes's novel *The Girl on the Via Flaminia*.[20] For Serra, this coverage is part of America's postwar cultural conquest of Italy: "In the magazine, Italy becomes a 'feminized country,' a country that is led back to submission by stressing its feminine features. American gave Italy food and culture, democracy and new kitchens. As its Pygmalion, it then symbolically transformed it into a beautiful woman in distress, ready to be rescued."[21] Published shortly after the first Italian war brides reached the United States, *Sposare lo straniero* disrupts this rhetorical tradition, which predates *Life*'s coverage; yet it has been left out of historiographies that include fictionalizations such as *Teresa*, Roberto Rossellini's *Paisà*, and John Horne Burns's *The Gallery*.[22]

By positioning this analysis between chapters on canonical, male-authored texts of the Allied-Italian encounter, I read Peverelli's novels as a corrective to the Italian neorealist narrative paradigm and to popular American representations. As these *rosa* recognize Italian women—irrespective of their sexual status—as actors in and transmitters of historical traumatic events, they position them as "borderline" spaces in which to negotiate postwar Italian identity rather than exclusively as metonyms for the nation.[23] With their multifocalized plots that include female and male perspectives, and their anomalous insistence on a contemporary backdrop, I also read these *rosa* as "borderline."[24] Asserting themselves as the privileged genre to represent the absurd realities of the historical moment, these *rosa* embrace the hybridity disavowed by the post-facto construction of canonical neorealism.[25] Here, then, I read them for what they say about the period they represent, as well as the context in which they were produced and received. In fact, *La lunga notte* evinces a central contradiction that shaped postwar Italian culture in concert with U.S.-Italian relations insofar as the solidification of the redemption paradigm was predicated on disavowing the link between the tacit, pervasive anti-Semitism in Italy and the Holocaust. Forgotten in Italy and inaccessible to an Anglophone audience, *La lunga notte* has produced no critical readings, leaving this blind spot unexplored; interrogating it, I show how *La lunga notte* concomitantly dispels the myth of the "good Italians" (*italiani brava gente*) by condemning Italian involvement in the Holocaust, even as its love story obeys anti-Semitic logic.

Finally, these *rosa* confront the genre's conventional happy ending, required to "allay whatever emotional tensions it elicited and bolster the hope that there may be a 'happily ever after.'"[26] However jarringly inappropriate in a Holocaust narrative, the *rosa*'s formal requirement replicates the Allies' redemptive rhetoric, making it an ideal narrative form through which to explore the tension between collective and individual experience. Rewriting the script of the Allies' rhetoric and the *rosa*'s conventions in the disjuncture between the "happy" "liberation" and the tragedies of the protagonists, *La lunga notte* is effectively a *rosa* "inhabited" by melodrama that "fail[s] to grant comforting closure or cure via resolutions and happy endings."[27] Then, as *Sposare lo straniero* shifts away from the trauma of the Holocaust, it seems to exhibit "the indifference shown for the tragedies experienced by the Jews after the liberation" that *La lunga notte* critiques.[28] Nonetheless, in *Sposare lo straniero*, as two heroines immigrate to the United States and England as war brides, their conventional happy end is haunted by the gendered violence of the encounter.

La lunga notte: An Italian Holocaust Romance Novel

La lunga notte starts in Milan the day before the armistice, as Andreina, a carefree, aristocratic orphan, gets pulled into the Roman resistance by her beloved Adriano, a partisan leader. In following him to Rome, Andreina steps away from her conventional counterparts who avoid travel, becoming an eyewitness to the German occupation.[29] She survives Allied aerial raids and psychological torture in the infamous Via Tasso prison and witnesses the destruction of a Jewish family at the hands of German and Italian soldiers. From the fascist soldiers who grab the postpartum mother to the neighbors who keep their doors shut, the novel makes Italian responsibility clear.[30] So, too, does it spell out the endpoint of the deportation: "every day thirty or forty Jews were found in their hideouts, sent to an unknown destination, or rather to a single destination: death."[31]

In addition to condemning the genocide beyond Italy's borders, *La lunga notte* depicts the Fosse Ardeatine massacre, offering "a key corrective to the tendency to conceptualize the Holocaust through the site of the concentration camp."[32] Starting from the preparation for the massacre, *La lunga notte* details the selection of the prisoners, their transportation to the Catacombs of San Callisto outside the city, their execution and, finally, the dissemination of the news throughout the city. Published prior to the "establishment of either a neorealist orthodoxy or any model for witness writing about the camps," *La lunga notte* expands the miniscule corpus of early Italian Holocaust narrative.[33] Moreover, it serves as a powerful counternarrative to the foundational text of neorealism, Rossellini's *Roma città aperta*, whose "structuring absence" is the Fosse Ardeatine.[34] Strikingly, *La lunga notte* names as the massacre's cause the partisan attack in via Rasella, a contentious event that served to "call into question the morality of the Resistance as a whole."[35] Peverelli writes, "People at the theatre, in pastry shops, but meanwhile in the jails, in the Gestapo headquarters, in the central office of the S.S., they were making the list of the 320 that were to be shot in retaliation for the 32 German soldiers killed by some bombs placed in via Rasella."[36] In one declarative sentence, *La lunga notte* affirms the responsibility of the partisans who staged the attack in via Rasella, and places guilt on the entire population of Rome that lived everyday life while the tragedy was unfolding. When the massacre takes place, however, both partisans and city are redeemed. Claudio, an imprisoned partisan becomes a Christ-figure by choosing to die in the place of an elderly Jewish prisoner. Intensifying the symbolism, Claudio serves as father-figure to the young boy killed beside him, and dies with a vision of his own martyred father who died to save fugitive partisans—thus serving as the central member of a patriarchal genealogy of martyrs.[37]

Although the reader follows these two victims until their death, within the diegetic framework the massacre is only witnessed by a young boy who hears an unearthly song emerging from a truck filled with "pale, spectral faces."[38] Despite this lack of witnesses, the news of the Fosse spreads throughout the city, in a chilling paragraph:

And news of the massacre began to leak: and Rome was horrified. It seemed as though the dead had been nearly buried still alive under a layer of a burning, sticky substance, and the day after the massacre, the quarries were blown up and sand and dirt fell on the bodies of those who may have still been in their death throes. And terror and stupor and agony weighed on the starving city. Curfew was moved up to five p.m. In the dark houses terrified citizens holed up like moles, and the most alarming news circulated from mouth to mouth, house to house.[39]

This description serves to mark the city's redemption: No longer blithely attending the theater, the city of Rome feels the Fosse Ardeatine profoundly. At the same time, it underscores which traumas are privileged at the expense of others. The news of the Fosse spreads despite the fear but by contrast, as Andreina witnesses her friend Ursula's family being hauled away by fascist police, "no doors were opened. Terror kept them closed," and then later, "life continued normally. Almost no one had noticed the drama of those poor human creatures who, loaded in trucks like animals to slaughter, were being taken to their deaths."[40] Side by side, *La lunga notte* gives portraits of contrasting Roman attitudes toward the Fosse Ardeatine, "the site of one of the first national monuments to victims of Nazi-Fascism in the postwar period," versus the Holocaust, subject to a long national amnesia.[41]

Looking at Peverelli's unflinching, widely disseminated representation, we must revisit such pillars of neorealist mythmaking, such as the assertion that Rossellini could not include via Rasella in his resistance films, because it was too raw a wound.[42] If we follow Karl Schoonover's contention that these films, produced with an eye on the North American alliance, needed to depict Italy as morally worthy of (economic) redemption, the question of audience becomes central.[43] As a popular text that circulated solely in Italian, *La lunga notte* had no concern of the foreign public nor, one might wager, the Italian intellectual elite. Without these constraints, it is not only able to name via Rasella, "a central wound in the national collective memory," but it also can implicate Italians—fascist and not—in every tragic turn of events and depict partisans with human foibles, rejecting what were to become central postwar myths.[44]

In Chapter 2, I discuss how Alfred Hayes's novel *All Thy Conquests* (1946)—accessible only to an Anglophone audience—critiques the "liberation" of Rome through the gruesome aftermath of the Fosse Ardeatine, while Roberto Rossellini's "Rome" episode of *Paisà*, originally conceived by Hayes, avoids reference to an event that threatens the foundational postwar myth of Italian redemption and instead focuses on the heroine's melodramatic fall. As unique as the representation of the Fosse in *All Thy Conquests*, introducing *La lunga notte* into the dialogue underscores that Hayes does not acknowledge "the real problems of alterity and the intolerance behind Jewish persecution," but instead, like most early postwar Italian narrative, emphasizes the political dimension of World War II.[45] These problems come into sharp focus in *La lunga notte* whose condemnation of religious persecution intertwines with an anti-Semitic plotline through the romantic rivalry between Andreina and Ursula, the assumed name of Wanda Levi, a Jewish girl who joined the Resistance after the racial laws upended her personal life. As it builds a love triangle where a "luxurious little doll" and a "Jew on the run" compete for the affections of the partisan, Adriano, *La lunga notte* distinguishes itself from early postwar representations where the female, Jewish partisan would have found herself doubly marginalized.[46] Indeed, it was not until his 1959 film *Generale della Rovere* that Rossellini acknowledged either the Jewish question or female participation in the *Resistenza*—and then only fleetingly.[47] In *La lunga notte*, the Jewish partisan finds herself in an unfamiliar genre: When Ursula falls under Adriano's spell, she is dismissive of the associations of gender and genre that come with the territory, reflecting, "I'm falling in love like the protagonist of a novel, like an idiot, like an old maid thirsty for love."[48] Yet it is precisely this fictional space that makes room for the Jewish partisan while affirming the veracity of her experience in contrast to the fantasies of Andreina. As Ursula tells her story, she describes how the racial laws destroyed her family and truncated her love story, which paradoxically affords her an active role in the Resistance: "I was a girl like you, Andreina: calm, carefree, happy to be alive. Now I am a monster. Capable of anything."[49] With respect to Ursula, Andreina's motives seem banal: "she believed she had come to Rome on a mission: by now she believed in that unrealistic love of hers, as if in a myth."[50] Although both girls are motivated by love, it is Ursula's tragedy, born out of the current political circumstances, that seems realistic, lending credence to the tragedies of her real-life counterparts.

Whatever sympathies the text gives Ursula in her parallel struggles to win over Adriano and fight the fascists who have destroyed her family, it is nonetheless governed by an anti-Semitic logic that denies her redemptive fantasy of transforming into a romantic heroine. When Andreina realizes that to commute Adriano's death sentence she must offer her body to a corrupt fascist official, the text self-consciously signals that this episode belongs to the realm of popular literature. Andreina wonders, "Oh, could it be?! Such a forbidden thing, this kind of adventure out of a serial novel . . . could situations of this sort [*genre*] still exist?"[51] As the official disparages her naiveté with similarly literary language, "what a big drama for such a little girl," Ursula steps into her role and sacrifices her virginity. Allowing Andreina to remain "pure," Ursula offers: "I will act in the comedy."[52] Casting herself as an able actress, Ursula disavows the anti-Semitic logic that she obeys when she agrees to contain the fascist contaminant for the sake of the purity of the Italian race. Nonetheless, the novel may signal that Ursula plays a socially constructed part—be it the "monster" or the seductress—but it does not allow her to achieve "comic closure, in the classical sense . . . the formulaic redemption of the fallen woman through marriage to a good man."[53] The anti-Semitic logic only sharpens with Adriano's revelation, moments before his execution. Envisioning the frivolous Andreina he once knew as a salvific Madonna, he realizes she is his true love rather than Ursula, "condemned to obey a secret law."[54] Ursula is left enacting revenge on the anti-Semitic fascist official by revealing he has made love to a Jew and setting his arrest in motion, before she prepares to embark on a suicide mission; recognized for her commitment to the Resistance, Ursula nonetheless remains entrapped as the stereotypical, vengeful Jew.

The tension between the novel's anti-Semitism together with its condemnation of the Holocaust speaks to its cultural context in which direct connections between Italian anti-Semitism and the events of World War II were repressed. According to Stefania Lucamante, this connection was not confronted by the public until it was brought out in the open in by Elsa Morante's *La storia* (1974; *History*), a popular novel set in German-occupied Rome that initially met with critical resistance. Reading Lucamante's assessment of *La storia*'s critics, we hear an uncanny echo of Banti's attack on Peverelli: "Lampoon[ed] for its Neorealist elements and melodramatic tones," *La storia* was "denounced . . . as a *romanzone* (roughly translatable as a populist, consumerist work)," by experimental artist Nanni Balestrini, who "subsequently cautioned would be readers."[55] With *La lunga notte* in the picture, a thirty-year silence in Italian culture is bookended by two popular, female-authored texts that challenge neorealist orthodoxy, using "generic transformations and hybridizations" to represent the traumatic events of the Holocaust within and outside Italy's borders from a gender-inclusive perspective.[56] In fact, as incongruent as it might seem, *La lunga notte* shares with survivor narratives "an emphasis on the concept of *vite romanzesche* (novel-like lives), intended as existences whose situations depend on a historical event of such proportions that life resembles fiction."[57] In this way, *La lunga notte* is uniquely positioned to represent recent events to its contemporary readership. Renegotiating the *rosa*'s familiar parameters to produce a "borderline" text, *La lunga notte* accommodates the destabilization of narrative codes precipitated by the armistice, where the continuation of violence confounds the expectations for a happy ending, and the public rhetoric of redemption collides with the private experience of unredeemable loss. Having considered the novel's treatment of the historical circumstances, I now turn to its representation of "female plight" through its melodramatic protagonist, Andreina, whose penchant for fantasy allows her to negotiate the absurdity of life during the occupation.

The Melodramatic Happy Ending: The Rebirth of Rome and the "Fall" of Andreina

Starting in Milan at the eve of the armistice, *La lunga notte* paints a backdrop of gutted buildings and anxious people, and introduces Andreina as a grammatical interruption: "But Andreina walked slowly, clinging to Adriano's arm."[58] "Drunk" with love, she "steals" her mysterious lover from his "extremely important" engagements: while she views Adriano as "a splendid conquest," he does not understand why he started a relationship with "that imp, so stupid and naïve in some things, so cunning and coquettish in others."[59] In describing her past as "that strange life poised between resorts and travel," the novel critiques Andreina and, by extension, the Italian upper-class; so, too, might it critique Peverelli's contemporaries who, precisely in this period, were retreating to the genre's facile commonplaces.[60] Then, with the announcement of the armistice, Andreina experiences relief tinged with uncertainty, rapid shifts of emotion common to wartime accounts: Is the armistice Italy's happy ending or the start of a national tragedy?[61] And how does this ill-defined national narrative impact individuals like Andreina who have been inured to the suffering of war? Learning that Adriano has fled to Rome and that she has been compromised by their association, she follows at his behest, blithely boarding a train only to face a rude awakening. Overwhelmed by her desperate fellow travelers with whom she survives an aerial bombardment, she arrives in Rome stripped of her final trappings of privilege.

Although Andreina's increasing engagement with the Resistance could be understood as a redemption for her past, *La lunga notte* rejects the misogynistic association of the "fall" with the sexual and the feminine, and "rebirth" with the political and the masculine. In fact, Peverelli's heroine displays a nascent political conscience even before she is impelled to follow Adriano, rejecting those "hundreds of women" who, "to live in peace, to not lose their wellbeing, would have put up with anything."[62] Her intrinsic worth is confirmed by another partisan, Antonello, who distinguishes her from those superficial women who "drink vermouth in pastry shops, organize afternoons at the theatre or the cinema," the habitats, in Peverelli's shorthand, for the politically disengaged.[63] Andreina will be repeatedly affirmed in her role as heroine not because she *sheds* these "inappropriate" qualities but because she uses them to productive end. Ursula disparages Andreina's fervent belief in "romantic and farfetched things" as a hindrance in "this era of sudden attacks and death," but by playing the pathetic girl, Andreina helps free imprisoned partisans.[64]

After this first heroic act, Andreina "performs" in the infamous via Tasso prison when she is taken in for questioning and, after refusing to comply, imprisoned. For a jealous Ursula, the arrest throws Andreina in an ill-fitting role: "It was so absurd that something so tragic and terrible happened to her, to the stupid, optimistic girl who had been playing on the partisan frontlines."[65] Ursula fears that via Tasso will transform the childish actress into a true heroine: "now Andreina would have the halo of martyrdom . . . everyone would consider her a heroine."[66] However, the experience in Via Tasso is more a negotiation than a transformation. While at first Andreina tries to dismiss the "fantastic" stories as the fruit of propaganda, she learns to confront reality thanks to the stories of her fellow female prisoners, which she verifies when she witnesses torture firsthand: "And with horror Andreina saw that the man was dripping blood. His face was a rainstorm of blood that fell in big drops on the floor, leaving a long trail."[67] Nonetheless, Andreina remains "incurable in her imaginative puerility," a quality that supports rather than hinders her role as witness.[68] The novel validates her vision when, on June 5, a group of women flood the prison in search of their loved ones. Although the brutalized bodies are gone, the reader knows how to interpret the traces of blood thanks to Andreina.[69]

As Andreina vouches for the truth of these stories, we might read the "borderline" heroine as a figure for Peverelli's "borderline" *rosa*, confirming the unbelievable horrors its readers may have heard about elsewhere. To this end, a lengthy description of Andreina watching an air raid suggests that her melodramatic subjectivity and her childlike fantasy facilitate her witnessing, "without fear but trembling with emotion."[70] Although Ursula disparages Andreina's recourse to tears as a sign of female weakness in contrast with her own "virility," this scene associates emotional excess with courage.[71] Moreover, while she initially seems to want to distance herself from the collective, this experience connects her to the emotions of others: "she thought of the terror of the population that had the bad luck to live in the targeted zones, but also of the wild joy with which the prisoners of Regina Coeli, of Via Tasso, greeted those booms."[72]

In contrast to this positive model of witnessing enabled by melodrama and fantasy, the novel depicts a boy witness, the neorealists' privileged symbol, with a certain anxiety.⁷³ In a gruesome chapter, Antonello is imprisoned by the Germans. Tormented by guilt for his role in inspiring a partisan attack on their headquarters, he digs his own grave alongside fellow prisoners, including a young boy he has just met. The passage spares no detail:

> The other five were given the order to throw dirt on the bodies of their dead fellow prisoners in the pit. They were still warm; some were still writhing, their nails scraping, their eyes dilated, staring at the distant sky. The spirit of one of the five could not bear it. He fell in a faint on the edge of the pit. A German soldier nudged him two or three times with his foot to make him stand up. But since he did not move, he, irritated, unloaded his pistol in his head.⁷⁴

When the two escape, they seek refuge in the nearby country house of his friend, Claudio, whose father hides them in a well. Emerging hours later, they see Claudio's father's brutalized body, in another gruesome passage: "The head of Claudio's elderly father fell in his hands like rotten fruit. Two little streams of blood still dripped slowly from his neck."⁷⁵ The sight triggers dark thoughts in Antonello: contemplating that his young companion would never heal from the experience, Antonello concludes that death would be preferable.⁷⁶ Refusing the symbol of the child witness that will be at the heart of Rossellini's redemptive neorealism, *La lunga notte* instead places its hope for Italy's future within the melodramatic-romantic heroine.

However, if the romantic heroine proves well-suited to the wartime context, the issue of genre comes to a head when a happy ending is dictated, both by the Allies' rhetoric and the *rosa's* formal constraints. At first, *La lunga notte* appears to comply with rhetoric not too distant from contemporary *New York Times* coverage discussed in Chapter 2: "Rome was born on that June morning over a sky of opal and roses, between the squeaks and chirps of happy birds: she was awake, quivering and vibrant, and the sun beat dazzlingly on Saint Peter's cupola as if in an apotheosis of joy and rebirth."⁷⁷ However, as the heroines chafe at the notion that their personal experience coincide with the collective, the melodramatic tension culminates when Andreina walks through the city as it pulses with life, bearing the weight of her unresolved trauma. Only when English Captain Edward Stones lays eyes on her does she start to share in the feeling of rebirth: "The man at the wheel smiled. His green eyes, so light, young, rested curiously on Andreina. And in a single moment, by virtue of that gaze, her old personality, feminine and flirtatious, malicious and tender, was reborn."⁷⁸ Encountering Captain Stones alongside her friend Antonello, she starts to inform her fellow Italian of all those they have lost—naming the specific sites of the murders—but trails off into ellipses: "Oh, Beppe shot at Forte Boccea, Claudio massacred at the Fosse Ardeatine, Colombi killed on the street like a dog . . . Oh, terrible . . . terrible, Antonello. . . . Better to say nothing. . . . Better to speak about you, Luciano, Berrini, Ghedini, who are alive. Don't think of all this sadness any more. . . . We have been fed, nourished, poisoned by tragedies for all these months. . . . I don't, I don't want to be sad any more . . ."[79] As Stones interjects in English to ask what she and Antonello are talking about, Andreina refuses to translate the Italian tragedy, deciding instead to use the intercultural encounter to facilitate the shift back to romance: "and she turned to him and smiled: 'Nothing: nothing at all . . .'"[80] Then, after learning of Adriano's execution and his emotional betrayal with Ursula, Andreina tries to complete this erasure, offering to Stones, "I will do what you want . . . Edward, oh anything, as long as you help me not to think."[81]

Andreina's sexual surrender to Stones undercuts Adriano's vision of her as a redemptive Madonna, but so too does it make a powerful suggestion about the constructed nature of the Italy-as-whore topos. When Andreina sexually sublimates her tragedy, she does so in order to conform to the collective narrative that equates liberation with redemptive rebirth. It is Antonello, instead, who reads her in that moment as a symbol of the fallen nation, despite his own earlier dalliance with a fascist woman. Comparing her to common Neapolitan prostitutes—"certain girls from Naples that he had hated and scorned, but that at least were driven by hunger, by poverty!"—he reads her behavior as an affront to all those Italian men like him who had fought and suffered.[82] Here, Antonello's moralism, commonplace to representations of the postliberation cities, is undermined by the readers' knowledge of Andreina's past as well as her motivations for her sexual encounter with Stones: not depravity or materialism, but simply a desire to forget death and to feel reborn.[83] In using the motivation ascribed to soldiers, *La lunga notte* signals that war does not only exist within the confines of a battlefield, nor does its cessation mean happiness.[84]

While Antonello genders suffering as masculine, *La lunga notte* closes with an emphatic refusal of redemption for the three remaining protagonists. Andreina, Antonella and Ursula all experience metaphorical death at the moment that Rome is "reborn," making the happy ending ring hollow. In the final words of the novel:

> But [Ursula] felt that she would never be peaceful nor pure again. Never. And nor would Antonello. And nor would Andreina, whatever they might

do to console themselves. That terrible, horrible war, and all that they had seen, suffered, and endured, had mangled their spirits, had extinguished in them all goodness and joy of life. Whatever happened, they would be other people, bitter and incredulous beings, from whom a terrible God had stolen something that no one would ever return.[85]

In refusing to allay the tension between individual loss and the Allies' redemptive ending, *La lunga notte* emerges as a *rosa* "inhabited" by melodrama insofar as it "understand[s] events of public history and private emotions being equally significant."[86] In the words of Andreina, "yes, it was terrible that her friends had been arrested. But her drama, her torment were equally important and decisive."[87] In this "melodramatic conjuncture of personal circumstance with decisive historical conditions," Peverelli's heroines resemble Rossellini's Francesca, as their "female plight symbolises the nation through romantic relations."[88] However, Rossellini feminizes the melodramatic fall only to cast redemption within a masculine neorealist sphere of northern partisans falling to their death. Peverelli, instead, privileges her "fallen" female characters and her hybrid genre as the "borderline" sites through which postwar Italian identity is to be negotiated, expanding the neorealist orthodoxy in content and form—a tendency that becomes all the more explicit in *Sposare lo straniero*. Despite the novel's shift away from the trauma of the occupation toward the romantic plotlines, it reasserts the underlying gendered violence within marriage, locating the true happy ending within the transnational correspondence of the Italian war brides.

Intercultural Marriage and the Transition from "Romance" to "Reality"

Picking up four months into the "dreamlike" Allied occupation of Rome, *Sposare lo straniero* shifts focus to romantic entanglements. However, even as it appears to enact the repression Andreina desires in *La lunga notte*, concomitantly, the novel exhibits a heighted interest in storytelling through metatextual comments on what kinds of genres can be used to transmit the destabilized reality of postliberation Rome. This concern is visible in the book's epistolary frame, opening with a letter from an American GI to his mother and ending with correspondence between war brides. In contrast to the final lines of *La lunga notte*, Jackie Larson's letter marks an abrupt shift, as he writes about his upcoming leave in Rome in search of romantic conquests. Declaring, "I feel as excited as a kid going to the theater for the first time," he evokes *La lunga notte*'s shorthand for a frivolous escapism.[89] Criticized by his new friend, the English Major Howard Whiter, Jackie looks in the mirror and sees "the image of a young, blond hero, with sparkling eyes, full lips, firm jaw," a subtle mockery of the American conqueror that indicates the novel's refusal to enact his escapist fantasy.[90]

Despite the disdain for Jackie's theatrics, the sexual encounter figures prominently in the novel's realist intentions, as it explores intercultural marriage. A blurb on the original cover announces, "Four girls impacted by the war: Gemma, Andreina, Luce, and Gesi live through their own novel. Each comes to a different conclusion. Is it a boon to marry a foreigner or not? Luciana will answer us, in her story that, like *La lunga notte*, only documents real events and characters based on real people."[91] Making good on its promise, the novel offers an array of opinions. Gesi and Andreina hold opposite attitudes that reverse over the course of the novel: Gesi rejects her American fiancé, Jackie, in favor of Antonello, while Andreina comes to feel at home in England with her husband, Howard. Gemma and Luce think about marriage in terms of interracial mixing: While Gemma's suicide is motivated by her "foreign" child, perceived as enemy inside her, Luce romanticizes the mystery of interracial love and the beauty of mixed-race children.[92]

In offering these answers—and insisting on its realist intentions—*Sposare lo straniero* engages with the question of how to negotiate gender roles in the transition from the "dream" of the Allied occupation to the "reality" of the postwar. Starting from the stereotypical premise that the lexicon of pleasure, dreams, and passion belongs to Italy while reality is in the Anglo-American domain, Andreina forges a hybrid Anglo-Italian identity parallel to the "true" *rosa* Peverelli fashions. As it emphasizes the seemingly fictional nature of life during "liberation," *Sposare lo straniero* shows awareness of the *rosa*'s penchant for excess through metaliterary references.[93] Self-consciously deploying and critiquing staples of the *rosa*, *Sposare lo straniero* affirms that its "unlikely" events are a product of that fabled time, thus casting itself as a novel that is, in its own words, life (*vita*). Andreina asks, "Why do novels usually end when the two protagonists marry? That's when the novel starts, that's when life starts."[94] Heeding her wishes, the latter half of *Sposare lo straniero* interrogates the novel of postwar life, envisioning the women who encounter the Allies as a "borderline" cultural space.

During the first act, every Allied-Italian encounter is characterized in terms of melodrama, comedy and the fairy tale.[95] Explicit in signaling the fablelike quality of its love stories, *Sposare lo straniero* more broadly asks the question Andreina poses about Gemma: "When the fairy tale ends, what will become of her?"[96] Indeed, those who envision the ending of the nightmarish German occupation as the fulfillment of a long-awaited dream only experience trauma. As the "liberation" demands further struggles from a wide swathe of the population, written out of the dominant discourse, the *romanzo rosa*, instead, can acknowledge reality's shortcomings: "Hundreds of girls had dreamed, had hoped, hundreds of girls had felt like little Cinderellas for whom phantasmagorical knights in shining armor had come, but now were returning to their homelands."[97] In this formulation, *Sposare lo straniero* dovetails with historical war bride accounts in which the first "act" of the narrative, set in Italy, promises a knight in shining armor, while the second, set in the adoptive country, is the time when the honeymoon ends.[98] Far from suggesting that her readers aspire to live within a dream as Banti accuses, Peverelli warns against this belief and suggests ways to manage this temporally circumscribed moment, as Andreina presciently speculates: "It was as though they all were living in a period outside of time, in which all the most unthinkable and extraordinary things could happen. Then, once the war was over, everything would go back to normal. And it would all seem like a dream."[99] For Andreina, the happy ending cannot be obtained by means of a rupture between the occupation and the postwar that Ben-Ghiat identifies as the prominent revisionist strategy in early representations of fascism.[100] Instead, it comes by negotiating the transition with open eyes.

In the novel, this transition is signaled by a long description of the final conflicts of the war where an uncharacteristic switch into the present tense heightens the intensity as the events tumble on top of one another with a series of "ands," linguistically evincing the "dizzying, rapid pace of events" it frantically describes:

> The Bologna front breached, the Allied troops gone down into the Po Valley, and the Germans' supposed resistance along the river quickly smashed, the first jeeps pushing into the Po Valley, and the partisans coming down from the valleys in triumph, and the cities in revolt, the Germans and Fascists in retreat, and before the Allies can reach the big cities of the North, justice has been done and the flags of freedom fly from the gutted houses, piazzas, churches where bells ring out in celebration.[101]

At a narrative speed that outstrips the pace of the novel's swiftest love affairs, this seemingly unending period abruptly concludes; as Andreina says, "an absurd and terrible period of our life has ended."[102] Indeed, this passage marks an important division: before, absurdities circle freely, if to some degree of criticism; after, those who are to end happily must figure out how to return to everyday life. In the first major scene after the war, Malcolm announces his departure with a warning to his onetime princess that melodramatic scenes have no place in this new reality.[103] However, if the Allied occupation is the *romanzo rosa*, a plot that "must evolve, without any great surprises or twists, toward a foreseeable happy ending," it proves to be a melodramatic *rosa*, haunted by the stories of those who did not achieve their own, such as Gemma.[104]

Andreina and Luce, in fact, face twists and turns as they negotiate their reality as war brides in what has been packaged as "a marvelous adventure."[105] When Andreina and Howard's marriage takes place, it is coded in language that suggests it is a risky continuation of the dreamlike world: "Thus the dream was coming true, that which had seemed unreal was coming to pass. Howard Whiter was marrying her, Andreina. All the obstacles had vanished, magically."[106] In this world, Howard sees himself as the unequivocal redeemer: "I arrived in a mangled country, mercilessly ravaged by war, and I saw a flower coming up out of the rubble, and so I picked it before other hands could destroy it, and I hold it near and dear so that it comes back to life."[107] In imagining Andreina's rebirth, Howard anticipates the protagonist of *The Girl on the Via Flaminia*, Robert, who dreams of "rebuilding" fallen Lisa, as discussed in Chapter 2, a fantasy as improbable for Hayes as for Peverelli. However, by extending the temporal parameters beyond the "fable" of "liberation," *Sposare lo straniero* envisions the possibility for rebirth that depends on Andreina's *self*-redemption when she negotiates a space for herself as an Italian woman in England high society and finds herself at home for the first time since she left Milan.[108]

Andreina's "marvellous adventure" in England begins with a rude awakening in the estate of her belligerent Duchess mother-in-law with a withdrawn husband who insists she repress everything "Italian" about her, from her makeup and clothes, to her passion. Howard's embittered old-maid sister, Mildred, disparages Italian war brides: "without merit and with great cunning, surrounding themselves with a halo of unhappy martyrs, they managed to snag themselves the best men of England and America."[109] Here, she voices a belief identified by Susan Zeiger who argues that, historically, war marriages provided a metaphor for the ambivalent relations between the spouses' respective countries; if marrying local women was a sign of military and economic power, foreign brides could also be seen as manipulators and infiltrators.[110] In her choice of words, *halo of unhappy martyrs*, Mildred echoes Ursula's disparaging comments in *La lunga notte* when she fears that Andreina's arrest will legitimate her participation in the resistance.[111] As I argued, *La lunga notte* refutes the perspective that a heroine need redemption for her romantic, melodramatic qualities; these intertextual references to *La lunga notte* allow *Sposare lo straniero* to further insist that Italian women do not need redemption from the Allies either. The night Andreina meets Howard, she rebukes him and his friends: "You know nothing of our desperate fight to gain our freedom, the right to fight for our ideas ... and how many of us have fallen, and how many of us have given our lives for this freedom before you came to offer it to us so ostentatiously."[112] However, in her new English home, where such lectures are deemed inappropriate, Andreina must adopt another approach. When Howard's mother and sister critique her makeup, voicing "a longstanding tradition of moral disapproval regarding female adornment," she wipes it off.[113] When Howard rebukes her indecorous demand for affection, she defends herself in terms of her traumatic wartime experience before being placated by a kiss: "But you know, when one goes through a war like this, and the fleeing and the bombings, and the risk of death, and prison, one cannot expect one's nerves not to be on edge."[114] This interaction serves as a measure of the impact the war has had on Andreina who insists the opposite in *La lunga notte*, imploring Adriano: "I don't want to hear talk of war, of Germans, of partisan frontlines ... I want to think that we two are the only ones who exist in the world, that we are happy, that we love each other, that ..."[115] Even as Andreina heads toward her happy ending, the events of *Lunga notte* continue to bubble to the surface when she discovers Howard has betrayed her with his former girlfriend, "With disconsolate anguish she thought back to that period of the Resistance against the Germans in Rome when she had suffered so much. And yet it seemed to her like nothing compared to this bitterness."[116] Nonetheless, as her memories fade, they hew more closely to the dominant postwar paradigm: The Italian enemy is gone without a trace, and only the Germans remain in sight.

Reshaping her Italian identity will be crucial to Andreina's "unveiling" scene (*svelamento*), a staple of the *rosa* when the heroine reveals "her beauty and other hidden qualities."[117] For Andreina, this initially means revealing her prewar state by erasing the trauma of the war: "She needed to be herself again, as she had been in happy times, before Italy was mangled by bombs, invaded by foreigners who were friends and enemies at the same time."[118] Dressed in blue—the same color she wears in Adriano's beatific vision—Andreina tries to return to her former self by turning to American fashion, emulating the cover of "Harper's Bazar" or "Vogue."[119] Andreina's performance dispels the "absurd legend" that she is a war refuge (and demonstrates that her public redemption depends on affirming not just her Italian authenticity but her upper-class status).[120] The war that has destroyed her country, renders her undeserving in the eyes of Howard's family; through elegant dress and unmatched charm, she earns even the grudging admiration of Mildred, who praises her by saying, "You seem fake."[121]

Even as Andreina rejects the compliment, asserting, "I'm not fake, this is the real me," this first unveiling is signaled as a performance, ending with her drunk and sleepwalking.[122] After the party, she strips off her costume and prepares her escape, walking to the train station, "like in fairy tales," only to fall asleep.[123] The final happy ending, then, involves one last awakening at the hands of a repentant Howard, a second unveiling, now out of costume. Only when she wakes up from the metaphorical and literal dream is Andreina redeemed. This cannot be achieved by recovering a past Italy through the complete erasure of the wartime experience. Indeed, when Andreina and Howard envision their happy ending by healing a *mangled Italy*, they fail, as anticipated by the conclusion of *La lunga notte* that warns the war that has "mangled her soul," cannot be forgotten; what has been stolen, cannot be restored.[124] Howard cannot transplant her to England like a flower; instead, by culling the best from each identity, Andreina manages to effect a change in Howard, transmitting to him the "Italian" trait that he had most rejected—passion.[125] Taking a conciliatory point of view, Howard emphasizes the symbolic status with which their relationship is invested: "Perhaps we were two enemy worlds until yesterday. But today no more. It is I who bow before you, and you must receive me in your arms. We must be—if it doesn't seem a bit ridiculous and presumptuous on my part to say it—we must be a little symbol of the world, Andreina."[126] When Andreina returns home with Howard, she confirms his transformation by reading his melodramatic apology letter—showing his prowess in a genre coded Italian and female. Upon this happy ending, Andreina finds additional letters that tell her the fate of the two remaining heroines. One letter brings news of Gesi's marriage to Antonello, and three tell the story of Luce and Freddy. Following these stories to their conclusions, then, I show how they leave question marks about marriage and instead, propose the redemptive power of female friendship and storytelling.

Female Storytelling as Redemption

As a counterpart to Andreina and Howard, Gesi and Antonello represent a happy ending within Italy's borders unfathomable to Hayes and Rossellini—but by no means unequivocally rosy. Like Hayes's Lisa and Rossellini's Francesca, Gesi begins the novel infatuated with the GI, in parallel with the "honeymoon" of Rome's liberation that gives way to the disillusionment of the occupation.[127] However, Peverelli elaborates the violence inherent in such a gendered formulation: When Jackie accompanies Gesi to her native Pescara in search of news of her family, he attempts to rape her; she staves him off but soon agrees to marry him, drawing a dubious line between conquest and consent. While Hayes and Rossellini depict a "honeymoon" followed by a precipitous breakup with no hint of redemption, in *Sposare lo straniero*, Gesi rejects the GI and embraces the Italian partisan; although Gesi envisions Jackie as mitigating the trauma of her town's devastation, it is when she decides to marry Antonello that she feels at home.[128] Nonetheless, Antonello, like Jackie, reads her symbolically, initially desiring her because he perceives her as war bounty being pillaged by Jackie.[129] Moreover, she distracts him at a crucial moment, interrupting the story he tells to Andreina about Ursula's fate, after being captured by the Nazis on her third parachute mission behind enemy lines:

> At first we thought they would shoot her. Then they found out she was Jewish, and they did not want to give her too quick a death. They took her to a concentration camp. I don't know if all the horrors that they describe about that world are true, but I assure you that the stories they tell make you shudder. Ursula is strong, she is used to everything, but those awful camps are called extermination camps, and in those places the most frightful, the slowest of deaths are calculated.[130]

This acknowledgment of Ursula's heroism and her tragic fate is cut short when Antonello catches sight of Gesi. Thus, reducing the story of Ursula's sacrifice and insidiously casting doubt on the full extent of the truth of the Holocaust's horrors, Antonello illustrates the phenomenon critiqued by historian David Ellwood, whereby the moralizing sexualization of women in representations of the occupation works to obscure a multitude of female roles.[131] While both novels offer a rejoinder to such beliefs, *Sposare lo straniero* suggests how they take hold. Moreover, that the repression of Ursula's story be performed by a male partisan is its own prescient commentary on decades of Italian cultural production.

Despite his "victory" in wresting Gesi from the American conqueror, Antonello appears trapped in his limited perceptions of Italian women. Instead, Jackie, returning to America without his Italian war booty, promises to provide a corrective in relaying stories of the occupation to an American audience that, like Andreina's adoptive English family, has prejudices against women who are "far-off foreigners, enemies."[132] A celebrity gossip columnist commissioned to write a military history, Jackie starts out conditioned by literary and cinematic norms: He views Gesi as the heroine of every American sentimental novel, and the girls of Rome as if they were American movie stars.[133] However, after his sexual conquests across Italy, he comes to defend Italian women who might appear to be prostituting themselves: "They said that they only gave themselves to the Americans for the thousand lire and cigarettes and chocolate. But Jackie knew it wasn't true. He knew they were much less greedy than American women."[134] As Jackie returns to the States to write his story, he functions as a symbol of the brief honeymoon of the liberation and as a fantastical projection of the American GI redeemed by his experience in Italy, not unlike John Horne Burns's narrator in *The Gallery*.[135]

Leaving readers to speculate what Jackie might have written, the novel focuses on the stories Italian women tell each other. In contrast to Jackie's letter to his mother about his plans for love in Rome, the following chapter introduces Gesi through her newfound friendship to Andreina. Whatever material assistance Andreina provides Gesi, Gesi helps Andreina start to come to terms with her trauma. Recognizing her former self in the childlike Gesi, Andreina also feels a renewed connection between Ursula and her present-day self:

> The drama that little Gesi told her about was like the echo of a drama she had already experienced, already suffered through, and it hurt her to wake up from the torpor in which she had fallen in those past months, much like a fearful but sweet sleep. It seemed to her that that girl with the little curls had brusquely called her back to the reality of an existence she had almost forgotten.[136]

Serving as her first audience, Gesi allows Andreina to experience the heady pleasure of narrating after four months of silence: "It was the first time that Andreina had told anyone about her tragedy: it gave her a kind of thrill."[137] Listening to Andreina's tale of betrayal without any personal experience, Gesi is "enchanted."[138] As the novel shows how both speaker and listener benefit, it also sets up another redemptive trajectory: "Confessing" to Gesi that she no longer believes in friendship, Andreina lays the groundwork the novel's happy ending when, as a war bride in England, she becomes the confidant of Luce, a war bride in Chicago.[139]

While Andreina plays an advisory role to the innocent Gesi, she relates to Luce as an equal. The parallels between them are apparent in their relationships with their respective foreign fiancés, the English Howard and the American Freddy, and in the paths that led to those relationships. Just as Andreina is betrayed by Adriano with Ursula only to be abandoned by Stones,

Luce loses her Italian fiancé to a Greek girl and then is left by Frank Smuth who goes back to his wife. After throwing herself too deeply into her fantasy world in an effort to forget her initial loss, Luce decides she has had enough "fantasy" and "romanticism."[140] She turns to Freddy, her sensible American colleague at the *Stars and Stripes* newspaper who revamps her social life and abruptly proposes marriage, despite his belief that she has been prostituting herself to the array of officers whom she frequents. Although Luce is, in fact, a virgin, the prostitute "haunts" her marriage, influencing how she and Freddy position themselves.[141] When Luce begins to regret her decision to marry a man who knows nothing of her cultural interests, she placates herself by considering what she stands to gain, using the Italian women who prostituted themselves to the Allies as a positive model of upward mobility. As she embraces the fantasy of these girls and their lavish lifestyle promised by illustrated magazines, she senses their presence in the cheap hotel room where she spends her wedding night:

> How many girls had already been there, with American soldiers, in that room? Girls who, like many that she had met, were good and simple and honest and then let themselves be swept away by that wave of folly, youth, and wealth that had crashed over the city. Girls who sold fish in the market and who then, all of a sudden, found themselves earning ten, twenty-thousand lire a day, and bought themselves furs, audacious and stunned.[142]

Caught in a momentary desire to emulate these girls' rags-to-riches trajectory, Luce has a change of heart when the moment comes to lose her virginity, and her upper-class background asserts itself: "Oh no, not like this, in that ugly room."[143] As Freddy forces himself on her, she submits while thinking, "but how to free herself from that grip?"[144] Just as Luce's ambivalent view toward her marriage is conditioned by her fantasies of the prostitute, so, too, is Freddy's attitude toward her. Startled by discovery that he has taken her virginity, Freddy enables a critique of those who assume that in Allied-occupied Italy, virginity is the rarest commodity (a belief satirized in Curzio Malaparte's *La pelle*, discussed in Chapter 5). In *Paisà*, Rossellini's Fred laments to the fallen Francesca, "Now you're all alike"; in fact, within the discursive realm of Italy-as-whore, the prostitute "haunts" gender, forcing every Italian woman to defend herself from the assumption—which Luce only can do by being raped.[145] Furthermore, this scene connects back to *La lunga notte*, echoing Ursula's seduction of the fascist official who expresses amazement that so convincing a seductress had been a virgin. Along with the parallel created between the American and the fascist, a link emerges between Luce and Ursula, casting a pall on Luce's ending and forcing the reader to question what is happy about it.

Positioned at the conclusion, the letters give Luce the final word and leave Andreina in the role of reader. Opening the pile, Andreina approaches them with the expectations of a reader habituated to romance but anxious insofar as life gives no such guarantees. After describing her fraught departure for the United States, Luce alludes to her wedding night, which she struggles to describe: "the taste of love that I got ... the taste was fast, painful, left me stunned."[146] She then details her transatlantic boat ride, dispelling the notion that it is "a romantic dream along the ocean."[147] Dedicating several pages to the stories of other war brides, she narrates the happy or tragic endings after their arrival.[148] In a subsequent tear-stained letter that Andreina reads with an ever-tightening feeling in her heart, Luce describes being overwhelmed with nostalgia as she agonizes about her struggles to adapt to working-class Chicago with a taciturn husband and an unsatisfying sex life.[149] Unable to withstand her solitude, she flees to New York to await a return ship only to realize she is pregnant, which pushes her to remain in America where Freddy's baby belongs: "my baby is Freddy's baby. It is an American baby. This is his country."[150] After she writes to him, he joins her in New York where she conveys her fears, allowing them to find a path to happiness that will include visiting Italy. Determined to raise the child as an American, Luce hopes to avoid transmitting "Italian" qualities to him, such as "sensitivity and poetry and art" that she perceives as ill suited to an American life.[151]

Luce's embrace of the American patriarchy offers ready-made fodder to critics who attack the conservative, misogynist tendencies of the romance. Her final words tout the superiority of men over all women and Italian women in particular, "so changeable and imaginative and full of strange whims," before telling her friend that she will subordinate herself to Freddy: "I told him that it's great, that from now on anything that makes him happy will be great."[152] As the final words of the novel express her hope that her child resemble his American father: "I hope that my baby looks like him," Luce's happy ending seems to encompass her capitulation to the patriarchy and, moreover, her renunciation of her child's Italian heritage, whom she envisions becoming an American tourist.[153] Apparently cured of her nostalgia, she seems ready to jump in the melting pot as American publications encouraged.[154]

However, the novel remains ambivalent about its heroines' status. On the one hand, it envisions the women who encounter the Allies as a "borderline" space between Italian and Anglo-American culture, fantasy and reality, occupation and postwar that may allow them to reappropriate the redemption narrative. On the other hand, in the Italian immigrant's promise to raise her child as an American, we see the postwar redemption narrative play out, once again, on the Italian woman's body, coopted into producing new American tourists. Even as the novel provides the conventions of a happy ending, it signals the violence of the encounter. In addition to Luce's discussion of prostitution, rape and suicide in the letter, we might read in her pregnancy the other pregnancies in *La lunga notte* and *Sposare lo straniero* that ended in tragedy: In addition to Gemma, who commits suicide rather than give birth to her "foreign" child, Mildred loses her American fiancé to the war and their baby in childbirth, and Ursula's brother and sister-in-law have their baby taken from them when they are deported, and given to an Italian family to be assimilated into Catholic Italian culture—another act of genocide. Early in the novel, Luce waxes poetic on the beauty of interracial children, "they say that children born of parents who belong to different races are beautiful," yet the novel presents them as sites of cultural conflict and, ultimately, loss.[155] Indeed, it stands to note that Andreina's successful positioning between Italian and English culture happens without any reference to motherhood, impending or desired.

With the marriage plot thus inhabited by melodrama, *Sposare lo straniero* locates redemption within the bounds of storytelling between Italian female friends.[156] This is not to be an intercultural exchange (it excludes the possibility for creating bonds with Howard or Freddy's family members), nor a nostalgic transnational link with those at home (both women want to cut all ties).[157] Nor is it to be found in intergenerational transmission, as the narrator speculates: "Much later, after many, many years, women who have become old would tell their disinterested granddaughters, 'Blonde tall boys came from America, who spoke loudly and laughed often.'"[158] In imagining women telling their stories of the Allied-Italian encounter in occupied Rome, *Sposare lo straniero* recognizes they may find the parameters of realism have shifted—with dire consequences for the preservation of the individual story and the collective memory. Even Peverelli herself describes rereading the autobiographically inspired *La lunga notte* at a distance of years and feeling disbelief "that everything had been so true."[159] Luce's letters, however, suggest that a *romanzo* may be true *and* pleasurable when read by an empathetic audience: not her mother-in-law, nor those she left at home, but Andreina, in whom she sees herself.[160] Here, Luce moves in opposite directions: while renouncing fantasy and romanticism, she articulates the importance of the pleasure of the word, enabled by the reader's connection to the events. For all her interest in truth, she does not advocate that writing be a spare chronicle of events (D'Annunzio, after all, remains her literary touchstone, *pace* Banti). On the contrary, she attributes her husband's lack of sexual refinement to a linguistic—and cultural—shortcoming: "Maybe it's the words that are missing, the damned words with which we in Europe, in Italy above all, cover everything, so the poorest and most naked of things appear splendid and luminous and fascinating, and even if these words are frills, it matters little, they give us pleasure."[161] After rejecting a lexicon of falsities—fables, novels, comedies, melodramas—the narrative ends by defending frilly Italian words as a legitimate source of pleasure; without them, Luce speculates, physical gratification may even be impossible.

How to read—and enjoy—frilly Italian words or dreamlike Italian moments without facing a rude awakening? Peverelli places the interpretive onus on her female protagonists, as she invests them with the power to negotiate reality and fantasy and to adapt accordingly, keeping those parts of themselves that will help them obtain a *real* happily ever after, a *romanzo* that is *vita*. At the same time, as the traumas of the occupation haunt the happy ending, it is a *rosa* that is also melodrama. Together *La lunga notte* and *Sposare lo straniero* function as a commentary on the power of the melodramatic *rosa* to intertwine art and life, fiction and truth, for the benefit of a contemporary audience that experienced the traumatic events it describes, even as they acknowledge that future generations may read their absurd realities as simply absurd. Mounting a proleptic defense against Banti's charge that the mix of American realism and Italian romance has a deleterious effect, these *rosa* locate redemption in the dialogue between Italian women as they negotiate their identity within Anglo-American culture.

La lunga notte and *Sposare lo straniero*, together with the texts explored in the previous chapter, *Paisà*, *All Thy Conquests*, and *The Girl on the Via Flaminia*, are at once a testament to the complexity of the Allied-Italian encounter in the space of Rome, and to the persistence of the gendering of redemption. Aware of the rhetorical tradition, Rossellini's Francesca puts on her costume and reads lines from a pocket dictionary, while Hayes's and Peverelli's heroines remark on the disorienting experience of playing a socially scripted part. Of the five texts, only *Paisà* has achieved transnational canonical status but within it, the "Rome" episode shares a similar critical fate to Peverelli's romances: Dismissed as melodramatic, it has been considered irrelevant to high-stakes cultural questions. Thus, the reception of these texts—produced and circulated shortly after the events they describe—suggests how the policing of generic borders helps consolidate the redemption paradigm. Here, instead, by reading them together in the context of representations of postliberation Rome, these chapters show how melodrama accommodates the gender-inclusive perspective that neorealism refuses and, moreover, how the melodramatic fallen woman helps repress historical trauma. Moreover, affirming *La lunga notte* and *Sposare lo straniero* as engaged *rosa*, this chapter expands the miniscule corpus of Italian Holocaust narrative and locates a patent demonstration of the anti-Semitism that coexists alongside denunciations of genocide; and it identifies a unique Italian war bride narrative, together with a transnational model for female redemption. Furthermore, making connections between American and Italian texts, novels and films, neorealist and "pink" texts, these chapters draw out each other's blind spots but also their insights; their capitulations but also their resistances. Comparatively, they show how the same events that threaten neorealism's redemptive arc, such as the massacre of the Fosse Ardeatine, freely circulate in an American novel like Hayes's *All Thy Conquests*, which, not coincidentally, was never translated into Italian. It also circulates in the pages of a romance novel like *La lunga notte*, which—under the reassuring cover of its "careless" genre—points an accusatory finger at all of Rome for its responsibility for the deportation of the Jews, and its privileging of the memory of the Fosse Ardeatine while repressing the Holocaust.

The remaining chapters, focused on the canonical texts of Allied-occupied Naples, are animated by similar concerns of cultural censorship but with a different bent, due to the intersection of the Neapolitan setting and the texts' autofictional genre. As the texts confront the unbelievable hell of Allied-occupied Naples—a city that faced the widespread destruction that Rome was spared—they affirm the first-person narrator's authority to tell the story. At the same time, however, the superlative drama of the Allied-occupied Naples lends itself to an allegorical reading that minimizes the texts' historical specificity. Seeking to discipline this hybridity, scholars tend to interpret in one of the two modes; continuing the approach taken here, I foreground the self-conscious, dynamic interplay between literature and history. Moreover, as they explore the gendering of redemption through this strategic blurring, the following chapters create dialogues between an American and an Italian novel and a British diary (and in the epilogue, an Italian diary). However, while Peverelli, Hayes, and Rossellini focus on heteronormative relationships between Anglo-Americans and Italians, in Allied-occupied Naples, John Horne Burns, Curzio Malaparte, and Norman Lewis confront the ways in which the gendering of redemption is troubled by sexuality and race, opening up the encounter to its transnational dimension.

4

A Queer Redemption
John Horne Burns's *The Gallery*

According to Italian critic Emilio Cecchi in a 1949 essay, of the countless novels written by American soldiers after their experience in Italy, one distinguishes itself from the mediocre pack: John Horne Burns's *The Gallery* (1947). American soldiers—in Cecchi's estimation—expected to go to Italy and see monkeys hanging from their tails off baobab trees; disappointed, they substituted their desire to laugh with a desire to "catechize" and "regenerate" the Italians.[1] John—the first-person narrator—also sets sail with jingoist convictions, but his wartime encounter produces the opposite effect, forcing him to question the American way of life. Mid-Atlantic on a convoy where he sees his companions stealing from one another, he writes, "I think I died as an American."[2] Starting with this spiritual death, John reconsiders his relationship to the Italians he has been sent to "liberate" and what kind of art that encounter might inspire. At the end, when his Italian lover urges him to tell his story, John realizes that Naples has been a "womb," allowing him to be reborn with an awareness of his shared humanity.[3] As *The Gallery*'s origin story, this moment articulates the novel's universalizing, redemptive ethos that differentiates it from other American World War II fiction. Singling it out in his retrospective, *After the Lost Generation* (1951), American critic John Aldridge reaffirms *The Gallery*'s uniqueness decades later: Whereas in the "classic pattern," the soldier's experience with the hell of war ends in his spiritual death, *The Gallery* is "virtually alone among war novels in arriving finally at an affirmation of the humanizing effects of the view of life as tragedy."[4]

After earning accolades for his first novel, Burns produced two high-profile flops and was dead of a cerebral hemorrhage at thirty-six.[5] Even after Burns's star burnt out, *The Gallery* retains its high repute: Revisiting *The Gallery* in 1964 on the occasion of a reedition, Brigid Brophy affirms, "in my very serious opinion, John Horne Burns was by far the most talented, and the most *attractively* talented, American novelist to emerge since the war."[6] Forty years later it was reissued again, this time by the *New York Review of*

Books, where it was introduced by American critic Paul Fussell as "an extraordinary contribution to American literature. Its structure is inventive and its prose is memorably energetic. There is nothing like it, and it thoroughly deserved the praise lavished on it in 1947, when it was one of the earliest works of fiction generated by the war just concluded."[7]

For all these sustained accolades, the novel remains understudied.[8] Although it is understood to be a story of "psychic, spiritual death and rebirth" in Allied-occupied Naples, the redemption narrative must be interrogated in terms of its intricate relationship to the setting.[9] This means at once zooming out from Naples to the Mediterranean and the world, and zooming in, to the city-within-a-city in Naples that gives the novel its name, an arcade called the Galleria Umberto I, introduced in the "Entrance." Crowded with architectural, corporeal, and naturalist metaphors, the prefatory "Entrance" signals that the novel's literary space will reflect the porous physical space to which it refers:

> There's an arcade in Naples that they call the Galleria Umberto Primo. It's a cross between a railroad station and a church. You think you're in a museum till you see the bars and the shops. Once this Galleria had a dome of glass, but the bombings of Naples shattered this skylight, and tinkling glass fell like cruel snow to the pavement. But life went on in the Galleria. In August 1944, it was the unofficial heart of Naples. It was a living and subdividing cell of vermouth, Allied soldiery and the Italian people.[10]

As a railroad station, a church, a heart, and a cell in the alcohol-ridden body of Naples, where civilizations "interpenetrat[e]," *The Gallery* is the scene of base encounters: "there were screams and coos and slaps and stumbles. There were the hasty press of kisses and sibilance of urine on the pavement. By moonlight shadows singly and in pairs chased from corner to corner."[11] Inviting the reader to walk around the Galleria as if it were a museum, *The Gallery* presents nine portraits of Italians and Americans who find themselves there in August 1944. These alternate with eight first-person promenades in which the narrator meanders the Mediterranean from North Africa to Naples—a journey that matches Burns's own experience as an intelligence officer. In each portrait and the three final promenades, readers return to the Galleria, traveling in time as they assemble the characters' and narrator's conflicting and complementary visions. Through these recurrent descriptions, the novel establishes the Galleria as a mise en abyme of the city: in the third portrait Hal observes, "It was like walking into a city within a city."[12] So, too, is it a mise en abyme of the novel: in the fourth portrait,

Chaplain Bascom remarks, "What a place that arcade is ... A great novel could be made of it."[13]

The theme of this "great novel" is the search for love in wartime. While five of the portraits tell love stories, the promenades recount John's journey to love in Naples, where he experiences a transcendent sexual communion with an unnamed Italian who inspires him to write *The Gallery*. Functioning as a frame, the "Entrance" together with the "Exit" bring the spiritual journey full circle, lending a narrative structure to what appears to be a plotless book. Reversing the hellish descent of a novel like Alfred Hayes's *All Thy Conquests*, *The Gallery* follows an upwards trajectory, as the banal encounter of the "Entrance" is elevated by the "Exit": "all the people in the Galleria were human beings in the middle of a war. They struck attitudes. Some loved. Some tried to love."[14] Read according to this arc, *The Gallery* is about the redemptive intercultural encounter. It touts the belief that, "In a war one has to love, if only to assert that he's very much alive in the face of destruction. Whoever has loved in wartime takes part in a passionate reaffirmation of his life," a sentiment that has made the book emblematic for war bride historians.[15] However, *The Gallery* spends only a few sentences on couples whose relationships continue during peacetime.[16] More apt is the attention it has received for "Momma," the portrait set in a clandestine gay bar nestled within the Galleria, a singular, open acknowledgment of homosexuality in the military in World War II.[17] At the geographical and affective heart of the novel, "Momma" articulates the paradigm of queer redemption John embraces at the conclusion in his sexual encounter with an Italian who is not only unnamed but ungendered. This redemption is about love that moves beyond the parameters of gender and nationality that the novel associates with American capitalism, occupation, and the narrator's spiritual death.

Serving as a womb for John, Naples is key to understanding *The Gallery*'s redemptive encounter. However, Brophy is quite right that Naples is "only a thematic center" that extends to North Africa as well as the United States.[18] Arguing that *The Gallery* is a transnational text, I start from Emma Bond's definition of "a stretching or going beyond the confines of national boundaries (be that in cultural, spatial or temporal terms)," similar to Mario Varricchio's, used in Chapter 3.[19] In the context of Naples, however, I relate the transnational to the concept of "porosity," a watchword in critical theory on Naples originating from Walter Benjamin and Asja Lacis's 1924 travel essay "Naples." Following John's promenades from North Africa to Naples in dialogue with the interrelated portraits, I argue that while the porosity of Naples confounds his fellow soldiers as they attempt to hold on to their egoistic notions, it is what allows John to move beyond the narrow confines of gender and nation, and experience a queer redemption, a concept that is also informed by Bond's transnational. Finally, after following John's redemptive journey, I use the recurrent space of the Galleria as the key to the novel's transnational poetics, allowing us to trace alternative textual journeys and consider what local identities are thus erased by his embrace of global humanism.

Transnationalism, Porosity, and *The Gallery*

The Gallery's transnationalism—taken as "a fundamental sense of exchange that is inherent in the term"—is visible on multiple levels.[20] At its most basic, *The Gallery* builds its representation of Allied-occupied Naples through journeys within and between the United States, French North Africa, and Italy, insisting on their vexed interrelationships as it zigzags through time and space. As *The Gallery* stages repeated crossings of the Atlantic and the Mediterranean within and between its portraits and promenades, the Galleria is not simply John's destination but also a geographical and temporal trans-space in which to engage the United States, Africa, and Italy, past, present, and future.

Within Naples, the transnational might also be figured in terms of porosity, a watchword for the city thanks to Benjamin and Lacis's essay; as Ruth Glynn summarizes: "Extrapolating from the permeability of the city's *tufo* stone to its architectural and urbanistic composition, Benjamin and Lacis extend the concept of porosity beyond the realms of the natural and built environments and project it onto the social fabric of the city, as well as onto the character and psychology of its inhabitants."[21] Recalling his arrival in Naples in August 1944, the narrator remembers confronting its "spatiotemporal" porosity as he tried to orient himself;[22] he writes, "I couldn't place Naples in any century because it had a taste at once modern and medieval."[23] Porosity, in John's vision, is reflected in the inhabitants' fluid sense of gender and in their interactions with the space. So, too, is it legible in the corporeal descriptions of the city's dwellings, "In the half shot houses what plaster remains in the eaves is as living and suppurating as human skin."[24] Here, he anticipates Serenella Iovino who argues that "Naples' porosity replicates the porosity of all bodies";[25] in *The Gallery*, the bodies of Naples and the body of Naples are in constant exchange, as when sewage-filled streets start vomiting like stomachs nauseated with war, and "clots of returning Neapolitans trek through the streets," or when bodies permeate the alleys and the alleys form part of the urban body: "Each alley had a different stench from many families with their own residua of body excretion, sweat, halitosis, and dandruff. And I remember alley after alley winding off Via Roma like a bowel."[26]

Beyond the thematic, the novel is porous in content and form. Built around journeys in and out of a porous arcade at the heart of a porous city, *The Gallery* is structurally hybrid.[27] As its promenades form intratextual dialogues with the alternating portraits, *The Gallery* shows a "fluidity of constructed styles and practices" that characterizes the transnational, including "bricolage, cultural translation and hybridity."[28] At the linguistic level, it is choral, as disembodied voices of soldiers and civilians, Allies and Italians intermingle, speaking different languages and dialects. Inspired by a Russian piece of music and an American poem, *The Gallery* is an intercultural, ekphrastic narrativization of an Italian arcade.[29] From the perspective of its reception, its presence within an interdisciplinary scholarly network further testifies to its transnationality: the novel's descriptions of the Galleria appear in scholarship of the Mediterranean, migration, architecture, cinema, and photography—often serving as an epigraph.[30]

As the "unofficial heart of the city," the Galleria embodies the porous, transnational space of Naples. Recurring in every portrait and the final three promenades, the Galleria makes the novel's time static and fluid, returning to August 1944 and traveling into the past and future.[31] By the "Exit," *The Gallery* zooms out from the individuals at the Galleria's center to the consider them "synecdoches for most of the people anywhere in the world."[32] Here, the novel affirms a similar message to Roberto Rossellini's *Paisà*, in which "the only viable means of escaping the catastrophes of war . . . is a form of belonging that blankets Italian and American lives with the protections of global humanism. . . . If you are human, it proposes, you are with us."[33] The redemption of *The Gallery* is precisely this embrace of global humanism that earned the novel distinctive praise from critics like Cecchi and Aldridge; toward the end of the novel, the narrator writes, "Perhaps we must soon all come to the point where we're proud only to say: I am a human being, a citizen of the world. For in Naples I and other Americans learned by a simple application of synecdoche that no one, in himself and by himself, is much better or much worse than anybody else."[34] Yet, its celebratory erasure of "local identity-based specificities within the transnational" requires further investigation in dialogue with the preceding episodes, pushing us to ask, what is the cost of this redemption?[35]

To do so, we must move inward one more concentric circle, from the Gallery as the city-within-the-city to "Momma's," the gay bar nestled within the Galleria. Despite holding a cache of stereotypes about her fellow Italians, Momma—a middle-aged, childless Milanese woman so named by her patrons—is the most forward-thinking of *The Gallery*'s cast of characters.[36] From her experience running the gay bar, she comes to believe that gender is a social construction: "The masculine and the feminine weren't nicely divided in Momma's mind as they are to a biologist. They overlapped and blurred in life."[37] This belief is reinforced by her patrons who go by "Magda" and "Esther," and radiates out to characters in other chapters, like the sergeant who appears, "almost as if Marisa had dressed herself in GI suntans and a blond tight wig," and even to the women of North Africa, "almost like pretty boys."[38] Her venue stands outside social convention, as its diverse patrons suggest alternate identities and narratives, distinct from the heteronormative plots that are passionately woven and tragically interrupted in Allied-occupied Naples. This group represents an "occult freemasonry" of "varied personalities" held together by a "subtle thread."[39] Despite their conflicts and clashes of nationality, race, class, and gender, they meld back into a single entity sharing a palpable energy. The diversity of the eclectic patrons is constantly emphasized and, as we are given brief glimpses into their lives and desires, the bar comes to form a Galleria within the Galleria Umberto I within *The Gallery*, a trans-space where local and global coexist. Nestled in the heart of the Galleria, "Momma's" is a microcosm of the space of the encounter; its celebration of gender fluidity provides a map to *The Gallery* and suggests how it uses the transnational, porous space of Naples to stage the narrator's redemption.

Using "Momma's" representation of wartime homosexuality as a point of departure, I understand the queering of the novel beyond the thematic, drawing on Bond's transnational as it intersects with critical theory on Naples. Thanks to its "peripheral status within Europe," Italy has long been characterized as premodern;[40] as a "multifaceted city attached to the edge of southern Europe,"[41] the position of Naples as internal other facilitates a disparaging conflation in which it is read as an "exaggerated version of Italy, that is, possessing all its defects in accentuated fashion."[42] The transnational, then, may reverse the logic of the Southern question and, instead, turn the city into a privileged site, as it "could conceivably contribute to its construction as a hyphenated 'trans-' or in-between space, as well as its ability to 'queer' fixed notions of a national time and space."[43] In understanding the transnational in terms of queer theory (where the hyphenated "trans-" prefix may also join with gender as well as national), Bond is not operating purely within the metaphorical but instead argues that "the body, as privileged site of lived subjectivity, yet also as a means of experiencing the local and the global simultaneously, becomes an important hinge of meaning within a mapping of the transnational."[44] When John and his Italian lover experience the ultimate encounter—simultaneous orgasm—their interpenetrated bodies are freed of the limitations of nationality and gender.

However, lest we end with a blind celebration of global humanism as enabled by the porosity of Naples (as the "Exit" encourages), Glynn offers a cogent corrective in an essay entitled, "Porosity and Its Discontents" where she investigates the privileged position given to Benjamin and Lacis's formulation by contemporary critical theorists who allow it to pass "uninterrogated into the field of critical analysis of cultural representations of Naples, where it has silently influenced and coloured interpretations of Neapolitan culture and cultural production without itself becoming subject to appropriate critical enquiry."[45] Demonstrating the ideological underpinnings of porosity extracted from their essay through "highly selective and strategic" readings, Glynn argues it instead be read "in relation to the long history of travel literature dedicated to journeys in Italy and the tendency therein to construct not only Naples but Italy more generally as 'a place that resists modernity.'"[46] Thus, if the porosity of Naples has come to represent a "positive model of postmodern Europeanness," it must also be understood in terms of a "contact zone," in Mary Louise Pratt's terms, "the space in which peoples geographically and historically separated come into contact with each other and establish ongoing relations, usually involving conditions of coercion, radical inequality, and intractable conflict."[47] Even as the ontological boundaries of redeemer/redeemed become porous in *The Gallery*'s Allied-occupied Naples to positive effect, the status of Naples as a contact zone underscores the asymmetrical power dynamics always at work. In light of Glynn's vital rereading, this chapter pushes back on the notion that *The Gallery*'s representation of Naples challenges the interrelated militaristic and touristic paradigms of redemption I explore in the military guidebooks in Chapter 1 and in Hayes's writing in Chapter 2. As its global humanism transcends the conventional gendering of United States and Italy, redeemer and redeemed, and shifts focus away from individual identities and local specificities, *The Gallery* nonetheless affords a crucial role to conventional gender dynamics, as Naples becomes a womb in which the burgeoning soldier-writer gestates and Italian, the maternal language at whose breast he suckles. Indeed, as I argue vis-à-vis Rossellini's *Paisà* in Chapter 2, *The Gallery*'s final redemption has a significant cost in terms of what is sacrificed in the name of global humanism.

In order to make the novel coincide with a redemptive journey from his departure from the United States (his death as a soldier-tourist) to his arrival in Naples (his rebirth as an authentic writer), one must smooth out its transgressive structure; to use Peter Brooks's Russian formalist terms, the novel must be read in terms of its *fabula* ("what really happened") rather than its *sjužet* (the plot of the narrative work).[48] Instead, following its transnational zigzagging—from Naples to Casablanca to Naples to Fedhala to Naples to Casablanca to Naples to Algiers to Naples—the reader has the uncanny perception of Naples and the Galleria as something at once new and familiar, "a vibrant curiosity," for Grand Tourists and their descendants, "unknown but within reach."[49] In this way, my reading takes advantage of *The Gallery*'s perceived weakness: the apparently lacking "fundamental relationship between the pieces in the two series."[50] Transposing Millicent Marcus's reading of the episodic *Paisà*, I show how *The Gallery*'s intratextual connections between promenades and portraits offer the possibility to queer the redemptive encounter.[51]

A Queer Journey to Naples: From Local to Global

With little detail about John's activities in North Africa or Italy—he appears to be an officer-*flâneur*—we might gauge his transformation in terms of his developing understanding of love. In fact, three promenades close with references to his own sexual encounters: The first promenade ("Casablanca") ends with the offhand mention of economic sexual exchanges with ambiguously gendered Moroccan women, "almost like pretty boys";[52] the fifth promenade ("Algiers") ends with an elliptical account of an evening spent in the bedroom of a Frenchman; and the final promenade ("Naples") concludes with a transcendent sexual encounter with a genderless Italian—the only person to name him "John"—who gives him the call to write. As we read each of these promenades with an adjacent portrait, the pairings elucidate the queer paradigm of redemptive love in porous Naples.

The first portrait, "Michael Patrick," provides a stark contrast for the "Casablanca" promenade that follows. For Michael Patrick, "Naples . . . spelled a certain freedom and relief to him, in opposition to that other idea of being flown up to south of Florence."[53] This freedom is synonymous with finding female company, but he makes an inept conqueror. After watching *La Bohème* alone through drunken tears, he finally experiences attraction at its simplest: a girl with a birthmark and red flower in her hair beckons to him across "some unbridgeable distance," as the chapter ends in a loving communion: "'Oh I think I love you' he said. Their tears mingled; he felt she was nodding her head."[54] From this happy ending, we move to the first promenade, "Casablanca," where the narrator is setting off to sea, a beginning that is also the end, as the narrator recalls his death as a jingoistic, egotistical American.

Face-to-face with a foreign culture in Casablanca, the narrator claims he held disdain for all other nationalities: "It didn't occur to me that they were members of the human race. Only Americans were."[55] When this stance collides with a heightened fear of death, his egotism sharpens as the narrator mocks his former self: "So I began to think of my Life with the tenderness of a great artist. I clasped myself fondly to myself. I retreated into my own private world with the scream of a spinster when she sees a mouse."[56] When he goes searching for company, neither love nor pleasure is at issue, but rather some unmet existential need: "My loneliness was that of a drunken old man sitting in a grotto and looking out on an icy sea at world's end. Then, sinking away under a weight of time, I'd be constrained to draw down the head of her on the bench beside me. I'd kiss her in an attempt to focus all my longing and my uneasiness."[57] "Casablanca" closes with an offhand reference to the bevy of local girls whose choral lines of dialogue in French, "you must moan when we make love and next time, please bring some chewing gum," reveal the economic underpinnings of the transaction.[58] While this first portrait—promenade pairing sets John at a temporal and emotional distance from the Naples of August 1944 of Michael Patrick and his wordless communion, by the time we reach the final portrait, Moe and the soon-to-be-narrator, instead, dovetail.

As lyrical and meandering as they are, the promenades move toward the Naples of August 1944 with a teleological determination, so that John can join the characters of the portraits. He, too, is in search of love, a quest rooted in his understanding of himself as an American and as an artist. These identities are at cross-purposes insofar as his egotistical jingoism results in "sterile" art. Essential to his transformation, North Africa gives John needed perspective about his American identity and serves as a counterpoint to Italy. The first five promenades, set in North Africa, all deal with the character's struggle to transform in the face of his alienation. Recurrent imagery reinforces the association of North Africa with this "death" and the first stages of his rebirth: In "Casablanca," the narrator "dies" amidst otherworldly metaphors, such as the "Caucasians" as "corpse intruders."[59] In "Fedhala," the narrator mentally x-rays the local American cemetery as he starts his personal autopsy by reflecting on the traces of American, French, and Spanish imperialism;[60] in "Casablanca-Algiers," where the narrator has his first encounter with Italian POWs and feels the stirrings of rebirth, the main setting is a hospital; in the two "Algiers," portraits, he takes his first tentative steps and learns how to walk as he prepares to arrive in Italy.

This transformation can be gauged in terms of his views of the foreign culture, starting from his bald colonialist attitude: "In North Africa I thought I could keep a wall between me and the people. But the monkeys in the cage reach out and grab the spectator who offers them a banana."[61] At the end of his time in North Africa, as he stares at the Mediterranean and "beg[ins] to ponder on variety and difference," he sheds his former self, yet cannot come into his own.[62] Reflecting on the differences between himself and the impoverished locals, John heads toward an existential crisis: "I found myself walking in a world in which I was an alien. I'd just come out of the womb, but there was no mother to take me by the hand."[63] Here, the narrative's divergent temporalities collide as John laments his absent mother, just after the reader has met a symbolic Italian mother in the previous portrait, "Momma." As yet unaware of the "Momma" who awaits him in Naples, John wanders the streets of Algiers and finds a "Frenchman of Algiers, not a man, not a boy."[64] A parental figure—John holds on to him, "like a little child"—this poet takes John to his bedroom, serves him wine, and recites his verses until the chapter trails off into ellipses.[65] Following "Momma," the sexual implication of the conclusion of "Algiers" becomes clear, as well as its role as a marker in John's journey. A more intimate encounter than the first promenade with the boyish women, it is nonetheless inconclusive: the Algerian father-figure does not prove enough, as John laments his absent mother. In Algiers he listens to another man's verses; in the final promenade, after the sexual encounter is narrated to its climax, he is called upon to create his own through the maternal Italian language. In contrast with the sterile experience of Africa, motherly Naples and Edenic Italian allow John to embrace the shared humanity of all those who have suffered in war.

As his boat approaches the harbor of Naples, the narrator recalls, "I peered with more interest than I had at Africa, for I had precise and confused ideas of what Italy'd be like."[66] Setting himself apart from the banalities of his fellow soldier tourists, he parrots the GIs' vision of Naples as they translate its icons into lowbrow terms:

> "That's Naples," said the voice that accompanies all travelers. "I'd know it from the postcards and the pitchers in the barbershops. Look, that's Vesuvius.... Yessir, the old anthill's smoking. Ain't got over the shock of Anzio yet.... And see that big thing that looks like a country club at the top of the city? That's Castel Sant'Elmo.... I been reading my guidebooks."[67]

The soldiers who travel from North Africa to Naples find little difference. For them, Africa and Europe are both sexualized lands of conquest, in their constant chorus of racist, misogynist clichés: "What I mean to say is, I'm going to start chasing some of this French stuff tonight"; "If a signorina comes to the door of my mess hall ... an says she's hungry, why I give her a meal.... But first I make it clear to her Eyetie mind that I'm interested in something she's got.... If she says ixnay I tell her to get the hell out."[68] Stripped of all pretense, the soldiers' notion of redemption is baldly sexualized, its power dynamics overtly asymmetrical. Here, then, Burns's narrator works to distinguish himself from his soldier-tourist companions who cling to the boundaries between male and female, American and foreign, redeemer and redeemed. If their heteronormative understanding of redemption depends upon such dynamics, it is undermined by the fluidity of gender in this porous trans-space.[69] However, John does not experience the disillusionment of Rossellini's or Hayes's American protagonists when they find their familiar points of reference destabilized, but instead experiences his queer redemption by embracing it.

As the narrator distinguishes himself from the chorus of soldier-tourists, *The Gallery* works within the rhetoric of (anti)tourism that is a staple of travel writing discourse.[70] His vision of Naples, too, is full of familiar tropes, in particular, the feminization of the space. As porous as Naples may be, *she* is as yet "a short girl with dark eyes and rich skin and body hair. Motherhood. Huge and inscrutable as the feminine Idea." From the idealized, maternal destination Italy, we tumble into the whorish Naples of the occupation, "legs open like a drunken trollop, tender in her ruin."[71] With Naples a feminized placeholder, "Edenic" Italian transforms him from sterile artist to productive writer: "Italian is an atavistic language. All the rest have been visited by some torture or trickery or introspection. *Italian alone is the language of the moment,* cunning yet unpremeditated. I learned Italian in order to make love. And I found Italian feminine and secret and grave and puzzled and laughing like a woman. Perhaps it came from the tit of Signora Eve in the Garden."[72] Returning John to a prelapsarian state, the dehistoricized Italian language allows him to express the evanescence of love in Allied-occupied Naples and, ultimately, in life.

As the "language of the moment," Italian is ideal for recounting the temporally circumscribed encounters happening in Momma's bar. Open for three hours per day and under threat of permanent closure, Momma's can offer love only within the narrowest of temporal parameters. In Allied-occupied Naples no one can craft a future, but in Momma's no one tries. One of the patrons, a British sergeant who goes by Magda, surveys the crowd and comments to another sergeant, who goes by Esther, "Since the desire to live, in its truest sense of reproducing, isn't in them, they live for the moment more passionately than most. That makes them brazen and shortsighted."[73] As Jonathan Vincent remarks, "Embracing rather than eschewing conditions of permeation and contingency, Burns's utopian netherworld serves as a sort of libidinal counternarrative to the frostbitten, socially cauterized normatives championed by the postwar suburban ideal: entrepreneurship, personal enrichment, and Protestant anti-Communism."[74] Demonstrating how the porosity of ontological boundaries in occupied Naples disrupts the bourgeois narratives of marriage and reproduction that are the underpinnings of nationalism and, by extension, war, "Momma" articulates a "queer time," outside "those paradigmatic markers of life experience—namely, birth, marriage, reproduction, and death." In parallel, it depicts Italian as a queer language of the moment that "leaves the temporal frames of bourgeois reproduction and family, longevity, risk/safety, and inheritance."[75]

The encounters in the promenades, "Michael Patrick," "Moe," and "Giulia" suggest that this temporality is not about homosexuality but about love in the trans-space of war that undermines heteronormative, reproductive plots that depend upon and reinforce the egotistic, materialistic logic of American capitalism. This ethos is articulated by Moe, who replays a story similar to Michael Patrick's. On his last night in Naples, Moe meets Maria, and they have a makeshift marriage where Moe bestows on her the cameo his mother wanted him to give to his future wife. Maria is embarrassed that she is no Virgin, but heirlooms and virginity are immaterial in a notion of love that lasts an evening. The day after, Moe travels to Tuscany, where he meets the death that Michael Patrick feared. However, his night with Maria has given him the necessary wisdom to accept it.[76]

In contrast to the first and ninth portraits about evanescent wartime love, the seventh is about love that demands to go beyond. Like Michael Patrick and Moe, Giulia and an American officer find love at first sight but have plans of marriage that the narrator mocks. The elaborate courtship ritual that leads to their engagement proceeds like "a clockwork juggernaut," presenting the American fiancé with "a scene as stylized as a Chinese play."[77] This "third and grim act" stars "the paternal grandmother [who] talked for twenty minutes, with gestures, on vice among young women," yet it comes to a preordained happy conclusion: "the air twittered with Italian delight. The world was good after all. And the paternal grandmother, in reaching greedily for her ninth éclair, fell into the hammered silver tray and got chocolate icing all over her lavender lace."[78] The ridiculousness of the grandmother's faceplant is subtended by a less humorous reality, making a grotesque juxtaposition of the family's gluttony and the dire circumstances of Naples. Giulia's captain plays along until he decides to go to the front and, on their last night together, he pleads to her, "I've got to make love to you, Giulia, and tonight.... Suppose... up there... they got me... and I died without ever having had you."[79] While he calls her foolish for holding onto "codes of respectability," she clings to her tradition saying, "I'm anything but a fool . . . I know all the arguments and all the answers. All women do. . . . We have to hold you off till we get a ring on our fingers. . . . My mother and her mother before her played that game. . . . And I shall do so too."[80] Here, then, in the contrast between "Moe" and "Giulia" we see the incompatibility of the bourgeois, reproductive conception of love oriented toward the future of the family across generations, and the notion of love in postliberation Naples that, hemmed in by war, cannot take tomorrow for granted. Indeed, virginity is immaterial if there's no tomorrow; for Giulia, who "knew he would be coming back to her," that concept holds her tightly in its sway.[81] Whether or not Giulia's intuition is right—and the tragic endings of the two successive portraits suggest that she may not be—the narrator's redemption depends upon rejecting her notion of time and instead, realizing that one is *potentially expendable*, and living and loving despite *and because* of this.

Along with its mockery of Giulia's intransigence (and its stinging portrait of the insufferable WAC, Louella), *The Gallery* is minimally interested in the women it portrays, whom the narrator describes as "(standing) for all the women and girls of the world."[82] Instead it favors the abstract womb of Naples and the maternal Italian language that facilitate John's rebirth in the final promenade where he remembers "love in Naples."[83] A fleeting paradise where "for one instant we were in a place where there was no difference between us," this love is an encounter that transcends gender:

> I remember lying there, lost and wondering. I put my hand out to encounter another hand, already reaching for mine. My mouth went out exploring, only to meet another mouth working toward mine in the darkness. . . . I think we were both a little sad when we kissed. In those kisses we tried to heal each other's souls.
>
> And I remember the sweet slowness of undressing one another, the longing and the languor. The clothes dropping whispering to the floor, the shadowy bodies gradually revealed.[84]

As John communes with his lover and with "all those who've ever loved and lived at all," their bodies interpenetrate and the narrative signals what it obscures from our view: the lovers reveal their shadowy bodies to one another, but the narrator's language keeps them from us. Without a gendered pronoun, his lover may be male (suggested by "Momma" and "Algiers," as well as Burns's biography) or female (supported by "Casablanca" and heteronormative convention). However, in that moment, the text makes both lovers genderless, suggesting that we reexamine all *The Gallery*'s homo- or heterosexual love stories and reimagine them as love stories, plain and simple.

Climaxing with a sexual encounter that converts the fallen narrator into a Dante, *The Gallery* paints Naples as an Edenic space outside history. However, no sooner is Italian erased through their amorous transcendence of difference, then it returns as John's lover issues the call to write in Italian; indeed, if the trans-space of Naples allows the narrator to queer the gendered paradigm that underwrites the soldiers' misogynist, racist, nationalism, it is the Italian he suckled from the breast of Momma Naples, understood as the "language of the moment," that inspires him to narrate his experience of redemptive rebirth: "Dear John, I advise you to tell everyone what you saw in Italy.... Because you know, the Italians don't hate you, they don't hate you, you Americans..."[85] John's story is no longer about men and women, America and Italy; the Galleria is no longer the heart of Naples but his mother's womb: "I must have spent at least nine months of my life there, watching and wandering. For I got lost in the war in Naples in August, 1944. Often from what I saw I lost the power of speech. It seemed to me that everything happening there could be happening to me. A kind of madness, I suppose."[86] As his mother's womb becomes a womb of humankind, the Galleria extends to Naples and to the Mediterranean as "a center of human life and thought." The inhabitants of Naples become "dots in a circle that never stops," closing the "Exit" with an affirmation of an infinite universality. However, even as the specificity of John's experience is erased, the presence of Italian is felt throughout this divine moment, an echo of Dante's final image in *Paradiso* of a "wheel moved evenly" ("*ruota che igualmente è mossa*").[87]

Creating this Dantean redemption, *The Gallery* embodies Italian transnationalism identified by Bond, insofar as it brings Italian literature's foundational text into the 20th-century American war novel.[88] Creating this *queer* Dantean redemption, it offers a direct challenge to early postwar Italian representations, most famously Rossellini's *Roma città aperta*, that make homosexuality synonymous with Nazi and fascist degeneracy.[89] However, even as *The Gallery*'s transnational narrative space works to challenge heteronormative conventions, its embrace of global humanism performs a dangerous erasure, a risk Bond locates in exclusively privileging the global nature of the transnational, thereby "potentially erasing local identity-based specificities."[90] When *The Gallery* tells us that military operations are not relevant and that Italy, instead, is the land of love, we hear resonances of Hayes's 1949 essay "Italy—Enchantress of Writers," in which he negates Italian colonialism in favor of tourism and romance.[91] Indeed, if the North African promenades point fingers at the inequities of French imperialism and the rest of the book rails against American aggressions abroad and at home, we might locate the redemptive powers of Naples in its historic association with the conquered. Here, then, in its readiness to make Naples and the Neapolitans a metonym for Italy and Italians, *The Gallery*, too, propagates a version of history that forgets Italian colonialism.

The Gallery provides a floor plan that encourages us to subsume its individual characters into a Dantean circle, inviting readers to walk through to the conclusion that "these people who became living portraits in this Gallery were synechdoches for most of the people anywhere in the world."[92] But on the way, it hurls readers across the Atlantic and the Mediterranean, within and between the chapters. No sooner do we reach Naples in the sixth promenade, then we travel back to the United States and the country's own unresolved North-South struggles that haunt Major Motes, the "Virginia gentleman," as he tries to negotiate his position within an occupying army that once occupied the land of his birth.[93] Or, in the pages right before the "Exit," we take a quick trip to Italian-occupied Africa, when Moe meets an Italian who spells out the myth of *italiani brava gente*, proclaiming, "I too have a good heart, even though I strafed the Ethiopian contadini. Under orders of the Duce, of course . . . I had also an amante, a Libyan black girl. I had two children by her. It broke my heart to leave my cugina di guerra and my bambini . . ."[94] In this sense, *The Gallery* does more than reverse the wartime redemption narrative and revert to the Grand Tour fantasy of a redemptive Italy. Enabling readers to move transnationally within and between the spaces of *The Gallery*, it locates multiple contact zones where unhealed traumas such as the Civil War and ongoing colonial conflicts intermingle with and destabilize the Allied-Italian encounter. Thus, as a counterpoint to the narrator's circular death-birth, I conclude with another possible trajectory that reads the Galleria as a transnational text-within-the-text, as it "allows for a reintroduction not only of other geographical locations, but also of different times, bringing the past back into the present."[95] Following characters in and out of the Galleria—Hal (a doppelganger for John), Giulia (the only Neapolitan character), and Moe (a Jewish soldier)—I use each iteration to contribute to an intratextual narrative path that suggests what is erased as part of his embrace of global humanism and what is to be gained in reading *The Gallery* beyond the narrator's redemption.

Reading *The Gallery* Transnationally through the Galleria

An officer plagued by a Jesus complex that plunges him into madness, Hal experiences the Galleria in near-identical terms as the narrator with whom he shares a travel itinerary. In fact, we might read his descent into madness as the narrator's journey (which also skirts madness) *in malo*. Hal's thoughts that, "There was no glass in the domed skylight" and "It was like all outdoors going on inside"—recall the "Entrance," anticipate the narrator's memory of his arrival in Naples one hundred-odd pages later, and foreshadow the "Exit."[96] Indeed, his visit to the Galleria reconfigures the novel's framing motifs: "These people, he said to himself, are all in search of love. The love of God, of death, or of another human being. They're all lost. That's why they walk so aimlessly. They all feel here that the world isn't big enough to hold them. And look at this place. Like a huge cross laid on the ground, after the corpus is taken off the nails."[97] As Hal underscores the spiritual dimension of the search for love in the Galleria, he foreshadows the eventual embrace of global humanism, yet Ian Wiblin notes within "this 'huge cross' . . . echoes of Walter Benjamin's polarities, pointing North, South, East and West." So, too, in the reference to the "corpus," does Wiblin find a connection to Naples, insofar as it "also suggests images of anatomical dissection, a science for which, as film theorist and historian Giuliana Bruno points out, Naples was famous if not notorious." An "accurate mapping of space," representing "a world in miniature," the passage speaks to the poetics of the text where the global can affirm the local: the cross pointing to a Christian universality and also to the built environment and history of Naples.[98]

As the only Neapolitan protagonist, Giulia is unique in having memories of the Galleria that predate the occupation. When, in the seventh portrait, Giulia observes, "On the pavement still lay the splinters of glass that had been bombed out of the skylight," she evokes the references to the shattered skylight throughout the text, as well as the memory of her childhood when it was still intact.[99] Giulia's experience of the Galleria during the occupation represents a traumatic loss, the place where she witnesses Italy's fall in gendered, sexualized terms: "In the exact center of the Galleria Giulia saw a sight that was new. It scored her with the fascination of a pimple on the back of one's neck. She saw many girls alone and in pairs, girls she'd never noticed on the streets of Naples before."[100] In a passage that could well have inspired Curzio Malaparte's *La pelle*, she watches these women and reflects in Italian, "We are defeated . . . in this war, not only soldiers have died . . . but the soul, women, the honor of each one of us."[101] The loss she perceives in the center of the Galleria becomes a talisman in her life, as she decides to keep herself apart from the "fallen" collective: her final act in the portrait is to refuse to cede her virginity, even in the face of the asymmetrical power dynamics that govern the relationship. Unlike Lisa of Hayes's *The Girl on The Via Flaminia*, Giulia resists playing her assigned part of the whore.

In the final portrait, Moe, an American Jewish soldier, has his own transformative experience in the center of the Galleria that allows him to recall his past and anticipate his death, by understanding himself as part of the collective that Giulia eschews:

> He walked till he was in the very center of the Galleria, under the dome. Slowly he spun round in his boots as though he were the needle of a compass orienting itself on the grid lines of a map. Thus he was the very center of that afternoon crowd in the Galleria. He was the nub of hundreds of persons, American, British, French, Polish, Moroccan, and Neapolitan. He smiled and said to himself that this was the first and last time he'd be the center of the world.[102]

Together, the iterations of the Galleria make the novel's time at once static and fluid, returning faithfully to August 1944 as they travel into the past and future. Individually, the passages serve as a key to each "Portrait," where they demonstrate the extent to which each character jibes with the ethos of the book: While the narrative mocks Giulia's stubborn refusal to abandon her prewar morality, it celebrates Moe's willingness to commune with the Galleria's global inhabitants.

Although they build to the narrator's redemption, when read in terms of their specific subjectivities, these individual portraits problematize the final embrace of global humanism. In the case of Giulia, we have a Neapolitan virgin, a figure so rare it becomes the subject of grotesque satire in *La pelle*, as I discuss in Chapter 5. In the case of Moe, we have a Jewish American soldier, shot by a German Luger pistol in the novel's only combat scene—a romanticized version of war. When Moe falls to the ground beneath German fire in the house of an Italian woman who calls him "*figlio mio*," his final moment is peaceful: "For a moment an agony plucked at his brain. He sensed a longing and a regret such as he could never have imagined. But then he saw his mother and Maria Rocco, and he knew he'd come a long long way. It wasn't really so long. But it was farther than most. So Moe smiled back at the German, and he felt his face dropping toward the floor."[103] In this most final of intercultural encounters—not incidentally between an American Jew and a German soldier—Moe dies amid a trinity of women: his mother, his "wife," and his adoptive Italian mother. This vision furthers his overdetermined christological status *and* recalls the symbolic role afforded women in the narrator's rebirth in the preceding promenade. Furthermore, if Moe is to be a symbol of a redemptive death that sacrifices individual identity for collective humanity, we must also recognize that it is achieved through a Jew dying like Christ at the hands of a German. Leaving no time to contemplate this death or reflect on its connection to the unfolding genocide, *The Gallery* reaches the "Exit," where it tells us that the portraits are all merely symbols, and it does so with a Dantean—and distinctly Christian—valence. In this case, the erasure of local specificities within the global amounts to a Jew subsumed within Christianity, a conversion that cannot be celebrated in light of the Holocaust.

My reading of *The Gallery* through the transnational space of the Galleria seeks to offer an alternative to the novel's final embrace of global humanism. However, Burns himself provided another alternative in a 1949 series of articles for the renowned American travel magazine, *Holiday*, in which he revisits North Africa and Italy. The allegorical dimension gone, each of the spaces he visits are concrete tourist destinations, with advice about food and lodging, together with general reflections on each city's culture, architecture, and politics (Figure 11). As he travels from Algiers to Casablanca to Tunis to Naples to Rome, Burns's Orientalizing tourist gaze is on view: He praises Algiers for its European feel and the segregation of the Arabs, celebrates Tunis's "tempo of the Middle Age," jokes about harems in Casablanca, romanticizes the turbulent ... violen[ce]" of Naples, and notes that Rome's trains are as "speedy as ever" but "no longer run on time, the chief boast of Mussolini's apologists."[104] Directly addressing the soldier returned as a tourist (himself included), the articles reflect on how soldiers and cities have changed in the intervening years: better food and accommodation, cleaner streets, more room on the sidewalks. He acutely registers this change in Naples, where "the beautiful harbor, once choked with half-submerged ships from the bombings, is now as fair and free of access as Marco Polo could desire," the bombed post office is now "napkin clean," and Via Roma "is almost orderly now."[105] The narrator does not hide his sadness, particularly when he finds the "only one true war souvenir in Naples—that arcade at the end of Via Roma known as the Galleria Umberto Primo," transformed beyond recognition: "And since this isn't the Naples you knew, you feel a little hurt, like a man attempting to relive his childhood."[106] After lamenting these signs of reconstruction, Burns starts to recognize Naples in the signs of violence reminiscent of fascism, as well as in the vendors of counterfeit items, the fortunetellers, the advertisements for quick cures for VD, and nuns leading orphan beggars.[107] Here, in stark contrast with Hayes's contemporary account of Italy in the *New York Times*,

THE GALLERIA, that arcade at the end of the Via Roma, is Naples' only true war souvenir.

NAPLES

The city below Vesuvius has become cleaner and less crowded in the last five years, but it continues to be a Fascist breeding ground

by JOHN HORNE BURNS

THERE'S ALWAYS a wispy smoke cloud over Vesuvius, as though to remind you of a dormant power nothing less than atomic; the gray mountain seems to say: "I did it in 79 A.D. and in March, 1944, and I can do it again." Perhaps the old volcano has a permanent pique against Naples, which is fast recovering from the madness you remember there five years ago. Only Vesuvius and the Bay are precisely as they were. When you get off the train in Garibaldi Square, your first impression is: "Why, this isn't the Naples that I and thousands of other Americans knew. It's cleaner; the streets seem more spacious." They are. For the simple reason of subtraction—when the Army left, there were fewer people in Naples. Today there's even room on the sidewalks. Only at five o'clock of a brilliant afternoon, with office workers hanging out of the trolleys on Corso Umberto, does Naples seem the bursting circus you once knew. Now she has even a certain flamboyant dignity.

Since you've read that Europeans have been slow about cleaning up their war rubble, you're surprised to find how many scars have been erased from Naples. True, there remain halves of buildings and empty spaces where apartments once were, but the plaster, the slag and

PHOTOGRAPHS BY ROGER COSTER

the debris have all been carted away. A great deal of reconstruction, or at least mopping up, has taken place here. The beautiful harbor, once choked with half-submerged ships from the bombings, is now as fair and free of access as Marco Polo could desire. The wharves have largely been rebuilt, and great ships ride in the roads, awaiting docking space. Where once there were LST's, Swedish, American and Canadian vessels glide importantly out of the Tyrrhenian Sea to rest. You're condescendingly pleased that the Neapolitans have done quite a piece of work in your absence. In the spring of 1949 the hoyden, sluttish city is probably as immaculate as she's (*Continued on Page 67*)

Figure 11. "Naples," by John Horne Burns, photographs by Roger Coster, *Holiday*, May 1949.

Burns's revised vision of the redemption of Naples is purely superficial; the restored glass skylight of the Galleria Umberto I that signifies economic progress is but a distraction from the essential continuity to Allied-occupied Naples. The only respite from the "squalor of Naples five years later" proves a jaunt to idyllic Capri, with which the Naples article closes.[108]

Then, extending his trip beyond Naples to end in Rome (no doubt to round out the series to five), Burns introduces the soldier-tourist to Trastevere, "a spot shunned by tourists," and to a typical struggling Trastevere family, "named Grimaldi—not for anonymity, but because there are thousands of Romans in this postwar pattern."[109] In this very brief portrait of sorts, Burns resurrects every conventional stereotype: the dominant mamma and nostalgic papa; the repressed musician daughter who makes the sign of the cross before going for a swim; and the vaguely criminal son who makes love with random Italian girls in the private changing cabins at the beach because it costs less than a brothel. When read in sequence with *The Gallery*, the *Holiday* articles substitute the novel's queer redemption with a heteronormative ending. No doubt conditioned by the magazine format, the articles of this revised *Gallery* construct a linear journey with no room for the transnational dimension of the novel, nor, indeed, the character's redemptive arc, that together unite the spaces as more than vignettes.[110] Thus, the articles further emphasize the power of *The Gallery*'s structure: offering open-ended paths through its porous, transnational space, it allows readers to follow John's queer redemptive journey and its embrace of global humanism but also to consider the local specificities that constitute the Galleria.

In the next chapter, I turn to the emblematic Italian narrative of Allied-occupied Naples, and the long-reviled counterpart to the beloved *Gallery*, Curzio Malaparte's *La pelle*, another autofictional novel whose first-person narrator is emphatic in directing the reader between the interpretive possibilities it proffers. As he affirms and undermines the veracity of the grotesque spectacles he recounts, the narrator suggests that they be read not as a reflection of the realities of occupation, but as a metaphor for the horrors of war. However, by asking why certain marginalized bodies are used to represent the encounter only to be transcended, I show how these novels insert the Allies and Italians alike into a transnational network where the gendering and racialization of redemption points to the traumatic legacy of slavery, colonialism, the Holocaust, and, as *La pelle* will add, mass rape.

5   Sleights of Hand, Black Skin, and the Redemption of Curzio Malaparte's *La pelle*

When Curzio Malaparte's literary counterpart reaches Naples on August 7, 1943, after a harrowing journey across Eastern Europe, he finds "a huge pile of debris and bloody rags."[1] Throughout *Kaputt* (1944), Malaparte serves as the first-person narrator, a contrast from the novel's final pages where an impersonal observer guides the reader into Naples.[2] Initially obscured by a black cloud of flies and the sun beating down on asphalt, Naples reveals itself through sound: "At first, the city looked deserted. Then, little by little, one distinguished a hum coming from the lanes and courtyards, a stifled chatter of voices, a faint and distant noise."[3] After this aural awakening, Naples divulges its secrets to the visitor's gaze; a lengthy description begins as such, "Then penetrating into the secret of the *bassi* with one's gaze, probing with one's eye the depths of the narrow clefts between the towering houses, one saw" swarming inhabitants attempt to meet their basic bodily needs.[4] An observer might blame these conditions on the war—the Allies' heavy bombings of the target-rich port city—but Malaparte soon dispels this belief. Repeating his initial description, he revises that impersonal vision and makes the ear and the gaze his own: "Not deserted, at first the city seemed silent. *I* saw people gesturing, moving their lips, and *I* did not hear a sound: But slowly, a confused rumble was born, in the dusty air, or so it seemed to *me*, acquiring shape and consistency in *my* ear."[5]

More than a grammatical revision, a larger narrative agenda emerges out of these first-person verbs, pronouns, and possessives that emphasize Malaparte's gaze, Malaparte's ears. Whereas the generic observer stops at the outward signs of devastation, Malaparte goes on to reveal the "real, the living Naples that had survived three years of bombardments, hunger and plague," a "Plutonic country" that continues its millennial existence deep within subterranean galleries, where the crash of bombs seems faint.[6] With this revelation, the conclusion of *Kaputt* lays the groundwork for its sequel, *La pelle* (1949; *The Skin*), arguably the most infamous of the Italian representations of Allied-occupied Naples.[7] First, *Kaputt* segues into

La pelle geographically but with a temporal gap that underscores the disjunction between pre- and post-armistice: In *Kaputt*, despite three years of the "plague" of war, Neapolitan life is unchanged; in *La pelle*, after less than six months of the "plague" of American occupation, the entire city has been infected. Second, as *Kaputt*'s narrator supplants the generic vision with his expert knowledge, he asserts his authority to guide readers through the infernal carnival of *La pelle*, in parallel with his job of liaison officer who acts as a cultural translator or a "Virgilian" guide to the disoriented American officers, Colonel Jack Hamilton and Captain Jimmy Wren.[8]

The Allied military's *Soldier's Guide to Naples* (1944) warns, "the Naples of prewar days is gone. It will be impossible for you to visit that Naples."[9] According to *Kaputt*, if we follow Malaparte into *La pelle*, the true Naples will be revealed. *La pelle*, for its part, ups the ante, as its characters claim that *Kaputt* (and by extension *La pelle*) is not interested in historical but artistic truth: when, in *La pelle*, Captain Malaparte meets a pair of incredulous readers of *Kaputt* (the French officers, General Augustine Guillaume and Lieutenant Pierre Lyautey), Colonel Hamilton retorts, "It does not matter at all if what Malaparte recounts is true or false. The question to pose is another: is what he does art or not?"[10] As we will see, this question functions as a sleight of hand that directs readers toward the novel's allegorical significance and away from its historical engagement. While recent critics have complied with this directive in their efforts to redeem the infamous author and polemical text, this chapter argues that it is precisely in its insistence on both literal and allegorical modes that *La pelle* makes its unparalleled contribution to the cultural corpus of Allied-occupied Italy.

La pelle's author, "one of the most controversial figures in modern Italian literature," was born Kurt Erich Suckert in Prato in 1897 to a German father and Italian mother.[11] A journalist and World War I veteran, he achieved literary notoriety by 1921, and joined the National Fascist Party in 1922.[12] In 1925, he adopted the pseudonym Curzio Malaparte—a reversal of "Bonaparte" that conveyed his attraction to the "bad part"—and soon earned the superlative "fascism's strongest pen," from noted antifascist Piero Gobetti. (At the time, it was not meant damningly.)[13] In the 1930s, Malaparte moved to France where he published an anti-Hitlerian text that got him expelled from the party and sentenced to five years exile on Lipari, of which he served less than two, due to his friendship with Galeazzo Ciano, Mussolini's son-in-law and foreign minister. During the war, he was a correspondent in Eastern Europe and, in 1944, he became a liaison officer to the Allies, experiences which form the basis of *Kaputt* and *La pelle* respectively. On his deathbed in 1957, he was granted membership in the Italian Communist Party and—

some believe—converted to Catholicism.[14] While his near-mythical career resists neat summary, American director Walter Murch does an apt job: "The contradictions and collisions of his life seem like a sped-up film of the first half of the twentieth century: German-Italian, Protestant-Catholic, soldier-pacifist, Fascist-Communist, journalist-novelist, editor-architect, film director-composer, diplomat-prisoner."[15]

With this resume, it is no surprise *La pelle*'s request that readers leave "truth" aside did not stave off Malaparte's fervent detractors.[16] In fact, for decades, all but his staunchest supporters disparaged *La pelle* as the work of an unscrupulous "chameleon" who deformed the reality of the occupation to erase his fascist past; even as the fiftieth anniversary of the war deflated Italy's wartime myths, *La pelle* remained in relative cultural exile.[17] Ultimately, critics outside of Italy appear to have altered the fortunes of the novel, reading its representations of the horrors of war as transcending history—a position that gained traction in 2009 when Milan Kundera crowned *La pelle* one of the greatest literary achievements of the 20th century.[18] In contrast with early readings that harped on how the novel deviated from historical truth and manipulated Malaparte's biography, scholars now recognize it as a form of autofiction,[19] as Ruth Glynn aptly puts it, an "unforgiving exposé of the ignoble struggle ... embellished by the inclusion of ambiguously fictionalized episodes."[20] Rather than cull *La pelle*'s fact from fiction, many argue that the blurring is the point, and rightly so: dense with intertexts from the epic and biblical to the surreal (to say nothing of its profound, as-yet unstudied fascination with the visual arts), *La pelle* represents historical events in an avowedly literary manner: To describe the Allies' landing at Salerno and a typhus outbreak in Naples, it evokes Virgil's *Aeneid* and Boccaccio's *Decameron*; the eruption of Vesuvius assumes biblical proportions, and an impoverished girl killed in an air raid is resurrected as Torquato Tasso's Clorinda.

After decades of marginalization, it seems safe to say that Malaparte has been redeemed, as evinced by a more widespread public interest and a robust presence of recent reprints and new translations.[21] So, too, has *La pelle*, as its critics adopt the interpretive approach requested by Officer Hamilton and, answering in the affirmative, assert *La pelle* represents "lies that show us the truth."[22] Yet in their recognition of the novel's literary engagement, some readers go so far as to dismiss "references to real facts and places" as "accidental, because of the emblematic and practically allegorical aim of the narration."[23] If *La pelle* was long thought to falsify the Allied occupation, today for many it transcends it; thus, the radical revision of *La pelle*'s critical fortunes instead proves to be the other side of the same coin: However welcome *La pelle*'s return from literary exile, its engagement with Allied-occupied Italy remains obscured.[24] A product of the cultural conventions in which the gendering of redemption is writ large, *La pelle* is singular in its self-awareness, thus offering an unparalleled site of critique.

In order to effect such a critique, this chapter adopts a twofold interpretive strategy that, on the one hand, takes seriously its engagement with the historical moment and, on the other—intimately related—hand, signals to how that intertwines with its allegorical mode. With regard to this first point, a brief structural summary will begin the work of understanding the novel's commitment to narrating the occupation. *La pelle* is composed of twelve chapters: the first nine are set in Naples, from the winter of 1944 as the Battle of Monte Cassino rages interminably to the March eruption of Vesuvius, which functions as a redemptive rebirth. Chapter 10, "The Flag," provides its own spectacularly grotesque ending when the joyous liberation of Rome turns mournful as a celebrating civilian is crushed beneath an Allied tank.[25] Chapter 11, "The Trial," strings together another series of endings: the liberation of Florence, Tuscany, and Milan. As readers stutter-step past the milestones, they experience the distended temporality of each "liberation" that promises but withholds peace: the end of the war brings Mussolini's execution in Piazzale Loreto and the brutal public lynching of his dead body. This passes in a flash before giving way to a surreal, posthumous trial, where the court and the defendant are all monstrous fetuses, and whose inconclusive ending prophecies Italy's defining postwar struggle to come to terms with the legacy of fascism. After this accumulation of rapidly undermined climaxes, "The Dead God," gestures toward the end of the occupation yet circles back to "The Rain of Fire," as the novel ends with a flashback of Jimmy and Malaparte contemplating Vesuvius. (Jack, we learn in passing, has died.)

This military progression is interrupted by frequent flashbacks that expand narrative time and space to include Malaparte's exile on the Sicilian island of Lipari in the 1930s, his experience on the Eastern front described in *Kaputt*, the announcement of Mussolini's arrest (July 25, 1943), and the liberation of Capri (September 16, 1943) and Naples (October 1, 1943). Atop the skeleton of these historical events, the novel's connective tissue—and the more common object of analysis—is the series of degraded, degrading spectacles that strain, and often shatter, the limits of credibility: Captain Malaparte and his Allied companions stand in line to meet the only virgin in all of Naples; they visit a shop selling blonde merkins to prostitutes to satisfy their "Negro" customers' sexual preference.[26] By "The Flag," Captain Malaparte himself has become the spectacle, claiming to his nauseated French companions who doubt the truth of *Kaputt* that he has eaten the hand of a colonial soldier (*goumier*) before their very eyes. As Captain Malaparte's companions grapple with the moral ambiguity of what they (think they) see, so too must *La pelle*'s readers decide whether these events were real occurrences or artistic invention, historical fact or literary allegory.

La pelle overflows with grotesque spectacles, yet I single these out insofar as they are moments when the text uses historically marginalized figures—the Neapolitan prostitutes, "Negro" soldiers, and the *goumiers*—as sites of intercultural encounter and concomitantly signals their respective significance as metaphors for the occupation and for art. Taking my cue from the text, then, I contextualize it within a cultural corpus that includes military documents, other literary texts and historiography, to point out the ways in which *La pelle* embraces, revises, or critiques national stereotypes and their gendering and racialization. I also read the episodes in terms of one another, asking why questions of truth and artistry are posed through representations of racialized, sexual violence: in "The Virgin of Naples" the finger of a 'Negro' soldier affirms a girl's unbelievable virginity; in "The Flag," the hand of a *goumier* validates Malaparte's literary authority, when he "proves" he has cannibalized it by arranging animal bones on his plate beneath the French officers' horrified gaze. Finally, my analysis is loosely structured around the novel's geographic architecture. The first part concentrates on the Negro-prostitute relationship in the Naples chapters from plague to redemptive rebirth, represented in terms of a subtle but unmistakable whitewashing of the Neapolitan women after their interracial sexual encounter. The latter part focuses on "The Flag," which unsettles any resolution as it jumps to another climax, the liberation of Rome. This narrative disturbance—which mirrors the stutter-step temporality of the occupation—forces us to set aside the redemptive ending and revisit the interracial sexual encounter. Thus, as I consider the *goumier* as he appears in the "The Flag," I suggest that the (avowedly false) representation of his hand points back to the earlier appearances of black hands (those of both the "Negroes" and the *goumiers*), introducing a self-critique of the racist assumptions held by cultural representations of Allied-occupied Italy, *La pelle* included.

The "Virgin of Naples" and the Ambivalence of "Liberation"

In the first pages of *La pelle*, throngs of prostitutes solicit soldiers in an interminable, infernal performance: "Parties of disheveled, painted women, followed by crowds of Negro soldiers with pale hands, were parading up and down Via Toledo, cleaving the air above the thronged street with shrill cries of 'Hi, Joe! Hi, Joe!'"[27] Unquestionably, *La pelle* is fascinated by these women and their clients, yet from the first chapter, street prostitution collides with the literary topos whereby the prostitute stands for fallen Italy. In this context, the "plague" of the first chapter's title refers to the medical epidemics debilitating the city and functions as a metaphor for the self-interested drive to save one's skin that turns every man, woman and child, into a prostitute: "Such was the baneful power of the contagion that self-prostitution had become a praiseworthy act, almost proof of patriotism, and all, men and women, far from blushing at the thought of it, seemed to glory in their own and the universal degradation."[28] In this hyperbolic formulation, every man, woman and child embodies fallen Italy, no metonymy but a perfect one-to-one correspondence. From this perspective, Italy remains not a conquered victim but instead, as in the preinvasion *Guide to the Occupation of Enemy Territory*, a gendered threat.

Taken to its logical conclusion, this paradigm turns women into combatants, an attitude satirized by *La pelle* through its biting description of "General Cork," a thinly veiled General Mark Clark, the showboating commander of the American Fifth Army. In the description of the Allies' arrival in Capri, the gun-toting troops are "frightened" by aristocratic women who "kidnap" the general and have their way with him.[29] Several chapters later, the motif recurs when the women celebrating the liberation of Rome become a series of body parts assailing the troops like a lyric poem gone wrong: "In a twinkling we were surrounded, assailed, overwhelmed, and the column disappeared beneath an inextricable tangle of legs and arms, a forest of black hair, and a soft mountain of ripe breasts, full lips and white shoulders."[30] In case the irony is lost, Malaparte punctuates it with a joke: "'As usual,' said the young curate of the Church of Santa Caterina, in Corso Italia, when delivering his sermon the next day. 'As usual Fascist propaganda lied to us when it predicted that if the American army entered Rome, it would assault our women. It is our women who have assaulted, and discomfited, the American Army.'"[31] The satire reaches its limits, however, when an Italian civilian is crushed beneath a tank of the "defeated" American army, flattening him into the titular "skin."

La pelle's grotesque reversals earned the novel no end of condemnation. However, read in the context of Allied military reports that blame Italian women for spreading a plague of venereal disease, *La pelle* seems less inflammatory than incisive. Even as a "war on syphilis" was being fought concurrently in the United States, the "army" of prostitutes in Naples was blamed as the source of the Italian epidemic, opening a new battlefield in this putative space of peace.[32] Armed with exceptionally "dangerous" germs, these women were considered biological weapons and—according to anecdote—denied treatment so as to be deployed against the Germans.[33] While the anecdote is quite possibly apocryphal, the military did go to extensive lengths to represent the singular threat posed by Italian women. In her reading of a U.S. military report, Mary Louise Roberts notes how it views Italian women "as agents of infection who 'descended upon' the camp, 'outflanking guards' and arousing men like so many parasites swarming down."[34] With such documents in mind, *La pelle* acquires greater satirical force, as it spectacularizes the gendering and sexualization of war that often takes place imperceptibly within the pages of official documents, passed off into the archives as if it were fact.

Reading *La pelle*'s representation of prostitution within its historical context becomes all the more important in light of the identity of the client: "Negroes," "buffalo soldiers" of the Ninety-Second Infantry Division.[35] Indeed, if the southern Italian woman provided a ready-made scapegoat for the VD epidemic, so too did the African American soldier, "a symbol of perversion within the US military."[36] In much the same way as it moves between prostitutes and the figuration of Italy-as-whore, *La pelle* explores blackness in the historical specific of the Negro soldier and as a generic category for the conqueror; when his Allied friends attempt to make a hierarchy of sexual encounters between "victors" and "vanquished" based on race, Captain Malaparte offers this pithy rejoinder: "To conquered peoples . . . all conquerors are men of color."[37] However, the presence of colored troops within the Allied forces means that all conquerors may be men of "color," but some are more "colored" than others, as the novel makes abundantly clear. The novel's metaphoric emphasis on the racialized conqueror is mirrored by its fascination with the "Negro," his ambivalent position as a conquered-conqueror makes him an attractive figure for a narrative keen on reversing conventional dynamics. Nominally, the "Negroes" commodify the Neapolitans but really, we soon discover, the Neapolitans trade them on an improvised slave market: "Fifty dollars was the maximum price that was paid for the hire of a Negro for a day, that is for a few hours—the time to make him drunk, to strip him of everything he had on, from his cap to his shoes, and then, after nightfall, to abandon him naked on the pavement of an alley."[38] Stripped of their spare parts, the "Negroes" become interchangeable with the Allies' inanimate machinery, as the Neapolitans dismantle them just as they do the tanks and ships.[39] This further reversal of the conqueror-conquered dynamic appears to reinforce Allied military beliefs about the threat posed by Neapolitans, an iteration of the prostitute-combatant motif discussed above. Yet this "slave market" also works to critique the racial inequity that structures U.S. society and the hypocrisy of a nation built on slavery that condemns Neapolitans for commodifying human flesh in the face of starvation. The carnivalesque world of *La pelle* unmasks the thin veneer of American redemptive discourse to reveal the racist underpinnings that it shares with fascism.[40]

In establishing a backdrop of the Allied-Italian encounter as an interracial, sexual, economic transaction that destabilizes conventional power dynamics, "The Plague" sets the stage for "The Virgin of Naples," a perversely intimate close-up of the soldier-prostitute encounter that starts with another reversal: In the lexicon of Allied-occupied Naples, soldiers lining up outside a door can only be waiting to have sex with a prostitute, whereas in *La pelle*, they line up to *not* have sex with a virgin. When Jimmy invites Captain Malaparte with a question, "Have you ever seen a virgin?"[41] he sets up the encounter that begins as an unveiling:

> The girl threw her cigarette on the floor, grasped the fringe of her petticoat with the tips of her fingers and slowly raised it. First her knees appeared, gently gripped by the silk sheath of her stockings, then the bare skin of her thighs, then the shadow of her sex. She remained for a moment in this posture, a sad Veronica, her face severe, her mouth half-open in an expression of contempt. Then, slowly turning on her back, she lay at full length on the bed and slowly opened her legs.[42]

More than a titillating experience, the spectacle gazes back at the spectator: "Just as the odious lobster when it mates slowly opens its pincerlike claws, staring at the male with its small, round, shining black eyes, motionless and threatening, so the girl slowly opened her fleshy pincers, rosy and black, and remained there, staring at the spectators. A profound silence reigned in the room."[43] However, an event so incredible cannot be seen to be believed; assuring the soldiers she is not the threat she appears to be, the man encourages them:

> "She is a virgin. You can touch. Put your finger inside. Just one finger. Go on, try. Don't be afraid. She doesn't bite. She is a virgin. A real virgin," said the man, thrusting his head into the room through a gap in the curtain.
>
> A Negro stretched out his hand, and slipped in a finger. Someone laughed, and seemed to repent of it. The "virgin" did not move, but stared at the Negro with eyes full of fear and loathing. I looked about me. Everyone was pale— pale with fear and loathing.

"Yes, she is like a child," said the Negro in a hoarse voice as he turned his finger slowly.

"Get your finger out of there," said the man's head thrust through the gap in the red curtain.

"Really, she is a virgin," said the Negro as he pulled out his finger.[44]

Staging the interracial sexual encounter through a fairly explicit depiction of penetration (*fairly*, insofar as it notes the finger's specific movements but avoids mention of the female genitalia), "The Virgin of Naples," has made readers uncomfortable. While working on the French translation, *La peau*, René Novella presented the chapter to a group of his colleagues at Malaparte's request, whose reactions were hostile: "They were almost unanimous in declaring that Malaparte pronounced an indictment of exaggerated violence and unacceptable cynicism against his country. Some scenes were even considered purely sadistic and everyone asked what would have been the public reception of such descriptions whose realism surpassed the limits of decency."[45] The U.S. publisher, Houghton Mifflin, chose not to find out, censoring key sentences about the finger that were restored in a 2013 reissue by the *New York Review of Books*.[46]

Moreover, even critics working from the unexpurgated Italian edition have avoided discussing the penetration or the interracial dimension: referring to the virgin on display, they leave unspecified the identity of the soldier who inspects her.[47] While possibly a sign of prurience, this aversion to the penetration is not simply imposed upon the text; instead, it is encouraged by *La pelle* as it shifts focus away from the "virgin" and the "negro" to the conquest-as-penetration metaphor. For two full pages, Captain Malaparte parses the connection between the military penetration of Italy and the "virgin": "when you go back to America . . . it will give you pleasure to talk about how your conqueror's finger passed beneath the triumphal arch of the poor Italian girls' legs."[48] This metaphor is meant to stabilize the relationship between Allies and Italians, yet it has the opposite result. In response to the virgin, Jimmy and the soldiers only laugh nervously. Existing to confirm the soldiers' superiority, the virgin's lobster claws cut off their power of speech, and undermine this banal metaphor for conquest: The impassive "virgin" shows no signs of distress, as she provides for her family through what is, effectively, prostitution.

Further layers of meaning are added by returning to a literal reading of the penetration, where the 'virgin' introduces a gendered critique: as the "Negro" penetrates her, he turns her into a whore at the precise moment he "proves" her virginity, thus foregrounding the interdependence of the concepts as products of the patriarchy that commodifies her regardless. Moreover, in staging the penetration as a spectacle, *La pelle* evokes the practice of the group medical exams conducted on Italian women suspected of prostitution—a reference that becomes more explicit when reading *La pelle* in dialogue with narratives that openly depict it, such as Alfred Hayes's *The Girl on the Via Flaminia* and Norman Lewis's *Naples '44*. Recalling this practice underscores the importance of reading *La pelle* both in a literary and historical context, in which the Italian woman as combatant functions as a symbolic reversal of the conventional wartime dynamic but also suffers material consequences. When a doctor pronounced a woman virgin or whore, healthy or diseased, the outcome was not a philosophical meditation on the occupation but a life-changing determination; as journalist Anna Garofalo reports from a hospital ward full of women, "Everyone awaits 'the results,' the certificate from the analysis that, having examined their 'slide' under a microscope, will declare if they are dangerous or innocuous. For them, 'the results,' mean liberty or internment, and it is more important than a love letter."[49]

In addition to erasing this humiliating historical practice, the conversion of the "virgin" into a metaphor works to whitewash the episode, in line with early scholarly readings.[50] Nonetheless, the first three chapters insist on the *interracial* sexual encounter. In "The Wigs," Captain Malaparte takes the same approach as with the "virgin," telling Jimmy to interpret the blonde pubic wigs created to facilitate couplings between the "Negroes" and the Neapolitan women as a symbol for victory: "The whole of Europe is nothing but a tuft of fair hairs. A crown of fair hairs for your victorious brows."[51] As the literal *covering figure* of the genitals, the wigs stand in for military conquest and the "Negro" soldiers, conquerors, yet this insistence on "discard[ing] the literal in order to concentrate on the figural" should be read with suspicion.[52] Why are the Neapolitan women and the "Negro" soldiers made the privileged site of truth only to be discarded? In the economy of *La pelle*, the racialized, sexualized encounter is called upon to restore clarity to an ambiguous historical situation. However, like the "virgin," the wigs muddy the question: underscoring the racialization of southern Italians, they signal the porous boundaries between the "Negro" and the Neapolitan—the American and the Italian other.[53] Thus, the wigs insist on the crucial function of the racialized other: if "Negroes" and Neapolitans are both "black," the Neapolitan women must become "white" where it matters, in order for the metaphor and the sex act to function. At the same time, it stresses that the Neapolitans' racial transformation is a ruse—successful only because the "Negroes" are naïve and/or sexually insatiable enough to believe it.

Can "blacks" turn "white"? With "The Wigs," *La pelle* completes its triptych of chapters that foreground the interracial sexual encounter, but the question returns briefly in "The Triumph of Clorinda," through a dinnertime anecdote in which the prostitutes become victims of the same ruse, suggesting that they and their clients are equally seduced by the mirage of whiteness:

> "In order to persuade the Neapolitan girls to become engaged to them," said Consuelo, "the Negro soldiers say that they are white like the others, but that in America, before sailing for Europe, they were dyed black so that they could fight at nighttime without being seen by the enemy. When they go back to America after the war they will scrape the black dye from their skins and become white again."[54]

In response, Jack laughs until the point of tears, a confident dismissal that contrasts the uncomfortable laughter elicited by the penetration of the virgin; after all, a southern "gentleman," such as Jack, requires the intransigence of racial identity. Nonetheless, the fact that racial transformation be singled out as a joke deserves consideration, positioned as it is within a chapter that ends as an impoverished girl, killed in an air raid, is transformed into Tasso's epic heroine through the princess Consuelo's ministering. In a novel where German women can turn into men, a man can become a woman in labor, a fetus in a jar can become Mussolini's dead body, a human body crushed beneath a tank can become the nation's flag, and a dog can become Christ, it is easy to miss the boundary that the text defends. The title shouts it, yet with its metaphorical valence, the importance of the skin proves surprisingly hard to see. Jack may laugh, but the reality this 'joke' glosses over is no laughing matter for *La pelle*. Indeed, if race is not subject to transformation, it is "contaminable," as Brackette F. Williams underscores in a reading of the "virgin" episode where she asserts the importance of the womb as a repository for cultural ideals—and the attendant preoccupation with its defense.[55]

In fact, if one such defense is the recurrent insistence on reading the interracial encounters allegorically, another can be found in "The Rain of Fire," the end of the nine-chapter Naples sequence that culminates in the eruption of Vesuvius—an event of biblical proportions that offers Jack a revelatory moment and fills his fellow soldiers with a sense of impending doom.[56] Amid the crowds of Americans, English, Polish, and French soldiers, the novel pays—once again—extra attention to the "Negroes" who, unfailingly accompanied by prostitutes, appear to return to a state of nature: "Scores of Negroes, their broad nostrils red and dilated, their round white eyes starting out of their black heads, milled around in the confusion, almost naked, as if they had rediscovered their ancient forests in the crowd. They were surrounded by swarms of prostitutes, also half-naked."[57] After a final reprisal of this interracial encounter, Captain Malaparte singles out individuals from the chorus of Neapolitans, a group of sleeping men and two women whom he says are the symbols of rebirth:

> That is Adam, and that is Eve. They have just been born out of the chaos, they have just returned from hell, they have just risen out of the grave. Look at them—they are newly born, and they have already taken upon themselves all the sins of the world. All the men and women in Naples, in Italy, in Europe are like these. They are immortal. They are born in sorrow, they die in sorrow, and they rise again, purified.[58]

Extending them to represent the people of Naples, Italy and Europe, *La pelle* employs a synecdoche similar to the conclusion of John Horne Burns's *Gallery*, although stopping short of universalizing them, so as to maintain the old/new world distinction. Here, as I argue in Chapter 4, the women singled out to play this symbolic role warrant consideration: a girl combing her hair and watching her reflection in the sea, and "a woman dressed in red ... suckling her child. Her snow-white breast protruded from her red blouse, splendid as the breast of the first woman in creation."[59] Linked to "The Virgin of Naples" with their red clothing but contrasting her with their snow-white skin, these women anchor an Edenic vision that reasserts Italian whiteness in the aftermath of the encounter with the racialized Allies.[60] Thus, even as the corporeal transformation of "blacks" to "whites" appears beyond the realm of imagination, *La pelle*'s shift from the black "virgin" to the "very white" Eve is just one of its many sleights of hand, functioning as a fantastical defense against the miscegenation threatened were the interracial, sexual encounter read literally.

In many ways, "The Rain of Fire," functions as an ending, with its redemptive thematics and the feeling of closure created by references to the opening chapters and to the end of *Kaputt*; yet this resolution is undone in the choppy transition to "The Flag," whose anomalous opening paragraph announcing victory at Cassino reads like the newsreel voiceovers that start each episode of Roberto Rossellini's *Paisà*.[61] With this unsettling continuation beyond the whitewashed redemption in "The Rain of Fire,"

La pelle revises the Naples chapters with another set of "black" fingers that simultaneously point to a violent, interracial, sexual encounter and to a metaliterary dimension. In "The Virgin of Naples," a black finger is called upon to penetrate the virgin, only to be converted by Captain Malaparte into an unstable metaphor for conquest. In "The Flag," the stakes are raised: as Captain Malaparte seeks to redeem his literary authority, he transforms the *goumier*'s black fingers into an allegory for his artistry, threatening to erase the historical encounter of mass rape to which those fingers also point. However, by reading the metatextual dimension together with the historical referent, I argue that "The Flag" offers a critique of colonialism and, moreover, the construction of the racialized other visible throughout cultural representations of the occupation.

The Goumier's Hand and the "Truth" of Malaparte's Fiction

Founded by the French in 1908 as a police force within Morocco, the *goumiers* participated "not only in French colonial expansion in Morocco, but also in overseas wars such as WWI, WWII and Indochina."[62] In Italy, they are most famous for their decisive role in the Battle of Monte Cassino, the historical backdrop for *La pelle*.[63] Their tenacity on the battlefield, however, is inseparable from their reputation of "savagery and dishonor." Built atop soldier and civilian tales of their indiscriminate cruelty, the *goumiers*' emblematic status was crystallized after May 1944, when they are said to have committed mass rape of the local civilian population in the Ciociara region near Rome with the permission of their French commanding officers.[64] Idealized as both valorous and evil, the *goumier* is uniquely vexed. From the perspective of the French colonial imaginary, he "occupies a particularly fraught position . . . with respect to the production of hierarchies of difference."[65] In World War II, "the presence of colonial soldiers in Europe had the effect of crossing the cultural boundaries that the colonial powers tried to maintain between the Europeans and the colonized peoples and therefore implicitly undermined the racialized, hierarchical colonial order."[66] In Italy, the colonial troops were at once the long-awaited "liberators" and the first people of color encountered by many Italians, who had long been exposed to fascism's racist rhetoric.[67] The mass rape and its aftermath reveals Italy's ambivalent position within a transnational network that shows the inadequacies of the occupied/liberated binary. According to one popular version of the story, the rape was a vendetta for Italian violence committed in North Africa and Corsica, tacitly accepted by the Americans in support of their French Allies.[68]

Until recently, the *goumier* and the mass rape remained the stuff of myth, thanks to the taboo nature of the subject and the multiple cultural competencies required to investigate it, including knowledge of Berber dialects, Arabic, French, Italian, and English.[69] Even a basic question about the number of victims remains unanswered, with official numbers ranging from 3,000 to 60,000, depending on the criteria.[70] While accurate figures will never be known, Moshe Gershovich concludes that "the collective picture of misery and despair (continued years after they had been raped due to the repressive attitude of their society) leaves no room for doubt about the broad scope of that phenomenon."[71] In Italy, efforts have been made to further understand this event with an emphasis on victims' narratives.[72] While many of these accounts perpetuate racist stereotypes about the *goumier*, studies by Gershovich and Driss Maghraoui work to counteract them, by adding oral histories from the *goumiers* and explaining the social and political conditions that keep them marginalized in multiple contexts: Reviled by the Italians and incompatible with both French and Moroccan national narratives, they were disinclined or unable to write their own version of the story.[73] Gershovich writes,

> While the story of the Italian victims of the *Marocchinate* has largely been recorded and made public, there has never been an attempt to extract testimonies from their likely assailants, Moroccan veterans from the French Army who had fought in Italy. Mostly illiterate, poor and largely marginalized within their own society after independence, given their association with Morocco's colonizers, these former soldiers rarely care to speak about their experiences abroad, let alone to discuss matters of sexual encounters, which remain by and large a taboo topic in public discourse.[74]

The oral testimony gathered by Gershovich and Maghrahoui stands alone in reporting a range of sexual encounters with Italians, including prostitution and romance, a testament to—and a small destabilization of—the prevailing *goumier*-rapist paradigm;[75] an invaluable contribution, these essays should be translated into Italian.

Contrary to this murky picture, the literary representations of the *goumier*—which predate the historical research—are in keen alignment: In Anglo-American and Italian cultural texts, the rape by the *goumiers* provides a ready-made ending that rewrites "standard histories of Italy's redemption by Allied forces, and mak[es] the antiwar argument that military occupations never have happy endings."[76] In *Private Angelo* (1946), a satirical novel by Eric Linklater, a Welsh-born Scot who served in Italy and wrote a military history of the campaign, *goumiers* rape Angelo and his wife, who bears a precociously deviant child whom she names Otello. *Goumiers* appear out of nowhere in the final pages of Tommaso Landolfi's *Racconto d'autunno* (1947; *An Autumn Story*) and rape the heroine, who dies. Mortimer Kadish's combat novel *Point of Honor* (1951) ends with American GIs guarding an Italian family from a group of lustful *goumiers*. In Alberto Moravia's novel *La ciociara* (1959), made famous by its film adaptation by Vittorio de Sica (1961), *goumiers* rape a mother and daughter in a church.[77] In *Within the Labyrinth* (1950), *The Sicilian Specialist* (1974), and *Naples '44* (1978) by Norman Lewis, *goumiers* are involved in brutal rapes and are the victims of heinous reprisals.[78] Their cultural portrayal appears in concert with (and no doubt served to reinforce) public opinion: as historian Sergio Lambiase writes, "to say 'Moroccans' means to evoke lightning-quick and dramatically, a situation 'at the limit.'"[79] So, too, does it make a commercially palatable scapegoat, as Millicent Marcus comments in terms of *La ciociara*: "If the rapists had to be Allies, at least make them exotic and 'other,' nonwhite and therefore capable of committing any bestiality that the racist mind thinks them capable of."[80] This reading easily extends to Liliana Cavani's cinematic adaptation of *La pelle* (1981), in which she spins a melodramatic scene out of a single-sentence description of a market where desperate mothers sell their children to the *goumiers*: "they felt them and lifted up their garments, sticking their long, expert, black fingers between the buttons of their knickers and holding them up to indicate their price."[81]

Unlike these texts, the baroque *La pelle* is uncharacteristically restrained, giving readers only fragments from which to piece together this shadowy figure: Blink, and they pass in a blur of the infernal carnival. In contrast to the "Negro," whose "glossy, massive, immense" body is subject to lengthy, aestheticizing descriptions,[82] the *goumiers* appear on few occasions; never a whole person, they are a series of body parts: "enveloped in their dark robes,"[83] as their long, black fingers palpate their potential victims, their eyes gleam with an evil desire.[84] And while the "Negro" speaks a few lines of infantilized dialogue, the *goumier* only communicates extralinguistically.[85] In this, *La pelle* is in alignment with texts such as Moravia's *La ciociara*, where they flash deviant smiles, and De Sica's film, where they are "completely incomprehensible."[86] In *Point of Honor* and *Racconto d'autunno*, despite a linguistic chasm, the *goumiers* are perfectly able to communicate their depravity.[87] However, much in the same way that *La pelle* uses the "Negro" soldier to critique the hypocrisy of the American "redeemer" even while reiterating the racist logic that underpins it, so, too, does it employ the *goumier*. Here, then, as important as it is to recognize the way in which *La pelle* perpetuates racist imagery, it is also essential to analyze the self-consciously symbolic ends to which these figures are put.

In "The Flag," as the *goumier*'s hand becomes the emblem for Malaparte's artistry, it also helps effect a critique of colonialism. At the start of the chapter, Captain Malaparte and Colonel Jack Hamilton meet up with General Guillaume and Lieutenant Lyautey as they are forced to keep an eye on their Moroccan division as they "gazed with avid eyes at the crowd of women promenading among the trees in the park of the papal villa."[88] At lunch, Guillaume tells his guests that he has received an order from the Vatican to keep the Moroccans out of the Eternal City, because they pose a threat to the Pope's "wives."[89] Much like the historiography that would follow, the officers emphasize the *goumiers*' hypersexual deviance to the exclusion of any reference to their role in the brutal fighting on the Gustav Line that opened the long-elusive road to Rome.[90] When the sound of an explosion interrupts the meal, the news reaches the table that the third *goumier* of the day has set off a landmine, but whereas the others died, this "lucky" soldier only loses his hand. The General's glib dismissal, "They haven't yet succeeded in finding the hand ... Who knows what will become of it?" critiques the historic practice of using the fearless *goumiers* as human mine-detectors and sets the scene of "cannibalism" that is to come.[91]

Unperturbed, Guillaume continues by speculating as to how Captain Malaparte might render their modest meal in his next book, based on what he has read—hot of the press—in *Kaputt*: "In his next book you will find our humble camp meal transformed into a regal banquet, while I shall become a kind of Sultan of Morocco."[92] Lyautey then inquires, "How much truth is there in all that you related in *Kaputt*?"[93] provoking Hamilton's retort: "It does not matter at all if what Malaparte recounts is true or false. The question to pose is another: is what he does art or not?"[94] Intransigent in their refusal to pose the proper question, the French officers are punished with a gruesome sleight of hand as Captain Malaparte recounts an event that has just taken place before their eyes. Describing the meal, he takes two pages to get to the couscous and the unusual piece of meat: "It was a man's hand. It was undoubtedly the hand of the unfortunate goumier, which the exploding mine had neatly severed and hurled into the great copper pot in which our kouskous was cooking.... If you don't believe me ... look here, on my plate. Do you see all these little bones? They are the knuckles. And these, ranged along the edge of the plate, are the five nails."[95] (See Figure 12.) In response to Captain Malaparte's declaration, the French officers are nauseated. However, if his declaration surprises them, it merely confirms the suspicions about "barbarous Italian people" expressed in "General Cork's Banquet," when Mrs. Flat refuses to eat a 'siren fish' who bears an uncanny resemblance to a girl, while implying that her dinner companions are com-

Figure 12. Captain Malaparte's sleight of hand is stripped of its racial connotations and metatextual symbolism in Liliana Cavani's 1981 film.

fortable eating Italian children.[96] In "The Flag," Captain Malaparte embraces this accusation but attributes it to social standards so intransigent as to dictate barbaric acts; he asks, "What could I do? I was educated at the Collegio Cicognini, which is the best college in Italy, and from boyhood I have been taught that one should never, for any reason, interrupt the general gaiety, whether at a dance, or a party or a dinner. I forced myself not to turn pale or cry out, and calmly began eating the hand."[97] On one level, the episode crystallizes the paradoxical perception of Italians as hypercultured and barbaric; it might also be read as a jab at the Italian upper class, where the extreme commitment to appearance—*bella figura*—justifies the most heinous behavior of which past decades have no shortage.[98]

However, the episode also works on a further level as it cordons off the ignorant French officers from those in the know (the reader and Jack). After they leave the group, Jack applauds Captain Malaparte's artistry, in a marked departure from previous scenes: Whereas no one in "General Cork's Banquet" determines whether the meal is a fish or a girl, in "The Flag," Malaparte congratulates himself: "Did you see how skillfully I arranged those little ram's bones on my plate? They looked just like the bones of a hand!"[99]

Abandoning the ambivalence that characterizes so many episodes, the novel affirms the officers' inability to distinguish; after all, they take animal for human bones, an artist for a cannibal. More than transforming Guillaume into a sultan, *La pelle* depicts him as the most banal of colonialists—and the least reliable of witnesses. Showing how racist beliefs color interpretation, the severed hand helps reframe the ubiquitous stories in soldiers' memoirs about the *goumiers*' penchant for dismembering enemies and friends: extracting gold teeth, castrating, severing limbs and heads, and selling jars of brandy-pickled fingers.[100]

However, for those who take their cue from Jack, the potential for reading this episode as a critique has been dampened. For instance, Giorgio Bàrberi Squarotti parses it into a "joke," a metaphor of the horrors of war, and a metatextual meditation about truth and literature, his concerns about the hand of the artist surpassing his interest in the *goumier*'s.[101] Similarly, Raffaele La Capria denounces Malaparte's "art of the prestidigitator," and Emilio Cecchi criticizes his "profane hands."[102] Tahar Ben Jelloun is a rare scholar who takes Malaparte's representation of the *goumier* seriously, yet he, too, uses similar rhetoric: as he laments Malaparte's racist representation, notes that "he forced his hand, as one does in literature."[103] Here, the rhetorical overlap points to a shared blind spot in these opposite approaches. Unmistakably, the depiction of the hypersexual *goumier* is racist. Unquestionably, the episode is metaliterary. Yet it is in the tension produced by their superimposition that the episode's power lies. Captain Malaparte's literary authority depends upon constructing the non-Western other out of animal bones, and yet, as he gloats about his artistry, he signals its fictionality. Might, then, it not suggest we read with suspicion the other black fingers and figures, within the pages of *La pelle* and beyond?

As *La pelle* stages an act of misreading on the part of the colonial masters and undermines their myths, it takes a distance from the cultural representations of the *goumier* I survey above. Insisting on the ambivalence of the Allied-Italian encounter, it opens the door to a reading of the *goumier* that problematizes his intertwined roles as rapist and symbol of absolute depravity. At the same time, "The Flag" points to the novel's other black finger as it suggests that, if all conquerors are men of "color" and conquest is figured as penetration, the belief that all men of color are rapists way well take root precisely where history and allegory are allowed to blur without interrogating how the one informs the other. Indeed, this logic goes a long way in explaining how *goumier* has become a synonym for rapist, in much the same way that the formulation of Italy-as-whore perpetuates generalizations about the ubiquity of prostitution.

As I argued in the case of the "Negro" soldier and the "virgin," limiting the *goumier* to an ahistorical metaphor for artistic "truth" obscures the text's insistence on the interracial sexual encounter, neutralizing anxieties about the threat he poses to established hierarchies. Thus, it becomes all the more crucial to read the episode metatextually and in terms of the historical context it obliquely provides, starting from the presence of the historic French officers with their actual names.[104] With this context, the *goumier*'s hand points, like the finger of the "Negro" soldier, to a sexual encounter: the mass rape of spring 1944. Although the rape is never discussed, the insistence on the fears of the locals and the Vatican makes it a credible—but inarguably oblique—referent that emerges through a few details within the story Captain Malaparte tells the French officers: Beyond a menu, the passage offers a complex portrayal of the relationships between the *goumiers*, their French commanders, their German enemies, and the Italian civilians. In the first course, prosciutto from the Frondi Mountains, Captain Malaparte recalls the battle sites the French officers have just traveled in Lazio, in the area known as Ciociaria. In the second course, the idyllic mountains give way to the Liri River, whose green banks are dotted with the corpses of the *goumiers*: "On its green banks many of your goumiers have fallen before the fire of the German machine guns—fallen face downward in the grass."[105] In this account, the battle is being fought between *your goumiers* and the Germans—with the French merely a possessive pronoun. In the third course—the (in)famous couscous—the mountains of Itri in Ciociaria return: "From it pregnant women make a potion that facilitates childbirth. It is a pungent herb, and the rams of Itri devour it greedily. It is, indeed, to this herb, kallimeria, that the rams of Itri owe their rich fat, so suggestive of pregnant women; because of it they have the weary, languid eyes of pregnant women and hermaphrodites."[106] More than a lesson on local flora, this insistence on pregnant women in Ciociaria resonates with the earlier suggestion that the Vatican's interest in keeping the *goumiers* out of Rome is due their sexual voracity. From this perspective, we can witness a circle of life and death linked by a series of violent acts: the *goumiers* rape the women of Ciociaria who, impregnated, eat the grass fertilized by the dead bodies of the *goumiers*. Subsequently, the French officers eat the mutton that, having gorged itself on that same plant, *tastes* like pregnant women. Thus, the colonizers are given a taste of their responsibility for their colonized subjects who have sacrificed themselves for—and transgressed against—the Italian people.

This reading, then, shows that to dismiss the historical referent of *La pelle* obfuscates these complex power dynamics between Italians, French,

Moroccans, Americans, and Germans; moreover, it elides the novel's strategically partial vision of history, with the usual amnesia about Italian colonialism and its blind eye toward the sexual violence perpetrated by "whites." At the same time, however, the move *between* historical referent and allegory is what allows these marginalized figures into the conversation about how the Allied-occupied Italy is represented and to what end. The text's dependence on the violent interracial, sexual encounter speaks to the role of race and gender in reestablishing boundaries in a situation where ontological boundaries are blurred: A black man penetrating a white woman excruciatingly simplifies one of World War II's most indeterminate spaces. The interracial rapes that appear throughout cultural representations of the Allied-Italian encounter serve to cement Italy as the victim and the Allies, the aggressor, while keeping colonialism a French vice, and rape, a Moroccan crime. Yet each of *La pelle*'s encounters troubles this narrative, showing how the "virgin" is no passive victim, the "white" woman not so white, the black fingers not what their racist viewers make them out to be.

At the same time, the characters' allegorical directive should not be obeyed but instead read as symptomatic of an anxiety toward the historical encounter—with the attendant threat of miscegenation. Thus, much in the same way that Captain Malaparte insists on figuring interracial penetrations as an allegory for the encounter, so too does he refuse to narrate the literal interracial penetrations *of* the encounter, leaving the pregnant women of Ciociara to "merge"—in Cynthia Enloe's characterization—"with the pockmarked landscape."[107] However, lest the fear of miscegenation function as its own sleight of hand, we should recall that the *goumiers* and their black fingers first appear in *La pelle* as they purchase Neapolitan boys, a proclivity emphasized in wartime memoirs. *La pelle*'s depiction of the *goumiers* "buying" Neapolitan boys seems genteel in comparison to this oft-cited, eyewitness account that attests, "The Moroccans flung themselves upon us like unchained demons. They violated, threatening with machineguns, children, women, young men, following each other like beasts in rotation."[108] Compared to the indiscriminate rape of the Italian people in this passage, the threat of miscegenation seems distant; reading the *goumier* in this historical context, it becomes apparent that the horror he evokes depends upon the misogynist logic that naturalizes wartime rape for reproductive females, as it designates it unspeakable for men, children and the elderly. The *goumier*'s emblematic status is not due to how many people he raped—but that he raped the wrong ones.

Thus, even as *La pelle*'s "porous Underworld" shows that "all bodies, human and nonhuman, are metamorphoses of each other," not all bodies are equal in its economy: As the title reminds us, skin matters.[109] Nor are all body parts equal: the privileged site of encounter is the genitals. In *La pelle*, the violent, interracial, sexual encounter functions as a commingling of self-conscious literary invention and historical referent, with the *goumier* and the "Negro" performing analogous roles. Read historically, "*La pelle* deploy[s] all the racist imagery of the time in the representations of blacks and Arabs" and their "inevitable lust for white 'flesh.'"[110] Yet the fact that their hands appear in the narrative when the text seeks to assert its *literary* status and to deny the historical referent, seems to demand an allegorical approach. While oftentimes the narrative chooses to leave readers questioning the significance of its grotesque spectacles, in these cases Captain Malaparte directs readers away from the "virgin-whore," the "Negro" soldier, and the *goumier* and toward questions of war and art. Thus, in its allegorical mode, the novel performs an act of whitewashing in which marginalized figures are foregrounded only to be silenced. This then, is the cost of following the sleight of hand through which the characters point toward allegory and Malaparte's literary redemption: the erasure of the violence in which these marginalized figures are implicated—as victim, perpetrator or something in between. However, by taking seriously the novel's historical engagement as it informs its allegorical directive, these episodes can become a site from which to examine the paradoxical status of the figures on whom redemption depends. Thus, the novel effects an astute critique of how gender, sexuality, and race constitute and trouble representations of this transnational contact zone—foremost, its own.

The way in which *La pelle* demands a reflection on the stereotypes it employs is important to keep in mind in the next chapter's analysis of Norman Lewis's *Naples '44*. A powerful cultural influence, *Naples '44* strategically revises *La pelle*, embracing an antifictional stance in contrast to Malaparte's and Burns's overtly allegorical pretensions. While all three texts walk a razor's edge between history and literature, *Naples '44*'s claim of nonfictionality proves problematic, as the narrator stages his own redemption in terms of his ability to identify the Neapolitan whores and Moroccan rapists who seem to be the city's sole inhabitants and, nonetheless, emerges "clear-eyed" in the minds of critics and historians.[111]

6

The Redemption of Saint Paul
Norman Lewis's *Naples '44*

According to critic Luigi Barzini in a 1980 *New York Times* review, out of the countless literary renditions of Naples, only one exceeds the mastery of John Horne Burns's *The Gallery*, and that is Norman Lewis's *Naples '44* (1978), a wartime diary whose descriptions have "the taste and smell of truth."[1] Based on Lewis's experience as a British intelligence officer stationed with the Allies, *Naples '44* starts with the September 9 landing on Paestum and, in 106 entries spanning thirteen months, details his encounter with the devastated city. He recounts dramatic events, such as the Germans' time-delay bombing of the Naples post office and the eruption of Vesuvius, as well as daily occurrences, such as the Allies' futile attempt to bring criminals to justice, the Neapolitans' ingenious efforts at avoiding starvation, and his job as a "wedding officer," vetting brides for British servicemen. Arriving in Italy as a "babe in the woods," Lewis is guided through this incomprehensible hell by Vincente Lattarullo, "a man steeped in the knowledge of the ways of Naples."[2] As a series of revelations distance him from the endemically corrupt Allies and warm him to the Neapolitans, by the end of his time in Naples, the hardnosed intelligence officer has "died" and wishes he could be reborn Italian.[3]

In the intervening years since Barzini's review, *Naples '44* has amassed a notable readership. A ubiquitous presence in popular and academic historiography, *Naples '44* is quoted extensively for its discussion of the black market, the mafia, prostitution, and mass rape committed by the Franco-Moroccan *goumiers*.[4] Among its vocal fans are two Neapolitan artists: Writer and critic Raffaele La Capria lauds it as an "extraordinary document of that time," and filmmaker Francesco Patierno, who produced a cinematic adaptation in 2017, celebrates it as "a sacred text . . . loved around the world."[5] While Patierno's adaptation garnered mixed reviews, its release became an occasion for a new chorus of critics on both sides of the Atlantic to voice their love of the book.[6]

For all its popularity, *Naples '44* has received minimal scholarly attention.[7] Excluded from the surfeit of studies on the immediate postwar period by its late publication date, it is doubly marginalized as a British-authored text in a cultural corpus heavy with Italian and American representations.[8] Helped by this outlier status, *Naples '44* has passed into the history books as an "antifictional" diary, as readers forget the long delay between the events described and the 1978 publication;[9] in Barzini's words: "*Naples '44* does not seem to have been written retrospectively, built from fading memories or interviews with elderly survivors. It purports to be the actual diary of a year in and around Naples, as written at the time of the Allied occupation . . . and barely edited."[10] For those critics who remark on it, the temporal distance adds to the book's credibility, as if its publication had been delayed because of the sensitive information contained within.[11] However, although Lewis's unpublished wartime notebooks are held by a private collector, there is no philological mystery surrounding *Naples '44*. Lewis's biographer, Julian Evans, confirms the vast changes between the notebooks and the "invented diary technique" of *Naples '44*, calling it "a narrative everywhere scored and colored by its detached and sensitive remaking. . . . More than three decades after the event, he used one-line entries to irrigate seeds of memory that, once germinated, could in his intentional hands be arranged into high display." In fact, Lewis returned there in order "to revive his memories" in preparation for writing, as Patierno's adaptation underscores with the device of an elderly man walking through present-day Naples.[12]

Naples '44's rhetorical strategy is an unquestionable success, as critics accept the fiction that Lewis "virtually banished himself" from his diary.[13] This "antifictional" stance positions *Naples '44* in diametric opposition to the allegorical pretensions of John Horne Burns's *The Gallery* and Curzio Malaparte's *La pelle*. Nonetheless, *Naples '44* is, like these other autofictional narratives of Allied-occupied Naples, very much a hybrid text that blurs the boundaries of historical referent and literary invention to its own strategic ends. Following Officer Lewis's transformation from an unwitting persecutor of the Neapolitan people to a uniquely sensitive cultural mediator, *Naples '44* is a conversion narrative, "written to lead to the ending."[14] Specifically, I read the "conversion" in Dantean terms using John Freccero's formulation, as a story that tells the journey of a pilgrim who "dies" at the end of the plot, thus giving birth to the narrator who tells the redemptive story.[15] As traces of hindsight emerge within the entries, they reveal the coexistence of—and underscore the spiritual distance between—Lewis-narrator and Lewis-character.

Furthermore, Officer Lewis's journey is punctuated by two transformative events that signal the text's Dantean affinity. Seated in a restaurant, the narrator recalls witnessing a group of blind orphans beg the impassive patrons. Using the past perfect that gives the feeling of distant hindsight, he writes:

> The experience changed my outlook. Until now I had clung to the comforting belief that human beings eventually come to terms with pain and sorrow. Now I understood I was wrong, and like Paul I suffered a conversion—but to pessimism. These little girls, any of whom could be my daughter, came into the restaurant weeping, and they were weeping when they were led away. I knew that, condemned to everlasting darkness, hunger and loss, they would weep on incessantly. They would never recover from their pain, and I would never recover from the memory of it.[16]

On the level of the plot, this episode marks the character's transformation: Rather than continue to submit the Neapolitans to the Allies' farcical justice, Officer Lewis takes a new approach toward those who have violated the letter of the law. On a rhetorical level, this metaphor reveals the text's Dantean aspirations, as Lewis compares himself to Saint Paul, a persecutor of the church who reverses course after being "blinded by the vision [of Christ] on the road to Damascus";[17] in *Paradiso*, Dante's pilgrim, too, compares himself to the emblematic figure of New Testament conversion as part of his strategy for establishing textual authority.[18] The second transformative moment also has a Dantean resonance, albeit indirect; when the narrator declares, "A year among the Italians had converted me to such an admiration for their humanity and culture that I realize that were I given the chance to be born again and to choose the place of my birth, Italy would be the country of my choice," he paraphrases the renowned American Dantista Charles Eliot Norton who wrote in his letters, "If I ever come back, may I be born Italian."[19] For Norton and other Anglo-American travel-writers, Italy, mediated through careful readings of Dante, "furnished . . . experience on the pulse by which they could examine, condemn and resist what they regarded as the evils in modernity."[20] Following this familiar trajectory of "death-and-renewal,"[21] in the last entry, Officer Lewis envisions his departure from Naples as a funeral, signaling the moment of "radical discontinuity" that is the hallmark of the Dantean conversion: "Death in life is closure in the story, but it is thanks to a spiritual resurrection that the story can be told."[22]

Using these textual landmarks, I track the character's journey as he rejects the hypocritical Allies and affirms his wish to be reborn Italian.

Nonetheless, this rejection does not catalyze a wholesale embrace of the Neapolitans, whom he views as subject to "mass hallucination."[23] Instead, Lewis distances himself from both groups, adopting the position of an "outsider [who], caught between competing worldviews but adhering to neither, can do nothing more than to observe."[24] It is precisely his *outsider* status that gives his book insider credentials as a "chronicle of war-ravaged woe and resilience under occupation," but he does not just position himself as distinct from the Allies and Neapolitans;[25] the narrator also separates from the character, telegraphing a "clear-eyed" authority in his critique of his former self.[26] As we will see, this transformation has consequences: As the narrator makes liberal use of Orientalizing topoi about Naples, he claims authority over them. Repeating them with more restrained language than Malaparte's *La pelle*, *Naples '44* appears a truthful account, even if its claims are ultimately more extreme. The success of this rhetorical strategy is measurable in its regular citation by historians as well as in its warm reception (particularly with respect to *La pelle*'s). So, too, is it evident in the response to Patierno's recent cinematic adaptation, as cultural publications further naturalize the narrator's power to arbitrate the truth of the Neapolitan women and the men whose status as lover or rapist depends on the color of their skin.

The Quasi-Conversion of Saint Paul

Arriving in Naples from North Africa, the first-person narrator of *Naples '44* resembles *The Gallery*'s in their unmasked disdain for the inept and cowardly Allies.[27] After landing, Lewis asserts, "we know nothing."[28] After an entire week, "Confusion is still intense."[29] All the while, he watches the Allies attempt to catalog their world, "hundreds of soldiers streaming like ants to bring typewriters and filing cabinets up from the beach," a quiet mockery that becomes explicit when Lewis reports that many of the dutifully filed documents were falsified. Worse, he details American hypocrisy in court trials that result in "appalling miscarriage(s) of justice," for instance, an elderly man who receives a three-year sentence for a misdemeanor while criminal masterminds go free.[30] Lewis concedes: "The days of Benito Mussolini must seem like a lost paradise compared with this."[31]

Rejecting their fellow Allies, the narrators of *Naples '44* and *The Gallery* look to the Italians for redemption, although in different ways and to different ends. John achieves redemption through an orgasmic communion with one Italian, the origin story of a text that concludes by distancing itself from the historical encounter in the Galleria Umberto in favor of a cosmic "Gallery." Officer Lewis gives no sign of his own sentimental life, as befits his outsider persona;[32] and in his professional life, his job is to erect boundaries between the Allies and Italians: As "wedding officer," he is tasked with distinguishing suitable wives from prostitutes, rather like finding a needle in the haystack of Allied-occupied Naples. Visiting their homes, he surveys their standard of living; if it seems too high, he asks, "Where does the money come from?" The question is destined to elicit an unsatisfactory answer; although they inevitably claim they are supported by a wealthy uncle, Officer Lewis knows that their husbands-to-be have been paying for their services and must reject their application.[33] Although his investigations continue to affirm the belief that the vast majority of Neapolitan women involved with servicemen do so with a financial motivation, he recognizes that the label "prostitute" is immaterial in determining a woman's potential for redemption through marriage, assuming they possess other key requirements: "Of the twenty-two failed candidates most seemed kindly, cheerful, and hardworking at their household tasks, and their standard of good looks was very high."[34]

Lewis comes to accept the possibility for a redemptive encounter between servicemen and Neapolitan women, a realization that leads to his "death"—his reassignment out of Naples—and "rebirth" as the author of *Naples '44*. The decisive case is a young widow named Liana Pagano, whose application Officer Lewis approves, even though her house is a little too spotless and her source of income a little too vague. This decision proves his undoing, when his supervisors send Officer Robert Parkinson to verify it.[35] In parallel descriptions of Lewis's naïve impressions versus his hypothetical but emphatic version of Parkinson's "rational" point of view, the men constrast one another. Having "achieved the deepest penetration of Italian life" while "remain[ing] aloof from it," Parkinson observes Italian holidays, quotes Leopardi, and speaks perfect Italian: "His curiosity was endlessly stimulated, but I felt his love was never awakened."[36] Yet the episode more crucially points to a distance between Lewis-character and Lewis-narrator, as the latter reflects on the shortcomings of the former. Whereas for Lewis, Liana's dead soldier husband appears in his photograph "buttoned into his tight uniform with his fine, young, upswept moustache," for Parkinson, his "vanished arrogance would have seemed to him contemptible."[37] For Lewis, "a moment of poetry" emerges in plaintive details such as "White walls, gloriously sculpted and dimpled by light. Women were hanging out washing above and below." For Parkinson, "there would have been no appeal in Liana's spotless linen hanging on the balcony, her whitewashed walls and the scrubbed floor tiles where linoleum should have been."[38] Whereas Lewis is swayed by Liana's "gamine charm," Parkinson is "immune." However, it is Lewis-narrator who makes these distinctions, distinguishing between his youthful lapse in judgment and his impression of Parkinson's "objective" interpretation.

This description climaxes in the second quasi-"conversion," the paraphrase of Norton's wish to be reborn Italian; yet this hypothetical rebirth (*were I given the chance*) does not connote Officer Lewis's "Neapolitanization," but merely his admiration.[39] In fact, his story with Lattarullo shows that he cannot embrace Neapolitans as the 'true' alternative to the false Anglo-Americans. If Lattarullo is Officer Lewis's Virgil, the space he guides him through is the upside-down world of *bella figura*—the "obsess[ion] with face" that guides everyday life in Naples, including Lattarullo's own precarious existence.[40] A typical member of the Neapolitan middle class, Lattarullo was allowed to study law because his parents wanted the honor of the title, despite their awareness of the nonexistent job prospects in the city's depressed economy.[41] Impoverished because of *bella figura*, Lattarullo also earns a small income thanks to its cultural stranglehold: hired to attend funerals with a nice suit and a patrician accent, Lattarullo plays the *zio di Roma* (uncle from Rome) so as to lend an air of dignity to the ceremonies of impoverished Neapolitan families. Although fascinated by the social fabric that facilitates this apparent ruse, Officer Lewis is troubled by what he views as a kind of collective detachment from reality. In countless entries, he details the Neapolitan devotion to saints in the face of the most dramatic crises, including a town's imminent destruction by the lava of Vesuvius.[42] The worse the situation, the stronger the belief; after the eruption, "miracles galore."[43] While Lewis accepts these beliefs in the lower classes, he is surprised when Lattarullo admits: "Much as I deplore the fact that living in the twentieth century we should be so obsessed by these relics of medievalism, I'm afraid that even I am not immune to mass suggestion."[44]

Having repeatedly characterized the Neapolitans as subject to "mass hallucinations," Lewis cannot embrace such a radical transformation, as much as he might deplore the Allies' hypocrisy. Instead, his *wish* highlights the fact that he has *not* become Italian; thus, he distinguishes himself from other officers who are "infect[ed] by the deviousness of the environment," or are pulled into the web of superstition, like Neil Armstrong, Lewis's former companion in Tunisia, who appears, "an Italian disguised in a British uniform." Lewis writes: "I watched the once straightforward English face which a year of solitary confinement in the heel of Italy had turned into such a marvelous barometer of wariness and skepticism. When one of the regulars came through the door and passed us muttering a polite ossequi, Armstrong's eyes swiveled cautiously, and although his hand did not move, I almost expected him to grope his testicles."[45] Armstrong, immersed in

Neapolitan superstition, and Parkinson, coldly in command of Italy's traditions, are the Scylla and Charybdis of travelers to Italy: one is all heart and the other all rationality.

Officer Lewis, too, occasionally doubts his own rationality. When he catches himself compromising ethically, he exclaims, "I am gradually becoming drawn into the system!"[46] Nonetheless if the character exhibits worrisome new behavior, the narrator is aware of the distance he takes from his original position; if the character makes mistakes, the narrator is aware of the ways in which he does not fit in: "The fact is we have upset the balance of nature here. I personally have been rigid when I should have been flexible."[47] Yet he is able to sail between these twin pitfalls; his moments of hindsight guarantee that he has not lost perspective, as is the fate of the protagonist of *Within the Labyrinth* (1950), a novel based on Lewis's time stationed in Benevento that shares many similarities with *Naples '44*. This authority is cemented when, in the final episode, Lewis imagines his Neapolitan sojourn ending with Lattarullo seeing him off at the train dressed in his funereal *zio di Roma* costume. Both within and outside Neapolitan culture, Officer Lewis is sent off by the *zio*, valorizing him as the essence of Neapolitan culture that he appreciates but is not tricked by; after all, he sees Lattarullo for who he is.

Returning to the start of *Naples '44* in light of the "death," the passive, impersonal syntax and the clipped prose of the first entries feel like a narrative strategy meant to vouch for the diary's antifictionality rather than the hurried scrawling of a soldier in the field. The first entry begins with the announcement of the armistice in the driest of terms: "It was announced to us at half past six today that an armistice with Italy had been signed and would take effect from tomorrow." The prose of the September 9 entry is even more clipped: "Landed on 'Red Beach,' Paestum, at seven o'clock."[48] Yet it gives way to a fuller description that belies *Naples '44*'s literary pedigree. For the British traveler, as for Lewis, "The initial image of Naples is often rendered in the language of the pictorially beautiful, if not the sublime,"[49] but Lewis warns us from the outset that "an extraordinary false serenity lay on the landward view." He writes:

> A great sweep of bay, thinly penciled with sand, was backed with distant mountains gathering shadows in their innumerable folds. We saw the twinkle of white houses in orchards and groves, and distant villages clustered tightly on hilltops. Here and there, motionless columns of smoke denoted the presence of war, but the general impression was one of a splendid and tranquil evening in the late summer on one of the fabled shores of antiquity.[50]

Evoking the Grand Tour, *Naples '44* treats southern Italy as "a vibrant curiosity, unknown but within reach; rarely visited by Northerners, but somehow familiar through ancient poetry and history."[51] When Officer Lewis and his fellow servicemen feel "as lost and ineffective as babies in the wood," ancient and idyllic imagery only offer temporary reassurance;[52] he does not lose an opportunity to emphasize the falseness of literary precedent, insisting that war has invalidated representations of Italy that trade in such idyllic terms, for instance, in his visit to the Sorrento peninsula: "This is a region on which all the guidebooks exhaust their superlatives, and the war had singed and scorched it here and there, and littered the green and golden landscape with the wreckage of guns and tanks."[53] Poetic visions of antiquity only go so far: "A few hundred yards away stood in a row the three perfect temples of Paestum, pink and glowing and glorious in the sun's last rays. It came as an illumination, one of the great experiences of life. But in the field between us and the temple lay two spotted cows, feet in the air."[54] Even as he evokes Anglo-American travel discourse, he takes his distance; as a soldier, he claims the role of antitourist who risks death to contemplate archeological wonders: "[we] were admiring the splendid husk of the Temple of Neptune when the war came to us in the shape of a single attacking plane. . . . We appreciated the contrasts involved and no one experienced alarm."[55]

Naples '44 insists on the insufficiency of past knowledge when even his native guide, Lattarullo, must reorient himself: "Everywhere there were piles of masonry, brought down by the air-raids, to be negotiated. . . . When we tried to take a short cut through a familiar vico, we found it freshly blocked by the collapse of tenements and filled with rubble to a depth of twenty feet."[56] It is fitting, then, that Officer Lewis successfully reads Naples when he gazes down on it from an elevated position. Likening the city to an "antique map, on which the artist had drawn with almost exaggerated care the many gardens, the castles, the towers and the cupolas," he is able to see beyond the destruction which leads him to reinforce the conventional representation of Italy's internal other: "for the first time I realized how un-European, how oriental it was."[57] Here, *Naples '44* announces its Orientalizing gaze that permeates the entire text: as Lewis compares the Neapolitans and those from the surrounding countryside to Africans, Bedouins, Chinese, Muslims, and primitive tribes, and their living conditions to the Dark, Bronze, and Middle Ages, *Naples '44* echoes Walter Benjamin and Asja Lacis's seminal travel essay, "Naples," macaroni-eating competitions and all.[58] Yet thanks to the Italian (quasi-)conversion, Officer Lewis seems like a compassionate insider; and thanks to the "plainspoken yet poetic" tone of the narrator, he seems like a sage outsider.[59] Through this pairing, *Naples '44* hides its status as a conversion narrative in dialogue with cultural representations of Naples, most significantly, Malaparte's *La pelle*, engaging it in an intertextual power play that has done much to perpetuate the gendered redemption of World War II Italy.

Naples '44 as a "Clear-Eyed" Revision of *La pelle*

After a month in the countryside, Lewis reaches Naples on October 6, 1943, a few days after the liberating army. While Captain Malaparte's first sight of Naples in *Kaputt* is an unfolding mystery, Lewis's reads as a matter-of-fact report: "The city of Naples smells of charred wood, with ruins everywhere, sometimes completely blocking the streets, bomb craters and abandoned trams."[60] As I discuss in Chapter 5, Malaparte establishes his authority to narrate Naples through two subtly revised passages; Lewis instead naturalizes his through his bureaucratic position, leading a recent publisher to affirm, "As an intelligence officer, he was granted extraordinary powers that allowed him to 'eavesdrop on humanity' and reveal all the divergent wonders of Naples."[61] Once the passive "granting" of such observational powers are interrogated, however, the clarity of his eye is clouded; Lewis's initial description continues, "Such has been the great public thirst of the past few days that *we are told* that people have experimented with seawater in their cooking, and families *have been seen* squatting along the seashore round weird contraptions with which they hope to distil seawater for drinking purposes."[62] Told by whom? Seen by whom? Bearing out the passage's ambiguity, Lewis answers the question differently when he rewrites the scene twenty years later in an essay, when he claims to have witnessed it personally.[63]

While the shared setting of Allied-occupied Naples is enough to encourage comparisons to *La pelle*, *Naples '44* openly signals its connection. Although it would have been impossible for Lewis not to be familiar with the infamous Malaparte, *Naples '44* dispels any doubt during an outing to Capri: "The haunted face of Curzio Malaparte whom I believed to be in the internment camp of Padula but from which he had clearly been released, appeared briefly, and among his courtiers I observed a British officer who, under the spell of his environment, grimaced and gesticulated in all directions."[64] In a single sentence, Lewis's equivocal portrait provides a blueprint of his engagement with the baroque novel and its untrustworthy author: associating Malaparte with the "escapist" world of Capri, "full of make-believe," he neglects to mention Malaparte's literary career but instead underscores his ill health, his political troubles, and his penchant for attracting sycophants. This single sentence depicts Malaparte as the stereotypically deceptive Italian that runs throughout *Naples '44* (and indeed, the guidebooks explored in Chapter 1); moreover, the enchanted British courtier emphasizes, by contrast, Lewis's sanity.

Beyond the mention of its author, *La pelle* is felt throughout *Naples '44* in descriptions that skirt the bounds of believability, for instance, the incomprehensible thefts plaguing the city. Among the feats of "Neapolitan kleptomania," Lewis includes scaling the thirty-foot walls of the Field Security Headquarters with the wheels of all of the Allies' vehicles and the day-by-day dismantling of an abandoned tank, a railway engine, buses, and trams.[65] In other "flamboyant acts of piracy," Neapolitans steal telegraph poles, vials of penicillin, an orchestra's instruments during intermission, and valuables out of a museum. He concludes: "Now the statues are disappearing from the public squares, and one cemetery has lost most of its tombstones. Even the manhole covers have been found to have a marketable value, so that suddenly these too have all gone, and everywhere there are holes in the road."[66] *La pelle*'s version of the thefts, instead, is rather succinct:

> In two hours the tank, which had been hidden in a yard, was stripped of all its bolts and dismantled. In two hours it disappeared: not a trace was left of it save for a patch of oil on the flagstones of the yard. One night a Liberty ship, which had arrived from America a few hours before in convoy with ten other ships, was stolen from Naples harbor. Not only was the cargo stolen, but the ship itself. It vanished and was never heard of again.[67]

Moreover, it concludes with Naples laughing at the news, all the way to the heavens: "All Naples, from Capodimonte to Posilipo, rocked with tremendous laughter at the news, as if convulsed by an earthquake. The Muses, the Graces, Juno, Minerva, Diana and all the Goddesses from Olympus . . . could be seen laughing and clasping their bosoms with both hands."[68] Veering into the surreal, it signals the need to read the episode with a critical eye. However, divine laughter notwithstanding, in one of the few histories of Allied-occupied Naples, Paolo De Marco privileges the description in *Naples '44*, saying that it puts *La pelle* in proper perspective.[69] In helping Lewis propagate a cache of stereotypes about Neapolitans, De Marco is not alone: Although Lewis ambiguously attributes the stories to generic reports, newspapers, and public rumor, a *New York Times* reviewer recounts the claims as if they were fact.[70]

Another ambivalent episode of *La pelle* revised by *Naples '44* is "General Cork's Banquet," where Captain Malaparte and Allied officials discuss the plagues of Naples—disease, prostitution, starvation—while being served an elaborate meal whose main dish is "a little girl or something that resembled a little girl."[71] Horrified, the guests refuse to believe Captain Malaparte that the "girl" is a siren fish and demand "she" be buried, while the narrator never confirms either identity, which, ultimately, is immaterial to *La pelle*'s objective to launch a multipronged critique against the Allies for suspecting the Italians of cannibalism; for wasting food in a famished city; for shedding tears over a cooked fish and disdaining the starving children forced to sell themselves to their liberators; for thinking that if the war had happened in America such things never would have happened. Lewis, instead, recounts the episode as part of his surprise at the Neapolitans' limitless capacity for eating even the most questionable items.[72] In contrast to Malaparte's uncomfortable juxtaposition between eating the flesh of a fish and "purchasing" a child, Lewis's straightforward explanation for the fish shortage avoids moral complexity. Yet the latter is taken as a "dry annotation" versus the former's "interminable embellishments."[73]

Lewis's description of the prostitution epidemic, starting from the exchange of sex for rations he witnesses in a municipal building outside Naples, also can be read in a similar dynamic with that of *La pelle*. Entering into "a vast room crowded with jostling soldiery," Officer Lewis observes "a row of ladies [sitting] at intervals of about a yard with their backs to the wall. . . . By the side of each woman stood a small pile of tins, and it soon became clear that it was possible to make love to any one of them in this very public place by adding another tin to the pile." At this unusual setup, the soldiers respond with "sheepish laughter, jokes that fell flat," while the women remain unmoved: "The women kept absolutely still, they said nothing, and their faces were as empty of expression as graven images."[74] Here, Lewis's description of the soldiers echoes Malaparte's "Virgin of Naples," where they laugh nervously in response to the girl's immutability.[75] His taciturn prostitutes, instead, revise the Malapartian "chorus" of prostitutes in *La pelle*'s opening chapter, "The Plague," an animalistic mob of splayed legs and mouths; while Malaparte's prostitutes spout obscenities as they bare their genitalia, Lewis's are silent and immobile: "They might have been selling fish, except that this place lacked the excitement of a fish market. There was no soliciting, no suggestion, no enticement, not even the discreetest and most accidental display of flesh." For the disappointed soldiers, "reality had betrayed the dream," a comment that pits Lewis's "matter-of-fact family-providers" against *La pelle*'s hysterical masses.[76] Indeed, to judge from the frequent citations of Lewis's scene, its sobriety has come to imply its veracity.[77] The next entry, however, retroactively casts suspicion on the women, as Officer Lewis emerges from the police archives with the conclusion that "most Italians [are] prone to sexual adventures."[78] Supported by "archival" documents, such a comment reinforces a long-held stereotype about the hypersexuality of Mediterranean people and hints that beneath the graven images, perhaps the women were enjoying it.[79]

Naples '44 also includes its own version of "The Virgin of Naples" and again deflates its spectacular nature and strips away, along with it, its multiple layers of meaning. Led to a *basso* by a Neapolitan woman, Officer Lewis discovers a thin girl standing in the corner of a windowless room: "This, said the woman, was her child, aged thirteen, and she wished to prostitute her. Many soldiers, it seems, will pay for sexual activity less than full intercourse, and she had a revolting scale of fees for these services. For example, the girl would strip and display her pubescent organs for twenty lire."[80] Compared to *La pelle*'s "Virgin of Naples" and its digital penetration of a Neapolitan girl by a "Negro" soldier, *Naples '44*'s sexual spectacles are low-key. In the preceding passage, *La pelle*'s baroque striptease becomes a simple statement of the price; the virgin with her menacing lobster claw legs becomes a thin girl standing in a corner; the avid, then embarrassed, public becomes an indignant but resigned Lewis. As I discuss in Chapter 5, *La pelle*'s striptease evokes a confluence of allegorical and historical meanings, from its critique of the metaphor of conquest-as-penetration and of the virgin/whore construction, to its allusion to the group medical exams performed on women suspected of prostitution. Here, instead, *Naples '44* adds one more piece of evidence that in Naples everyone is a prostitute, even the virgins.

In a separate incident, however, *Naples '44* does recount something intimate and spectacular—an incident that speaks to the narrator's self-construction. As part of a sting, Officer Lewis witnesses a gynecological inspection meant to verify whether a group of girls and women are prostitutes, a medical striptease that evokes the splayed legs in "The Virgin of Naples": "The first six women, some of them sobbing and protesting, were led forward, ordered to remove their knickers, pull up their skirts, and settle themselves in the chairs in which their legs, held in stirrups, were grotesquely raised and separated." Lewis then turns to the individual women: "Among them were a few bejeweled courtesans and some obvious bargirls, but the majority looked like young housewives, some with their shopping-bags on their arms, and there were some very young girls who were certain to be virgins." Condemning the "ugly and most depressing experience," the narrator nonetheless sees fit to distinguish virgins from whores.[81] Even though the "fish-market" scene shows housewives with shopping bags and young girls prostituting themselves, and even though we learn in the Pagano episode that Officer Lewis is too influenced by "poetry" to discriminate between respectable women and prostitutes masquerading as fiancés, the narrator declares courtesans and bargirls to be whores, housewives and young girls to be innocent.

I signal these contradictory assumptions to redress the historical record built upon *Naples '44*. While *La pelle* uses hyperbole to satirical effect and, in so doing, demands a negotiation of its relationship to the historical events it recounts, *Naples '44* is pernicious in its subtlety. *La pelle*'s allegory, at turns epic and surreal, disrupts the realist pretensions that the sparsely written diary-novel courts. *Naples '44* not only appears credible enough to dispatch official statistics that claim 42,000 out of 150,000 of the women of Naples to be prostitutes, but it does so while depicting nearly *every* woman in the text as prostituting herself, from housewives to virginal girls, from princesses to orphans. Yet the contrast between *Naples '44*'s "matter-of-fact precision" and *La pelle*'s baroque prose maps onto a true/false, British/Italian dualism that grants the former permission to reflect the reality of a city it Orientalizes if not openly mocks, a reminder that the national stereotypes explored throughout this book also inflect the authors' status.[82] As a result of this privileged perspective, *Naples '44* becomes the arbiter of the sexuality of the Neapolitan women; even while Officer Lewis sympathizes with them, the narrator—much like Alfred Hayes's—unmasks them all as whores.

Most problematically, this judgment extends to rape victims whose claims Officer Lewis is sent to investigate, when his ability to do so proves to be colored by his view of Neapolitans as hypersexualized and obsessed with appearance. Confessing that he does not understand the Neapolitans' "exotic mating rituals," Lewis dismisses the notion of rape for southern Italian women: "Rape is a fairly everyday event in this part of the world, and is not necessarily a serious business for the victim. Peasant girls in some of the big estates are raped by their overseers as a matter of course every day of the week. . . . Concealment of what has happened is what matters, to avoid a personal slump in value in the sexual market."[83] Sent to investigate an anomalous report of rape, Lewis confirms his doubts: "The rape turned out to have been prolonged, almost a leisurely affair, occupying some hours."[84] The anecdote concludes with the phony victim being willingly auctioned off to marry any Allied soldier interested in the hefty dowry offered by her former lover. However, the intended humor is troubling in light of historical evidence about the underreported nature of rape during the occupation where "white" perpetrators were concerned, and about the psychological, economic and social consequences for the victims.[85]

As historians demonstrate, the accused perpetrator, too, faced a range of consequences, dependent on his race and class rather than concrete evidence. Wartime sexual encounters involving white, upper-class officers were more likely to be deemed prostitution, whereas those involving black, lower-class soldiers were rape.[86] The one acknowledged rape in *Naples '44* speaks to this point when, on the backdrop of the historical mass rape by the *goumiers*, Lewis singles out a mother-daughter pair of victims: "The French colonial troops are on the rampage again. Whenever they take a town or a village, a wholesale rape of the population takes place. Recently all females in the villages of Patricia, Pofi, Isoletta, Supino, and Morolo were violated."[87] In contrast to the *everyday affair* of a master raping a servant, the interracial rape acquires a serious pall:

> Today I went to Santa Maria a Vico to see a girl said to have been driven insane as the result of an attack by a large party of Moors. I found her living alone with her mother (who had also been raped a number of times), and in total poverty. Her condition had improved, and she behaved rationally and with a good deal of charm, although she was unable to walk as a result of physical injuries. The Carabinieri and the PS said that she had been certified as insane, and would have been committed to an asylum had a bed been available.[88]

In its sketchy attempt at portraying the nameless victim and her parenthetically raped mother, the description is peculiar: although she is "said to have been driven insane," Lewis finds her rational and charming but physically impaired and comes away with the reflection that "She would be unlikely in the circumstances ever to find a husband."[89] Offering no help, the narrator suggests that the sight of the victims serve a symbolic purpose, "At last one had faced the flesh-and-blood reality of the kind of horror that drove the whole female population of Macedonian villages to throw themselves from cliffs rather than fall into the hands of the advancing Turks. A fate worse than death: it was in fact just that."[90]

Claiming to present the flesh-and-blood reality of the victims, the narrator turns their plight into a generic nationalist conflict: Macedonians versus Turks, Italians versus Moroccans. As he distinguishes rape victims from scam artists under the guise of objectivity with such success that his "report" is accepted as true, he casts blanket assumptions that for Italian women rape is not really rape, unless the rapist is a racialized foreigner.[91] Moreover, the narrator forecloses any identity for the Moroccan soldiers beyond sexual deviants, as he asks, "What is it that turns an ordinary decent

Moroccan peasant boy into the most terrible of sexual psychopaths as soon as he becomes a soldier?"[92] Here, then, in *Naples '44*, not only is it impossible for white men to be rapists, but all Moroccans must be. Pushing the distinction further, Lewis depicts the emblematic rapist as violating gender norms: "I learned that the attackers of the Santa Maria a Vico family were roaming the countryside in several jeeps, led by a sergeant-chef who fancied himself as a dancer, and dressed up as a female when not in action."[93] Thus, rape becomes the exclusive crime of transgender/crossdressing, racialized *goumiers*. *Naples '44* propagates the same representation of the *goumier* traced in Chapter 5, stressing that the horror he evokes comes from the fact that they exceed the bounds of acceptable wartime violence by raping the wrong victims: "In Lenola, which fell to the Allies on May 21, fifty women were raped, but—as these were not enough to go round—children and even old men were violated. It is reported to be normal for two Moroccans to assault a woman simultaneously, one having normal intercourse while the other commits sodomy."[94] Considering all the ways in which rape is excused in contrast to the ways in which it is condemned, a hierarchy emerges that excludes white, heterosexual men from being rapists, and affords victim status only to those who suffer sexual violence at the hands of racialized, homosexual, pederast, or transgender/crossdressing foreigners. While these stereotypes circulate in *La pelle*, the metaliterary discourse interrupts careful readers from assimilating them wholesale and instead encourages their critique; when they emerge in *Naples '44*, the diary's "matter-of-fact precision" reassures readers that they are true.

Naples '44 walks a razor's edge between truth and fiction, like *La pelle*, yet in order to fashion itself as an authoritative *Commedia* of Allied-occupied Naples, *Naples '44* rewrites and disavows *La pelle* as an outlandish *Aeneid*.[95] The consequences of this intertextual powerplay are significant: under the cover of British objectivity, *Naples '44* represents all women in Naples as whores and all Moroccans feminized rapists, and yet it emerges as a "clear-eyed" account of Naples, to this day, as reviews of Patierno's cinematic adaptation remind us. Eliciting celebrations of the diary-novel, the film becomes a useful intertext as the pastiche of Italian and Hollywood film clips, archival material, and contemporary shots of Naples signals *Naples '44*'s constructed status, albeit unevenly: perfectly conveying the diary-novel's attitudes toward prostitution, it chooses instead to be silent on its racialized portrayal of rape.

Saint Paul on Screen: Francesco Patierno's *Naples '44*

Adapting a text as multifaceted as *Naples '44* can be no easy task. Francesco Patierno took it on in 2017, eliciting further praise for the book and its author, even as his film received mixed reviews: the *New York Times* calls Lewis "a remarkable chronicler of life" and the text "plainspoken yet poetic," while the *Los Angeles Times* finds it "justifiably acclaimed as a chronicle of war-ravaged woe and resilience under occupation," only to conclude, "At most, *Naples '44* makes a solid case for turning to Lewis's prose and getting the full effect of his year there that way."[96] In Patierno's film, British actor Benedict Cumberbatch reads heavily condensed episodes that combine and jump between different entries. Together with an eclectic soundtrack that hurries from nostalgic to jazzy to psychedelic, this voiceover accompanies a montage of archival footage, clips from Italian and American films set during the occupation, shots of contemporary Naples, and sequences where a silent actor meant to represent an elderly Lewis revisits the scenes of his youth. *Naples '44* covers a range of events, such as the devastating explosion of the city's post office, the typhus epidemic, the black market, the eruption of Vesuvius, the miracle of Saint Gennaro, and a healthy dose of the Lattarullo character (whose cinematic doppelgänger becomes the legendary Neapolitan actor Totò). However, at just over eighty minutes and with long stretches given to film clips, it is necessarily selective. While it does include the literary landmarks I signaled (the two "conversions" and the "death"), it eliminates entire plot lines that help locate Lewis's narrative authority in his evaluation of the Neapolitan women and the *goumier*: the "Liana" story, the "virginity" exam, and the rape investigations.

Calling it an "affectionate yet misguided tribute," Jay Weissberg of *Variety* critiques the exclusion of certain kinds of material: "Curiously, Lewis's not infrequent passages about massive corruption among the Allied officers are largely absent, and his gut-wrenching evocation of the female population's degradation is passed over far too quickly." The representation of prostitution is circumscribed, but more pressing are questions raised by the images that accompany Cumberbatch's voiceover: During the four minutes dedicated to the "serious" sex lives of the occupants of Naples (including an expurgated description of the group prostitution scene), the vast majority of the archival photographs and film clips show groups of women, young and old, alternating with images of soldiers. Apart from one photo of a sailor groping two women standing on either side, there is no sign of sexual activity in these images as the women are shown walking about a ruined landscape.[97] Yet the voiceover suggests that the random girls and women that flash upon the screen were involved in prostitution.[98] Here, Pa-

Figure 13. "The women kept absolutely still, they said nothing, and their faces were as empty of expression as graven images." Archival images accompany text from Norman Lewis's *Naples '44* that describes a scene of group prostitution with housewives accepting rations as payment, in the 2017 film, directed by Francesco Patierno.

tierno is in line with his source text, repeating its widespread generalization about the female population of Naples; yet the use of archival images puts specific faces to the generic accusation, raising ethical questions about his montage (Figures 13 and 14). In addition to these chaste archival images, Patierno turns to contemporary cinema in order to represent the explicit sexual encounter, excerpting clips from Mike Nichols's 1970 adaptation of Joseph Heller's *Catch-22* (1961) and Liliana Cavani's 1981 adaptation of Malaparte's *La pelle*. Robert Abele of the *Los Angeles Times*, Derek Smith of *Slant*, and Luke Y. Thompson of the *Village Voice* all question this decision, the latter arguing he "consciously avoids the true horrors of hooking in favor of a tee-hee bedroom-comedy approach common to the appropriated clips."[99] However "jarring," these cinematic adaptations of novelizations of the Allied-Italian encounter remind the viewer that *Naples '44* is a post-facto reconstruction and not an unmediated testimonial.[100] Moreover, the clips from *Catch-22* and *La pelle* offer an astute commentary on Lewis's tone, which appears "affectionate and fascinated," thanks to his character's conversion narrative but is often, in fact, satirical.[101] For instance, the appearance of *Catch-22*'s protagonist, Yossarian, reminds viewers of the tongue-in-cheek nature of many of Lewis's observations, particularly the veritable catch-22s that colored American justice during the occupation; the shared ironic vision between Heller and Lewis could well be worth exploring.

Figure 14. "Here a row of ladies sat at intervals of about a yard with their backs against the wall." Archival images accompany text from Norman Lewis's *Naples '44* that describes a scene of group prostitution with ordinary housewives accepting rations as payment, in the 2017 film, directed by Francesco Patierno.

In a similar vein, Patierno's inclusion of Cavani's *La pelle* proves useful in pointing a finger at the Malapartian intertext within *Naples '44*. Patierno avoids Cavani's invented or enhanced plotlines and female characters that subversively add a feminist vein to Malaparte's androcentric novel, which would have struck an odd note for an adaptation of Lewis's text.[102] Instead, he includes Cavani's version of Malaparte's infamous hand-eating scene, accompanying Lewis's comments on the resourcefulness of the starving Neapolitans, a clip that speaks to the problematic treatment of race shared by Cavani, Lewis and Patierno. As I discuss in Chapter 5 (see Figure 12), in Malaparte's version, the "cannibalized" "hand" supposedly belongs to a *goumier* who lost it in a landmine accident, as part of a critique of the clueless French colonizers, together with a metatextual commentary on Malaparte's artistry that points to the fictionalized construction of other black fingers in the text and beyond. Cavani's version removes all racial discourse and metatextual commentary; the episode is simply one more uncomfortable encounter between Captain Malaparte and the American officers whom he frequents, making it a perfect fit for Lewis's narrative as it marvels on the Neapolitans' willingness to eat anything. Moreover, the inclusion of this episode in Patierno's film signals an unexpected proximity between the feminist Italian film and the roughly contemporary British diary in their shared attitude toward the *goumier* as a shorthand for the depravity of war.

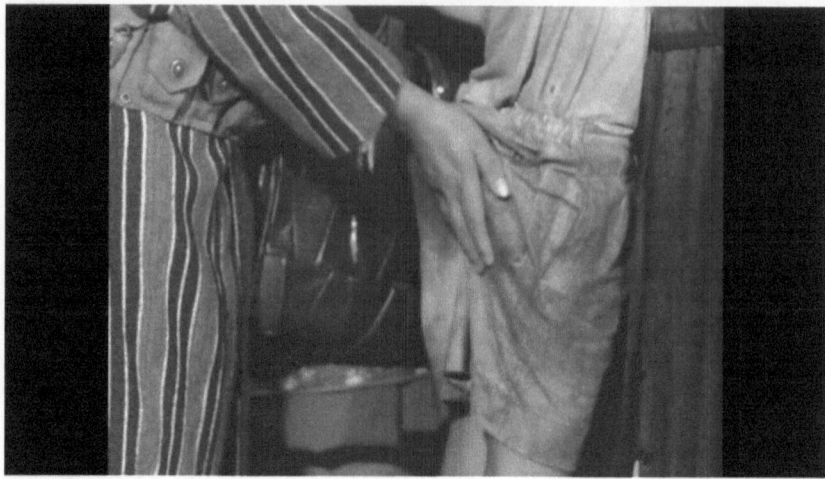

Figure 15. Liliana Cavani represents the Moroccan *goumier* pederast as a symbol of the absolute depravity of the Allied occupation of Naples in her 1981 film, *La pelle*.

However, while Cavani and Lewis take a distance from Malaparte's self-conscious construction of the *goumier*, Patierno removes the *goumier* altogether. Whether he did so in order to skirt Lewis's blatant racism or to avoid controversy, the exclusion constitutes a lost opportunity to engage with an unhealed wound in our memories of World War II, both in terms of the wholesale accusations against an entire population of soldiers and in terms of the silencing of the victims who were converted into a symbol of Italy's suffering. In this way, Patierno replicates the problem of Christopher Nolan's 2017 World War II blockbuster *Dunkirk*, which erases all trace of the colonial soldier.[103] Had Patierno wanted an honest cinematic rendering of Lewis's vision of the *goumier*, he could have chosen the scene from Cavani's *La pelle* where they are depicted as hypersexual pederasts (Figure 15). Had he desired to avoid whitewashing *and* perpetuating racist stereotypes, he might have included clips from *Days of Glory* (2006), directed by Rachid Bouchareb, the only film to consider the heroism of colonial soldiers in World War II, albeit without mention of the rapes.[104]

In addition to encouraging dialogue between Lewis, and well-known texts such as *La pelle* and *Catch-22*, Patierno's eclectic collage introduces viewers to a wealth of film, turning his closing credits into a veritable filmography that might inspire future exploration: *Napoli Milionaria!* (1950) by Eduardo De Filippo, *Il re di Poggioreale* (1961) by Duilio Coletti, and *Le quattro giornate di Napoli* (1962) by Nanni Loy. Among the list we also

Figure 16. Francesca (Maria Michi) from Roberto Rossellini's *Paisà* (1946) becomes an unexpected spokeswoman for Neopolitans suffering a postwar water crisis in Francesco Patierno's film *Naples '44*.

find Roberto Rossellini's *Paisà*, but while we might expect to see clips from its "Naples" episode, Patierno surprisingly chooses to excerpt "Rome." A further surprise comes the way in which Patierno uses Francesca—not in the segments dedicated to prostitution but instead to segue from the joy of liberation to the suffering faced by Naples in their lack of drinking water, a realistic detail from the episode that is often overlooked in favor of the melodramatic plot (Figure 16). Certainly, one might want to be careful in exchanging Naples for Rome, as also occurs in the use of *Catch-22*; a reviewer's comment on how Patierno's clip from *Paisà* "present[s] Naples and its people in the same raw, unadorned fashion as the archival footage," is doubly jarring in light of the episode's Roman setting and its melodramatic mode.[105] Still, that geographical slippage might be outweighed by the fact that Patierno incorporates texts generally excluded from analyses of cultural representations of the occupation.[106] Reframing them within an unorthodox context, Patierno thus invites further consideration of this intertextual network. While critics respond to Patierno's film by asserting the supremacy of Lewis's diary, positioning them as intertexts yields insights into both—and into the larger body of cultural representations of Allied-occupied Italy.

Throughout this book, I outline and critique the gendering of redemption in cultural texts, showing how it conditions our understanding of Allied-occupied Italy in terms of what it foregrounds and what it marginalizes. In some cases—as in *Paisà*, *All Thy Conquests*, *The Girl on the*

Via Flaminia, *The Gallery*, *La pelle*, and *Naples '44*—this means revisiting critical consensus about canonical texts. In other cases—as in the military guidebooks and the novels of Luciana Peverelli—this means reintroducing widely distributed texts that remain unstudied. It was never in my sight to undertake the encyclopedic task of combing the reaches of this unruly corpus, but instead to focus on those that made the widest cultural impact vis-à-vis this paradigm. However, in the following epilogue, I introduce one little-known text, a diary that provides a powerful counterpoint to *Naples '44*: Maria Luisa D'Aquino's *Quel giorno trent'anni fa* (1975; *That Day Thirty Years Ago*). A proleptic rejoinder to *Naples '44*, *Quel giorno trent'anni fa* shows a different way of revising redemption. Creating her own Dantean conversion in which she is author, protagonist, and (ambivalently gendered) symbol of the Italian nation, D'Aquino deploys and subverts commonplace notions of Italian womanhood and the contradictory cultural ends to which Italian women have long been put.

Epilogue

September 8, 1943. The Italian government announces an unconditional surrender to the Allied forces that invaded the peninsula only days earlier. Inside the walls of Vatican City an American nun, Mother Mary Saint Luke, begins her diary, *Inside Rome with the Germans* (1945), with the news: "Armistice! A sigh of relief went up from the crowds around the loudspeakers. Then a pause. People looked at each other questioningly—Armistice or Armageddon?"[1] A similar ambivalence emerges from the diary of British-American aristocrat Iris Origo, *War in Val d'Orcia* (1947).[2] Writing from her Tuscan villa, Origo notes that the festivities end almost as soon as they begin:

> Outside the peasants are rejoicing, the bonfires continue, we hear sounds of laughter and merrymaking. The household look at us with excited faces, in which delight is marred by a dawning uneasiness. 'What do you think will happen next? What about the Germans?' What, indeed, about the Germans? Presumably they will at once occupy the chief Italian towns. Presumably, too, they will continue fighting at Naples, and later on form another line of defence along the Apennines. But what is to be the Italian part in all this?[3]

In the town of San Lorenzello, in the province of Benevento, Campania, Neapolitan aristocrat Maria Luisa D'Aquino starts her diary, *Quel giorno trent'anni fa* (1975; *That Day Thirty Years Ago*), by signaling the same collective joy: "People are saying it's divine intervention, running to church to thank the Virgin, oblivious to the gravity of the moment, unaware of its tragic consequences."[4] From Rome to Tuscany to Campania, long-awaited relief proves short-lived, evaporating with the realization that the armistice marks a new chapter in the country's drawn-out plot of suffering; in D'Aquino's ominous assessment, the Italians have merely exchanged the yoke of fascism for the ball and chain of the Allies.[5] Despite their divergent vantage points as an American nun cloistered in the Vatican, an Irish American landowner in the Tuscan countryside, and a Neapolitan aristocrat in Campania, these diarists attest to the country's ambivalence toward the armistice: at turns salvation and Armageddon, freedom and enslavement, a happy ending and an uncertain new beginning.[6]

For all their initial uncertainty, however, all three diaries end optimistically and with surprisingly consonant rhetoric. Concluding on June 4, 1944, with the sight of the first Allied troops to quietly enter Rome, the nun envisions religious rebirth: "Fascism was gone; Nazism was gone; and the horror of war had passed from Rome. Italy is on the eve of a new era. She has suffered in the crucible of pain and humiliation. She will put her affairs in order and begin life afresh."[7] Origo concludes on July 5, 1944, with a similar sentiment: "Destruction and death have visited us, but now—there is hope in the air," a vision of renewal that concentrates on restoring the ravaged land and its devastated inhabitants. Speaking eloquently of the "industry and resourcefulness of the Italian workman," the landowner invests them with the power to "bring the land back to life again."[8] However, her optimism stands in tension with her depiction of the arrival of the U.S. Fifth Army in the penultimate entry: The soldiers who liberate Val d'Orcia are not the mythic American GIs but the Franco-Moroccan *goumiers* who "regard loot and rape as the just reward for battle."[9] This tragic moment segues into the final entry, opening in medias res: "But now, at once, we must begin again."[10] Following her description of mass rape, "but," a strained grammatical suture, makes a stark juxtaposition between the physical violence suffered by countless women and the abstract promise of rebirth. In her final entry, D'Aquino also employs the topos of rebirth, refracted through a Dantean lens congenial with her identity as a poet.[11] Concluding with a moment of personal significance, her long-awaited return to Naples on February 28, 1945, D'Aquino marks the start of "a new cycle of my existence" that she punctuates with the opening words of Dante's autobiography, "INCIPIT VITA NOVA" (Here begins a new life).[12] Even as the conclusions appear to resolve the initial uncertainties, their gendered redemption foregrounds the tensions of World War II Italy, particularly when the universal suffering experienced by the feminized nation is juxtaposed with specific trauma. Origo represents the depths of Italy's suffering through the women raped by their supposed liberators; D'Aquino creates parallels between herself and Italy, both mutilated by their tremendous loss.

These diaries add a further dimension to our understanding of the Allied-Italian encounter—and, indeed, the gendering of redemption—but while the English-language texts, *Inside Rome with the Germans* and *War in Val d'Orcia*, have received some attention, *Quel giorno trent'anni fa* is virtually unknown.[13] Published in 1975, the story of a widowed aristocrat in southern Italy never gained the attention afforded to oral and written texts about women's contributions to the *Resistenza* in the north that the Italian feminist movement brought to light in the same years.[14] A carefully crafted piece of literature and an invaluable historical artifact, D'Aquino's diary also creates a fruitful dynamic with Norman Lewis's *Naples '44*: set in the same geographical region and published in the same years, both diaries claim to have been written without the benefit of hindsight or (much) editing.[15] However, D'Aquino's diary signals its central concern with personal and collective memory, and their intersections. In referring to "that day thirty years ago," D'Aquino positions her intimate reflections within the collective. The transformative experience of the individual who lives through the occupation is the narrative thread of D'Aquino's diary, which, like Lewis's, is a conversion narrative. However, whereas Lewis establishes distance from, and authority over, the events he describes, D'Aquino inscribes herself within them: through the hellish experience, she becomes a contemporary Dante who uses the distance between the present-day "poet" she has become and the past "pilgrim" that she was, to renegotiate her relationship to the nation.

In so doing, D'Aquino relies on conventionally gendered rhetoric, comparing herself to "the ground that received [her husband's] seed to be fertilized," and puritanically chastening Italian women whose sexual mores are not as laudable as her own.[16] Nonetheless, within cultural representations of the Allied-Italian encounter, dominated by male voices, D'Aquino is singular. Foregrounding the strength of her intellect, her literary capacity, and her body's materiality, she offers a different paradigm for redemption: Her spiritual death and rebirth are in dialogue with—not reducible to—the nation's.[17] Creating a Dantean conversion narrative, D'Aquino carves an unorthodox space for herself. She is her diary's pilgrim, who finds herself at the edge of an abyss and lives to tell the tale. At the same time, she is (quiet literally) a poet, in search of the redemption of her literary value that she claims has lied dormant since becoming a wife and mother. As poet, she fashions herself as allegory, revising the trope of Italy-as-whore as she positions herself as faithful wife and steadfast helmsman.

Revising Redemption in Maria Luisa D'Aquino's *Quel giorno trent'anni fa*

September 8, 1943. In the small town of San Lorenzello where she and her five children have sought refuge from the bombings that are devastating Naples, Maria Luisa D'Aquino starts her diary in opposition to the Allies' rhetoric: "Is it a date of liberation? I don't think so."[18] In the 539 days that follow, D'Aquino dedicates three hundred pages to the results of this "decisive turning point."[19] A loyal monarchist, she refutes the promise of American redemption at every opportunity: "It is for fools to have faith in what is only American propaganda. Some evenings ago, in fact, an American journalist said that in Southern Italy one already can see the signs of rebirth. Nothing could be more false."[20] By the time D'Aquino returns to Naples in late 1944, her negative feelings about the "liberators" have only intensified; at the sight of Umberto's old barracks her heart falls:

> In place of our tricolor, the American flag waved arrogantly. And I said in revulsion: "Not here too!"—Because the face of Naples has changed: it is a beautiful devastated city and one has the impression that it is mostly inhabited by people in uniform. Races from every country rub elbows in the crowded city, giving it the feel of a colony. The Allies say that they are our friends, and one must accept, "for better or for worse" their officiousness. But when one has lost a war, as we have, how can one smile at our victors, at those who bombed our cities, even if today they are our liberators?
>
> I close my eyes so as not to see, and look inside myself: these are the streets that I walked on Umberto's arm. What pain! Sometimes I walk as if in a trance. There's the Vomero, where we had our lovers' hideaway.[21]

Consonant with this turn inward, D'Aquino does not conclude with another event of (inter)national significance but instead, the start of her personal *vita nova*. However, as we will see, this final disavowal of politics results in an unorthodox dynamic between diarist and country as several redemptions intertwine to create the diary's upward trajectory from the "fall" of the nation to her personal rebirth.

As the protagonist of this harrowing tale, D'Aquino-pilgrim faces all-consuming economic concerns. She must redeem her few remaining items of value for the largest possible quantity of food in an ever-inflating black market: "I gave away my sheet for a thousand lire and ten kilos of bread. That way I can cope with daily life for a while."[22] This preoccupation rhetorically permeates her reflections on her personal situation, in the metaphor of her year as a ledger with a "disastrous" balance.[23] However, in spite of her obvious financial difficulties, signs of her privilege surface with references to the household staff she employs, the powerful figures she contacts for financial assistance, and the valuables she holds onto until the very last moment.[24] Sympathy for D'Aquino's "via crucis"[25] is further tempered by her disparaging representation of American and colonial soldiers as sex-crazed drunks:

> This evening the spectacle of the drunken American soldiery was nauseating. Tonight inebriated soldiers knocked on every door on the street in search of women. This is a rather clean place and there exist no sellers of love. At a late hour, a native from the colored troops regiment, whose drunkenness led to desire, broke down a door looking to enter a house, but luckily he was taken away in time by the patrol.[26]

Moreover, her hostile attitude toward foreigners extends to Italian peasants whom she views as belonging to an inferior race:

> This morning a woman from here came, a certain Carmela with a confusing nickname. I always look at her with a certain repugnance: perhaps because I insist she plays the part of the Vampire because of her contraband trade. Her physiognomy differs from that of our race: her elongated eyes and dull gaze make her look like a Mongol. She always has a smile on her bloodless lips that makes you want to slap it into a grimace, once you realize how devious she is.[27]

D'Aquino emerges from these daily struggles with the contradictions one might expect in such a three-dimensional portrayal. Although judgmental about overt displays of femininity from other women, she is in touch with her own sexuality and femininity; she discusses her desire to make love to her husband, relays her erotic dreams, recalls her pregnancies and childbirth experiences, reflects on the joys and challenges of breastfeeding and weaning, and celebrates her menstrual cycle: "Blood. Vivid, warm blood gushing from my most secret depths. The more it flows, the more it reveals to you the force of your healthy, female nature."[28] Yet because she must "substitute He who took care of everything," she embraces conventionally masculine roles, performing grueling physical labor, conducting high-level financial negotiations and offering detailed analyses of the unfolding political events.[29] By no means discordant, her hybrid identity manifests itself in simple descriptions that bring together her identity as mother and citizen: "While I nursed, I listened to the radio."[30] Although she claims to be like most women in her lack of a political conscience and feels one burgeoning only at the end of the diary, her detailed analyses of unfolding events, starting from the first entry, suggest otherwise.[31]

Such dismissive self-characterizations also mark her commentary on the diary she is writing. At the start, D'Aquino claims to have mental space only to write about the day's events, yet her depiction as a humble scribe proves a mere posture.[32] As she gazes backward to reflect on her milestones as wife and mother, she also sketches her early years as a poet (a career interrupted by all those gendered milestones), and wrestles with her present identity as a diarist who desires to remember and to forget. She remarks with sadness when she is unable to keep up her daily writing practice, yet as the diary preserves a melancholy array of anniversaries, she laments: "Why did men invent the calendar? If it didn't exist, today I would not remember that, one year ago, Umberto was here for the last time."[33] However, even as she longs for "the secret of some magic potion to make me forget everything around me," the diary's very existence attests to the fact that for her, the power of written memory has triumphed over the pull of oblivion, a power connected to her deep-seated identity as a poet.[34] As she opens space for her own story within the chronicle of war, she recounts formative encounters with her "artistic godfather," Roberto Bracco, and returns to writing poetry for the first time in years.[35] Later, she insists on the central place writing holds in her life, in her account of the household drama that ensues when her servant quits without warning:

> I realized that, sometimes, when my maid found me writing or reading she looked at me askance, deeming me an idler.... Despite my former serving girl's opinions, I cannot only think of the cleaning, the cooking, the children; I also need to do all those things that provoked disdain in her: to read a book, to take up the pen, to laze in bed, letting my mind occupied with other thoughts wander.[36]

As D'Aquino affirms her right to nurture her creative life, her elitism bubbles over, as she quotes Hegel and attributes her maid's disapproval to her "inferior condition."[37] Here, then, without detracting from D'Aquino's accomplishment, the conditions that made such writing possible should not be overlooked. It is no accident that the women able to record and publish their stories were affluent, like D'Aquino and Origo, or affiliated with the church, like Mother Mary Saint Luke.

D'Aquino's concerns with the power of written memory, together with her emphasis on her literary identity, underscore her role as creator of a carefully crafted text—in spite of her prefatory claim to have written spontaneously without regard for form or style.[38] As the diary enters its second year, she notes that the calendar creates intratextual links between entries, providing a more intentional structure than the passing of days. As she insists that she has not moved beyond the tragedy of her husband's death, she exerts a backward pull against the forward march of time, creating a dialectical narrative movement not unlike John Freccero's description of Dante's *terza rima*: "The spring will return and I will needlessly feel it in the accelerated flow of my blood. And the memories of love will come back to me again, like after a shipwreck the debris of a vessel float to the surface."[39] Imagining the future in which her past will resurface like shipwrecked debris, she creates further intratextual connections through the nautical imagery, pulling the reader back to the start of the diary where she affirms that thanks to her struggles, "I feel stronger: it is certainly my age, and the knowledge of the helmsman who steers the course of his ship and brings the many lives entrusted to him to port."[40] As she compares herself to a steady helmsman, D'Aquino echoes Dante's purgatorial invective with which *Allied Encounters* begins: "Ah, slavish Italy, dwelling of grief, ship without a pilot in a great storm, not a ruler of provinces, but a whore!"[41] In cementing an allegorical connection between herself as "mutilated" widow and the "mutilated" nation, she affirms the role as helmsman and concomitantly staves off any critique of her moral rectitude that might characterize her as fallen: She defends herself against gossip when she begins to receive regular visits from "Captain Bob," a Scottish officer who brings sustenance for her family and emotional support for her, and lashes out against a friend who chooses to date Allied officers.[42] D'Aquino's rebirth is not to be located in a new marriage but in negotiating her identity as faithful wife, steadfast helmsman—and poet.

D'Aquino frames her own narrative and Italy's in terms of the gendered, redemptive language explored throughout *Allied Encounters*. However, if Italy as faithful wife seems little more than a reversal of Italy as whore, D'Aquino's text does not let stand a disembodied figure but addresses the physicality of her female subjectivity. If she is Italy, she is also a subject who experiences sexual pleasure, menstruates, bears the weight of pregnancy, the pain of labor, the challenges of breastfeeding, and the ambivalence of weaning. At the same time as she foregrounds her female subjectivity, she also forges a hybrid identity in the day-to-day descriptions of her life where she claims to have "abolished her femininity."[43] Here, as she embraces the role of helmsman, we might remember that Dante's helmsman was Beatrice.

D'Aquino does not let herself be subsumed by her symbolic relationship to Italy, as she demonstrates in her treatment of September 8. Like diarists such as Origo, Mother Mary Saint Luke and Norman Lewis, D'Aquino foregrounds the importance of September 8, 1943, but surprisingly, on September 8, 1944, she chooses not to reflect on this national anniversary. In her September 7 entry, she starts with a reflection on the power of the calendar to preserve her *personal* memories: "If I didn't look at the calendar, I wouldn't remember many dates, but nor would I relive my past in its every detail."⁴⁴ Describing a night out in Naples, she ends the entry with a titillating promise: "It was also the eve of my first experience of love."⁴⁵ While her family interprets this event as D'Aquino's fall, she details the transcendent physical and emotional gratification of her first sexual encounter: "In vain Umberto tried to calm my indomitable trembling. It stopped only after I had known love completely, only to become a convulsive weeping that confounded Umberto, leading him to mistakenly believe that he had hurt or offended me, and that made him drop to his knees at my feet to ask, crying, for my absurd forgiveness for having made me happy."⁴⁶ Comparing herself to Eve in the garden, she refuses any guilt by insisting on the private nature of her decision. D'Aquino's September 8 was an event that, to the outside world, seemed like a sin that must be redeemed through marriage; instead, she makes it "a goal of my life as a woman."⁴⁷ In dislocating the nation's tragic September 8 and privileging her own happy ending, D'Aquino uses the gendered, sexualized terms of this formulation to revise national and private events. Just as people wrongly saw her September 8 as a fall, so too do they see Italy's, a charge she answers with her husband's post-armistice sacrifice.

In forging this intersection between the national September 8 and the personal September 8, D'Aquino underscores its conventional terms but also her unique insight into both, whether she is belittling the locals for their misinterpretation of "the historic announcement that made so many hearts rejoice and that put a foreboding anxiety in mine" or gently teasing her husband when interprets her pleasure as pain.⁴⁸ Indeed, overshadowed by the "bomb" of the armistice or the "trembling" of the orgasm, these quiet commentaries reveal D'Aquino's double game: If she is to be read as the allegory of the nation, it is because she, herself, is writing it. She may be Beatrice, the stern admiral of her family's ship, but she is also the pilgrim who finds her way, which allows her to become the poet who writes the story.

In the final pages, the Dantean resonances intensify. In June 1944 she diagnoses her mourning as a fatal illness: "many believe I am recovering and don't realize that I am sick enough to die."⁴⁹ By August, however, she refers to herself as a survivor: "I am like a convalescent who overcame a crisis that seemingly should have destroyed her."⁵⁰ Then, two months later, she reflects upon rereading her entry from the year prior when she first learned of Umberto's death, "I feel as though I walked along the edge of an abyss, unconscious like a sleepwalker, without falling in."⁵¹ As D'Aquino recognizes her transformative journey over the year of mourning, she underscores that it is thanks to her ability to reread her diary that she is able to gauge the distance she has traveled. Using this tragic experience as a source of authority, she claims it allows her to see, "under a light of truth and from the top of a summit that not all can reach, if not through an ordeal such as mine."[52]

In her affirmation of the privileged perspective afforded by her suffering (acquiring christological resonances in the word "*calvario*," ordeal), D'Aquino depicts herself as the pilgrim-turned poet. Simultaneously, she embraces the role of author, past, present, and future: as wartime diarist, she looks back to her development as poet and signals ahead to the journalist she was to become during the thirty years in which her diary went unpublished.[53] Thus, when she concludes with a *vita nova*, her Dantean language at once positions her as part of an Italian literary tradition and provides a reminder of how that tradition has long depended on gendered, sexualized rhetoric that relegates women to symbols of a literary and civic tradition. Her personal redemption, then, is embodied by this singular diary; indeed, even as she claims that the premarital consummation of her relationship with Umberto represents a point of arrival in terms of her identity as woman, the diary's final pages emphasize that her transformation into wife and mother have left her striving toward one more conquest: "I need to regain my individual personality, to become a woman with a new place to conquer in the world. Maybe the same one that I aspired to become if destiny hadn't changed my name, making me take on the one that my children would have and that led me to give up, in part, that dream of art I harbored during my unquiet adolescent years."[54] Today, it is not so much ironic as predictable that D'Aquino's place in history wedges her between her saintly ancestor Tomaso, and her successful journalist sons. However, *Quel giorno trent'anni fa* should earn itself a place in the cultural corpus of World War II Italy that *Allied Encounters* seeks to broaden: Both the helmsman of her home and of her text, D'Aquino makes Italy a woman who bleeds, lactates, orgasms, navigates, reads, remembers, and writes.

Acknowledgments

I could not have undertaken this project without having learned, in and out of the classroom at the University of California, Berkeley: from Barbara Spackman, whose model of brilliant, witty, and critical scholarship serves as an ideal, every time I sit down to read or write; from Albert Ascoli, whose warm mentorship provides a sure point of reference for which I will always be grateful; and from Mia Fuller, whose confident vision of what it means to be an interdisciplinary scholar has long been my touchstone. Timothy Hampton, Ramona Naddaff, and Naomi Seidman modeled a diversity of scholarly approaches and encouraged me to develop my own. At Columbia University, Teodolinda Barolini guided me through my first close reading in Italian with a passion and a precision that made it feel inevitable that I set off on this journey.

From her first serendipitous email inviting me to present on a panel to the present day, Ruth Glynn has been an essential interlocutor of uncommon insight and generosity. David Ellwood, Maggie Fritz-Morkin, Danielle Hipkins, Regina Longo, Giorgio Mariani, and Francesca Parmeggiani generously offered feedback on early drafts, and Jessica Tanner not only gave patient counsel but also the book's subtitle. Charles Leavitt IV has been a wonderful colleague with whom to explore the seemingly boundless cultural production of the Allied occupation. Roberto Dainotto, Ellen Welch, and Esther Gabarra unfailingly gave insight, intellectual support, and advice on matters large and small, and Rebecca Falkoff always had the right words to help me keep going. I owe Erin Bauer a debt of gratitude for her encouraging response to (and late-night editing of) the embryonic version of this research. So, too, do I thank the undergraduate and graduate students, and my Graduate Research Consultant, Giuliano Migliori, whose spirited debate on these texts continuously reaffirmed their contemporary resonance.

At Fordham University Press, I thank my editors Kurt Piehler, Frederic Nachbaur, and Will Cerbone for including my manuscript in this series and for their skilled handling of the editorial process from start to finish. Thanks to managing editor Eric Newman and manuscript editor Gregory

McNamee, who were wonderful resources. I am grateful to feedback from anonymous peer reviewers whose comments helped me hone my argument. My thanks to the editors and anonymous peer reviewers at *Italian Studies* and *California Italian Studies* for their reports on articles about Luciana Peverelli's *Sposare lo straniero* and Curzio Malaparte's *La pelle,* which served as the seeds for Chapters 3 and 5. Jamie Richards was an invaluable help in editing my translations of Peverelli's novels and Maria D'Aquino's diary. Her eye for detail, command of language and creativity make her an exemplary translator and an unparalleled collaborator.

I am grateful to the Institute for the Arts and Humanities at the University of North Carolina, Chapel Hill, for a fellowship that helped with the completion of this book. Our leader, Michele Berger, was steadfast in her mentorship, and our cohort, insightful and encouraging: Claude Clegg, Banu Gokariksel, Corey Johnson, Betsy Olson, Charles Price, and Matt Taylor. A thank you to the members of the summer faculty writing groups organized by the Center for Faculty Excellence who helped me advance the project. The Office of Research Development generously contributed funds to the cost of publication.

The day-to-day work of writing would never have gotten done without the patient counsel, generous encouragement, and warm presence of colleagues who make North Carolina feel like home: Michele Berger, Cristina Carrasco, Amy Chambless, Maggie Fritz-Morkin, Heather Knorr, Lilly Nguyen, Susan Page, Carolina Sá Carvalho, Jessica Tanner, Ariana Vigil, and Ellen Welch. In Berkeley, I have been luckily for relationships that began in the Dwinelle Hall seminar room and spread beyond it: Chris Atwood, Rebecca Falkoff, Aileen Feng, Janaya Lasker-Ferretti, Anthony Martire, Emily Rabiner, and Rhiannon Welch.

I am infinitely rich thanks to lifelong friends spread far and wide: Shelley Barandes, Erin Bauer, Emanuele Belfiore, Cristiano Cardinali, Michele Gambini, Gabriele Gardenale, Aurora Meneghello, Chiara Nava, Lando Pieragostini, Francesca Pieroni, Isabella Tombolini, and Silvia Veroli. In Chapel Hill, my extended family has saved the day on more than one occasion: Heather, Alba, Jeff, Vanessa, Karen, Fabio, Jenny, Brian, Esther, Pedro, Sam, and Irene. Infinite gratitude to Arianna di Florio, who at every crossroads pushed me onward with exactly the right emoji.

My deepest thanks go to my first language teacher, my mother, Gayle, and to my father, Carlos, who gave me a love of language, a curiosity for the foreign, and the freedom to let passion guide my studies. To Rachel, Michael, Sarah, Franca, Lamberto, Gregg, Carol, Max, Nat, Lily, and my extended family for their warmth, humor, and cooking. Gratitude and love seem like small words to give to Lorenzo, who always asks to share my books; to Dylan, who was taking shape at the same time as this project; and to Gianluca, who generously gave me support from start to finish. Beginning and ending every day with three such exquisite people has made these years infinitely sweet. And although I only picked up his beloved *Catch-22* after he was gone, this book is for Aaron and for Sylvia, my grandparents, my first and most enthusiastic readers, who kept my library plentifully stocked.

Notes

Preface

1. On the contact zone, see Mary Louise Pratt, *Imperial Eyes*. Ruth Glynn adopts this terminology in the context of Allied occupied Naples in "Naples and the Nation," 6.
2. Millicent Marcus, "Miss Mondina, Miss Sirena, Miss Farina," 297. See also Marcus, "The Italian Body Politic Is a Woman."
3. Teodolinda Barolini, *The Undivine Comedy*, 16.
4. Shoshana Felman, *What Does a Woman Want?* 26.

Introduction

1. On the history of Italy of this period, see David Ellwood, *Italy*.
2. On the multifaceted significance of the armistice, see Elena Agarossi, *A Nation Collapses*.
3. *New York Times*, "Americans in First."
4. Herbert L. Matthews, "Naples Goes Mad with Joy"; on diverse responses to the Allies' arrival, see Paola Gambarota, "The Fall of Naples."
5. *New York Times*, "The Victory of Rome."
6. Roy Palmer Domenico, *Italian Fascists on Trial*, 49.
7. Ellwood, "Liberazione/occupazione," 15. While I refer to the liberation of Naples and Rome as the expulsion of the Germans in October 1943 and June 1944, when referring to the months that followed, I put "liberation" in quotation marks in recognition of the term's interdependence with occupation (a belief generally shared by the texts I analyze).
8. David Ellwood, *The Shock of America*, 281.
9. Susan L. Carruthers, *The Good Occupation*.
10. *New York Times*, "The Victory of Rome."
11. Jonathan Vincent, "America e Italia," 25.
12. Linda Munk, *The Devil's Mousetrap*, 4–5.
13. Carole Emberton, *Beyond Redemption*, 3.
14. David M. Ward, *Antifascisms*, 103.
15. Sam B. Girgus, *Levinas and the Cinema of Redemption*, 33.
16. Franco Baldasso, "Against Redemption," 24.
17. *New York Times*, "Italy's Liberation Is Acclaimed Here."

18. Ellwood, *Italy*, 219.
19. Andrew Buchanan, "Good Morning, Pupil!" 219.
20. Emberton, *Beyond Redemption*, 3–4.
21. On such a distinction in Italian partisan narratives, see Robert S. C. Gordon, "The Italian War," 130.
22. Baldasso, "Against Redemption," 27.
23. Herbert L. Matthews, "Italy Seeks to Cut All Fascist Ties"; "Italians Fought Germans Fiercely."
24. *New York Times*, "The Great Reversal." A similar assertion can be found in an October 15, 1943, memo from General Taylor: "By maintaining a vigorous resistance to the German forces, the Italian Nation, through its armed forces and its civilian population, may hasten the redemption of Italy," as cited in Harry L. Coles and Albert K. Weinberg, *Civil Affairs*, 246.
25. *New York Times*, "The Great Reversal," 20.
26. "State Department Is Inclined to End Harsh Armistice Regime," as cited in Coles and Weinberg, *Civil Affairs*, 497.
27. Ruth Glynn, "Naples and the Nation," 2.
28. Gordon, "The Italian War," 130. For a discussion of the same, see Baldasso, "Against Redemption," 27–28. On the topos of self-sacrifice, see Rosaria Forlenza, "Sacrificial Memory and Political Legitimacy in Postwar Italy." On the exclusion of the South from this redemptive postwar narrative, see Glynn, "Naples and the Nation."
29. Anne McClintock, "Family Feuds," 62.
30. Vernadette Gonzalez, *Securing Paradise*, 7.
31. "Ahi serva Italia, di dolore ostello,/nave sanza nocchiere in gran tempesta,/non donna di province, ma bordello!" Dante Alighieri, *Purgatorio*, 96–97.
32. Millicent Marcus, "The Italian Body Politic Is a Woman." On the gendering of Italy in Anglo-American travel writing, see Robert Viscusi, "The Englishman in Italy"; James Buzard, "A Continent of Pictures"; Chloe Chard, "Grand and Ghostly Tours." On the feminization of Italians in American culture in the lead-up to the war through the early postwar period, see Buchanan, "Good Morning, Pupil!" In *Life Magazine* in the early postwar period, see Ilaria Serra, "Italy: America's War Bride."
33. On the construction of Italy's "backwardness," see John Agnew, "The Myth of Backward Italy in Modern Europe." On the romantic/nativist visions of Italy in America, see John P. Diggins, *Mussolini and Fascism*.
34. Marcus, "Miss Mondina, Miss Sirena, Miss Farina," 297.
35. John Russo, "The Unbroken Charm," 127.
36. Ibid., 126.
37. Ellwood, "The American Challenge in Uniform," 5.
38. On the genealogy of Italian national character as a negative, feminized formulation, produced within and outside Italy's borders, see Silvana Patriarca, *Italian Vices*.

39. The black market is generally recognized today as the cause of prostitution. See Ellwood, "Liberazione/occupazione."

40. Thomas H. Sternberg et al., *Preventative Medicine in World War II*, 216–217.

41. Ibid., 218 (emphasis mine).

42. Eric Sevareid, *Not so Wild a Dream*, 421–422.

43. For a defense of the GIs' "normal" preoccupation with sex in World War II Europe, see Peter Schrijvers, *The Crash of Ruin*, 53–54. For a critique of this double standard between European women and GIs, see Mary Louise Roberts, *What Soldiers Do*; Cynthia Enloe, *Maneuvers*, 63. Such logic has been identified within a domestic, American context in John Parascandola, "Quarantining Women," 436.

44. Patriarca, *Italian Vices*.

45. Enloe, *Maneuvers*, 63. For a description of the unhygienic, chaotic, retrograde, humiliating treatment available to the Italian women, see Sergio Lambiase and Gian Battista Nazzaro, *L'odore della guerra*, 113. For the perspective of the women in one of these Roman hospitals, see Anna Garofalo, *L'italiana in Italia*, 67–68. For a fictionalization of a soldier's hellish yet curative experience getting penicillin, see John Horne Burns, *The Gallery*, 269–297.

46. Ellwood, "The American Challenge in Uniform," 6.

47. David Forgacs, "Fascism and Anti-Fascism Reviewed," 191–192.

48. Moshe Gershovich, "Collaboration and 'Pacification'"; "Memory and Representation of War and Violence"; Driss Magraoui, "Moroccan Colonial Soldiers" and "The Goumiers in the Second World War."

49. On the racialization of southern Italian immigrants in the United States, see Shelleen Greene, *Equivocal Subjects*, 174–175.

50. Emberton, *Beyond Redemption*, 3.

51. Carruthers, "Produce More Joppolos," 1097.

52. *A Guide to Occupation of Enemy Territory*, 10.

53. On "destination Italy," see Stephanie Hom, *The Beautiful Country*.

54. On the popularity of the feminized Italian male in the United States, see Jacqueline Reich, *Beyond the Latin Lover*.

55. This book is neither historically exhaustive nor thematically bound. Although most of these texts have become emblems of the Allied Italian encounter, canonicity is not my interest in and of itself. Most notably, I do not analyze John Hersey's *A Bell for Adano* (1944), set in occupied Sicily, a text of profound cultural importance whose negligible treatment of the sexual aspect of the encounter—as Carruthers remarks in her definitive reading—puts it outside my thematic focus. Carruthers, "Produce More Joppolos." Another iconic text from this period, Eduardo De Filippo's play *Napoli milionaria!* (1945), represents "the Allied occupation and its effects as a form of moral malady, closely associated with the emasculation or feminization of Italian society," but "disregard[s]" the intercultural encounter and "interrogate[s] instead the behavior and responsibility of ordinary Neapolitans." Glynn, "Naples and the Nation," 15. Other texts that fit historically and thematically but fall outside my theoretical concerns include

Scottish writer Eric Linklater's *Private Angelo* (1946), a satirical novel set across Italy (briefly discussed in Chapter 5) and the novel *Casualty* (1946) by American writer Robert Lowry.

56. To mention only a scant few novels: Italian texts like *Mille tradimenti* (1957; *A Thousand Betrayals*) by Ugo Pirro, a collaborator of Rossellini's and an important presence in the Italian film industry; British texts like Alexander Barons's *There's No Home* (1950), set in Sicily, or Norman Lewis's own novel *Within the Labyrinth* (1950), which uses much of the same material as *Naples '44*; American classics like *The Man in the Gray Flannel Suit* (1955) by Sloan Wilson, *Catch-22* (1961) by Joseph Heller, or the now-forgotten but once popular *Secret of Santa Vittoria* (1966) by Robert Crichton, all of which became films.

57. Ellwood, "You Too Can Be Like Us."

58. Gordon, *The Holocaust in Italian Culture,* 87.

59. Catharine Edwards, *Roman Presences,* 1.

60. Forgacs, *Rome Open City*; Michael P. Rogin, "Mourning, Melancholia, and the Popular Front"; Philip Cooke, *The Legacy of the Italian Resistance*; Lara Pucci, "Shooting Corpses"; Giuliana Minghelli, *Landscape and Memory in Post-Fascist Italian Film.*

61. Anna Banti, "Storia e ragioni del 'romanzo rosa.'" On Banti, see Robbin Pickering-Iazzi, *Politics of the Visible,* chap. 3.

62. Ruth Ben-Ghiat, "Fascism, Writing, and Memory."

63. Here I draw on Danielle Hipkins's premise in *Italy's Other Women* whereby "the female prostitute is particularly important to Italian national cinema as a 'borderline identity' used to establish, but also to destabilize, the hegemony of respectable femininities, almost entirely premised as they are on a certain kind of sexual behavior," 10.

64. Maria Pia Pozzato, *Il romanzo rosa,* 26–29.

65. Stefania Lucamante, *Forging Shoah Memories,* 119.

66. Alfred Hayes's *All Thy Conquests* refers to relationships between "negroes" and prostitutes, 38. Luciana Peverelli's *Sposare lo straniero* refers to an interracial marriage between an Italian woman and a "negro" millionaire, 349. In Roberto Rossellini's *Paisà*, the interracial encounter takes place in Naples and plays out within the confines of a nonsexual relationship between an African American military policeman and a Neapolitan boy.

67. In *All Thy Conquests*, the least sympathetic character is a morally bankrupt, bisexual Marchese. As Derek Duncan argues, in early postwar Italian cinema, "homosexual acts form a panoply of degenerate activities that indict a morally bankrupt society." "The Queerness of Italian Cinema," 473.

68. Glynn, "Naples and the Nation," 2.

69. Lambiase and Nazzaro, *L'odore della guerra,* 79.

70. Curzio Malaparte, *The Skin,* 53; "gridando in cento strane, sconosciute favelle." *La pelle,* 47.

71. "Razze di tutti i paesi si danno gomito ... dandole l'aspetto di un paese

coloniale." Maria Luisa D'Aquino, *Quel giorno trent'anni fa*, 295–296 (translation mine).

72. On the contact zone, see Mary Louise Pratt, *Imperial Eyes*; in the context of Allied-occupied Naples, see Glynn, "Naples and the Nation," 6.

73. My understanding of the queer as linked to the trans- of transnational comes from Emma Bond, "Towards a Trans-National Turn in Italian Studies?"

74. John Aldridge, "For Novelist John Horne Burns, War Was Hell—and Much More," 5.

75. Raffaele La Capria compares the "honest" writer of *The Gallery* to the "excessive" writer of *La pelle*. *Ultimi viaggi nell'Italia perduta*, 42.

76. John Gatt-Rutter, "Liberation and Literature," 256.

77. Norman Lewis, *Naples '44*, 131.

78. Gatt-Rutter, "Liberation and Literature," 256.

79. John Freccero, *Dante*, 104, as cited in Teodolinda Barolini, *The Undivine Comedy*, 16–17.

80. La Capria, *Ultimi viaggi nell'Italia perduta*, 40 (translation mine).

81. Glynn, "Naples and the Nation," 13.

1. Redeeming Destination Italy: A Guide to the Occupation of Enemy Territory

1. *A Guide to Occupation of Enemy Territory*, 1.

2. Italy's age-old superlative status is attested by the first English-language edition of the seminal *Baedeker* guide: "From the earliest ages down to the present time Italy has ever exercised a powerful influence on the denizens of more northern lands, and a journey thither has often been the fondly cherished wish of many an aspiring traveller," Karl Baedeker, *Italy*, xi.

3. The definition of "destination Italy" comes from Stephanie Hom, *The Beautiful Country*. On the Allies' perceptions of the Italians in the lead-up to war, see Ilaria Favretto and Oliviero Bergamini, "Temperamentally Unwarlike," 114.

4. *A Guide to Occupation of Enemy Territory*, 29, 6.

5. Ibid., 26.

6. Favretto and Bergamini, "Temperamentally Unwarlike," 16.

7. Max Corvo, *OSS in Italy*, 65; Peter Tompkins, *A Spy in Rome*, 20.

8. As with most of the military pamphlets, the *GOETI*'s authorship is unattributed. Marshall is listed as the author of "*Guide to Occupation of Enemy Territory* and other official manuals," in *Who Knows, and What, among Authorities, Experts and the Specially Informed*, 434; Marshall's memoir has no specific reference to the pamphlet's title. S. L. Samuel Lyman Atwood Marshall, *Bringing Up the Rear*, 50.

9. John Mason Brown, *To All Hands*, 91.

10. Ibid., 95. *The Soldier's Guide to Sicily*'s plethora of offensive stereotypes about Sicilians earned it a scathing condemnation from Sicilian writer Leonardo Sciascia (who mistakenly attributes it to the Americans) in the introduction to a recent Italian translation, *Guida del soldato in Sicilia*, 2013.

Notes to pages 18–20

11. Ray Ward, *With the Argylls*, 200.

12. *A Guide to Occupation of Enemy Territory*, 33–34.

13. On the construction of Italy's "backwardness," see John Agnew, "The Myth of Backward Italy in Modern Europe."

14. Emma Bond, "Towards a Trans-National Turn in Italian Studies?" 421; on this point, Bond cites Roberto Dainotto, *Europe (in Theory)*.

15. John Russo, "The Unbroken Charm."

16. This tension is perhaps attributable to the *GOETI*'s coauthorship between the Civil Affairs Division (CAD) and the SSD. The CAD had the mission "to transform the inhabitants of liberated countries into fighting allies," George C. Marshall, *Biennial Reports of the Chief of Staff of the United States Army to the Secretary of War*, 187. Such efforts are traceable to lines in the *GOETI* that encourage troops to help "convert enemies into friends" and to counteract twenty years of antidemocratic fascist propaganda by behaving according to the principles of the "Four Freedoms"—printed, legend had it, on the Allies' military banknotes. *A Guide to Occupation of Enemy Territory*, 31, 2. On the banknote legend, see David Ellwood, *The Shock of America*, 278. In contrast to this forward-looking mission, the coauthoring SSD had a goal of "maintaining the mental and physical stamina of their troops for combat," which included helping them enjoy Italy's touristic patrimony through the provision of "pocket guides to foreign countries," "Special Service Division," 1, 5.

17. Andrew Buchanan, "I Felt Like a Tourist instead of a Soldier," 595.

18. Vernadette Gonzalez, *Securing Paradise*, 7. The illusion of the war/travel opposition has been explored by scholars of tourism and travel in dialogue with postcolonial theory; for instance, James Buzard recognizes that Mary Louise Pratt's *Imperial Eyes* makes it imperative to problematize the notion of "travel as a great peacemaker." "What Isn't Travel," 56.

19. Gonzalez, *Securing Paradise*, 7. Here, Gonzalez makes use of McClintock's notion of "porno-tropics." Anne McClintock, *Imperial Leather*, 21–24.

20. Hom, *The Beautiful Country*, 53.

21. The redemption of "fallen" Italy has been imagined as a revirilization in the procolonialist discourses of the liberal and fascist states. For the relationship between attempts to "virilize" Italy and colonialism, see Silvana Patriarca, *Italian Vices*, esp. 114 and 134. Buzard notes that Henry James gives Italy a rhetorical sex change in describing its modernization, post-Risorgimento. *The Beaten Track*, 133.

22. *A Guide to Occupation of Enemy Territory*, 10. On the hypocritical attitudes toward prostitution in World War II Europe, see Cynthia Enloe, *Maneuvers*.

23. *A Guide to Occupation of Enemy Territory*, 25.

24. Kaeten Mistry, *The United States, Italy and the Origins of Cold War*. Published in 1952 with minor revisions in 1954 and 1956, the *PGI* was completely revised in terms of the text and illustrations in 1964 and 1981, with more minor revisions in 1987. Military guides to other countries receive similar overhauls at roughly the same time, suggesting regular State Department updates.

25. Horn, *The Beautiful Country*, 44. On the conventional guidebook's predilection for "Culture" (monuments, museums etc.) over "culture" (signs of daily life), naturalized by guides such as Baedeker's, see Buzard, "A Continent of Pictures," 31.

26. *A Guide to Occupation of Enemy Territory*, 37.

27. Ibid., 39, 37–38.

28. Ibid., 15.

29. Ibid., 16.

30. "It is by no means impossible to travel through Italy without an acquaintance of Italian or French, but in this case the traveller cannot conveniently deviate from the ordinary track and is moreover invariably charged (alla Inglese) by hotel keepers and others, considerably in excess of the ordinary prices. . . . For those . . . who desire to confine their expenditure within the average limits a slight acquaintance with the language of the country is indispensable," Baedeker, *Italy*, xii.

31. On "winning" souvenirs, see *A Guide to Occupation of Enemy Territory*, 7–8. On avoiding purchase, see ibid., 15, 28. On deferring and limiting purchases, see ibid. 33, 16. In his memoir, a U.S. sonar operator recalls purchasing souvenirs in Sicily. His motivation? "An act of charity to the destitute." His concern? That behind the amateurish needlework of a needy woman might lurk the mafia. H. G. Jones, *The Sonarman's War*, 136.

32. *A Guide to Occupation of Enemy Territory*, 10.

33. Ibid.

34. Margaret Bourke-White, *They Called It Purple Heart Valley*, 104.

35. From an American perspective, see Favretto and Bergamini, "Temperamentally Unwarlike"; from a British perspective, see Owain Wright, "Orientalising Italy."

36. *Pocket Guide to France* (1944), 15.

37. Ibid., 19.

38. Ibid., 10.

39. *A Guide to Occupation of Enemy Territory*, 27.

40. Ibid., 12, 17.

41. Ibid., 31, 41.

42. The sum total of the Allied military policy toward the Italian language certainly cannot be reduced to the *GOETI*. The military also distributed English-to-Italian and Italian-to-English phrasebooks, and subsequent guidebooks contain brief language sections, as I will discuss. On the importance of military policy toward language in the context of war, see Hilary Footitt and Michael Kelly, *Languages at War*, 123.

43. *A Guide to Occupation of Enemy Territory*, 7, 12.

44. Ibid., 30.

45. Ibid., 41.

46. Ibid., 40.

47. *Pocket Guide to Germany* (1944), 12–16. On language policy in Germany, see Footitt and Kelly, *Languages at War*, 125.

48. *A Guide to Occupation of Enemy Territory*, 16, 2.

49. As cited in Merle Fainsod, "The Development of American Military Government Policy during World War II," 30. Fainsod underscores the inherent contradiction in such instructions.

50. A *New York Times* article announces the distribution of these guidebooks as preparation for the Salerno landings and summarizes their contents. Daniel de Luce, "Invasion Weapon Is 'Guide to Italy.'"

51. *A Guide to Occupation of Enemy Territory*, 1–2. *Soldier's Guide to Italy*, 6, emphasis mine. Another significant change for the *SGTI* is that it represents a collaboration between the British and U.S. armies; ibid., 5. Although the text of the *SGTI* is mostly original, one entire section is copied from the *GOETI* as well as a few from the British *Soldier's Guide to Sicily*, as I later discuss.

52. *Soldier's Guide to Italy*, 9.

53. Ibid. 9, 20.

54. Ibid., 24.

55. Ibid., 26.

56. Ibid., 20.

57. *A Guide to Occupation of Enemy Territory*, 32; *Soldier's Guide to Italy*, 9.

58. *Soldier's Guide to Italy*, 27.

59. Ibid., 28, 30. De Luce signals the touristic component in his summary of the *SGTI*, "Invasion Weapon Is 'Guide to Italy.'"

60. *Soldier's Guide to Italy*, 14; *A Guide to Occupation of Enemy Territory*, 16. I am grateful to Dominique Reardon, who made this observation during an undergraduate seminar presentation at the University of North Carolina, Chapel Hill.

61. *Soldier's Guide to Italy*, 19.

62. De Luce's summary of the *SGTI* confirms this perception with a subhead, "Discussion to be avoided." De Luce, "Invasion Weapon Is 'Guide to Italy.'"

63. *Soldier's Guide to Sicily*, 13.

64. Ibid., 12; *Soldier's Guide to Italy*, 31.

65. *Soldier's Guide to Sicily*, 2; for the historic conflation between Italy and its own south, see Hom, *The Beautiful Country*, 57.

66. *Soldier's Guide to Italy*, 13.

67. On the false, necessary opposition between respectable and dirty women in a military context, see Enloe, *Maneuvers*, 52.

68. *Soldier's Guide to Italy*, 13. No doubt with an eye toward the domestic audience, De Luce's summary avoids mention of the section on prostitution but emphasizes the precautions against "flirting" and concludes with this passage. "Invasion Weapon Is 'Guide to Italy.'"

69. *Soldier's Guide to Sicily*, 6.

70. *Pocket Guide to France* (1944), 19–20; *Pocket Guide to Germany* (1944),

12–16. The success of the official attempts at dissuading soldiers from marrying Italians is borne out in the statistics of Italian war brides; Susan Zeiger, *Entangling Alliances*, 102. Maria Porzio writes of attempts to discourage marriages between servicemen and Italian women who were seen as untrustworthy. *Arrivano gli alleati!* 59. On the Italian war bride in Italian literature, see Chapter 3.

71. Regina M. Longo, "Between Documentary and Neorealism," 12 n. 31.

72. *A Pocket Guide to Italy* (1981), 6.

73. John P. Diggins, *Mussolini and Fascism*, 6. David Forgacs challenges the concept of the Americanization of Italy in, "Americanisation."

74. David Vine, *Base Nation*.

75. While the wartime guidebooks were initially classified "restricted," the 1950s *Pocket Guide* series were, in fact, sold by the military to the public as conventional guidebooks, Herbert Mitgang, "G.I. Travel Guides Become 'Poor Man's Baedekers.'"

76. *A Pocket Guide to Italy* (1952), 1–2.

77. On the Allies' scapegoating of Mussolini in the postwar, see Patriarca, *Italian Vices*, 189; Favretto and Bergamini, "Tempermentally Unwarlike," 117.

78. *A Pocket Guide to Italy* (1952), 7–8.

79. Ibid., 8.

80. On American soldiers' perceptions of Italians as singers and poor soldiers, see Peter Schrijvers, *The Crash of Ruin*, 54 and 123. See also Buchanan, "Good Morning, Pupil!" 224.

81. The same images appear in the 1952 and 1956 editions of the *Pocket Guide to Germany*.

82. *A Pocket Guide to France* (1951), 35.

83. Ibid., 34.

84. *A Pocket Guide to Italy* (1952), 4.

85. *A Pocket Guide to Italy* (1964), 7–8. This reprises a sentiment from the *Soldier's Guide to Sicily*: "Morals are superficially very rigid, being based on the Catholic religion and Spanish etiquette of Bourbon times; they are, in actual fact, of a very low standard, particularly in the agricultural areas. . . . The Sicilian is still, however, well known for his extreme jealousy in so far as his womenfolk are concerned, and in a crisis still resorts to the dagger," 6.

86. *A Pocket Guide to Germany* (1965), 1.

87. *A Pocket Guide to Italy* (1964), 8. On the figure of the prostitute in postwar film as symptomatic of the shift of the societal roles of Italian women brought on by war, see Danielle Hipkins, "Francesca's Salvation or Damnation?"

88. *A Pocket Guide to Italy* (1964), 6, 10.

89. Ibid., 11.

90. Ibid., 1.

91. *A Pocket Guide to Greece* (1966), 10, 33.

92. *A Pocket Guide to Italy* (1964), 1.

93. Ibid., 28–29.

94. *A Pocket Guide to Italy* (1981), 7.

95. Ibid., 15–16. The 1946 referendum abolished the monarchy and established the republic (as the guide correctly states earlier on page 15), not the 1948 constitution.

96. *A Guide to Occupation of Enemy Territory*, 18.

97. *A Pocket Guide to Italy* (1981), 9.

98. Ibid., 6.

99. Vine, *Base Nation*, 234–235.

100. Contemporary military guides to most other nations have much more substantial tourist sections.

101. *A Pocket Guide to Italy* (1981), 38.

102. Ibid.

103. Loredana Polezzi, *Translating Travel*, 29.

104. *A Pocket Guide to Italy* (1981), 40.

105. Ellwood, "You Too Can Be Like Us."

106. *A Pocket Guide to Italy* (1952), 72; *A Pocket Guide to Italy* (1981), 28. The 1867 *Baedeker's* similarly cautions that not speaking Italian will impinge on one's "true enjoyment," more so than in any other country. *Italy from the Alps to Naples*, xiii.

107. *A Pocket Guide to Italy* (1964), 4; *A Pocket Guide to Italy* (1981), 28.

108. *A Pocket Guide to Italy* (1981), 27; *A Pocket Guide to Italy* (1952), 3.

109. Buzard, *The Beaten Track*, 134.

110. *A Pocket Guide to Italy* (1981), 40.

111. *A Pocket Guide to Italy* (1964), 14.

112. *Soldier's Guide to Italy*, 10; *A Pocket Guide to Italy* (1964), 1, 47; *A Pocket Guide to Italy* (1981), 41.

113. *A Pocket Guide to Italy* (1964), 46; *A Pocket Guide to Italy* (1981), 27. On the need to treat Italians with extra sensitivity, see ibid., 47. On the oversensitivity of the Italians during wartime, see *Soldier's Guide to Italy*, 20.

114. Favretto and Bergamini, "Temperamentally Unwarlike," 114.

115. Henry Stuart Hughes, *The United States and Italy*, 13.

116. Chloe Chard, "Grand and Ghostly Tours"; Hughes, *The United States and Italy*, 3; Diggins, *Mussolini and Fascism*, 6.

117. *A Guide to Occupation of Enemy Territory*, 41.

2. "Liberated" Rome beyond Redemption: Roberto Rossellini's *Paisà* and Alfred Hayes's *All Thy Conquests* and *The Girl on the Via Flaminia*

1. In an effort to protect Rome's treasures, Pope Pius XII petitioned the Allies and the Germans to keep the city "open," protecting it from becoming a battleground.

2. Alfred Hayes, *All Thy Conquests*, 247.

3. Millicent Marcus, "The Italian Body Politic Is a Woman," 336–337.

4. The two surviving versions produced by Hayes and Mann are accessible in Adriano Aprà, *Rosselliniana*.

5. On early reviews of *Paisà* from Italy, France, the United States, and the United Kingdom, see Aprà, *Il dopoguerra di Rossellini*. On *Paisà*'s "groundbreaking" role in Italian cinematic neorealism, see Marcus "Rossellini's *Paisà*." *All Thy Conquests* was lauded in the *New York Times* as "a penetrating, truthful and compassionate novel," particularly in its "honest and accurate" portraits of "real Italians, not caricatures." Howard Taubman, "The Eternal City and Its Liberators." See also Anthony M. Gisolfi, "The Beach of Heaven," 206–207. Critic John Aldridge called *All Thy Conquests* "the first important novel of World War II." *After the Lost Generation*, 133. Years later, John P. Diggins celebrated it for its "historical verisimilitude." *Mussolini and Fascism*, 434.

6. Marcus, "Rossellini's *Paisà*," 296.

7. Among such contemporary revisitations of *Paisà* that privilege the first and last episodes, see Giuliana Minghelli, *Landscape and Memory in Post-Fascist Italian Film*, 86; Karl Schoonover, *Brutal Vision*, chap. 3.

8. On the episode as a "alien body" see David Bruni, "Il classicismo nella modernità," 73. Danielle Hipkins critiques these early dismissive readings, "Francesca's Salvation or Damnation?" 155. See also Siobhan S. Craig, *Cinema after Fascism*, and Louis Bayman, *The Operatic and the Everyday in Postwar Italian Film Melodrama*.

9. Marcus, "Rossellini's *Paisà*," 295.

10. Marcus, "Liberating the Garden," 552; Bayman, *The Operatic and the Everyday in Postwar Italian Film Melodrama*, 87; Fabio Ferrari, "Americana," 129.

11. Hipkins, "Francesca's Salvation or Damnation?" 163–164.

12. Ruth Ben-Ghiat, "Fascism, Writing, and Memory"; Lorenzo Fabbri, "Neorealism as Ideology."

13. Minghelli, *Landscape and Memory in Post-Fascist Italian Film*, 86.

14. Bruni notes that the lengthy flashback is a one-off in Rossellini's work, "Il classicismo nella modernità," 75.

15. On the historical practice of rounding up women in this manner, see Charles Maurice Wiltse, *The Medical Department*, 258.

16. Roy Palmer Domenico, *Italian Fascists on Trial*, 92. On the "significant political consequences for the new Italy" "triggered" by the liberation of Rome, see ibid., 45–46.

17. Alessandro Portelli, *The Order Has Been Carried Out*, 9.

18. On the fear of the "specter of Communism" behind the violent mob, and its influence on U.S. diplomacy, see Diggins, *Mussolini and Fascism*, 379–380. For related documents including the joint statement, see Harry L. Coles and Albert K. Weinberg, *Civil Affairs*, 478.

19. Fellow American novelist John Hersey, whose novel *A Bell for Adano* (1944), set in postinvasion Sicily, won him a Pulitzer Prize, describes the text

rather aptly on its 1946 book flap: "Mr. Hayes has written a kind of impression of failure—a many-toned failure: failure to purge the fascists or their ideas; failure to live up in personal terms to the demands of democracy; failure to live up even to certain minimum requirements of humanity—to a minimum generosity, to a least amount of loyalty, selflessness, and understanding."

20. Tag Gallagher, *The Adventures of Roberto Rossellini*, 723 n. 16. Peter Bondanella, while less polemical, refers to Hayes by way of partial justification for the episode's "conventional" nature, *The Films of Roberto Rossellini*, 76. Hayes is also briefly mentioned by Hipkins, "Francesca's Salvation or Damnation?" 166.

21. Gallagher, *The Adventures of Roberto Rossellini*, 181.

22. Schoonover, *Brutal Vision*, xxi.

23. Fabbri, "Neorealism as Ideology," 194.

24. Ibid.

25. Hipkins, *Italy's Other Women*, 7.

26. Hayes dates the genesis of *The Girl on the Via Flaminia* to late winter of 1945 when he was on an aircraft carrier home from Italy. He claims he first wrote it as a play, then—failing to have it published—he revised and published it as a novel in 1949. The film rights to the novel were bought by Anatole Litvak, who produced it as *An Act of Love* (1954), set in Paris. Hayes then revised it once again into a play, also produced that year. Hayes, "Wartime Story."

27. Herbert L. Matthews, "Conquerors' Goal Reached by Allies."

28. *New York Times*, "The Victory of Rome."

29. Anne O'Hare McCormick, "The Americans Lead the Way into Rome."

30. *Life Magazine*, "Rome Falls."

31. Anne O'Hare McCormick, "France and Italy in the Drama of Liberation"; Herbert L. Matthews, "Rome Is up at Dawn to Cheer 5th Army."

32. Herbert L. Matthews, "A New Chapter in Eternal Rome." See also Matthews, "Stimson in Rome on Symbolic Day"; McCormick, "France and Italy in the Drama of Liberation"; McCormick, "Duce's Palace a Gallery as Press Mourns for Italy."

33. McCormick, "France and Italy in the Drama of Liberation."

34. Herbert L. Matthews, "Rome Mob Lynches Fascist Official after Seizing Him in Open Court." In a letter to the editor in the next day's edition of the *Times*, intellectual Lewis Mumford censured Matthews for his "self-righteous" judgements against the Roman people. "Roman Account Stirs Reader." In his memoir, *The Education of a Correspondent* (1946), Matthews acknowledges the validity of such criticism and tempers his moral outrage. A different version of the lynching emerged from Austrian journalist Paul Hofmann, who claims to have been with Matthews, suggesting that they happened upon the crowd and were unaware of what was happening until later, *The Seasons of Rome*, 119.

35. *Life Magazine*, "Lynching in Rome."

36. A report from the Allied Control Commission files, dated September 22, 1944, entitled "A Gory Episode—Can This Government Maintain Order?"

describes Carretta unsympathetically: "Carretta, who had been director of the Regina Coeli Jail until dismissed by AMG on 18 June, had aroused great hatred by turning over Italians to the Germans, who then slaughtered them," cited in Coles and Weinberg, *Civil Affairs*, 478 n. 17. In its early coverage, *Life* calls Carretta an "offensive, flabby lipped sadist." "Lynching in Rome," 36. After the Italian government issued its exonerating report, descriptions tend to be more neutral or positive. Diggins calls him "an innocent prosecution witness," *Mussolini and Fascism*, 379; William Vance goes farther to call him "an antifascist hero." *America's Rome*, 395.

37. Domenico, *Italian Fascists on Trial*, 94. Matthews changes his opinion, first asserting, "This was no mob of hooligans." "Rome Mob Lynches Fascist Official after Seizing Him in Open Court." He later stresses that the most ardent members of the mob were "former jailbirds for common crimes." "Italian Government Report Shows Carreta, Lynched as Fascist, Was Entirely Innocent."

38. Domenico, *Italian Fascists on Trial*, 96.

39. Matthews, *The Education of a Correspondent*, 481.

40. On the Piga report, see Domenico, *Italian Fascists on Trial*, 27 nn. 43–44.

41. Matthews, *The Education of a Correspondent*, 467. See also Eric Sevareid, *Not so Wild a Dream*, 421–422, discussed in the Introduction.

42. *New York Times*, "Two Italian Generals Are Sentenced in Rome." On this disproportionate tendency to prosecute crimes of morality and the continued fascination with the mistresses of Fascist *gerarchi*, see Domenico, *Italian Fascists on Trial*, 50.

43. Ibid.

44. Lara Pucci, "Shooting Corpses." See also Philip Cooke, *The Legacy of the Italian Resistance*, 35.

45. David Forgacs, *Rome Open City*, 65. Michael P. Rogin calls the massacre "the structuring absence of Rome Open City's story and its mood," "Mourning, Melancholia, and the Popular Front," 145. Minghelli cites screenwriter Ugo Pirro's recollection about the birth of *Roma città aperta* "as an expression of a compromise out of the impossibility of speaking about the tragedy of the Fosse Ardeatine." *Landscape and Memory in Post Fascist Italian Film*, 72.

46. Ibid., 87.

47. Ben Ghiat, "Fascism, Writing, and Memory," 660–661.

48. On the significance of the epigraph, see Vance, *America's Rome*, 392.

49. On the proceedings as show trials and Caruso as a spectacle "presented at the very least as much for public and Allied consumption as they were an effort to rid the Roman bureaucracy of Fascists" see Domenico, *Italian Fascists on Trial*, 90. See also Pucci, "Shooting Corpses," 363.

50. Hayes, *All Thy Conquests*, 9, 8.

51. Ibid., 11.

52. Ibid., 12, 13.

53. Ibid., 102.

54. Ibid., 103.

55. Ibid., 96.

56. Ibid., 105, 106. "Hayes's version of the life of Pietro Caruso . . . reads as the life of Italy itself during the twenty-five years of the Fascist party." Vance, *America's Rome*, 394.

57. Hayes, *All Thy Conquests*, 109. On Benedetto Croce and the fascist parenthesis, see Ben-Ghiat, "Fascism, Writing, and Memory," 660 n. 124.

58. Hayes, *All Thy Conquests*, 291.

59. On the foregone nature of Caruso's sentence, see Domenico, *Italian Fascists on Trial*, 96.

60. McCormick, "Signs in Italy of Anarchy in Europe."

61. Hayes, *All Thy Conquests*, 288.

62. Ibid., 292.

63. Ibid., 292–293; McCormick, "Signs in Italy of Anarchy in Europe."

64. Hayes, *All Thy Conquests*, 294.

65. On the connection between the Carretta and Mussolini lynchings, and the negative impact on U.S. perceptions of Italians, see Andrew Buchanan, "Good Morning, Pupil!" 237.

66. Italian politicians evoked the U.S. domestic context in defense of their own situation. Matthews's account quotes Sforza, high commissioner for the punishment of fascist crimes, as saying, "This is like the lynching of the Negros, and we will not have it in Italy." Matthews, "Rome Mob Lynches Fascist Official After Seizing Him in Open Court." In a subsequent article, he reports, "Palmiro Togliatti, incidentally, took the trouble at yesterday's Cabinet meeting to look up in an encyclopedia how many lynchings the United States has in an average year after he had been reproached with condoning the lynching of Signor Carretta." "Italy To Declare War on Japanese."

67. Vance, *America's Rome*, 394.

68. Matthews, "Rome Mob Lynches Fascist Official after Seizing Him in Open Court," 10.

69. Hayes, *All Thy Conquests*, 34.

70. Ibid., 21.

71. Ibid., 44.

72. Ibid., 46.

73. Ibid., 50.

74. Stefania Parigi, *Paisà*, 26 (translation mine). See also Craig, *Cinema after Fascism*, 38.

75. Hayes, *All Thy Conquests*, 53.

76. Ibid., 277.

77. Ibid., 280, 273.

78. Ibid., 272.

79. On this tendency among publishers of early postwar American-authored novels set in Italy and Germany, and the resulting misrepresentation of books

such as John Horne Burns's *The Gallery*, see Susan Carruthers, *Good Occupation*, 116. *All Thy Conquests* was reprinted only through 1958, whereas *The Girl on The Via Flaminia* was reissued in 2007 by Europa Editions. The novel appears to have been translated only into German, as *Alle deine Siege*.

80. Hayes, *All Thy Conquests*, 53.

81. *Life Magazine*, "Movie of the Week," 41. On the use of sexualized imagery to sell Italian neorealism, see Nathaniel Brennan, "Marketing Meaning, Branding Neorealism," 88 and 94; Tulio Balio, *The Foreign Film Renaissance on American Screens*, 47–48; and Schoonover, *Brutal Vision*, chap. 2. Although images of Michi feature prominently in the posters Schoonover analyzes, he does not analyze her characters, Marina and Francesca.

82. On the prostitute as a reassuring symbol in the context of war, see Cynthia Enloe, *Maneuvers*, 108.

83. On *Paisà*'s participation in a "memorialist tradition crowned by Ugo Foscolo's *Dei Sepolchri*," see Marcus, "Rossellini's *Paisà*," 298–299.

84. Hayes, *The Girl on the Via Flaminia*, 37, 52–53.

85. Ibid., 127.

86. Jonathan Vincent, "America e Italia," 87.

87. Hayes, *The Girl on the Via Flaminia*, 198.

88. Ibid., 139. For an historical case of a Neapolitan landlady arrested under the suspicion of running an informal brothel out of her apartment as well as the letters of local citizens denouncing such activity, see Maria Porzio, *Arrivano gli alleati!*, 106–107.

89. On the origins and development of this belief, first advanced by a doctor in Naples in 1495, see John Parascandola, "Quarantining Women."

90. Hayes, *The Girl on the Via Flaminia*, 195.

91. Ibid., 162–165.

92. Ibid., 163.

93. On the (anti)tourist/traveler and the search for authenticity, see Jonathan Culler, *Framing the Sign*.

94. Hayes, *The Girl on the Via Flaminia*, 211.

95. Ibid., 68. On Leopardi in this tradition, see Marcus, "The Italian Body Politic Is a Woman," 332–334.

96. Hayes, *The Girl on the Via Flaminia*, 188. On the historical instance of head-shaving as punishment for sleeping with the enemy, see Porzio, *Arrivano gli alleati!*, 118–140.

97. On the paradox of gendered nationalism, see Anne McClintock, "Family Feuds."

98. Hayes, *The Girl on the Via Flaminia*, 180, emphasis mine.

99. Ibid., 191. Ellipses in original. On the experience of the medical exam, see Anna Garofalo, *L'italiana in Italia*, 67–68; Sergio Lambiase and Gian Battista Nazzaro, *L'odore della guerra*, 113–114.

100. Hayes, *The Girl on the Via Flaminia*, 123.

101. Ibid., 132. Hayes's stage adaptation of *Girl on the Via Flaminia* in 1954 seems to capitulate to such pressures: the description of the medical exam is condensed, and Lisa's reflection on her transformation into a prostitute during her "first time" with Robert is eliminated. Garofalo also writes of her need to keep discussions of prostitution off the radio. *L'italiana in Italia*, 10.

102. Hayes, *The Girl on the Via Flaminia*, 192.

103. Hipkins, "Francesca's Salvation or Damnation?" 162. See also Craig, *Cinema after Fascism*, 34–38.

104. Vincent, "America e Italia," 27.

105. Hayes, "Italy—Enchantress of Writers."

106. Hayes, *The Girl on the Via Flaminia*, 207–208, emphasis mine.

107. Ibid., 131, 183.

108. Hayes, "Italy—Enchantress of Writers."

109. Ibid.

110. Ibid.

111. Catherine O'Rawe, "Back for Good," 1.

112. Ibid. 6.

3. Happily Ever after Redemption: Luciana Peverelli's "True" Romance Novels of Occupied Rome

1. A brief history of the romance novel is found in Robin Pickering-Iazzi, *Politics of the Visible*, 98–99.

2. For a reading of Liala that redresses the legacy of Banti's essay, see ibid., 89–123.

3. Anna Banti, "Storia e ragioni del 'romanzo rosa,'" 78–79.

4. "Il colore della velocità, della folla, e anche della disattenzione: letto, se le statistiche non ingannano, da tre milioni di individui." Ibid., 75, all translations of Banti mine.

5. "meccanica inventrice di innumerevoli collisioni fra donne oziose e ricche, donne povere e ambiziose, e uomini dalla mascella volitiva." Ibid.

6. "la dattilografia cui sta per capitare la grande avventura, verbigrazia l'amore del ricco principale ammogliato, si fermerà al bar, comprerà la matassa di lana a tre capi, si cuocerà due uova al tegame, coi gesti e le parole di ciascuna delle lettrici: le quali, risalendo da quel controllato verosimile al delizioso rischio del romanzesco, assimileranno se stesse all'eroina con una approssimazione piena di speranza." Ibid., 80.

7. "il romanzo alla Peverelli, tanto dire il romanzo spicciolo attuale," "Una costante di conformismo e di banalità nell'intrigo necessario ad accaparrare lettori inesperti e impazienti, non toglie che nella squallida pagina si annidino tuttavia una quantità di gesti minuti e verdici, di reazioni previste, ma naturali, specchio di una esperienza reale, vissuta." Ibid.

8. Anna Bravo, *Il fotoromanzo*, 116 (translation mine). On the importance of Banti's essay in the context of Italian literary criticism of the 1950s, see Pickering-

Iazzi, *Politics of the Visible*, 91. In the field of English romance studies, Pamela Regis was among the first to redress the widespread negative attacks on the conventions of the romance, particularly the happy ending, *A Natural History of the Romance Novel*.

9. Pickering-Iazzi, *Politics of the Visible*, 99.

10. Ibid., 91.

11. On the gendering of neorealism and the limited discursive space it leaves for women, see Catherine O'Rawe, "Back for Good," esp. 139 n. 62. See also Danielle Hipkins, "Francesca's Salvation or Damnation?" Although Banti does not mention neorealism in this essay, she enthusiastically embraces Rossellini's *Roma città aperta* in another, describing it as a long-awaited cinematic redemption of the insensitive American comedies such as Charlie Chaplin's *The Great Dictator* that circulated during the occupation, in what she characterizes as a veritable form of punishment of the Italian people, "Neorealismo nel cinema italiano."

12. Ruth Ben-Ghiat, "Fascism, Writing, and Memory."

13. Rita Verdirame, *Narratrici e lettrici*, 174 (translation mine). In his survey of the global reception of *The Moon Is Down*, Donald V. Coers locates three early Italian translations, suggesting "unusual interest in the novel in that country." In addition to Peverelli's version published by Editoriale Roma, "Heinemann and Zsolnay published in London a version entitled *Notte senza luna* (*Night without Moon*), with the translator's name not given. In 1945, yet another Italian edition, translated by Giorgio Monicelli, was published in Milan by Mondadori under the title *La luna tramonta* (*The Setting Moon*)." *John Steinbeck Goes to War*, 116.

14. Bravo, *Il fotoromanzo*, 116 (translation mine). For a summary of this output, see Eugenia Roccella, *La letteratura rosa*, 141–142. General discussions of Peverelli can be found in Verdirame, *Narratrici e lettrici* and Bravo, *Il fotoromanzo*.

15. On the marginalization of postwar cinematic melodrama through this process outlined by Ben-Ghiat, see O'Rawe, "Back for Good," 125–126.

16. As cited in Roccella, *La letteratura rosa*, 78 (translation mine). The last reprinting of *La lunga notte* was by Rizzoli in 1975, and *Sposare lo straniero* was last issued by Garzanti in 1977.

17. Anna Bogo, "Romanzo rosa," 1602; see also Maria Pia Pozzato, *Il romanzo rosa*, 79–80.

18. Robert Gordon's exhaustive survey *The Holocaust in Italian Culture*, with a chapter dedicated to Rome, does not include *La lunga notte*, despite his willingness to include literary texts with "contrasting" pretensions, such as Debendetti's "semidetached chronicle" and Curzio Malaparte's *Kaputt*, which he judges a "melodramatic and narcissistic elaboration," 48. Recent attempts to widen the canon of Italian Holocaust narrative fail to mention *La lunga notte*: Risa B. Sodi, *Narrative and Imperative*; Stefania Lucamante, *Forging Shoah Memories*. *La lunga notte* deserves to be read in the context of narratives of the *Resistenza* by authors such as Italo Calvino, Elio Vittorini, Beppe Fenoglio,

Luigi Meneghello, and, particularly Renata Viganò, offering a counterpoint to her canonical, conservative, *L'Agnese va a morire* (1949). Within the Roman context, it might dialogue productively with texts such as Roberto Rossellini's film *Roma città aperta* (1945) and Fulvia Ripa di Meana's diary *Roma Clandestina* (1945), or Carla Capponi's partisan memoir *Con cuore di donna* (2009). Later, I discuss its relevance to Elsa Morante's *La storia* (1974; *History*).

19. Nonfictional war bride accounts in English have emerged in recent years, including soldiers' memoirs. See Leonard H. Poppelsdorff, *Say Your Prayers Dear*; Eric Newby, *Love and War in the Apennines*. Mario Varricchio and Silvia Cassamagnaghi both draw on recent self-published narratives from the perspective of the Italian war bride: Varricchio, "Il sogno e le radici"; Cassamagnaghi, *Operazione spose di guerra*.

20. *Teresa*, focused on a returning veteran's psychological adjustment, is based on a story written by Alfred Hayes with Stewart Stern, and was nominated for the Academy Award for best story. See Cassamagnaghi, *Operazione Spose di guerra*, 246–252.

21. Ilaria Serra, "Italy: America's War Bride," 452.

22. The first arrival of Italian war brides can be dated by a *New York Times* article from October 10, 1945. Varricchio, "Il sogno e le radici," 115–116 n. 1. While one might expect historians working outside of Italian to exclude Peverelli, it is surprising not to see a mention in a study like Cassamagnaghi, *Operazione spose di guerra*, who makes Burns's novel *The Gallery* one of her most frequent sources. Varricchio does not mention Peverelli, but his sources are exclusively nonfictional. A brief reading of *Sposare* is found in Roccella, *La letteratura rosa*, 77–81; Maria Porzio, *Arrivano gli alleati!*, 194; Alberto Traldi, *Fascism and Fiction*, 203–204. Hipkins's reading of the novel in dialogue with my own earlier analysis, "Marry the Allies?" has helped me reframe my reading of the novel's treatment of the prostitute. *Italy's Other Women*, 10.

23. Here I draw on Hipkins's premise in *Italy's Other Women* whereby "the female prostitute is particularly important to Italian national cinema as a 'borderline identity' used to establish, but also to destabilize, the hegemony of respectable femininities, almost entirely premised as they are on a certain kind of sexual behavior," 10.

24. Pozzato, *Il romanzo rosa*, 26–29.

25. On the commingling of *verismo*, *rosa*, and melodrama in Peverelli's texts, see Bravo, *Il fotoromanzo*, 23.

26. Pickering-Iazzi, *Politics of the Visible*, 98.

27. O'Rawe, "Back for Good," 128.

28. Lucamante, *Forging Shoah Memories*, 119.

29. On the general immobility of the romance heroine, see Pozzato, *Il romanzo rosa*, 22. Andreina's status as orphan, instead, likens her to the conventional heroine. Ibid, 19.

30. Peverelli, *La lunga notte*, 72, 74.

31. "ogni giorno trenta quaranta ebrei venivano scovati nei loro rifugi, spediti per ignota destinazione: o meglio per un'unica destinazione: la morte." Ibid., 234. Another explicit reference to the extermination camps reads: "in the gas chambers, Jews die by the hundreds, like flies, like ants." Ibid., 141, "Nelle camere a gas gli ebrei muoiono a centinaia, come le mosche, come le formiche" (all translations of Peverelli mine).

32. Gordon, *The Holocaust in Italian Culture*, 10. The novel also refers to pogroms in Eastern Europe. Peverelli, *La lunga notte*, 146.

33. Gordon, *The Holocaust in Italian Culture*, 48.

34. Michael P. Rogin, "Mourning, Melancholia, and the Popular Front," 145.

35. Lara Pucci, "Shooting Corpses," 366. Maja Mikula writes about the decades long legal battle surrounding the classification of the via Rasella attack and its implications for one partisan, Carla Capponi: while it was considered an act of war, victims' families filed lawsuits into the late 1990s in order to reclassify it as a crime. "Gender and Patriotism in Carla Capponi's *Con Cuore di Donna*," 71.

36. Peverelli, *La lunga notte*, 226.

37. Ibid., 230–231.

38. "facce pallide, spettrali." Ibid., 229.

39. "E qualche notizia di quel massacro cominciava a trapelare: e Roma inorridiva. Pareva che i morti fossero stati seppelliti quasi ancor vivi sotto uno strato di una sostanza bruciante e adesiva: il giorno seguente al massacro, le cave erano state fatte saltare e sabbia e terra erano franati sui corpi di coloro che forse non avevano ancora finito di agonizzare. E terrore e stupore a angoscia pesavano sulla città affamata. Il coprifuoco era stato portato alle cinque. Nelle case buie si rintanavano come talpe i cittadini atterriti, e le notizie più allarmanti circolavano di bocca in bocca, di casa in casa." Ibid., 233.

40. "Nessuna porta si aprì. Il terrore le teneva chiuse." Ibid., 74; "La vita proseguiva normalmente. Quasi nessuno si era accorto di quel dramma, di quelle creature umane, che caricate come bestie pel macello venivano portate alla morte." Ibid., 75.

41. Pucci, "Shooting Corpses," 357.

42. Ugo Pirro, *Celluloide*, 72, as cited in Giuliana Minghelli, *Landscape and Memory in Post Fascist Italian Film*, 216 n. 49.

43. Karl Schoonover, *Brutal Vision*.

44. Gordon, *The Holocaust in Italian Culture*, 11.

45. Lucamante, *Forging Shoah Memories*, 160.

46. "bambolina di lusso," "fuggiasca ebrea." Peverelli, *La lunga notte*, 30.

47. For a history of Italian Holocaust cinema, "a genre that was slow to start," see Giacomo Lichtner, "For the Few, Not the Many," 236.

48. "Mi sto innamorando come la protagonista di un romanzo, come un'idiota, come una vecchia zitella assetata d'amore." Peverelli, *La lunga notte*, 48.

49. Ibid., 31–32; "Io ero una ragazza come te, Andreina: tranquilla, spensierata, felice di vivere. Adesso sono un mostro. Capace di qualsiasi cosa." Ibid., 31.

50. "credeva di essere giunta a Roma per una missione: credeva in quel suo amore inverosimile, ormai, come in un mito." Ibid., 68.

51. "Oh, possibile? ! Questa cosa così vieta, questo genere d'avventure da romanzo a dispense . . . possibile che esistessero ancora situazioni di quel genere?" Ibid., 199.

52. "Che grosso dramma per una bambina così piccola." Ibid., 201; "Reciterò la commedia." Ibid., 204.

53. Millicent Marcus, "The Italian Body Politic Is a Woman," 337.

54. "condannata a soffrire una segreta legge." Peverelli, *La lunga notte*, 269.

55. Lucamante, *Forging Shoah Memories*, 156, 157.

56. Ibid., 4.

57. Ibid., 12.

58. "Ma Andreina camminava adagio, aggrappata al braccio di Adriano." Peverelli, *La lunga notte*, 5.

59. "una splendida conquista," "quella sbarazzina così stupida e ingenua in talune cose, così scaltra e civetta in altre." Ibid., 6.

60. "quella strana vita in bilico tra la villeggiatura e la vacanza." Ibid., 9; Pozzato, *Il romanzo rosa*, 79–80.

61. See the Epilogue.

62. "per il quieto vivere, per non perdere il loro benessere si sarebbero accomodate di qualsiasi cosa." Peverelli, *La lunga notte*, 19.

63. "bevono vermut nelle pasticcerie, organizzano pomeriggi al teatro e al cinematografo." Ibid., 41.

64. "le cose romantiche e inverosimili." Ibid., 80; "quest'epoca di agguati e di morte." Ibid., 94.

65. "Era così assurdo che qualcosa di tragico e di tremendo fosse capitato a lei, alla stupida bambina ottimista che giocava al fronte clandestino." Ibid., 123.

66. "ora Andreina avrebbe avuto l'aureola del martirio . . . tutti l'avrebbero considerata come un'eroina." Ibid., 125.

67. Ibid., 131, 138; "E con orrore Andreina vide che l'uomo grondava sangue. La sua faccia era tutta una pioggia di sangue che cadeva a grosse gocce sull'impiantito, segnando una lunga scia." Ibid., 152.

68. "inguaribile nella sua fantasiosa puerilità." Ibid., 202. See also ibid., 239.

69. Ibid., 253.

70. "senza paura, ma tremante di emozione." Ibid., 202.

71. Ibid., 255.

72. "Pensava al terrore della popolazione che aveva la mala sorte di abitare le zone prese di mira, ma anche alla gioia selvaggia con cui i carcerati di Regina Coeli, di via Tasso, salutavano quegli schianti." Ibid., 202.

73. For a summary of the redemptive significance of the boy witness in *Roma città aperta* (and its exclusion of the girl), see Lesley Caldwell, "Ragazzo Fortunato?" 65–66.

74. "Agli altri cinque venne dato ordine di gettar della terra sui corpi dei

compagni caduti nella fossa. Erano ancora caldi; qualcuno agonizzava ancora, raspando con le unghie, gli occhi dilatati, fissi al cielo lontano. Ad uno di quei cinque non resse l'animo. Cade svenuto sull'orlo della fossa. Un soldato tedesco lo urtò due o tre volte col piede per obbligarlo a rialzarsi. Ma come quello non si muoveva, irritato, gli scaricò la pistola nel cervello." Peverelli, *La lunga notte*, 179.

75. "La testa del vecchio padre di Claudio ricadde nelle sue mani come un frutto marcio. Due piccoli rivoli di sangue gocciolavano ancora lenti dal collo." Ibid., 185.

76. Ibid., 180, 186.

77. "Nacque Roma in quella mattina di giugno su un cielo d'opale e di rose, tra uno stridìo e un cinguettare di uccellini felici: era sveglia, e fremente e vibrante, e il sole batté folgorante sulla cupola di San Pietro come in un'apoteosi di gioia e di rinascita." Ibid., 263.

78. "L'uomo al volante sorrise. Gli occhi verdi, chiarissimi, giovani, si posarono curiosi su Andreina. E in un solo istante, per virtù di quello sguardo, la sua personalità di un tempo, femminile e civetta, maliziosa e tenera, rinacque." Ibid., 265.

79. "Oh, Beppe fucilato a Forte Boccea, Claudio massacrato alle Fosse Ardeatine, Colombi ucciso per la strada come un cane . . . Oh, terribile . . . terribile, Antonello . . . Meglio non parlare . . . Parlare di te, parlare di Luciano, di Berrini, di Ghedini, che sono vivi. Non pensare più a tanta tristezza . . . Ci siamo cibate, nutrite, avvelenate di tragedie in tutti questi mesi . . . Non voglio, non voglio più essere triste. . . ." Ibid., 266.

80. "Ed ella si volse a lui, e gli sorrise: 'Nothing: nothing at all . . .'" Ibid.

81. "Faccio quello che vuoi . . . Edward, oh tutto, purché tu mi aiuti a non pensare!" Ibid., 282.

82. "talune ragazze di Napoli che egli aveva odiate e disprezzate, ma che almeno erano state spinte dalla fame, dalla miseria!" Ibid., 284. As Hipkins notes, Antonello also makes the assumption that Gesi, his love interest in *Sposare lo straniero*, is prostituting herself when he sees her dancing at a club. *Italy's Other Women*, 98–99.

83. Eric Sevareid, *Not So Wild a Dream*, 421–422, discussed in the Introduction; see also Herbert L. Matthews, *The Education of a Correspondent*, 467, discussed in Chapter 2.

84. On the gendered spaces of war and the need to renegotiate them beyond the battlefield, see Chris Cuomo, "War Is Not Just an Event."

85. "Ma [Ursula] sentì che non sarebbe mai più ritornata né serena né limpida. Mai più. E neppure Antonello: e neppure Andreina, qualsiasi cosa avessero fatto per consolarsi. Quella terribile, orribile guerra, e ciò che avevano veduto, sofferto, patito, aveva maciullato le loro anime, aveva spento in loro la bontà e la gioia della vita. Qualsiasi cosa fosse accaduta, essi sarebbero stati altre persone, esseri amari e increduli, a cui un Dio terribile aveva rubato qualcosa che nessuno avrebbe restituito mai più." Peverelli, *La lunga notte*, 287.

86. O'Rawe, "Back for Good," 128. Here, she draws from Louis Bayman, *The Operatic and the Everyday in Postwar Italian Film Melodrama*, 81.

87. "Sì, era terribile che gli amici fossero stati arrestati. Ma il suo dramma, il suo tormento erano altrettanto importanti e decisivi." Peverelli, *La lunga notte*, 92.

88. Bayman, *The Operatic and the Everyday in Postwar Italian Film Melodrama*, 87.

89. "Mi sento eccitato come un bambino che vada per la prima volta a teatro." Peverelli, *Sposare lo straniero*, 5; "All of Rome knew that in the prisons languished innocents subjected to torture, but all of Rome kept on going to the bars, cinemas, theatres. This seemed to her at once inhuman and absurd." Peverelli, *La lunga notte*, 131, "Tutta Roma sapeva che nelle carceri languivano, torturati, degli innocenti, ma tutta Roma continuava a frequentare i bar, i cinematografi, i teatri. Questo le parve ad un tratto inumano e assurdo."

90. Peverelli, *Sposare lo straniero*, 11–12; "l'immagine di un giovane eroe biondo, con gli occhi sfavillanti, le labbra carnose, la mascella decisa." Ibid., 34.

91. "Quattro ragazze che la guerra ha colpito: Gemma, Andreina, Luce e Gesi vivono il loro romanzo. Ognuna giunge a una conclusione diversa. Sposare lo straniero è una fortuna o no? Luciana ce lo dice in questo suo racconto che, come 'La lunga notte,' si documenta solo di episodi reali e di personaggi realmente esistiti," as cited in Roccella, *La letteratura rosa*, 78.

92. Peverelli, *Sposare lo straniero*, 212, 222.

93. Ibid., 57, 177, 308.

94. "Perché i romanzi finiscono di solito quando i due protagonisti si sposano? Comincia allora il romanzo, comincia allora la vita." Ibid., 271.

95. Ibid., 58, 59, 64, 106.

96. "Quando la fiaba finirà, che sarà di lei?" Ibid., 84. Jackie has a similar concern about a girl he meets in a club; ibid., 51–52.

97. "Centinaia di ragazze avevano sognato, avevano sperato, centinaia di ragazze si erano sentite come piccole cenerentole per cui erano giunti da paesi lontani e fantasmagorici principi azzurri, ma adesso se ne ritornavano alla loro patria." Ibid., 259.

98. See Cassamagnaghi, *Operazione Spose di guerra*, esp. 9–14. She finds the "principe azzurro" characterization in a 1951 essay by Oriana Fallaci as well as in Vittorio De Sica's 1946 film *Abbasso la ricchezza!* Ibid., 10 and n. 6.

99. "Era come vivessero tutti un periodo fuori del tempo, in cui tutte le cose più impensate e più straordinarie potevano accadere. Poi, una volta finita la guerra, tutto sarebbe tornato nella normalità. E tutto sarebbe sembrato un sogno." Peverelli, *Sposare lo straniero*, 64.

100. Ben-Ghiat, "Fascism, Writing, and Memory," 660.

101. "ritmo vertiginoso e incalzante di avvenimenti," "Il fronte di Bologna sfondato, le truppe alleate scese nelle valle del Po, e la supposta resistenza dei tedeschi lungo il fiume subito infranta, le prime jeep che si spingono nella pianura padana, e i partigiani che calano trionfanti dalle valli, e le città che

insorgono, i tedeschi e i fascisti in fuga, e prima che gli alleati giungano nelle grandi città del nord giustizia è fatta e le bandiere delle libertà sventolano sulle case sventrate, sulle piazze, sulle chiese dove tutte le campane suonano a festa." Peverelli, *Sposare lo straniero*, 203.

102. "Un periodo assurdo e tremendo della nostra vita si è chiuso." Ibid., 204.

103. Ibid., 207.

104. Bogo, "Romanzo Rosa," 1602.

105. "una meravigliosa avventura." Peverelli, *Sposare lo straniero*, 243.

106. "Così il sogno si avverava, quello che era sembrato inverosimile accadeva. Howard Whiter sposava lei, Andreina. Tutti gli ostacoli erano scomparsi, magicamente." Ibid., 264.

107. "Sono arrivato in un paese maciullato, martoriato dalla guerra senza pietà, e dal cumulo di rovine ho visto sorgere un fiore, e allora l'ho colto, prima che altre mani lo distruggessero, e lo tengo caro e prezioso perché riprenda vita." Ibid.

108. Ibid., 345.

109. "Senza merito alcuno e con molta scaltrezza, circondandosi dell'aureola delle infelici martiri, sono riuscite a beccarsi gli uomini migliori d'Inghilterra e d'America." Ibid., 318.

110. Susan Zeiger, *Entangling Alliances*, 7.

111. Peverelli, *La lunga notte*, 125.

112. "Non sapete niente della nostra disperata lotta per conquistarci la libertà, il diritto di batterci per le nostre idee . . . e quanti di noi sono caduti, e quanti di noi hanno dato la vita per questa libertà prima che voi veniste ad offrircela con tanta ostentazione." Peverelli, *Sposare lo straniero*, 82.

113. Hipkins, *Italy's Other Women*, 54; Peverelli, *Sposare lo straniero*, 314–315.

114. "Ma sai, quando si è patita una guerra simile, e fughe e bombardamenti, e minacce di morte, e prigione, non si può pretendere che i nervi siano a posto." Peverelli, *Sposare lo straniero*, 314.

115. "Io non voglio sentir parlare di guerra, di tedeschi, di fronte clandestino . . . Voglio pensare solo che esistiamo noi due al mondo, che siamo felici, che ci vogliamo bene, che . . ." Peverelli, *La lunga notte*, 122.

116. "Ripensò con desolato affanno a quel periodo della resistenza contro i tedeschi in Roma in cui aveva tanto sofferto. Eppure le sembrava che fosse nulla in confronto a questa amarezza." Peverelli, *Sposare lo straniero*, 326.

117. Pozzato, *Il romanzo rosa*, 27 (translation mine).

118. "Doveva essere di nuovo lei stessa, come era stata ai tempi felici, prima che l'Italia fosse maciullata dalle bombe, fosse invasa da stranieri amici e nemici al tempo stesso." Peverelli, *Sposare lo straniero*, 336.

119. Ibid., 337.

120. Ibid., 339.

121. "Sembri finta." Ibid., 337.

122. "Non sono finta, così, sono vera." Ibid.

123. "come nelle fiabe." Ibid., 342.
124. Peverelli, *La lunga notte*, 287.
125. Peverelli, *Sposare lo straniero*, 345.
126. "Siamo forse stati due mondi nemici fino a ieri. Ma oggi non più. Sono io che piego davanti a te, e tu devi accogliermi nelle tue braccia. Dobbiamo essere, se non ti sembra un po' ridicolo e presuntuoso da parte mia dirlo, dobbiamo essere un piccolo simbolo del mondo, Andreina." Ibid., 344.
127. Herbert L. Matthews, *The Education of a Correspondent*, 467.
128. Peverelli, *Sposare lo straniero*, 258.
129. Ibid., 88, 169.
130. "Dapprima pensammo che la fucilassero. Poi seppero che era ebrea e non vollero darle quella morte che era troppo rapida. L'hanno portata in un campo di concentramento. Non so se tutti gli orrori che ci descrivono di quel mondo siano veri, ma ti assicuro che i racconti ti fanno accapponare la pelle. Ursula è forte, è abituata a tutto, ma quei tremendi campi si chiamano di eliminazione, e vi è studiata laggiù la più spaventosa, la più lenta delle morti." Ibid., 168–169.
131. David Ellwood, "The American Challenge in Uniform," 6.
132. "la straniera lontana, la nemica." Peverelli, *Sposare lo straniero*, 261.
133. On Jackie's past and present writing activities see ibid., 6, 204; on his perceptions of Italian women see ibid., 72, 43.
134. "Si diceva che si dessero agli americani soltanto per le thousand lire, e le sigarette e la cioccolata. Ma Jackie sapeva che non era vero. Sapeva che erano tutte assai meno avide delle americane." Ibid., 193.
135. Ibid., 260.
136. Ibid., 23; "Il dramma di cui la piccola Gesi le parlava era come l'eco di un dramma già vissuto, già sofferto da lei, e le faceva male risvegliarsi dal torpore in cui era caduta negli ultimi tempi, molto simile a un vile ma dolce sonno. Le sembrava che quella ragazza dai riccioletti corti l'avesse bruscamente richiamata alla realtà di un'esistenza che aveva quasi dimenticata." Ibid., 20–21.
137. "Era la prima volta che Andreina parlava della sua tragedia a qualcuno: vi provava una specie di ebbrezza." Ibid., 25.
138. Ibid., 26.
139. Ibid., 28.
140. Ibid., 126, 307.
141. Hipkins, *Italy's Other Women*, 98. Hipkins's discussion of this haunting in terms of Gesi's relationship with Antonello is apt in the case of Luce as well.
142. "Quante ragazze erano già state lì, con dei soldati americani, in quella stanza? Ragazze che, come molte che aveva conosciute, erano state brave e semplici e oneste e poi si erano lasciate travolgere da quella specie di ondata di follia, di giovinezza e di ricchezza che si era abbattuta sulla città. Ragazze che vendevano il pesce ai mercati, e che poi, ad un tratto, si erano trovate a guadagnare diecimila, ventimila lire al giorno, e si comperavano le pellicce, spavalde ed esterrefatte." Peverelli, *Sposare lo straniero*, 300–301.
143. "Oh no, non così in quella brutta camera." Ibid., 302.

144. "Ma come scogliersi da quella stretta?" Ibid.

145. Hipkins, *Italy's Other Women*.

146. "l'assaggio di amore che ho avuto . . . l'assaggio fu rapido, doloroso, mi lasciò stordita." Peverelli, *Sposare lo straniero*, 348.

147. "un romantico sogno lungo l'oceano." Ibid.

148. While American newspapers preferred to celebrate the happy marriages, some brief reports of war bride suicides appeared in early postwar publications, Varricchio, "Il sogno e le radici," 118.

149. Peverelli, *Sposare lo straniero*, 353.

150. "Il mio bambino è il bambino di Freddy. È un bambino americano. Questa è la sua patria." Ibid., 360–361.

151. "la sensibilità, e la poesia e l'arte." Ibid., 361.

152. "così mutevoli e fantasiose e piene di strani capricci." Ibid., 362; "gli ho detto che va benissimo, che tutto quello che gli fa piacere andrà benissimo d'ora in poi." Ibid.

153. "io spero che il mio bambino assomigli a lui." Ibid.

154. Varricchio, "Il sogno e le radici," 125.

155. "Si dice che i bambini nati da genitori che appartengono a razze diverse siano bellissimi." Peverelli, *Sposare lo straniero*, 222.

156. A common critique of the romance genre is that it privileges heteronormative marriage and refuses female relationships. Regis, *A Natural History of the Romance Novel*, 4–5. This model of friendship among war brides also distinguishes itself from the affective transnationalism of the historical war bride that privileges the family back in Italy. Varricchio, "Il sogno e le radici," 129.

157. Although Varricchio identifies letter writing as a transnational coping strategy that historically enabled war brides to handle the trauma of immigration, he specifies these letters were meant to maintain affective ties to their families. Ibid., 128–129.

158. "Molto più tardi, dopo molti e molti anni, le donne fatte vecchie avrebbero raccontato alle nipoti distratte: 'vennero dall'America dei ragazzi biondi, alti, che parlavano a voce alta e ridevano spesso . . .'" Peverelli, *Sposare lo straniero*, 260.

159. "Che tutto sia stato così vero." Peverelli, "Autobiografia," 316.

160. Peverelli, *Sposare lo straniero*, 355, 347, 305.

161. "Forse sono le parole che mancano, le parole maledette di cui noi in Europa, in Italia sopra tutto, rivestiamo tutto, così che le più povere e nude cose appaiono splendide e luminose e affascinanti, e anche se queste parole sono orpelli, poco importa, ci fanno piacere." Ibid., 356.

4. A Queer Redemption: John Horne Burns's *The Gallery*

1. Emilio Cecchi, "La 'Galleria' di J. H. Burns," 371. Originally translated in 1949 by Anna Voing and reprinted in multiple editions, it was reissued in 1992 with a revised translation by Liu Saraz.

2. John Horne Burns, *The Gallery*, 18.

3. Ibid., 311.

4. John W. Aldridge, "For Novelist John Horne Burns, War Was Hell—and Much More," 5.

5. There are three biographies on Burns: John Mitzel, *John Horne Burns*; Mark T. Bassett's unpublished dissertation "John Horne Burns," and most recently, David Margolick, *Dreadful*.

6. Brigid Brophy, "John Horne Burns," 192.

7. Paul Fussell, Introduction, vii.

8. *The Gallery* is beloved by scholars of American literary representations of Allied-occupied Italy, earning favorable comparisons to John Hersey's *Bell for Adano*. See Henry Stuart Hughes, *The United States and Italy*, 12; Anthony M. Gisolfi, "The Beach of Heaven"; John P. Diggins, *Mussolini and Fascism*, 435; Frederick Robert Karl, *American Fictions*, 99–101. For the most comprehensive (and highly favorable) Italian analysis of the novel, see Laura Coltelli, "L'Italia nel romanzo di guerra americano." While he initially loved it, Raffaele La Capria finds it slightly less "sincere" today and sees more overlaps between Burns's honesty and Malaparte's excess, *Ultimi viaggi nell'Italia perduta*, 25. The most thorough literary analyses can be found in John Gatt-Rutter, "Liberation and Literature"; Jonathan Vincent, "America e Italia" and *The Health of the State*; Clive Baldwin, "The Orgasm of a Frigidaire." Historians also love *The Gallery*, citing it as a nonfictional source. See John Costello, *Virtue Under Fire*, 226; Sergio Lambiase and Gian Battista Nazzaro, *L'odore della guerra*, 79; Gloria Chianese, "Italiani liberati dalla Sicilia a Napoli," 104; Paolo De Marco, *Polvere di piselli;* Maria Porzio, *Arrivano gli alleati!* Diggins warns precisely against this kind of reading. *Mussolini and Fascism*, 441

9. Bassett, "John Horne Burns," 52.

10. Burns, *The Gallery*, 1.

11. Brophy, "John Horne Burns," 193; Burns, *The Gallery*, 1.

12. Ibid., 85.

13. Ibid., 109.

14. Ibid., 342.

15. Ibid., 307. Citations of this affirmation are ubiquitous in war-bride historiography: Susan Zeiger, *Entangling Alliances*, 2; Elfrieda Berthiaume Shukert and Barbara Smith Scibetta, *The War Brides of World War II*; Silvia Cassamagnaghi, *Operazione spose di guerra*. This quotation appears, unattributed, in Costello, *Virtue under Fire*, 7; and also in Patricia J. Anderson, *Passion Lost*, x.

16. Burns, *The Gallery*, 267–268. On war-bride scholarship in the Italian context, see Chapter 3.

17. Winston Leyland, *Gay Roots*; Allan Bérubé, *Coming Out Under Fire*; Anthony Slide, *Lost Gay Novels*; Drewey Wayne Gunn, *Gay American Novels*. A substantive analysis in the context of masculinity studies is found in Baldwin, "The Orgasm of a Frigidaire."

18. Brophy, "John Horne Burns," 193.

19. Emma Bond, "Towards a Trans-National Turn in Italian Studies?" 416.
20. Ibid.
21. Ruth Glynn, "Porosity and Its Discontents" (*Critical Inquiry*, forthcoming 2019, cited by permission of the author).
22. Serenella Iovino, *Ecocriticism and Italy*, 17.
23. Burns, *The Gallery*, 207.
24. Ibid.
25. Iovino, *Ecocriticism and Italy*, 18. Here, Iovino is discussing a passage from Curzio Malaparte's *La pelle*.
26. Burns, *The Gallery*, 220, 209.
27. Remarking that Benjamin and Lacis's essay makes no mention of the Galleria Umberto I, despite Benjamin's extensive study of arcade, Ian Wiblin applies their description of the "porous" city to the space of the Galleria, "Confronting the Void," 141–142.
28. Bond, "Towards a Trans-National Turn in Italian Studies?" 416. Here, Bond draws from Steven Vertovec, *Transnationalism*.
29. Bassett identifies sources of inspiration for *The Gallery*, including a poem entitled "The Gallery" by Andrew Marvell and a musical mode, Modest Petrovich Moussorgsky's *Pictures at an Exhibition*, which alternates promenades and portraits, "John Horne Burns," 181, 183.
30. Iain Chambers opens his chapter on Naples with a quote from Burns, *Mediterranean Crossings*, 71. Johann Friedrich Geist includes an entry on *The Gallery* in his tome, *Arcades: The History of a Building Type*, 437. In an essay on Neapolitan filmmaker Elvira Notari, Giuliana Bruno cites Burns's description of the *Gallery* from Geist. Giuliana Bruno, "Streetwalking around Plato's Cave." Drawing on Bruno, Lidia Curti also cites Burns's description of the Galleria in "Female Literature of Migration in Italy." Also drawing on Bruno, photographer Ian Wiblin returns to the original text in his astute analysis. "Confronting the Void."
31. Although most of the book is oriented toward the past and present, Wiblin points out that *The Gallery* looks to the (fairly near) future, imagining Neapolitans in 1960, a year Burns never lived to see. *The Gallery*, 308, as cited in Wiblin, 151.
32. Burns, *The Gallery*, 342.
33. Karl Schoonover, *Brutal Vision*, 144–145.
34. Burns, *The Gallery*, 309.
35. Bond, "Towards a Trans-National Turn in Italian Studies?" 418.
36. Burns, *The Gallery*, 128.
37. Ibid., 145.
38. Ibid., 293, 42.
39. Ibid., 130, 148.
40. Bond, "Towards a Trans-National Turn in Italian Studies?" 417.
41. Chambers, *Mediterranean Crossings*, 72.

42. Silvana Patriarca, *Italian Vices*, 9. For this historic conflation between Italy and its own south, see also Stephanie Hom, *The Beautiful Country*. Patriarca and Hom both draw from Nelson Moe, *The View from Vesuvius*. See also the Introduction and Chapter 1.

43. Bond, "Towards a Trans-National Turn in Italian Studies?" 417.

44. Ibid., 416.

45. Glynn, "Porosity and Its Discontents."

46. Hom, *The Beautiful Country*, 50, as cited in Glynn, "Porosity and Its Discontents."

47. Glynn, "Porosity and Its Discontents"; Mary Louise Pratt, *Imperial Eyes*, 6–7. Glynn uses Pratt's contact zone to discuss Allied-occupied Naples in "Naples and the Nation."

48. "We must . . . recognize that the apparent priority of *fabula* to *sjužet* is in the nature of a mimetic illusion, in that the *fabula*—'what really happened'—is in fact a mental construction that the reader derives from the sjuzet, which is all that he ever directly knows." Peter Brooks, *Reading for the Plot*, 13.

49. Sharon Ouditt, *Impressions of Southern Italy*, 3.

50. Aldridge, *After the Lost Generation*, 142. Gatt-Rutter also describes the attempt to unify the portraits and promenades as a "gamble that doesn't . . . come off," "Liberation and Literature," 254. For Karl, the unity is achieved two-thirds of the way through with the "Giulia" portrait. *American Fictions*, 100. Fussell also calls it a "plotless book less like a novel than a memoir, or even a travel book, or a collection of sketches illustrating a double theme," but recognizes this plotlessness as part of the novel's "unique structure," insofar as the "discontinuity . . . suggest[ed] incoherence as a contemporary social characteristic." Introduction, ix.

51. Millicent Marcus, "Rossellini's Paisà." See also Chapter 2.

52. Burns, *The Gallery*, 24.

53. Ibid., 3.

54. Ibid., 17.

55. Ibid., 21.

56. Ibid.

57. Ibid., 24.

58. "Il faut gémir quand nous faison l'amour. Et la prochaine fois je te prie de m'approter un peu de chewing gum." Ibid., 24 (translation mine).

59. Ibid., 19.

60. Ibid., 45, 52–53.

61. Ibid., 49.

62. Ibid., 156.

63. Ibid., 158.

64. Ibid.

65. Ibid., 159.

66. Ibid., 206.

67. Ibid., 83.

68. Ibid., 20, 261–262, ellipses in original.
69. "The novel may then be considered as attempting to develop a narrative that challenges and reworks contemporary expectations of gender and sexual identity, of self and 'other,' but without being able to establish a consistent alternative vision." Baldwin, "The Orgasm of a Frigidaire," 154.
70. On the hierarchical opposition between tourists and travelers as constitutive of travel discourse, see Jonathan Culler, *Framing the Sign*.
71. Burns, *The Gallery*, 207.
72. Ibid., 210.
73. Ibid., 149.
74. Vincent, "America e Italia," 26.
75. Judith Halberstam, *In a Queer Time and Place*, 2, 6.
76. Burns, *The Gallery*, 331.
77. Ibid., 253, 254.
78. Ibid., 254, 255.
79. Ibid., 257.
80. Ibid., 258.
81. Ibid., 257.
82. Ibid., 211.
83. Ibid., 305.
84. Ibid., 306.
85. Burns, *The Gallery*, 210; "Caro John, ti consiglio di dire a tutti quel che hai visto in Italia . . . Perché sai, gl'Italiani non vi odiano, non vi odiano, voi altri Americani . . ." Ibid., 311 (translation mine).
86. Ibid., 311.
87. Dante Alighieri, *Paradiso*, 572–573.
88. Bond, "Towards a Trans-national Turn in Italian Studies?" 418.
89. Derek Duncan, "The Queerness of Italian Cinema," 473.
90. Bond, "Towards a Trans-national Turn in Italian Studies?" 418.
91. "For though we Americans were a conquering army, when history is written it will show that the Neapolitans conquered many of us. They beat us down with love. They loved love. There were Italian boys and girls who slashed their wrists for us, whether we deserved it or not." Burns, *The Gallery*, 304.
92. Ibid., 342.
93. I am grateful to Megan Fenrich, who brought these Civil War references to my attention in a graduate seminar at the University of North Carolina, Chapel Hill.
94. Burns, *The Gallery*, 318.
95. Bond, "Towards a Trans-National Turn in Italian Studies?" 423.
96. Ibid., 85; "Once this Galleria had a dome of glass, but the bombings of Naples shattered this skylight." Ibid., 1.
97. Ibid., 85–86.
98. Wiblin, "Confronting the Void," 152.

99. Burns, *The Gallery*, 12; Ibid., 227.
100. Ibid., 228.
101. "Siamo vinti . . . in questa guerra sono morti non soltanto i soldati . . . ma l'anima, le donne, e l'onore di tutti quanti." Ibid., 229 (translation mine).
102. Ibid., 315.
103. Ibid., 341.
104. Burns, "Algiers," 131; "Tunis," 65; "Casablanca," 64; "Naples," 70; "Rome," 65.
105. Burns, "Naples," 65, 67.
106. Ibid., 67–68.
107. Ibid., 70, 154.
108. Ibid., 156.
109. Burns, "Rome," 67.
110. Although *Holiday* is famous for its high-caliber literary contributors, Burns's articles are surrounded by advertisements for vacations and alcohol. The American magazine was published between 1946 and 1977, and in 2014 it resumed publication as a biannual based in Paris.

5. Sleights of Hand, Black Skin, and the Redemption of Curzio Malaparte's *La pelle*

1. Curzio Malaparte, *Kaputt*, 410; "Un enorme mucchio di macerie e di stracci insanguinati." *Kaputt*, 940.
2. On *Kaputt* and Malaparte's self-construction as narrator, see Charles Burdett, "Changing Identities through Memory"; Franco Baldasso, "Curzio Malaparte and the Tragic Understanding of Modern History."
3. Malaparte, *Kaputt*, 410; "La città, sulle prime, pareva deserta. Ma poi, a poco a poco, si udiva uscir dai vicoli e dai cortili un ronzio, un clamore soffocato di voci, uno strepito fioco e lontano." *Kaputt*, 940.
4. Malaparte, *Kaputt*, 410, emphasis mine, translation modified (the Foligno translation eliminates the repetition of the passage, especially where the two descriptions contradict one another); "Penetrando allora con lo sguardo nel segreto dei 'bassi,' frugando con l'occhio in fondo alle strette, altissime spaccature aperte fra palazzo e palazzo che son le nobili vie dell'antica Napoli, si vedeva . . ." *Kaputt*, 940.
5. Translation mine, emphasis mine (the Foligno translation leaves out those phrases in the second part of the description that contradict the sequence of the first); "Nonché deserta, sulle prime la città mi apparve silenziosa. Vedevo la gente correre gesticolando, vedevo muover le labbra, e non udivo un suono, uno strepito, una voce: ma a poco a poco un clamore confuso nasceva, o mi parve, nell'aria polverosa, prese al mio orecchio forma e sostanza." *Kaputt*, 941.
6. "Era la Napoli vera, la Napoli, viva, sopravvissuta a tre anni di bombardamenti, di fame, di pestilenze, era la Napoli popolare, quella dei vicoli, dei 'bassi,' dei tuguri, dei rioni senza luce, senza sole, senza pane." *Kaputt*, 947.
7. Ruth Glynn counts just five others, including Liliana Cavani's 1981 film

adaptation of *La pelle*: Eduardo De Filippo's *Napoli milionaria!* (1945) and its adaptations, the Naples episode of Roberto Rossellini's *Paisà* (1946), Duilio Coletti's film *Il re di Poggioreale* (1961), and Roberto De Simone's *Satyricon a Napoli '44* (2014)—the only other literary narrative amid plays and films. Glynn, "Naples and the Nation," 1. A recent addition to this corpus is Francesco Patierno's *Naples '44* (2017), a "documentary" adaptation of Norman Lewis's 1978 diary of the same title. See Chapter 6.

8. Baldasso, "Curzio Malaparte and the Tragic Understanding of Modern History," 295.

9. *Soldier's Guide to Naples* (1944), 1.

10. Malaparte, *The Skin*, 283; "Non ha alcuna importanza se quel che Malaparte racconta è vero o falso. La questione da porsi è un'altra: se quel ch'egli fa è arte o no." *La pelle*, 268.

11. Alessandro Scarsella, "Curzio Malaparte," 1111.

12. On the scandal surrounding Suckert's *Viva Caporetto!*, see Guido Bonsaver, *Censorship and Literature in Fascist Italy*, 17–18.

13. On the (friendly) relationship between Gobetti and Malaparte, see Giuseppe Pardini, *Curzio Malaparte*, 63.

14. Luigi Martellini, Introduction. For a complete political biography, see Pardini, *Curzio Malaparte*. For a fictionalization of Malaparte, based on the author's personal experience, see Percy Winner, *Dario*.

15. Walter Murch, "Malaparte's 'Partisans, 1944.'"

16. In an appendix to the 1959 Vallechi edition of *La pelle*, editor Enrico Falqui published a letter Malaparte wrote to a critic in which he made a similar request, Luigi Baldacci. Introduction, vi.

17. The originator of the "chameleon" epithet was Antonio Gramsci, *I quaderni*, 205. The "chameleon" has justified decades of dismissive readings of Malaparte's oeuvre, see Pardini, *Curzio Malaparte*, 16 n. 5; Francesco Perfetti, "Introduction," 9; Giordano Bruno Guerri, *L'arcitaliano*, 97. Particularly hostile readings can be found in Edmondo Cione, *Napoli e Malaparte*; Emilio Cecchi, "Curzio Malaparte." An early supporter was Malaparte's sister, Edda Ronchi Suckert, who edited a twelve-volume collection of his papers and related material, *Malaparte*. The 1997 Mondadori volume, *Opere*, and Pardini's *Biografia politica* represent an effort to return Malaparte to the public eye that took over a decade to gain traction.

18. Milan Kundera, *Encounter*. Kundera generated widespread interest in the novel as well as a new round of negative editorials in Italy. Other scholars outside of Italy whose appreciation of Malaparte and *La pelle* predates Kundera's high-profile endorsement include John Gatt-Rutter, "Liberation and Literature"; Murch, "Malaparte's 'Partisans, 1944'"; Gary Indiana, *Utopia's Debris*. The republication of *Kaputt* in 2005 by the *New York Review of Books* no doubt helped fuel this renewed interest in Malaparte outside of Italy. See Tim Parks, "The Horrors of War."

19. For the earliest such reading, see Gatt-Rutter, "Liberation and Literature," 61. See also Indiana, *Utopia's Debris*, 178; Kundera, *Un incontro*; Jenny McPhee, Foreword.

20. On the early reviews of *La pelle*, most of which took its nonfiction status for granted (with some suspicion), see Marisa Escolar, "Sleights of Hand"; Glynn, "Naples and the Nation," 5.

21. Malaparte's works are now being regularly published in Italian, English, French, and Spanish. To speak just of some recent English publications, Murch translated the collection, *The Bird That Swallowed Its Cage*, in 2014. *The New York Review of Books* published an unexpurgated translation of *The Skin* in 2013, and *The Kremlin's Ball*, translated by Jenny McPhee, in 2018. His name also graces a popular Manhattan Italian restaurant, opened in 2011, and he is the protagonist of a novel that was a finalist for the prestigious Premio Strega in 2016, Rita Monaldi and Francesco Sorti's *Malaparte*.

22. Indiana, *Utopia's Debris*, 179.

23. Scarsella, "Curzio Malaparte," 1112.

24. Notable exceptions include Baldasso, "Curzio Malaparte and the Tragic Understanding of Modern History"; and in terms of Allied-occupied Naples, Gatt-Rutter, "Liberation and Literature," and Glynn, "Naples and the Nation."

25. Cavani ends her cinematic adaptation of *La pelle* with this episode.

26. The novel uniformly uses the term *negri*.

27. Malaparte, *The Skin*, 13. "Torme di donne spettinate e imbellettate, seguite da turbe di soldati negri dalle mani pallide, scendevano e salivano per Via Toledo, fendendo la folla con stridi acuti: 'ehi, Joe! Ehi, Joe!'" Malaparte, *La pelle*, 8–9.

28. Malaparte, *The Skin*, 32. "Tanta era l'iniqua forza del contagio, che prostituirsi era divenuto un atto degno di lode, quasi una prova di amor di patria, e tutti, uomini e donne, lungi da arrossirne, parevano gloriarsi della propria e della universale abbiezione."

29. Malaparte, *The Skin*, 200; *La pelle*, 191–192.

30. Malaparte, *The Skin*, 298; "Scendevan di corsa, discinte, scarmigliate, deliranti, agitando le braccia, ridendo, piangendo, gridando: in un attimo fummo circondati, assaliti, soverchiati, e la colonna sparí sotto un groviglio inestricabile di gambe e di braccia, sotto una foresta di capelli neri, sotto una tenera montagna di seni floridi, di bocche carnose, di spalle bianche." *La pelle*, 282–283.

31. Malaparte, *The Skin*, 298; "('Come al solito' disse il giorno dopo nella sua predica, il giovane curato della Chiesa di Santa Caterina in Corso Italia 'come al solito la propaganda fascista mentiva, quando annuziava che l'esercito americano, se fosse entrato in Roma, avrebbe assalito le nostre donne: sono le nostre donne che hanno assalito, e sconfitto l'esercito americano')." *La pelle*, 283.

32. John Parascandola, "Quarantining Women." The (losing) battle metaphor appears in John Costello, *Love, Sex, and War*, 224; Paolo De Marco, *Polvere di piselli*, 43; Peter Schrijvers, *The Crash of Ruin*, 179.

33. Charles Maurice Wiltse, *The Medical Department*, 215–216. On the

weaponizing of Italian women, see Norman Lewis, *Naples '44*, 87–88. On Lewis, see Chapter 6.

34. Roberts, *What Soldiers Do*, 164. Roberts analyzes the Wiltse report cited above, *The Medical Department*, 258. On the "ambivalence and fragmentation" of the Allies' policy toward prostitution, see Cynthia Enloe, *Maneuvers*, 62–63.

35. See Hondon B. Hargrove, *Buffalo Soldiers in Italy*. In "The Trial," Malaparte refers explicitly to spending time with the Ninety-Second Division when it was stationed near Livorno.

36. Roberts, *What Soldiers Do*, 165. In Alfred Hayes's *All Thy Conquests*, the narrator remarks on the *negri* who frequent prostitutes in the Roman Forum, 34. See also Edmund Wilson, *Europe without Baedecker*, 68. In the "Naples" episode of Roberto Rossellini's *Paisà*, the African American soldier is represented as a drunkard but has no involvement with prostitutes who, curiously enough, are not present in this male-dominated episode.

37. Malaparte, *The Skin*, 217; "Per i popoli vinti . . . tutti i vincitori sono uomini di colore." *La pelle*, 206.

38. Malaparte, *The Skin*, 21–22. "Cinquanta dollari erano il prezzo massimo che si pagava per comprarsi un negro a giornata, cioè per poche ore: il tempo necessario per ubriacarlo, spogliarlo di tutto quel che aveva addosso, dal berretto alle scarpe, e poi, scesa la notte, abbandonarlo nudo sul lastrico di un vicolo." *La pelle*, 17.

39. This slave-trade motif appears in the "Naples" episode of Rossellini's *Paisà* and, as Peter Bondanella remarks, contains a similar irony, *A History of Italian Cinema*, 73. On this episode and its racial significance, see Shelleen Greene, *Equivocal Subjects*, 167–170.

40. Stephanie Depaola traces convincing overlaps between Italian and American anti-black racism, "Sexual Violence, Racism, and the Allied Occupation of Italy."

41. Malaparte, *The Skin*, 42; "Non hai mai visto una vergine?" *La pelle*, 37.

42. Malaparte, *The Skin*, 48; "La ragazza gettò la sigaretta per terra, afferrò con la punta delle dita i lembi della sottana, e lentamente li sollevò: prima apparvero i ginocchi, stretti dolcemente nella guainia di seta delle calze, poi la pelle nuda delle coscie, poi l'ombra del pube. Rimase un istante in quell'atto, triste Veronica, col viso severo, la bocca sprezzantemente socchiusa. Poi lentamente rovesciandosi sulla schiena, si distese sul letto e aprì adagio adagio le gambe." *La pelle*, 43.

43. Malaparte, *The Skin*, 48; "Come fa l'orrenda aragosta in amore, quando apre lentamente la tenaglia delle branche guardando fisso il maschio con i piccoli occhi rotondi neri e lucenti, e sta immota e minacciosa, così fece la ragazza aprendo lentamente la rosea e nera tenaglia delle carni, e rimase così, guardando fisso gli spettatori. Un profondo silenzio regnava nella stanza." *La pelle*, 43.

44. Malaparte, *The Skin*, 48–49. "'She is a virgin. You can touch. Put your finger inside. Only one finger. Try a bit. Don't be afraid. She doesn't bite. She is a virgin. A real virgin,' disse l'uomo spingendo la testa dentro la stanza per lo

spacco della tenda. Un negro allungò la mano, e provò col dito. Qualcuno rise, e pareva si lamentasse. La 'vergine' non si mosse, ma fissò il negro con uno sguardo pieno di paura e di odio. Mi guardai intorno: tutti erano pallidi, tutti erano pallidi di paura e di odio. 'Yes, she is like a child' disse il negro con voce rauca, facendo roteare lentamente il dito.' 'Get out the finger,' disse la testa dell'uomo infilata nello spacco della tenda rossa. 'Really, she is a virgin' disse il negro ritraendo il dito." *La pelle*, 43–44.

45. Malaparte and Novella, *Mi scriveva Malaparte*, 50 (translation mine).

46. The British version, also translated by David Moore, published by Alan Redman, censors other parts of the book, including an entire chapter representing a homosexual birthing ritual turned orgy, but leaves the "Virgin."

47. Giampaolo Martelli, *Curzio Malaparte*, 154; Gatt-Rutter, "Liberation and Literature," 249; Gianni Grana, *Curzio Malaparte*, 108.

48. Malaparte, *The Skin*, 50; "quando tornerai in America . . . ti piacerà raccontare che il vostro dito di vincitori è passato sotto l'arco di trionfo delle gambe delle povere ragazze italiane." *La pelle*, 45.

49. Anna Garofalo, *L'italiana in italia*, 67 (translation mine).

50. Gatt-Rutter, "Liberation and Literature," 61; Grana, *Curzio Malaparte*, 108.

51. Malaparte, *The Skin*, 80; "Tutta l'Europa non è che un ciuffo di peli biondi. Una corona di peli biondi per la vostra fronte di vincitore." *La pelle*, 78.

52. Barbara Spackman, *Decadent Genealogies*, 165.

53. On the racialization of the Italians in the United States in response to immigration, see Greene, *Equivocal Subjects*, 175.

54. Malaparte, *The Skin*, 233–234; "'I soldati negri' disse Consuelo 'per convincere le ragazze napoletane a fidanzarsi con loro, raccontano di esser bianchi come gli altri, ma che in America, prima di imbarcarsi per l'Europa, sono stati tinti di nero, per poter combattere di notte senza esser visti dal nemico. Quando, dopo la guerra, torneranno in America, si raschieranno via dalla pelle la tintura nera, e torneranno bianchi." Malaparte, *La pelle*, 223. John Horne Burns mentions a similar story in *The Gallery*, 267.

55. Brackette F. Williams, *Women out of Place*, 22.

56. Jack's revelation is in *The Skin*, 261; *La pelle*, 247–248; the soldiers' hellish realization is in *The Skin*, 263–264; *La pelle*, 250.

57. Malaparte, *The Skin*, 266–267; "Negri quasi nudi, come se avessero in quella folla ritrovata l'antica foresta, si aggiravano nel tumulto con le froge dilatate e rosse, i tondi occhi bianchi sporgenti dalla nerra fronte, attorniati da branchi di prostitute mezze nude anch'esse." *La pelle*, 253.

58. Malaparte, *The Skin*, 273; "Quello è Adamo e quella è Eva, appena partoriti dal caos, appena risaliti dall'inferno, appena risorti dal sepolcro. Guardali, sono appena nati, e già hanno sofferto tutti i peccati del mondo. Tutti gli uomini, a Napoli, in Italia, in Europa, sono come quegli uomini. Sono immortali. Nascono nel dolore, muoiono nel dolore, e risorgono puri." *La pelle*, 259.

59. Malaparte, *The Skin*, 272; "Una donna vestita di rosso, seduta sotto un

albero, allattava il suo bambino. E il seno, sporgente fuor del corpetto rosso, era bianchissimo . . . , come il seno della prima donna della creazione." *La pelle*, 258.

60. On the malleable perception of Italians' racial identity, see Silvana Patriarca, "Fear of Small Numbers," 541.

61. Malaparte, *The Skin*, 274; *La pelle*, 260.

62. Driss Maghraoui, "Moroccan Colonial Soldiers," 26.

63. On Monte Cassino, see John Ellis, *Cassino*.

64. Maghraoui, "The Goumiers in the Second World War," 580.

65. Karl Ashoka Britto, "L'Esprit de Corps," 145.

66. Eric Storm and Ali Al Tuma, "Introduction," 2.

67. Sergio Lambiase and Gian Battista Nazzaro, *Napoli*, 140.

68. Giuseppe Speciale, "Il risarcimento dei perseguitati politici e razziali," 116–117; Gershovich, "Memory and Representation of War and Violence," 83; Eric Morris, *Circles of Hell*, 329. On the decades long repression of the victims' stories in order to preserve Franco Italian relations and the "myth" of the Allies, see Michela Ponzani, *Guerra alle donne*, 248–249.

69. On the difficulty in obtaining (and historiographical lack of interest in) the *goumiers*' perspective, see Gershovich, "Memory and Representation of War and Violence," 85. With the exception of a one page chapter in Lambiase and Nazzaro, *Napoli*, 140, that recognizes the racism faced by the *goumier*, the earliest Italian scholarship on the topic is from the 1990s and the perspective is heavily weighted toward the victims: Massimo Lucioli and Davide Sabatini, *La ciociara e le altre*; Roberto Gremmo, *Le marocchinate*; Michele Strazza, *Senza via di scampo*; Gigi Di Fiore, *Controstoria della liberazione*. A fascinating legal perspective about reparations is Speciale, "Il risarcimento dei perseguitati politici e razziali." Recent, more balanced, studies include Maria Porzio, *Arrivano gli alleati!*, 82–89 and Ponzani, *Guerra alle donne*, 223–252. A hybrid text between victims' fictionalized testimony and historical fictions, laden with racist stereotypes, is Stefania Catallo, *Le marocchinate*. Depaola offers a much needed historical contextualization and critique of this Italian body of scholarship, "Sexual Violence, Racism, and the Allied Occupation of Italy." In English, we see a more sustained effort to engage with the *goumier*. In addition to Gershovich's "Collaboration and 'Pacification'" and "Memory and Representation of War and Violence," and Maghraoui's, "Moroccan Colonial Soldiers" and "The Goumiers in the Second World War," other English language studies include: Robert G. Weisbord and Michael W. Honhart, "A Question of Race"; Isobel Williams, *Allies and Italians under Occupation*. An early English-language study is, Edward L. Bimberg, *The Moroccan Goums*, which Gershovich singles out for his "anachronistic and distinctly paternalistic colonial attitude," "Collaboration and 'Pacification,'" 142.

70. Speciale, "Il risarcimento dei perseguitati politici e razziali," 116.

71. Gershovich, "Memory and Representation of War and Violence," 83. Maghraoui claims that fifty nine *goumiers* were punished for such crimes, out of a colonial army of about 13,000 men. "The Goumiers in the Second World War," 580.

72. On this victim-centric approach and its limitations, see Depaola, "Sexual Violence, Racism, and the Allied Occupation of Italy."

73. Gershovich, "Memory and Representation of War and Violence," 85. See also Storm and Al Tuma, "Introduction," 4. On the incompatibility of the *goumier* with both French and Moroccan national discourse, see Maghraoui, "Moroccan Colonial Soldiers," 32.

74. Gershovich, "Memory and Representation of War and Violence," 85.

75. See Maghraoui, "Moroccan Colonial Soldiers"; Gershovich, "Memory and Representation of War and Violence," 86–87.

76. Millicent Marcus, "The Italian Body Politic Is a Woman," 335.

77. Mitchell Goodman's novel *The End of It* (1961) briefly represents the *goumier* through a soldier's letter home, signaling their fierce nature, their unusual garb and their hypersexuality.

78. A rare cinematic counter-narrative is the 2006 film *Indigènes* (Natives) by Rachid Bouchareb, a French director of Algerian descent.

79. Lambiase and Nazzaro, *Napoli*, 140 (translation mine). On the fear and hatred of the *goumier* among Italian civilians see Ponzani, *Guerra alle donne*, 232.

80. Marcus, *Filmmaking by the Book*, 284 n. 30.

81. Malaparte, *The Skin*, 120; "Li tastavano, alzavano loro le vesti, ficcavano le loro lunghe, esperte dita nere fra i bottoni dei calzoncini, contrattavano il prezzo mostrando il dito della mano." *La pelle*, 120.

82. For example, Malaparte, *The Skin*, 21; *La pelle*, 16.

83. Malaparte, *The Skin*, 13; "avvolti nei loro scuri mantelli," *La pelle*, 9.

84. Malaparte, *The Skin*, 125; *La pelle*, 117.

85. There is a reference to French colonial soldiers speaking French amongst one another, which Malaparte and Jack cannot understand and lament is not "real" French. Malaparte, *The Skin* 25; *La pelle* 21.

86. Moravia, *La ciociara*, 266; *Two Women*, 281; Gershovich, "Memory and Representation of War and Violence," 4.

87. Kadish, *Point of Honor*, 299–300; Tommaso Landolfi, *An Autumn Story*, 139; Landolfi, *Racconto d'autunno*, 145. Although she expresses a hatred toward the *goumiers*, Irish-American expatriate and landowner Iris Origo describes one of few examples of the *goumier* communicating something other than sexual desire: "He can speak only a few words of English and Italian and is very completely lost—travelling north, although he says he wants to get to Rome. We give him food and shelter for the night and point out the road to the south. 'Me ship,' he says. 'Me not swim.'" *War in Val d'Orcia*, 98–99. On Origo's condemnation of the rape, see the Epilogue.

88. Malaparte, *The Skin*, 275; "i *goumiers* miravano con occhi avidi la folla femminile che passeggiava tra gli alberi nel parco della villa papale." *La pelle*, 261.

89. Malaparte, *The Skin*, 280; *La pelle*, 265–266. This order by the Vatican has since been recovered in the archives. Weisbord and Honhart, "A Question of Race," 405–406.

90. Maghraoui, "The Goumiers in the Second World War," 580.

91. Malaparte, *The Skin*, 282; "Non sono ancora riusciti a ritrovar la mano . . . chi sa dove sarà andata a finire!" *La pelle*, 267–268. On the *goumiers* as human mine detectors, see A. J. Liebling, *Mollie, and Other War Pieces*, 22; Alice Hoffman and Howard S. Hoffman, *Archives of Memory*, 66.

92. Malaparte, *The Skin*, 283; "nel suo prossimo libro, la nostra povera mensa da campo diventerà un banchetto regale, e io diventerò una specie di Sultano del Marocco." *La pelle*, 268.

93. Malaparte, *The Skin*, 283; "cosa c'è di vero in tutto quel che raccontate in *Kaputt*." *La pelle*, 268.

94. Malaparte, *The Skin*, 283. "Non ha alcuna importanza se quel che Malaparte racconta è vero o falso. La questione da porsi è un'altra: se quel ch'egli fa è arte o no." *La pelle*, 268.

95. Malaparte, *The Skin*, 286–287; "Era una mano d'uomo. Certamente era la mano del disgraziato *goumier*, che lo scoppio della mina aveva recisa di netto, e scagliata dentro la grande marmitta di rame, dove cuoceva il nostro *kouskous*. . . . Se non mi credete . . . guardate qui, nel mio piatto. Vedete questi ossicini? Sono le falangi. E queste, allineate sull'orlo del piatto, sono le cinque unghie." *La pelle*, 271–272.

96. Malaparte, *The Skin*, 226; *La pelle*, 214. I further discuss this episode in Chapter 6.

97. Malaparte, *The Skin*, 286; "Che potevo fare? Sono stato educato nel Collegio Cicognini, che è il migliore collegio d'Italia, e fin da ragazzo mi hanno insegnato che non bisogna mai, per nessuna ragione, turbare una gioia comune, un ballo, una festa, un pranzo. Mi son fatto forza per non impallidire, per non gridare, e mi son messo tranquillamente a mangiar la mano." Ibid., 271–272.

98. On *bella figura* in Italian culture, see Jacqueline Reich, *Beyond the Latin Lover*, chap. 1.

99. Malaparte, *The Skin*, 288; "Hai visto con che arte avevo disposto nel piatto quegli ossicini di montone? Parevan proprio le ossa di una mano!" *La pelle*, 273.

100. See Schrijvers, *The Crash of Ruin*, 47; Charles Scheffel and Barry Basden, *Crack! and Thump*, 75; Morris, *Circles of Hell*, 329; Rick Atkinson, *The Day of Battle*, 529; Hoffman and Hoffman, *Archives of Memory*, 66.

101. Giorgio Bàrberi Squarotti, "L'allegoria degli orrori della guerra," 287; see also Baldacci, Introduction, vii.

102. Raffaele La Capria, "Malaparte gran bugiardo," 37 (translation mine). In his recent book, La Capria makes his peace with Malaparte and *La pelle*. *Ultimi viaggi nell'Italia perduta*, 34–36; Cecchi, "Curzio Malaparte," 689 (translation mine).

103. Tahar Ben Jelloun, "'Segnorine' e marocchini" (translation mine). Marino Biondi also converts Captain Malaparte's plate into Curzio Malaparte's canvas, *Scrittori e miti totalitari*, 75.

104. On Guillaume's and Lyautey's association with the *goumiers*, see Bimberg, *The Moroccan Goums*, 19 and 123. On Guillaume's highly prejudiced

vision of the *goumiers*, see Ellis, *Cassino*, 372. In his diary, Lyautey alludes to a nocturnal "crisis" brought on by the proximity of some beautiful Italian women, curious to see the "color" of the *goumiers*. Pierre Lyautey, *La campagne d'Italie*, 85.

105. Malaparte, *The Skin*, 285; "Sulle sue verdi rive molti dei vostri *goumiers* sono caduti col viso nell'erba, sotto il fuoco delle mitragliatrici tedesche." *La pelle*, 270.

106. Malaparte, *The Skin*, 285; "è un'erba con la quale le donne incinte fanno una bevanda propiziatrice dei parti, un'erba ciprigna, di cui i montoni di Itri sono ghiottissimi. È appunto quell'erba, la *kallimeria*, che dà ai montoni di Itri quell'adipe ricco di donna incinta, e quella pigrizia muliebre, quella voce grassa, quello sguardo stanco, e languido, che hanno le donne incinte e gli ermafroditi." *La pelle*, 271.

107. Enloe, *Maneuvers*, 108. Nelson Moe locates a similar disavowal in his analysis of the text of a popular Neapolitan song of the period, "Tammurriata nera," "Naples '44/'Tammurriata Nera'/Ladri Di Biciclette."

108. Raleigh Trevelyan, *Rome '44*, 277. Trevelyan quotes the passage without attributing it to any source. Ellis also cites this passage and gives Trevelyan as a source, *Cassino*, 371. The Italian version of the quotation reads: "i marocchini si sono precipitati su di noi come demoni scatenati, hanno violentato, minacciando con mitragliatrici, bambine, donne, ragazzini, susseguendosi come bestie nei turni," Nota per S. E. il Marseciallo Badoglio, 25 maggio 1944, in *Morals & Conduct, French colonial troops* as cited in Ponzani, *Guerra*, 233. Strazza cites this passage without attributing it in *Senza via di scampo*, 113.

109. Serenella Iovino, *Ecocriticism and Italy*, 31.

110. Patriarca, "Fear of Small Numbers," 551.

111. Gatt-Rutter, "Liberation and Literature," 256.

6. The Redemption of Saint Paul: Norman Lewis's *Naples '44*

1. Luigi Barzini, "Una grande calamità."
2. Norman Lewis, *Naples '44*, 12, 35.
3. Ibid., 183.
4. Anglo-American historians who treat Lewis as an historical source include Roy Palmer Domenico, *Italian Fascists on Trial*; John Costello, *Virtue Under Fire*; Raleigh Trevelyan, *Rome '44*; Peter Caddick-Adams, *Monte Cassino*; Douglas Porch, *The Path to Victory*; Tony Judt, *Postwar*; Lloyd Clark, *Anzio*; David Vine, *Base Nation*. Amongst Italian historians, Maria Porzio cites his diary fourteen times, her second most cited source, and relays his statistics on prostitution and marriage vetting; Paolo De Marco quotes him thirty-nine times, his most cited source, on the black market, theft, famine as well as prostitution. Sergio Lambiase and Gian Battista Nazzaro repeat De Marco's statistic on prostitution (which comes from Lewis), *L'odore della guerra*, 108–109; see also Gigi Di Fiore, *Controstoria della liberazione*, and Camillo Albanese, *Napoli e la seconda guerra mondiale*.

5. Raffaele La Capria, *Ultimi viaggi nell'Italia perduta*, 39 (translation mine). Francesco Patierno, "How They Did It." *Naples '44* first appeared in Italian in 1993 as *Napoli '44*.

6. Aside from the adaptation, it has inspired Anthony Capella's *The Wedding Officer*, a loose, commercial novelization. Adam Foulds's historical novel *In the Wolf's Mouth* uses Lewis as a frequent source.

7. For a brief analysis of Lewis in the context of early postwar representations of Allied-occupied Naples, see John Gatt-Rutter, "Liberation and Literature." Sharon Ouditt contextualizes *Naples '44* in terms of travel writing in *Impressions of Southern Italy*. For popular readings of Lewis in a travel writing context, see Ben Taylor, *Naples Declared*; La Capria celebrates Lewis in *Ultimi viaggi nell'Italia perduta*, 37–40; Paola Villani analyzes Lewis together with Malaparte's *La pelle* and Burns's *The Gallery*, as well as the journalist Alan Moorehead's *Eclipse* and official Allied reports, finding significant overlap among their representations of Naples. "The Redemption of the Siren," 272–273.

8. Two other unstudied, British-authored literary narratives are Eric Linklater's *Private Angelo* (1946), discussed in Chapter 5, and Alexander Baron's *There's No Home* (1950).

9. Philippe Lejeune includes the diary among other "antifictional" narratives, including autobiography, biography, and history, yet singles the diary out from among them: "The diary grows weak and faints or breaks out in a rash when it comes into contact with fiction." *On Diary*, 204.

10. Barzini, "Una grande calamità." Remarking on Eric Newby's *Love and War in the Apennines*, a diary that has been treated as antifictional despite being published in 1971, Silvia Ross writes: "this long lag between the actual events and their full narrative representation . . . undermines to a certain extent the 'referential pact' that some . . . consider fundamental to travel writing, in that recreating the past many years after the fact, relying heavily on one's memory, has the potential to encourage fabrication." "Conflict, Mobility and Alterity," 151.

11. Gatt-Rutter asserts that the delay was caused by its status as true. "Liberation and Literature," 256. Barnaby Rogerson also sees the delay as strengthening the text's veracity. "Norman Lewis's Acknowledged Masterpiece about the Human Cost of War."

12. Julian Evans, *Semi Invisible Man*, 232, 569.

13. Rogerson, "Norman Lewis's Acknowledged Masterpiece about the Human Cost of War."

14. Lejeune, *On Diary*, 207.

15. John Freccero, *Dante*.

16. Lewis, *Naples '44*, 49.

17. Teodolinda Barolini, *The Undivine Comedy*, 149. On Dante's privileging of Saint Paul, see Albert Ascoli, *Dante and the Making of a Modern Author*, 383 n. 115.

18. Barolini, *The Undivine Comedy*, 57.

19. Lewis, *Naples '44*, 183; Charles Eliot Norton, *Letters of Charles Eliot*

Norton, 440. According to John Russo, Norton, Henry Wadsworth Longfellow, and James Russell Lowell "are the Big Three" who epitomize the American tradition of travel writing on Italy through the 1850s. "The Unbroken Charm," 125.

20. Ibid., 127.
21. Ibid., 126.
22. Freccero, *Dante,* 265.
23. Lewis, *Naples '44,* 99.
24. Ouditt, *Impressions of Southern Italy,* 29.
25. Robert Abele, "Benedict Cumberbatch Coolly Narrates Norman Lewis's Visual War Diary in 'Naples '44.'"
26. Gatt-Rutter, "Liberation and Literature," 256. La Capria also describes him in such terms: "the attentive eye is infallible . . . it observes, investigates, records." *Ultimi viaggi nell'Italia perduta,* 37 (translation mine).
27. Lewis, *Naples '44,* 18.
28. Ibid., 11.
29. Ibid., 18.
30. Ibid., 82.
31. Ibid., 169.
32. According to Rogerson, "He was also a crack shot and a determined and successful lover of women—to the extent that at one period of his life he was running three separate 'establishments.' If it wasn't such a corny old chestnut, I would claim him as a real James Bond." "Norman Lewis's Acknowledged Masterpiece about the Human Cost of War."
33. Lewis, *Naples '44,* 104–105.
34. Ibid., 105.
35. Ibid., 182–183.
36. Ibid., 184.
37. Ibid., 183, 184.
38. Ibid., 183, 184–185.
39. La Capria, *Ultimi viaggi nell'Italia perduta,* 38.
40. Lewis, *Naples '44,* 36. On *bella figura* in Italian culture, see Jacqueline Reich, *Beyond the Latin Lover,* chap. 1.
41. Lewis, *Naples '44,* 50.
42. Ibid., 94–96.
43. Ibid., 101.
44. Ibid., 120.
45. Ibid., 182, 170.
46. Ibid., 156.
47. Ibid., 168.
48. Ibid., 11.
49. Ouditt, *Impressions of Southern Italy,* 11.
50. Lewis, *Naples '44,* 11–12.
51. Ouditt, *Impressions of Southern Italy,* 3.

52. Lewis, *Naples '44*, 12.
53. Ibid., 23.
54. Ibid., 12.
55. Ibid., 13.
56. Ibid., 47.
57. Ibid., 40.
58. Comparisons to non-Western peoples can be found on ibid., 43, 55, 80, 109, 168, and 186. For temporal metaphors, see ibid., 43, 47, 80, 99, 120, 155, and 158. On the macaroni-eating competition, see Walter Benjamin and Asja Lacis, "Naples," 167. Lewis, *Naples '44*, 56. For more on Benjamin and Lacis, see Chapter 4.
59. Ben Kenigsberg, "'Naples '44' Chronicles Life during Wartime."
60. Lewis, *Naples '44*, 25.
61. Rogerson, "An Intelligence Officer in the Italian Labyrinth."
62. Lewis, *Naples '44*, 25.
63. Lewis, "Travel: See Naples and Die."
64. Lewis, *Naples '44*, 102.
65. Ibid., 78.
66. Ibid., 79–80.
67. Malaparte, *The Skin*, 24; "In due ore, il carro armato, nascosto dentro un cortile, fu sbullonato e smontato. In due ore sparì, non ne rimase traccia: soltanto una chiazza d'olio sul lastrico del cortile. Nel porto di Napoli, una notte, fu rubata una *Liberty ship*, giunta alcune ore prima dall'America in convoglio con altre dieci navi: fu rubato non solo il carico, ma la nave. Scomparve, e non se n'è mai saputo più nulla." *La pelle*, 20.
68. Malaparte, *The Skin*, 24–25; "Tutta Napoli, da Capodimonte a Posillipo, fu scossa, a una tal notizia, da un formidabile riso, come da un terremoto. Si videro le Muse, le Grazie, e Giunone, e Minerva, e Diana, e tutte le Dee dell'Olimpo . . . ridere reggendosi il seno con ambe le mani." *La pelle*, 20.
69. De Marco, *Polvere di piselli*, 154.
70. Richard Rovere, "A City Bleeding."
71. Malaparte, *The Skin*, 209. "Una bambina, qualcosa che assomigliava a una bambina." *La pelle*, 208.
72. Lewis, *Naples '44*, 55.
73. Peter Robb, *Street Fight in Naples*, 92. De Marco uses Lewis's story as a confirmation of the truth of the dinner, *Polvere di piselli*, 162.
74. Lewis, *Naples '44*, 24.
75. See Chapter 5.
76. Lewis, *Naples '44*, 24.
77. See De Marco, *Polvere di piselli*, 132; Lambiase and Nazzaro, *L'odore della guerra*, 109; Porzio, *Arrivano gli alleati!*, 61; Silvia Cassamagnaghi, *Operazione Spose di guerra*, 111; Albanese, *Napoli e la seconda guerra mondiale*, 158. For a literary refiguration of this scene set in Palermo, see Foulds, *In the Wolf's Mouth*, 187.

78. Lewis, *Naples '44*, 26.

79. On the sexualized southerner stereotype, see Ouditt, *Impressions of Southern Italy*, 5.

80. Lewis, *Naples '44*, 100.

81. Ibid., 180.

82. When attending a meeting of southern separatists, plotting their secession from the North, Lewis writes, "I listened with all the gravity I could manage, but found it hard to keep a straight face." Ibid., 55.

83. Ibid., 175; 171. A character in *Within the Labyrinth* makes a similar assertion: "In my opinion . . . and I give it after mature reflection, a girl who travels on a bus at night unaccompanied by her family, cannot be raped. The thing's a contradiction in terms. I'll go so far as to say that in my young days, if we'd ever come across a girl in such a situation—which, of course, would have been impossible—we should have felt that an overture of some kind was expected of us. Rape! That's a hard word. How on earth do they expect you to distinguish between a little routine and playful resistance and genuine disinclination." *Within the Labyrinth*, 241.

84. Lewis, *Naples '44*, 172–173.

85. On the consequences of rape for the victims, see Giuseppe Speciale, "Il risarcimento dei perseguitati politici e razziali," and Michela Ponzani, *Guerra alle donne*. See also Chapter 5.

86. On how the perpetrator's class influences whether he is judged to be a rapist or a John, see Cynthia Enloe, *Maneuvers*, 111; in regard to race, see Mary Louise Roberts, *What Soldiers Do*, 195–221; Raphaëlle Branche and Fabrice Virgili, "Writing the History of Rape in Wartime," 8. Stephanie Depaola explores the extreme disparities in the Italian context, where all those executed for rape were African Americans. "Sexual Violence, Racism, and the Allied Occupation of Italy." See also the Introduction.

87. Lewis, *Naples '44*, 130–131.

88. Ibid., 131.

89. Ibid.

90. Ibid.

91. See De Marco, *Polvere di piselli*, 240; Porch, *The Path to Victory*, 565; Fabrizio Carloni, *Il corpo di spedizione francese in Italia*, 21; La Capria, *Ultimi viaggi nell'Italia perduta*, 39.

92. Lewis, *Naples '44*, 131.

93. Ibid., 131–132.

94. Ibid., 130. Lewis's *The Sicilian Specialist* opens with a more graphic depiction of such a rape set in Sicily, 3–4.

95. On Dante's strategic use of discrediting the *Aeneid* in order to make his truth claims, see Barolini, *The Undivine Comedy*.

96. Kenigsberg, "'Naples '44' Chronicles Life During Wartime"; Abele, "Benedict Cumberbatch Coolly Narrates Norman Lewis' Visual War Diary in 'Naples '44.'" Other reviewers concur, "Even at its best, *Naples '44* works most

effectively as an advertisement for Lewis's book, making room for the text to breathe and allowing the writer's unique perspective to shine through." Derek Smith, "Naples '44"; "Still, the doc delivers enough arresting Neapolitan moments that many viewers will consider tracking down the source material." John DeFore, "Naples '44. Film Review."

97. This image appears to be the same as one that appears in Lambiase and Nazzaro, *Napoli*, 137.

98. For the text of this passage, see Lewis, *Naples '44*, 24.

99. Luke Y. Thompson, "Found-Footage Documentary 'Naples '44' Is Brought Together by Benedict Cumberbatch's Voice." See also Abele, "Benedict Cumberbatch Coolly Narrates Norman Lewis' Visual War Diary in 'Naples '44,'" and Smith, "Naples '44."

100. Ibid.

101. Ibid.

102. Ruth Glynn, "Engendering Occupation."

103. Sunny Singh, "Why the Lack of Indian and African Faces in Dunkirk Matters."

104. For a positive take on the film, see Gershovich, "Memory and Representation of War and Violence," 88. On a critique of the film's removal of the rape, see Gigi Di Fiore, *Controstoria della liberazione*, 217.

105. Smith, "Naples '44." Abele also refers to *Catch-22* as being set in Naples. "Benedict Cumberbatch Coolly Narrates Norman Lewis' Visual War Diary in 'Naples '44.'" While the prostitute character is Neapolitan, the scene of Yossarian's infernal wanderings is Rome.

106. On the subject of geographical slippage, it stands to note that Rossellini himself used footage of the liberation of Livorno to stand in for Rome in *Paisà*. Peter Bondanella, *The Films of Roberto Rossellini*, 67.

Epilogue

1. Jane Scrivener, *Inside Rome with the Germans*, 2. Published under a pseudonym, the diary is introduced by a family friend, an ambassador to Spain and Columbia University professor of European history, who vouches: "She is an American citizen and a cultivated lady. . . . She is a staunch American, as the diary amply demonstrates. She is also a Catholic religious." Carl J. H. Hayes, Foreword, x–xi. Raleigh Trevelyan uses her diary as a source in *Rome '44* and names her as Mother Mary Saint Luke, born Jessica Lynch in Brooklyn. For a reading of Scrivener's diary in the context of the dearth of American accounts of Rome during the German occupation, see William L. Vance, *America's Rome*, 364–403.

2. For a critical analysis of Origo's diary, see Silvia Ross, "Conflict, Mobility and Alterity." Origo, a prolific writer and biographer, is the subject of a biography: Caroline Morehead, *Iris Origo*. In 2018, her earlier war diary, *A Chill in the Air*, was published by the *New York Review of Books*, which also reissued *War in Val d'Orcia*.

3. Iris Origo, *War in Val d'Orcia*, 64–65. Scrivener also asks, "What about the Germans?" *Inside Rome with the Germans*, 2.

4. "Si parla di intervento divino, si corre in chiesa a ringraziare la Vergine, incoscienti dell'ora grave, inconsapevoli delle sue tragiche conseguenze." Maria Luisa D'Aquino, *Quel giorno trent'anni fa*, 10 (all translations mine).

5. Ibid.

6. On the multifaceted meanings of the armistice in Italy, see Elena Agarossi, *A Nation Collapses*, 10.

7. Scrivener, *Inside Rome with the Germans*, 203–204.

8. Origo, *War in Val d'Orcia*, 239.

9. Ibid., 236. On the *goumier* and the accused historic mass rape after the May 1944 victory at Monte Cassino, see Chapters 5 and 6.

10. Origo, *War in Val d'Orcia*, 239.

11. On D'Aquino's published collections of poetry, see Lucia Gangale, *Donne nel Sannio*.

12. "Un nuovo ciclo della mia esistenza." D'Aquino, *Quel giorno trent'anni fa*, 304.

13. A brief biography, found at the end of her journalism collection, claims that her diary was well received upon publication. *La mia Napoli*, 124. The only other published biography is an entry in Gangale, *Donne nel Sannio*, 51–54.

14. Fiona M. Stewart, "We Will Build a Better World Together."

15. In the opening dedication, D'Aquino claims to have only edited a limited amount of "superfluous" material.

16. "Io sono stata come la terra che ha accolto il suo seme per fecondare." D'Aquino, *Quel giorno trent'anni fa*, 78; for her critiques of Italian women, see ibid., 11, 289.

17. For instance, she compares herself to Baudelaire, ibid., 89.

18. "È una data di liberazione? Non lo credo." Ibid., 9.

19. "svolta decisiva." Ibid.

20. "È da ingenui prestar fede a quella che è solo una propaganda degli americani. Sere fa, infatti, un giornalista americano ha detto che nell'Italia meridionale si vedono già i segni di una rinascita. Nulla di piú falso." Ibid., 156.

21. "Al posto del nostro tricolore, sventolava con arroganza una bandiera americana. E ho detto con raccapriccio: 'Anche qui!'—Poiché Napoli ha cambiato volto: è una bella città devastata e si ha l'impressione che sia abitata, nella maggior parte da gente in uniforme. Razze di tutti i paesi si danno gomito nelle strade affollate, dandole l'aspetto di un paese coloniale. Gli alleati dicono che sono i nostri amici, e bisogna accettare, 'bon gré mal gré' la loro invadenza. Ma quando si è perduta una guerra, come l'abbiamo perduta noi, come si può sorridere ai nostri vincitori, a coloro che hanno bombardato le nostre città, anche se oggi essi sono i nostri liberatori? Chiudo gli occhi per non vedere, e guardo dentro di me: sono le strade che ho percorso al braccio di Umberto. Che pena! Cammino talvolta come in 'trance.' Ecco il Vomero, dove avevamo il nostro rifugio d'amore." Ibid., 295–296.

22. "Ho dato il lenzuolo per mille lire e per dieci chili di pane. Così potrò far fronte per qualche tempo alla vita quotidiana." Ibid., 153.

23. Ibid., 135.

24. On her various babysitters, cooks, servants, and breadmakers, see ibid., 20, 30, 57, 103; on her request for assistance, 116; on the jewels, 294.

25. Ibid., 118.

26. "Questa sera lo spettacolo della soldataglia americana ubriaca era stomachevole. Stanotte soldati ebbri hanno bussato a tutte le porte che affacciano sulla strada in cerca di donne. Questo è un luogo piuttosto pulito e non esistono venditrici d'amore. A tarda ora, un indigeno delle truppe di colore, che l'ubriachezza aveva portato all'erotismo, ha sfondato un portone cercando di penetrare in una casa, ma per fortuna è stato portato via in tempo dalla ronda." Ibid., 59; see also 150.

27. "Stamane è venuta una donna di qui, una certa Carmela dal soprannome confuso. La vedo sempre con una certa ripugnanza: forse perché ritengo faccia la parte del vampiro per il suo commercio di generi di contrabbando. Ha una fisionomia che differisce dalla nostra razza; gli occhi allungati, dallo sguardo scialbo, la fanno somigliare ad una mòngola. Ha sempre sulle labbra esangui un sorriso che ti verrebbe la voglia di trasformarglielo in smorfia con uno schiaffo, tanto ti accorgi quanto sia súbdolo." Ibid., 22.

28. "Il sangue. Un sangue vivo, caldo, sgorgato dalle mie piú segrete viscere, che quanto piú fluisce piú ti rivela la forza della tua natura femmina e sana." Ibid., 199. On her sexual desires, see ibid., 32 and 227; on breastfeeding, childbirth, and weaning see ibid., 66–67, 86 and 192.

29. "sostituire Colui che pensava ad ogni cosa." Ibid., 294.

30. "Mentre lo allattavo, ho ascoltato la radio." Ibid. 13.

31. Ibid., 261.

32. Ibid., 32–33.

33. Ibid.,145, 159; "Perché gli uomini hanno inventato il calendario? Se non esistesse, io oggi non ricorderei che, un anno fa, Umberto fu qui per l'ultima volta." Ibid., 253.

34. "il segreto di qualche filtro magico per smemorarmi da tutto quello che mi circonda." Ibid., 183.

35. Ibid., 199–203.

36. "Mi sono accorta, qualche volta, che quando la mia domestica mi trovava a scrivere o a leggere mi guardava in tralice, giudicandomi una perdigiorno.... Malgrado le opinioni della mia ex cameriera, io non posso pensare soltanto ad occuparmi del rassetto, della cucina, dei bambini; io ho bisogno di fare anche tutte quelle cose che ad essa ispiravano disprezzo: leggere un libro, prendere la pena in mano, oziare sdraiata sul letto, vagabondando con la mente occupata da altri pensieri." Ibid., 238–239.

37. Ibid., 238.

38. The one critic who discusses the diary paraphrases this claim and agrees. Gangale, *Donne nel Sannio*, 54.

39. "Tornerà la primavera e io inutilmente la sentirò nel corso accelerato del mio sangue. E ritorneranno ancora i ricordi d'amore come dopo un naufragio

salgono a galla i rottami di una imbarcazione." D'Aquino, *Quel giorno trent'anni fa,* 152.

40. "sento di essere piú forte: è certo l'età, ed è la stessa consapevolezza che ha il nocchiero che guida la rotta della sua nave e che conduce in porto tante vite a lui affidate." Ibid., 26. See also ibid., 271–272.

41. Dante Alighieri, *Purgatorio,* "Ah, slavish Italy, dwelling of grief, ship without a pilot in a great storm, not a ruler of provinces, but a whore!"; "Ahi serva Italia, di dolore ostello,/nave sanza nocchiere in gran tempesta,/non donna di province, ma bordello!" 96–97. On the importance of these verses in terms of the gendering of the Italian body politic, see Millicent Marcus, "The Italian Body Politic Is a Woman" and the Introduction.

42. The comparison between herself and Italy is made in D'Aquino, *Quel giorno trent'anni fa,* 169; she frequently describes Italy as mutilated (ibid., 244), as well as herself and other widows (ibid., 247). On gossip surrounding "Captain Bob," see ibid., 217. On her criticism of her friend, see ibid., 269–270.

43. "Io ho abolito la mia femminilità." Ibid., 222.

44. "Se non guardassi il calendario non ricorderei tante date, ma non rivivrei nemmeno il mio passato in ogni suo dettaglio." Ibid., 263.

45. "ero anche alla vigilia della mia prima esperienza d'amore." Ibid.

46. "Invano Umberto cercava di calmare quel tremito indomabile. Esso cessò solo dopo che ebbi conosciuto tutto l'amore per sfociare in un pianto convulso che disorientò Umberto, traendolo nell'inganno di avermi arrecato male o offesa e che lo portò a cadere genuflesso ai miei piedi per chiedermi, piangendo, l'assurdo perdono di avermi resa felice." Ibid., 264.

47. "un traguardo della mia vita di donna." Ibid., 263.

48. "lo storico annuncio che fece esultare tanti cuori e che mise nel mio un'ansia presaga." Ibid., 265.

49. "molti mi credono convalescente e non si accorgono che sono ammalata da morirne." Ibid., 222.

50. "Sono come una convalescente che abbia superato una crisi che pareva dovesse squassarla." Ibid., 248.

51. "mi pare di aver camminato sull'orlo di un abisso con la stessa incoscienza dei sonnambuli, senza esservi precipitata dentro." Ibid., 283.

52. "sotto una luce di verità e dall'alto di una sommità che non tutti possono raggiungere se non attraverso un calvario come il mio." Ibid., 272.

53. Some of those writings can be found in *La mia Napoli.*

54. "Bisogna che io riprenda la mia personalità individuale, che io diventi una donna con un nuovo posto da conquistare nel mondo: forse quella stessa che aspiravo a diventare se il destino non avesse cambiato il mio nome, facendomi acquistare quello che avrebbero avuto i miei figli e che mi portò a rinunziare parzialmente a quel sogno d'arte covato negli anni inquieti dell'adolescenza." D'Aquino, *Quel giorno trent'anni fa,* 277.

Works Cited

Abele, Robert. "Benedict Cumberbatch Coolly Narrates Norman Lewis' Visual War Diary in 'Naples '44.'" Review of *Naples '44*, directed by Francesco Patierno. *Los Angeles Times*, December 7, 2017.
Agarossi, Elena. *A Nation Collapses: The Italian Surrender of September 1943*. Translated by Harvey Fergusson II. Cambridge: Cambridge University Press, 2006.
Agnew, John. "The Myth of Backward Italy in Modern Europe." In *Revisioning Italy: National Identity and Global Culture*, edited by Beverly Allen and Mary J. Russo, 23–42. Minneapolis: University of Minnesota Press, 1997.
Albanese, Camillo. *Napoli e la seconda guerra mondiale: Vita quotidiana sotto le occupazioni dei Nazisti e degli Alleati*. Formigine: Infinito Edizioni, 2014.
Aldridge, John. *After the Lost Generation: A Critical Study of the Writers of Two Wars*. New York: Arbor House, 1985.
———. "For Novelist John Horne Burns, War Was Hell—and Much More." *Chicago Tribune*, May 12, 1985.
Alighieri, Dante. *The Divine Comedy of Dante Alighieri: Paradiso*. Translated by Robert M. Durling and Ronald L. Martinez. New York: Oxford University Press, 2010.
———. *The Divine Comedy of Dante Alighieri: Purgatorio*. Translated by Robert M. Durling and Ronald L. Martinez. New York: Oxford University Press, 2003.
Anderson, Patricia J. *Passion Lost: Public Sex, Private Desire in the Twentieth Century*. Markham, ON: Thomas Allen, 2001.
Aprà, Adriano. *Il dopoguerra di Rossellini*. Rome: Cinecittà International, 1995.
———. *Rosselliniana: Bibliografia Internazionale: Dossier Paisà*. Rome: Di Giacomo, 1987.
Ascoli, Albert Russell. *Dante and the Making of a Modern Author*. Cambridge: Cambridge University Press, 2008.
Atkinson, Rick. *The Day of Battle: The War in Sicily and Italy, 1943–1944*. New York: Macmillan, 2008.
Baedeker, Karl. *Italy: Handbook for Travellers—Third Part, Southern Italy, Sicily, the Lipari Islands*. London: Karl Baedeker, 1867.
———. *Italy from the Alps to Naples: Handbook for Travellers*. New York: Charles Scribner's Sons, 1909.

Baldacci, Luigi. Introduction to *La Pelle* by Curzio Malaparte. Milan: Mondadori, 1978.

Baldasso, Franco. "Against Redemption: The Early Postwar Debate over the Transition from Fascism to Democracy in Italy." PhD dissertation, New York University, 2014.

———. "Curzio Malaparte and the Tragic Understanding of Modern History." *Annali d'italianistica* 35 (2017): 279–303.

Baldwin, Clive. "'The Orgasm of a Frigidaire': Male Sexuality and the Female Other in Post–World War II American Fiction." In *Masculinity and the Other: Historical Perspectives*, edited by Heather Ellis and Jessica Meyer, 138–160. Cambridge: Cambridge Scholars Publishing, 2009.

Balio, Tullio. *The Foreign Film Renaissance on American Screens, 1946–1973*. Madison: University of Wisconsin Press, 2010.

Banti, Anna. "Neorealismo nel cinema italiano." In *Opinioni*, 90–101. Milan: Saggitore, 1961.

———. "Storia e ragioni del 'romanzo rosa.'" In *Opinioni*, 75–82. Milan: Saggitore, 1961.

Bàrberi Squarotti, Giorgio. "L'allegoria degli orrori della guerra." In *Curzio Malaparte: Il narratore, il politologo, il cittadino di Prato e dell'Europa*, edited by Biblioteca comunale "Alessandro Lazzerini" di Barili, 285–306. Naples: CUEN, 2000.

Barolini, Teodolinda. *The Undivine Comedy*. Princeton: Princeton University Press, 1992.

Baron, Alexander. *There's No Home: A Novel*. London: Sort of Books, 2011.

Barzini, Luigi. "Una Grande Calamità." Review of Four Days of Naples by Aubrey Menen and Naples '44 by Norman Lewis. *New York Review of Books* 27, no. 1 (February 7, 1980), 47–49.

Bassett, Mark T. "John Horne Burns: Towards a Critical Biography." PhD dissertation, University of Missouri, Columbia, 1985.

Bayman, Louis. *The Operatic and the Everyday in Postwar Italian Film Melodrama*. Edinburgh: Edinburgh University Press, 2014.

Ben-Ghiat, Ruth. "Fascism, Writing, and Memory: The Realist Aesthetic in Italy, 1930–1950." *Journal of Modern History* 67, no. 3 (1995): 627–665.

Benjamin, Walter, and Asja Lacis. "Naples." In *Reflections: Essays, Aphorisms, Autobiographical Writing*, edited by Peter Demetz, translated by Edmund Jephcott, 163–173. New York: Schocken Books, 1986.

Ben Jelloun, Tahar. "'Segnorine' e marocchini. Storia di un pregiudizio. Interview with Pietro Treccangoli." *Il Mattino*, September 10, 1993.

Bérubé, Allan. *Coming Out Under Fire: The History of Gay Men and Women in World War II*. Chapel Hill: University of North Carolina Press, 2010.

Bimberg, Edward L. *The Moroccan Goums: Tribal Warriors in a Modern War*. Westport, CT: Greenwood Press, 1999.

Biondi, Marino. *Scrittori e miti totalitari: Malaparte, Pratolini, Silone*. Florence: Polistampa, 2002.

Bogo, Anna. "Romanzo Rosa." In *Encyclopedia of Italian Literary Studies*, edited by Gaetana Marrone and Paolo Puppa, 1600–1603. New York: Routledge, 2006.

Bond, Emma. "Towards a Trans-National Turn in Italian Studies?" *Italian Studies* 69, no. 3 (2014): 415–424.

Bondanella, Peter. *The Films of Roberto Rossellini*. Cambridge: Cambridge University Press, 1993.

———. *A History of Italian Cinema*. New York: Continuum, 2009.

Bonsaver, Guido. *Censorship and Literature in Fascist Italy*. Toronto: University of Toronto Press, 2007.

Bourke-White, Margaret. *They Called It "Purple Heart Valley": A Combat Chronicle of the War in Italy*. New York: Simon & Schuster, 1944.

Branche, Raphaëlle, and Fabrice Virgili. "Writing the History of Rape in Wartime." In *Rape in Wartime*, edited by Raphaëlle Branche, Isabelle Delpla, John Horne, Pieter Lagrou, Daniel Palmieri, and Fabrice Virgili, translated by Helen McPhail, 1–16. New York: Palgrave Macmillan, 2012.

Bravo, Anna. *Il fotoromanzo*. Bologna: Il Mulino, 2003.

Brennan, Nathaniel. "Marketing Meaning, Branding Neorealism: Advertising and Promoting Italian Cinema in Postwar America." In *Global Neorealism: The Transnational History of a Film Style*, edited by Saverio Giovacchini and Robert Sklar, 87–102. Jackson: University Press of Mississippi, 2011.

Britto, Karl Ashoka. "L'Esprit de Corps: French Civilization and the Death of the Colonized Soldier." In *Empire Lost: France and Its Other Worlds*, edited by Elisabeth Mudimbe-Boyi, 145–161. Lanham, MD: Lexington Books, 2009.

Brooks, Peter. *Reading for the Plot: Design and Intention in Narrative*. Cambridge, MA: Harvard University Press, 1992.

Brophy, Brigid. "John Horne Burns." In *Don't Never Forget: Collected Views and Reviews*, 192–202. London: Jonathan Cape, 1966.

Brown, John Mason. *To All Hands: An Amphibious Adventure*. New York: Whittlesey House, 1943.

Bruni, David. "Il classicismo nella modernità: Il terzo episodio." In *Paisà: Analisi del film*, edited by Stefania Parigi, 73–84. Venice: Marsilio, 2005.

Bruno, Giuliana. "Streetwalking around Plato's Cave." *October* 60 (1992): 111–129.

Buchanan, Andrew. "'Good Morning, Pupil!' American Representations of Italianness and the Occupation of Italy, 1943–1945." *Journal of Contemporary History* 43, no. 2 (2008): 217–240.

———. "'I Felt like a Tourist instead of a Soldier': The Occupying Gaze—War and Tourism in Italy, 1943–1945." *American Quarterly* 68, no. 3 (2016): 593–615, 855.

Burdett, Charles. "Changing Identities Through Memory: Malaparte's Self-Figurations in Kaputt." In *European Memories of the Second World War*, edited by Helmut Peitsch, Charles Burdett and Claire Gorrara, 110–119. New York: Berghahn Books, 1999.

Burns, John Horne. "Algiers." *Holiday*, February 1949, 65–70, 131–134.

———. "Casablanca." *Holiday*, January 1949, 64–70, 130–131.

———. *The Gallery*. Introduction by Paul Fussell. New York: New York Review of Books, 2013.
———. *La galleria*. Translated by Anna Voing. Milan: Garzanti, 1949.
———. *La galleria: Un americano a Napoli*. Translated by Anna Voing and revised by Liu Saraz. Milan: Baldini & Castoldi, 1992.
———. "Naples." *Holiday*, May 1949, 65–70, 154–156.
———. "Rome." *Holiday*, June 1949, 65–70, 132–134.
———. "Tunis." *Holiday*, March 1949, 65–70, 122–124.
Buzard, James. *The Beaten Track: European Tourism, Literature, and the Ways to Culture, 1800–1918*. Oxford: Clarendon Press, 1993.
———. "A Continent of Pictures: Reflections on the 'Europe' of Nineteenth-Century Tourists." *PMLA* 108, no. 1 (1993): 30–44.
———. "What Isn't Travel." In *Unravelling Civilisation: European Travel and Travel Writing*, edited by Hagen Schulz-Forberg, 43–62. Brussels: Peter Lang, 2005.
Caddick-Adams, Peter. *Monte Cassino: Ten Armies in Hell*. New York: Oxford University Press, 2013.
Caldwell, Lesley. "Ragazzo Fortunato? Children in Italian Cinema." In *New Visions of the Child in Italian Cinema*, edited by Danielle Hipkins and Roger Pitt, 59–78. Oxford: Peter Lang, 2014.
Capella, Anthony. *The Wedding Officer*. New York: Random House, 2006.
Carloni, Fabrizio. *Il corpo di spedizione francese in Italia, 1943–1944*. Milan: Mursia, 2006.
Carruthers, Susan L. *The Good Occupation: American Soldiers and the Hazards of Peace*. Cambridge, MA: Harvard University Press, 2016.
———. "'Produce More Joppolos': John Hersey's A Bell for Adano and the Making of the 'Good Occupation.'" *Journal of American History* 100, no. 4 (2014): 1086–1113.
Cassamagnaghi, Silvia. *Operazione Spose di guerra: Storie d'amore e di emigrazione*. Milan: Feltrinelli Editore, 2014.
Catallo, Stefania. *Le marocchinate*. Rome: Sensibili alle Foglie, 2015.
Cecchi, Emilio. "Curzio Malaparte." In *Storia della letteratura italiana*, edited by Natalino Sapegno and Emilio Cecchi, 687–690. Milan: Garzanti, 1965.
———. "La 'Galleria' di J. H. Burns." In *La Galleria: Un americano a Napoli* by John Horne Burns, translated by Anna Voin and revised by Liù Saraz, 369–374. Milan: Baldini & Castoldi, 1992.
Chambers, Iain. *Mediterranean Crossings: The Politics of an Interrupted Modernity*. Durham, NC: Duke University Press, 2008.
Chard, Chloe. "Grand and Ghostly Tours: The Topography of Memory." *Eighteenth-Century Studies* 31, no. 1 (1997): 101–108.
Chianese, Gloria. "Italiani liberati dalla Sicilia a Napoli. 1943." In *1943–1945, la lunga liberazione*, edited by Eric Gobetti, 95–104. Milan: FrancoAngeli, 2007.
Cione, Edmondo. *Napoli e Malaparte*. Naples: Pellerano-Del Gaudio, 1950.

Clark, Lloyd. *Anzio: Italy and the Battle for Rome—1944*. New York: Grove/Atlantic, 2007.
Coers, Donald V. *John Steinbeck Goes to War: The Moon Is Down as Propaganda*. Tuscaloosa: University of Alabama Press, 1991.
Coles, Harry L., and Albert K. Weinberg. *Civil Affairs: Soldiers Become Governors*. Washington, DC: Center of Military History, United States Army, 1986.
Coltelli, Laura. "L'Italia nel romanzo di guerra americano." *Rivista di letterature moderne e comparate* 28 (1975): 47–73, 132–145.
Cooke, Philip. *The Legacy of the Italian Resistance*. New York: Palgrave Macmillan, 2011.
Corvo, Max. *OSS in Italy, 1942–1945: The War Memoirs of Max Corvo*. New York: Enigma Books, 2005.
Costello, John. *Love, Sex, and War: Changing Values, 1939–45*. London: Collins, 1985.
———. *Virtue under Fire: How World War II Changed Our Social and Sexual Attitudes*. Boston: Little, Brown and Company, 1987.
Craig, Siobhan S. *Cinema after Fascism: The Shattered Screen*. New York: Palgrave Macmillan, 2010.
Crichton, Robert. *The Secret of Santa Vittoria*. New York: Simon & Schuster, 1966.
Culler, Jonathan. *Framing the Sign: Criticism and Its Institutions*. Oxford: Blackwell, 1988.
Cuomo, Chris. "War Is Not Just an Event: Reflections on the Significance of Everyday Violence." *Hypatia* 11, no. 4 (2003): 30–45.
Curti, Lidia. "Female Literature of Migration in Italy." *Feminist Review*, no. 87 (2007): 60–75.
Dainotto, Roberto. *Europe (in Theory)*. Durham, NC: Duke University Press, 2007.
D'Aquino, Maria Luisa. *La mia Napoli. 'Mosconi' 1945–1976*. Preface by Pasquale Nonno. Naples: Mario Raffone, 1990.
———. *Quel giorno trent'anni fa*. Naples: Guida Editori, 1975.
DeFore, John. "Naples '44." Review of *Naples '44*, directed by Francesco Patierno. *Hollywood Reporter*, December 6, 2017.
De Luce, Daniel. "Invasion Weapon Is 'Guide to Italy.'" *New York Times*, September 7, 1943.
De Marco, Paolo. *Polvere di piselli: La vita quotidiana a Napoli durante l'occupazione alleata, 1943–1944*. Naples: Liguori, 1996.
Depaola, Stephanie. "Sexual Violence, Racism, and the Allied Occupation of Italy: History and the Politics of Memory." PhD dissertation, Fordham University, 2018.
Di Fiore, Gigi. *Controstoria della liberazione: Le stragi e i crimini dimenticati degli Alleati nell'Italia del sud*. Milan: Rizzoli, 2012.
Diggins, John P. *Mussolini and Fascism: The View from America*. Princeton: Princeton University Press, 1972.
Domenico, Roy Palmer. *Italian Fascists on Trial, 1943–1948*. Chapel Hill: University of North Carolina Press, 1991.

Duncan, Derek. "The Queerness of Italian Cinema." In *A Companion to Italian Cinema*, edited by Frank Burke, 467–483. Chichester, UK: John Wiley & Sons, 2017.

Edwards, Catharine. *Roman Presences: Receptions of Rome in European Culture, 1789–1945*. Cambridge: Cambridge University Press, 1999.

Ellis, John. *Cassino, the Hollow Victory: The Battle for Rome, January–June 1944*. New York: McGraw-Hill, 1984.

Ellwood, David. "The American Challenge in Uniform: The Arrival of America's Armies in World War II and European Women." *European Journal of American Studies* 7, no. 2 (2012).

———. *Italy, 1943–1945*. New York: Holmes & Meier, 1985.

———. "Liberazione/occupazione." In *1943–1945, la lunga liberazione*, edited by Eric Gobetti, 13–25. Milan: FrancoAngeli, 2007.

———. *The Shock of America: Europe and the Challenge of the Century*. Oxford: Oxford University Press, 2012.

———. "'You Too Can Be Like Us': Selling the Marshall Plan." *History Today*, October 1, 1998.

Emberton, Carole. *Beyond Redemption: Race, Violence, and the American South after the Civil War*. Chicago: University of Chicago Press, 2013.

Enloe, Cynthia. *Maneuvers: The International Politics of Militarizing Women's Lives*. Berkeley: University of California Press, 2000.

Escolar, Marisa. "Marry the Allies? Luciana Peverelli's 'True' Romanzo Rosa in 'Liberated' Rome." *Italian Studies* 70, no. 2 (2015): 228–248.

———. "Sleights of Hand: Black Skin and Curzio Malaparte's." *California Italian Studies* 3, no. 1 (2012).

Evans, Julian. *Semi Invisible Man: The Life of Norman Lewis*. London: Jonathan Cape, 2008.

Fabbri, Lorenzo. "Neorealism as Ideology: Bazin, Deleuze, and the Avoidance of Fascism." *The Italianist* 35, no. 2 (2015): 182–201.

Fainsod, Merle. "The Development of American Military Government Policy during World War II." In *American Experiences in Military Government in World War II*, edited by Carl Friedrich, 23–51. New York: Rinehart, 1948.

Favretto, Ilaria, and Oliviero Bergamini. "'Temperamentally Unwarlike': The Image of Italy in the Allies' War Propaganda, 1943–45." In *War and the Media: Reportage and Propaganda, 1900–2003*, edited by Mark Connelly and David Welch, 112–126. London: I. B. Tauris, 2005.

Felman, Shoshana. *What Does a Woman Want? Reading and Sexual Difference*. Baltimore: Johns Hopkins University Press, 1993.

Ferrari, Fabio. "Americana: The American(ized) Woman as Represented by Five Italian Directors since 1945." In *Pagina pellicola pratica: studi sul cinema italiano*, edited by Rebecca West, 127–145. Ravenna: Angelo Longo Editore, 2000.

Footitt, Hilary, and Michael Kelly. *Languages at War: Policies and Practices of Language Contacts in Conflict*. Basingstoke, UK: Palgrave Macmillan, 2012.

Forgacs, David. "Americanisation: The Italian Case (1938–1954)." In *Americanisation and the Transformation of World Cultures: Melting Pot or Cultural Chernobyl*, edited by Philip H. Melling and Jon Roper, 81–96. Lewiston, NY: Edwin Mellen Press, 1996.

———. "Fascism and Anti-Fascism Reviewed: Generations, History and Film in Italy after 1968." In *European Memories of the Second World War*, edited by Helmut Peitsch, Charles Burdett, and Claire Gorrara, 185–199. New York: Berghahn Books, 1999.

———. *Rome Open City (Roma città aperta)*. London: British Film Institute, 2000.

Forlenza, Rosario. "Sacrificial Memory and Political Legitimacy in Postwar Italy. Reliving and Remembering World War II." *History and Memory* 24, no. 2 (2012): 73–116.

Foulds, Adam. *In the Wolf's Mouth*. New York: Harper Collins, 2014.

Freccero, John. *Dante: The Poetics of Conversion*. Cambridge, MA: Harvard University Press, 1986.

Gallagher, Tag. *The Adventures of Roberto Rossellini*. Boston: Da Capo Press, 1998.

Gambarota, Paola. "The Fall of Naples: Percezioni e rappresentazioni americane della liberazione di Napoli." In *Leggere il tempo negli spazi: 1943 a Napoli, in Campania, nel Mezzogiorno e Mediterraneo*. Special issue of *Meridione, Sud e Nord nel Mondo*, edited by Francesco Soverino, 2–3 (2015): 255–268.

Gangale, Lucia. *Donne nel Sannio: Una ricerca storico sociale*. Naples: Guida Editori, 2004.

Garofalo, Anna. *L'italiana in Italia*. Bari: Editori Laterza, 1956.

Gatt Rutter, John. "Liberation and Literature: Naples 1944." *Journal of Modern Italian Studies* 1, no. 2 (1996): 245–272.

Geist, Johann Friedrich. *Arcades: The History of a Building Type*. Cambridge, MA: MIT Press, 1985.

Gershovich, Moshe. "Collaboration and 'Pacification': French Conquest, Moroccan Combatants, and the Transformation of the Middle Atlas." *Comparative Studies of South Asia, Africa and the Middle East* 24, no. 1 (2004): 139–146.

———. "Memory and Representation of War and Violence: Moroccan Combatants in French Uniforms during the Second World War." In *Colonial Soldiers in Europe, 1914–1945: "Aliens in Uniform" in Wartime Societies*, edited by Eric Storm and Ali Al Tuma, 77–94. New York: Routledge, 2015.

Girgus, Sam B. *Levinas and the Cinema of Redemption: Time, Ethics and the Feminine*. New York: Columbia University Press, 2010.

Gisolfi, Anthony M. "'The Beach of Heaven': Italy 1943–1945 in American Fiction." *Italica* 27, no. 3 (1950): 199–207.

Glynn, Ruth. "Engendering Occupation: The Body as Warzone in Liliana Cavani's La Pelle." *Romance Notes* 55, no. 3 (2015): 345–355.

———. "Naples and the Nation in Cultural Representations of the Allied Occupation." *California Italian Studies* 7, no. 2 (2017).

———. "Porosity and Its Discontents." *Cultural Critique*, forthcoming 2019.

Gonzalez, Vernadette. *Securing Paradise: Tourism and Militarism in Hawai'i and the Philippines.* Durham, NC: Duke University Press, 2013.

Goodman, Mitchell. *The End of It.* New York: New American Library, 1963.

Gordon, Robert S.C. *The Holocaust in Italian Culture, 1944–2010.* Stanford, CA: Stanford University Press, 2012.

———. "The Italian War." *The Cambridge Companion to the Literature of World War II,* edited by Marina MacKay, 123–136. Cambridge: Cambridge University Press, 2009.

Gramsci, Antonio. *I quaderni: Letteratura e vita nazionale.* Rome: Editori Riuniti, 1996.

Grana, Gianni. *Curzio Malaparte.* Milan: Marzorati, 1961.

Greene, Shelleen. *Equivocal Subjects: Between Italy and Africa—Constructions of Racial and National Identity in the Italian Cinema.* New York: Continuum, 2012.

Gremmo, Roberto. *Le marocchinate, gli alleati e la guerra ai civili: Le vittime dell'occupazione militare straniera nell'Italia liberata, 1943–1947.* Biella: Storia Ribelle, 2010.

Guerri, Giordano Bruno. *L'arcitaliano: Vita di Curzio Malaparte.* Milan: Mondadori, 2000.

Guida del soldato in Sicilia. Palermo: Sellerio Editore, 2013.

A Guide to Occupation of Enemy Territory—Italy. Washington, DC: Special Service Division, Army Service Forces in cooperation with Civil Affairs Division, War Department, 1943.

Gunn, Drewey Wayne. *Gay American Novels, 1870–1970: A Reader's Guide.* Jefferson, NC: McFarland, 2016.

Halberstam, Judith. *In a Queer Time and Place: Transgender Bodies, Subcultural Lives.* New York: New York University Press, 2005.

Hargrove, Hondon B. *Buffalo Soldiers in Italy: Black Americans in World War II.* Jefferson, NC: McFarland, 2003.

Hayes, Alfred. *All Thy Conquests.* Bel Air, CA: Howell, Soskin, 1946.

———. *All Thy Conquests.* New York: Lion Books, 1950.

———. *All Thy Conquests.* New York: Lion Books, 1956.

———. *Alle deine Siege.* Translated by Heinrich Maria Ledig-Rowohlt and Susanne Lepsius. Hamburg: Rowohlt, 1954.

———. *The Girl on the Via Flaminia.* New York: Harper, 1949.

———. "Italy—Enchantress of Writers." *New York Times,* April 10, 1949.

———. *La ragazza della via Flaminia.* Turin: Einaudi, 1954.

———. "Wartime Story: 'Via Flaminia's' Author Gives Play's History." *New York Times,* May 16, 1954.

Hayes, Carl J. H. Foreword. In *Inside Rome with the Germans,* by Jane Scrivener, vii–xi. New York: Macmillan, 1945.

Hegarty, Marilyn. *Victory Girls, Khaki-Wackies, and Patriotutes: The Regulation of Female Sexuality during World War II.* New York: New York University Press, 2008.

Heller, Joseph. *Catch-22.* New York: Simon & Schuster, 1961.

Hersey, John. *A Bell for Adano*. New York: Knopf, 1944.
Hipkins, Danielle. "Francesca's Salvation or Damnation? Resisting Recognition of the Prostitute in Roberto Rossellini's *Paisà* (1946)." *Studies in European Cinema* 3, no. 2 (July 2006): 153–168.
———. *Italy's Other Women: Gender and Prostitution in Italian Cinema, 1940–1965*. New York: Peter Lang, 2016.
Hoffman, Alice M., and Howard S. Hoffman. *Archives of Memory: A Soldier Recalls World War II*. Lexington: University Press of Kentucky, 2015.
Hofmann, Paul. *The Seasons of Rome: A Journal*. New York: Henry Holt, 1997.
Hom, Stephanie Malia. *The Beautiful Country: Tourism and the Impossible State of Destination Italy*. Toronto: University of Toronto Press, 2015.
Hughes, Henry Stuart. *The United States and Italy*. Cambridge, MA: Harvard University Press, 1979.
Indiana, Gary. *Utopia's Debris: Selected Essays*. New York: Basic Books, 2008.
Iovino, Serenella. *Ecocriticism and Italy: Ecology, Resistance, and Liberation*. London: Bloomsbury, 2016.
Jones, H. G. *The Sonarman's War: A Memoir of Submarine Chasing and Mine Sweeping in World War II*. Jefferson, NC: McFarland, 2010.
Judt, Tony. *Postwar: A History of Europe since 1945*. New York: Penguin, 2006.
Kadish, Mortimer Raymond. *Point of Honor*. New York: Random House, 1951.
Karl, Frederick Robert. *American Fictions, 1940–1980: A Comprehensive History and Critical Evaluation*. New York: Harper & Row, 1983.
Kenigsberg, Ben. "'Naples '44' Chronicles Life during Wartime." Review of *Naples '44*, directed by Francesco Patierno. *New York Times*, November 28, 2017.
Kundera, Milan. *Encounter*. Translated by Linda Asher. New York: HarperCollins, 2010.
La Capria, Raffaele. "Malaparte gran bugiardo. Il trucco c'è e si vede." *Corriere della Sera*, April 21, 2009.
———. *Ultimi viaggi nell'Italia perduta*. Milan: Bompiani, 2015.
Lambiase, Sergio, and Gian Battista Nazzaro. *L'odore della guerra: Napoli 1940–1945*. Naples: Avagliano, 2002.
———. *Napoli 1940–1945*. Milan: Longanesi & Co, 1978.
Landolfi, Tommaso. *An Autumn Story*. Translated by Joachim Neugroschel. Hygiene, CO: Eridanos Press, 1989.
———. *Racconto d'autunno*. Florence: Vallecchi, 1947.
Lejeune, Philippe. *On Diary*. Honolulu: University of Hawaii Press, 2009.
Lewis, Norman. *Naples '44: A World War II Diary of Occupied Italy*. Boston: Da Capo Press, 2004.
———. *Napoli '44*. Translated by Matteo Codignola. Milan: Adelphi, 1993.
———. *The Sicilian Specialist*. New York: Perseus Books Group, 1986.
———. "Travel: See Naples and Die." *The Observer*, January 11, 1998.
———. *Within the Labyrinth*. London: Jonathan Cape, 1950.
Leyland, Winston. *Gay Roots: Twenty Years of Gay Sunshine: An Anthology of Gay History, Sex, Politics, and Culture*. San Francisco: Gay Sunshine Press, 1993.

Lichtner, Giacomo. "For the Few, Not the Many: Delusion and Denial in Italian Holocaust Films." In *Holocaust and the Moving Image: Representations in Film and Television since 1933*, edited by Toby Haggith and Joanna Newman, 236–242. London: Wallflower Press, 2005.

Liebling, A. J. *Mollie, and Other War Pieces*. New York: Ballantine Books, 1964.

Life Magazine. "Lynching in Rome." October 9, 1944, 36–37.

———. "Movie of the Week: Paisan." Review of *Paisan*, directed by Roberto Rossellini. July 19, 1948, 41.

———. "Rome Falls. Liberators Get a Wild Welcome." June 12, 1944, 38–39.

Lilly, Robert J. *Taken by Force: Rape and American GIs in Europe during World War II*. London: Palgrave Macmillan UK, 2007.

Linklater, Eric. *Private Angelo*. London: Buchan & Enright, 1986.

Longo, Regina M. "Between Documentary and Neorealism: Marshall Plan Films in Italy (1948–1955)." *California Italian Studies* 3, no. 2 (2012).

Lowry, Robert. *Casualty*. New York: New Directions, 1946.

Lucamante, Stefania. *Forging Shoah Memories: Italian Women Writers, Jewish Identity, and the Holocaust*. New York: Palgrave Macmillan, 2014.

Lucioli, Massimo, and Davide Sabatini. *La ciociara e le altre: il corpo di spedizione francese in Italia: 1943–1944*. Rome: Monte Porzio Catone, 1998.

Lyautey, Pierre. *La campagne d'Italie, 1944: Souvenirs d'un goumier*. Paris: Plon, 1945.

Maghraoui, Driss. "The Goumiers in the Second World War: History and Colonial Representation." *Journal of North African Studies* 19, no. 4 (2014): 571–586.

———. "Moroccan Colonial Soldiers: Between Selective Memory and Collective Memory." *Arab Studies Quarterly* 20, no. 2 (1998): 21–41.

Malaparte, Curzio. *Kaputt*. In *Opere scelte*, edited by Luigi Martellini, 427–963. Milan: Mondadori, 1997.

———. *Kaputt*. Translated by Cesare Foligno. New York: New York Review of Books, 2005.

———. *La pelle*. Milan: Mondadori, 2001.

———. *Malaparte*. Edited by Edda Ronchi Suckert. Florence: Ponte alle Grazie, 1991.

———. *The Skin*. Translated by David Moore. New York: New York Review of Books, 2013.

Malaparte, Curzio, and René Novella. *Mi scriveva Malaparte*. Florence: Shakespeare and Co., 1994.

Marcus, Millicent. "The Italian Body Politic Is a Woman: Feminized National Identity in Postwar Italian Film." In *Sparks and Seeds*, edited by Dana E. Stewart and Alison Cornish, 329–347. Turnhout: Brepols, 2000.

———. "Liberating the Garden: Eden and The Fall from *Paisà* to *Mediterraneo*." In *Italy and America, 1943–1944: Italian, American and Italian American Experiences of the Liberation of the Italian Mezzogiorno*, edited by John Anthony Davis, 549–570. Naples: La Città del Sole, 1997.

———. "'Miss Mondina, Miss Sirena, Miss Farina': The Feminized Body-Politics from *Bitter Rice* to 'La voce della luna.'" *Romance Languages Annual* 4 (1992): 296–300.

———. "Rossellini's *Paisà*: National Identity by Means of Montage." *Italian Quarterly* (2000): 295–302.

Margolick, David. *Dreadful: The Short Life and Gay Times of John Horne Burns*. New York: Other Press, 2013.

Marshall, George C. *Biennial Reports of the Chief of Staff of the United States Army to the Secretary of War, 1 July 1939–30 June 1945*. Washington, DC: Center of Military History, 1996.

Marshall, Samuel Lyman Atwood. *Bringing Up the Rear: A Memoir*. San Rafael, CA: Presidio Press, 1979.

Martelli, Giampaolo. *Curzio Malaparte*. Turin: Borla, 1968.

Martellini, Luigi. Introduction to *Opere scelte* by Curzio Malaparte, xliii–lxxvi. Milan: Mondadori, 1997.

Matthews, Herbert L. *The Education of a Correspondent*. New York: Harcourt, Brace and Company, 1946.

———. "Italian Government Report Shows Carreta, Lynched as Fascist, Was Entirely Innocent." *New York Times*, November 11, 1944.

———. "Italians Fought Germans Fiercely." *New York Times*, December 12, 1943.

———. "Italy Seeks to Cut All Fascist Ties." *New York Times*, November 7, 1943.

———. "Italy to Declare War on Japanese." *New York Times*, September 28, 1944.

———. "Naples Goes Mad with Joy as Grim Allied Push Ends." *New York Times*, October 2, 1943.

———. "A New Chapter in Eternal Rome." *New York Times*, June 18, 1944.

———. "Rome Is up at Dawn to Cheer 5th Army." *New York Times*, June 6, 1944.

———. "Rome Mob Lynches Fascist Official After Seizing Him in Open Court." *New York Times*, September 19, 1944.

———. "Stimson in Rome on Symbolic Day." *New York Times*, July 5, 1944.

McClintock, Anne. "Family Feuds: Gender, Nationalism and the Family." *Feminist Review* 44 (1993): 61–80.

———. *Imperial Leather: Race, Gender, and Sexuality in the Colonial Contest*. New York: Routledge, 1995.

McCormick, Anne O'Hare. "The Americans Lead the Way into Rome." *New York Times*, June 5, 1943.

———. "Duce's Palace a Gallery as Press Mourns for Italy." *New York Times*, September 9, 1944.

———. "France and Italy in the Drama of Liberation." *New York Times*, June 7, 1944.

———. "Signs in Italy of Anarchy in Europe." *New York Times*, September 20, 1944.

McPhee, Jenny. Foreword to *The Kremlin Ball* by Curzio Malaparte, translated by Jenny McPhee, vii–xvi. New York: New York Review of Books, 2018.

Mikula, Maja. "Gender and Patriotism in Carla Capponi's Con cuore di donna." In *Across Genres, Generations and Borders: Italian Women Writing Lives*, edited by Susanna Scarparo and Rita Wilson, 70–85. Newark: University of Delaware Press, 2004.

Minghelli, Giuliana. *Landscape and Memory in Post-Fascist Italian Film: Cinema Year Zero*. New York: Routledge, 2014.

Mistry, Kaeten. *The United States, Italy and the Origins of Cold War: Waging Political Warfare 1945–1950*. Cambridge: Cambridge University Press, 2014.

Mitgang, Herbert, "G.I. Travel Guides Become 'Poor Man's Baedekers.'" *New York Times*, May 18, 1952.

Mitzel, John. *John Horne Burns: An Appreciative Biography*. Dorchester, MA: Manifest Destiny Books, 1974.

Moe, Nelson. "Naples '44/Tammurriata Nera/Ladri Di Biciclette." In *Italy and America, 1943–1944: Italian, American and Italian American Experiences of the Liberation of the Italian Mezzogiorno*, edited by John Anthony Davis, 433–454. Naples: La Città del Sole, 1997.

———. *The View from Vesuvius: Italian Culture and the Southern Question*. Berkeley: University of California Press, 2002.

Monaldi, Rita, and Francesco Sorti. *Malaparte: Morte come me*. Milan: Baldini & Castoldi, 2015.

Moravia, Alberto. *La ciociara*. Milan: Bompiani, 1957.

———. *Two Women*. Translated by Angus Davidson. New York: Farrar, Straus & Cudahy, 1958.

Morehead, Caroline. *Iris Origo: Marchesa of Val d'Orcia*. Boston: David R. Godine, 2004.

Morris, Eric. *Circles of Hell: The War in Italy 1943–1945*. London: Hutchinson, 1993.

Mumford, Lewis. "Roman Account Stirs Reader." *New York Times*. September 21, 1944.

Munk, Linda. *The Devil's Mousetrap: Redemption and Colonial American Literature*. New York: Oxford University Press, 1997.

Murch, Walter. *The Bird That Swallowed Its Cage: The Selected Writings of Curzio Malaparte*. Berkeley, CA: Counterpoint Press, 2014.

———. "Malaparte's 'Partisans, 1944.'" *Zoetrope. All Story* 2, no. 3 (1998).

Neale, Steve. "Melodrama and Tears." *Screen* 27, no. 6 (1986): 6–23.

Newby, Eric. *Love and War in the Apennines*. New York: Penguin Books, 1999.

New York Times. "Americans in First." June 5, 1944.

———. "The Great Reversal." October 14, 1943.

———. "Italy's Liberation is Acclaimed Here." September 9, 1943.

———. "Two Italian Generals Are Sentenced in Rome." December 23, 1944.

———. "The Victory of Rome." June 6, 1944.

Norton, Charles Eliot. *Letters of Charles Eliot Norton*. New York: Houghton Mifflin, 1913.

O'Rawe, Catherine. "Back for Good: Melodrama and the Returning Soldier in Post-War Italian Cinema." *Modern Italy* (2017): 123–142.

Origo, Iris. *A Chill in the Air: An Italian War Diary, 1939–1940*. New York: New York Review of Books, 2018.

———. *War in Val d'Orcia: An Italian War Diary, 1943–1944*. Boston: David R. Godine, 1984.

Ouditt, Sharon. *Impressions of Southern Italy: British Travel Writing from Henry Swinburne to Norman Douglas*. New York: Routledge, 2013.

Parascandola, John. "Quarantining Women: Venereal Disease Rapid Treatment Centers in World War II America." *Bulletin of the History of Medicine* 83, no. 3 (2009): 431–459.

Pardini, Giuseppe. *Curzio Malaparte: Biografia Politica*. Milan: Luni Editrice, 1998.

Parigi, Stefania. *Paisà: Analisi del film*. Venice: Marsilio, 2005.

Parks, Timothy. "The Horrors of War. Review of Kaputt by Curzio Malaparte, Translated by Cesare Foligno." *New York Review of Books*, December 1, 2005.

Patierno, Francesco. "How They Did It: The Director of *Naples '44* on Blending Adaptation, Documentary, and Fiction." *Movemaker.com*, December 12, 2017, https://www.moviemaker.com/archives/moviemaking/directing/naples-44/.

Patriarca, Silvana. "Fear of Small Numbers: 'Brown Babies' in Postwar Italy." *Contemporanea* 18, no. 4 (2015): 537–567.

———. *Italian Vices: Nation and Character from the Risorgimento to the Republic*. Cambridge: Cambridge University Press, 2010.

Perfetti, Francesco. Introduction to *Curzio Malaparte: Biografia Politica*, 7–22. Milan: Luni Editrice, 1998.

Peverelli, Luciana. "Autobiografia." In *Narratrici e lettrici (1850–1950): Le letture della nonna dalla Contessa Lara a Luciana Peverelli*, edited by Rita Verdirame, 273–325. Padua: libreriauniversitaria.it, 2009.

———. *La lunga notte: Romanzo*. Milan: Rizzoli, 1951.

———. *Sposare lo straniero*. Milan: Garzanti, 1977.

Pickering-Iazzi, Robin. *Politics of the Visible: Writing Women, Culture, and Fascism*. Minneapolis: University of Minnesota Press, 1997.

Pirro, Ugo. *Celluloide*. Milan: Rizzoli, 1983.

———. *Mille tradimenti: Romanzo*. Milan: Bompiani, 1959.

———. *A Thousand Betrayals*. Translated by Frances Frenaye. New York: Simon & Schuster, 1961.

A Pocket Guide to France. Washington, DC: United States Army Service Forces, Information and Education Division, 1944.

A Pocket Guide to France. Washington, DC: Office of Armed Forces Information and Education, Department of Defense, 1951.

A Pocket Guide to Germany. Washington, DC: United States Army Service Forces, Information and Education Division, 1944.

A Pocket Guide to Germany. Washington, DC: United States Armed Forces Information and Education Division, 1965.

A Pocket Guide to Greece. Washington, DC: United States Armed Forces Information and Education, 1966.

A Pocket Guide to Italian Cities. Washington, DC: United States Army Service Forces, Information and Education Division, 1944.
A Pocket Guide to Italy. Washington, DC: Office of Armed Forces Information and Education, Department of Defense, 1952.
A Pocket Guide to Italy. Washington, DC: Office of Armed Forces Information and Education, Department of Defense, 1964.
A Pocket Guide to Italy. Washington, DC: American Forces Information Service, 1981.
A Pocket Guide to Italy. Washington, DC: American Forces Information Service, 1987.
Polezzi, Loredana. *Translating Travel: Contemporary Italian Travel Writing in English Translation.* Farnham, UK: Ashgate, 2001.
Ponzani, Michela. *Guerra alle donne: Partigiane, vittime di stupro, "amanti del nemico," 1940–45.* Turin: Einaudi, 2012.
Poppelsdorff, Leonard H. *Say Your Prayers Dear: The True Romance of an Englishman and an Italian Girl Set in Italy During the Second World War.* Ilfracombe, UK: Stockwell, 1985.
Porch, Douglas. *The Path to Victory: The Mediterranean Theater in World War II.* New York: Farrar, Straus, and Giroux, 2004.
Portelli, Alessandro. *The Order Has Been Carried Out: History, Memory and Meaning of a Nazi Massacre in Rome.* New York: Palgrave Macmillan, 2003.
Porzio, Maria. *Arrivano gli alleati! Amori e violenze nell'Italia liberata.* Bari: Laterza, 2011.
Pozzato, Maria Pia. *Il romanzo rosa.* Milan: Espresso Strumenti, 1982.
Pratt, Mary Louise. *Imperial Eyes: Travel Writing and Transculturation.* London: Routledge, 1992.
Pucci, Lara. "Shooting Corpses: The Fosse Ardeatine in Giorni Di Gloria (1945)." *Italian Studies* 68, no. 3 (2013): 356–377.
Regis, Pamela. *A Natural History of the Romance Novel.* Philadelphia: University of Pennsylvania Press, 2003.
Reich, Jacqueline. *Beyond the Latin Lover: Marcello Mastroianni, Masculinity and Italian Cinema.* Bloomington: Indiana University Press, 2004.
Robb, Peter. *Street Fight in Naples: A City's Unseen History.* London: Bloomsbury, 2011.
Roberts, Mary Louise. *What Soldiers Do: Sex and the American GI in World War II France.* Chicago: University of Chicago Press, 2013.
Roccella, Eugenia. *La letteratura rosa.* Rome: Editori Riuniti, 1998.
Rogerson, Barnaby. "Naples '44: An Intelligence Officer in the Italian Labyrinth." Review of *Naples '44* by Norman Lewis. *Geographical*, January 1, 2004, https://www.theguardian.com/books/2011/may/28/naples-44-norman-lewis-rereading.
———. "Naples '44—Norman Lewis's Acknowledged Masterpiece about the Human Cost of War." *The Telegraph*, October 6, 2009, https://www.telegraph.co.uk/expat/expatlife/6262513/Naples-44-Norman-Lewiss-acknowledged-masterpiece-about-the-human-cost-of-war.html.

Rogin, Michael P. "Mourning, Melancholia, and the Popular Front: Roberto Rossellini's Beautiful Revolution." In *Roberto Rossellini's Rome Open City*, edited by Sidney Gottlieb, 131–160. Cambridge: Cambridge University Press, 2004.

Ross, Silvia. "Conflict, Mobility and Alterity: World War II and the Italians in Eric Newby and Iris Origo." *Studies in Travel Writing* 16, no. 2 (2012): 149–162.

Rovere, Richard. "A City Bleeding: Naples." Review of *Naples '44* by Norman Lewis. *New York Times*, March 18, 1979.

Russo, John. "The Unbroken Charm: Margaret Fuller, G. S. Hillard, and the American Tradition of Travel Writing on Italy." In *Margaret Fuller: Transatlantic Crossings in a Revolutionary Age*, 124–155. Madison: University of Wisconsin Press, 2007.

Scarsella, Alessandro. "Curzio Malaparte (Kurt Erich Suckert)." In *Encyclopedia of Italian Studies*, edited by Gaetana Marrone, Paolo Puppa, and Luca Somigli, 1111–1115. New York: Routledge, 2006.

Scheffel, Charles, and Barry Basden. *Crack! And Thump*. Melbourne: Camroc Press, 2007.

Schoonover, Karl. *Brutal Vision: The Neorealist Body in Postwar Italian Cinema*. Minneapolis: University of Minnesota Press, 2012.

Schrijvers, Peter. *The Crash of Ruin: American Combat Soldiers in Europe During World War II*. New York: New York University Press, 2001.

Scrivener, Jane. *Inside Rome with the Germans*. New York: Macmillan, 1945.

Serra, Ilaria. "Italy: America's War Bride—How Life Magazine Feminized Italy in the 1950s." *Italica* 86, no. 3 (2009): 452–470.

Sevareid, Eric. *Not so Wild a Dream*. Columbia: University of Missouri Press, 1995.

Shukert, Elfrieda Berthiaume, and Barbara Smith Scibetta. *The War Brides of World War II*. San Rafael, CA: Presidio Press, 1988.

Singh, Sunny. "Why the Lack of Indian and African Faces in Dunkirk Matters." *The Guardian*, August 1, 2017.

Slide, Anthony. *Lost Gay Novels: A Reference Guide to Fifty Works from the First Half of the Twentieth Century*. New York: Routledge, 2013.

Smith, Derek. "Naples '44." Review of *Naples '44*, directed by Francesco Patierno. *Slant Magazine*, November 26, 2017.

Sodi, Risa B. *Narrative and Imperative: The First Fifty Years of Italian Holocaust Writing (1944–1994)*. New York: Peter Lang, 2007.

Soldier's Guide to Italy. Washington, DC: War Department, 1943.

Soldier's Guide to Naples. Naples: Metropolitan Area Peninsular Base Section, 1944.

Soldier's Guide to Naples. Naples: Metropolitan Area Peninsular Base Section, 1945.

Soldier's Guide to Sicily. Cairo: Printing and Stationery Services, M.E.F., 1943.

Spackman, Barbara. *Decadent Genealogies: The Rhetoric of Sickness from Baudelaire to D'Annunzio*. Ithaca, NY: Cornell University Press, 1989.

The Special Service Division. Washington, D.C.: War Department, 1943.

Speciale, Giuseppe. "Il risarcimento dei perseguitati politici e razziali: L'esperienza italiana." In *Riparare, risarcire, ricordare: Un dialogo tra storici e giuristi*, edited by Giorgio Resta and Vincenzo Zeno Zencovich, 115–138. Naples: Editoriale Scientifica, 2012.

Sternberg, Thomas H., et al. "Chapter X. Venereal Disease." In *Preventative Medicine in World War II: Vol. 5, Communicable Diseases Transmitted Through Contact or Through Unknown Means,* edited by Leonard D. Heaton, et. al. Washington, D.C., Office of Surgeon General, Department of The Army, 1960.

Stewart, Fiona M. "'We Will Build a Better World Together': Female Partisans' Memories of Their Resistance to Fascism (1943–1945)." In *Italian Women at War: Sisters in Arms from the Unification to the Twentieth Century*, edited by Susan Amatangelo, 113–132. Madison, NJ: Farleigh Dickinson University Press, 2016.

Storm, Eric, and Ali Al Tuma. "Introduction: Colonial Soldiers in Europe, 1914–1945." In *Colonial Soldiers in Europe, 1914–1945: "Aliens in Uniform" in Wartime Societies*, edited by Eric Storm and Ali Al Tuma, 1–19. New York: Routledge, 2015.

Strazza, Michele. *Senza via di scampo: Gli stupri nelle guerre mondiali*. Potenza: Consiglio Regionale della Basilicata, 2010.

Taubman, Howard. "The Eternal City and Its Liberators." Review of *All Thy Conquests* by Alfred Hayes. *New York Times*, November 17, 1946.

Taylor, Ben. *Naples Declared: A Walk Around the Bay*. London: Penguin, 2012.

Thompson, Luke Y. "Found-Footage Documentary "Naples '44" Is Brought Together by Benedict Cumberbatch's Voice." Review of *Naples '44*, directed by Francesco Patierno. *Village Voice*, December 1, 2017.

Tompkins, Peter. *A Spy in Rome*. New York: Simon & Schuster, 1962.

Traldi, Alberto. *Fascism and Fiction: A Survey of Italian Fiction on Fascism (and Its Reception in Britain and the United States)*. Lanham, MD: Scarecrow Press, 1987.

Trevelyan, Raleigh. *Rome '44: The Battle for the Eternal City*. New York: Viking Press, 1982.

Vance, William L. *America's Rome: Catholic and Contemporary Rome*. Vol. 1. New Haven, CT: Yale University Press, 1989.

Varricchio, Mario. "Il sogno e le radici: Nostalgia e legami transnazionali delle spose di guerra italiane." In *Lontane da casa: Donne italiane e diaspora globale dall'inizio del Novecento a oggi*, edited by Stefano Lucconi and Mario Varricchio, 115–147. Turin: Accademia University Press, 2015.

Verdirame, Rita. *Narratrici e lettrici (1850–1950): Le letture della nonna dalla Contessa Lara a Luciana Peverelli: Con testi rari e documenti inediti*. Padua: libreriauniversitaria.it, 2009.

Vertovec, Steven. *Transnationalism*. London: Routledge, 2009.

Villani, Paola. "The Redemption of the Siren." In *Sites of Exchange: European Crossroads and Faultlines*, edited by Maurizio Ascari and Adriana Corrado, 263–278. Amsterdam: Rodopi, 2006.

Vincent, Jonathan. "'America e Italia': U.S. World War II Novels and the Occupation of Italy." *Fictions: Studi sulla narratività* 13 (2014): 17–30.

———. *The Health of the State: Modern US War Narrative and the American Political Imagination, 1890–1964*. Oxford: Oxford University Press, 2016.

Vine, David. *Base Nation: How U.S. Military Bases Abroad Harm America and the World*. New York: Metropolitan Books, 2015.

Viscusi, Robert. "'The Englishman in Italy': Free Trade as a Principle of Aesthetics." *Browning Institute Studies* 12 (1984): 1–28.

Ward, David M. *Antifascisms: Cultural Politics in Italy, 1943–49—Benedetto Croce and the Liberals, Carlo Levi and the Actionists*. Madison: Farleigh Dickinson University Press, 1996.

Ward, Ray. *With the Argylls: A Soldier's Memoir*. Edinburgh: Birlinn, 2014.

Weisbord, Robert G., and Michael W. Honhart. "A Question of Race: Pope Pius XII and the 'Coloured Troops' in Italy." *Historian* 65, no. 2 (2002): 403–417.

Who Knows, and What, among Authorities, Experts and the Specially Informed. Chicago: A. N. Marquis & Co., 1954.

Wiblin, Ian. "Confronting the Void: Photographic Experience of the Naples Arcade." *History of Photography* 30, no. 2 (2006): 140–154.

Williams, Brackette F. *Women out of Place: The Gender of Agency and the Race of Nationality*. New York: Routledge, 1996.

Williams, Isobel. *Allies and Italians under Occupation: Sicily and Southern Italy 1943–45*. Houndmills, UK: Palgrave Macmillan, 2013.

Wilson, Edmund. *Europe Without Baedeker: Sketches Among the Ruins of Italy, Greece & England, Together with Notes from a European Diary*. New York: Macmillan, 1966.

Wilson, Sloan. *The Man in the Gray Flannel Suit*. New York: Simon & Schuster, 1955.

Wiltse, Charles Maurice. *The Medical Department: Medical Service in the Mediterranean and Minor Theaters*. Washington, DC: Office of the Chief of Military History, Dept. of the Army, 1965.

Winner, Percy. *Dario, 1925–1945: A Fictitious Reminiscence*. New York: Harcourt, Brace and Company, 1947.

Wright, Owain. "Orientalising Italy: The British and Italian Political Culture." In *Locating Italy: East and West in British–Italian Transactions*, edited by Kirsten Sandrock and Owain Wright, 33–57. Amsterdam: Rodopi, 2013.

Zeiger, Susan. *Entangling Alliances: Foreign War Brides and American Soldiers in the Twentieth Century*. New York: New York University Press, 2010.

Index

Abele, Robert, 148
An Act of Love (Litvak), 178n26
African American soldiers, 7–8, 12, 14, 115–123, 170n66
After the Lost Generation (Aldridge), 91
Aldridge, John, 91, 95, 177n5
Algiers (North Africa), 13, 98, 99–100, 105, 108
allegories of Allied Italian encounters: about, ix–x, 90; in diary entries, 155, 159–160; in *La pelle*, 112–115, 119–121, 123, 126–128, 130–131, 143–144; in *Paisà*, 43–44; post-liberation Naples described in terms of, 12, 14, 90, 112–115
Allied-Italian encounters, gender dynamics of: about, x, xi; in borderline spaces, 11 (see also *La lunga notte*; *Sposare lo straniero*); defined, 1–2; as financial transactions, x, 2, 5–6, 21 (see also Italian prostitutes); as horrors of war, 13–14 (see also *La pelle*); as rapes (see rapes); redemption paradigm for, 14–15 (see also *Naples '44*; redemption); through rebirth (see *Quel giorno trent'anni fa*; rebirth); through soldier tourism, 9 (see also destination Italy); through unresolved traumas, 9–10 (see also *All Thy Conquests*; Fosse Ardeatine massacre; *The Girl on the Via Flaminia*; *Paisà*); in transnational spaces, 13 (see also *The Gallery*)
Allied military guidebooks, 17–41; about, 8–9, 171n8; on culture and industries of Italy, 17, 30–31, 30–32f, 33–34; on false Italy, 8–9, 20–24, 25, 27–28, 40–41; on foreign language use, 21, 25–26, 37–40, 39f, 173n42; militarism and tourism juxtaposition in, 19–21, 25, 28–29, 36–37, 172nn16,18; on Naples, post-armistice, 112; on southern Italy, 33; on venereal disease, 22, 26–27; on women, 22, 26–27, 28, 31–33, 174n68, 175n70. See also *Guide to the Occupation of Enemy Territory—Italy*; specific "soldier's guide" and "pocket guide" titles
All Thy Conquests (Hayes): about, 42–43, 44–46, 177n5, 181n79; Caruso trial inclusion in, 10, 45–46, 50, 71–72, 90; critical interpretations of, 46; flashback use in, 44–45, 54; as liberation drama, 50–55; marketing strategy for, 55, 56f; *Paisà* comparison to, 42–43, 44–47, 54; sexualized interracial encounters in, 199n36
American Special Service Division (SSD), 18
American war novel: *All Thy Conquests* as, 43, 71–72, 90; *The Gallery* as, 91–92; Peverelli's novels as contrast to, 68–69, 71–72
anti-Semitism: in *La lunga notte*, 69, 72–73, 90; literary treatment of, 11; in *Sposare lo straniero*, 88, 90
armistice: as betrayal, 1, 4–5; as redemptive act, 1, 2–3, 167n2, 168n24
autofictional narratives, 12–13, 14. See also *The Gallery*; *La pelle*; *Naples '44*
Autumn Story (Landolfi), 125

Badoglio, Pietro, 3
Baldasso, Franco, 2, 3
Balestrini, Nanni, 73
Banti, Anna, 66–67, 73, 183n11
Bàrberi Squarotti, Giorgio, 128
Barolini, Teodolinda, x–xi
Barzini, Luigi, 132, 133
Battle of Monte Cassino, 114, 123
A Bell for Adano (Hersey), 169n55, 177–178n19
Ben-Ghiat, Ruth, 67, 80
Benjamin, Walter, 93, 94, 97, 106, 139, 193n27
Ben Jelloun, Tahar, 128
Bond, Emma, 93, 94, 96–97, 104–105
Bondanella, Peter, 178n20, 199n39
"borderline" texts: about, 11, 69, 170n63; *La lunga notte* as, 73–74, 75, 78; *Sposare lo straniero* as, 79–80, 87–88
Bouchareb, Rachid, 150
Bourke-White, Margaret, 22
Bracco, Roberto, 158
British government: colonialism legacy of, 7–8; on Italian occupation, 1–3; military guidebooks of, 18, 26, 174n51; on soldier–civilian sexual encounters, 7
Brooks, Peter, 97–98
Brophy, Brigid, 91, 93
Bruni, David, 177n14
Buchanan, Andrew, 19
buffalo soldiers, 7–8, 12, 14, 115–123, 170n66
Burns, John Horne: about, 91–92; travel articles by, 108–110, 109f, 196n110. See also *The Gallery*

Calvino, Italo, 183n18
Capella, Anthony, 205n6
Capponi, Carla, 184n18, 185n35
Carretta, Donato, lynching of, 45–46, 48–50, 52–53, 55, 178n34, 178–179nn36–37, 180n66
Carruthers, Susan, 1–2, 7, 8
Caruso, Pietro, 10, 45, 48, 49
Caruso trial and mob action: literary treatment of, 10–11, 45–47, 50–53, 55, 71–72, 180n56; media's treatment of, 48–50, 178n34, 178–179n36, 180n66; sentencing, 180n59; symbolic value of, 179n49
Casablanca (North Africa), 98–99, 108
Cassamagnaghi, Silvia, 7
Casualty (Lowry), 170n55
Catch-22 film adaption (Nichols), 148, 151
Cavani, Liliana, 125, 127f, 148, 149–150, 150f, 196–197n7, 198n25
Cecchi, Emilio, 91, 95, 128
Ciano, Galeazzo, 112
Clark, Mark, 1, 2, 47, 116
Coers, Donald V., 17
Cold War military guidebooks. See *Pocket Guide to Italy* (1952–87)
Coletti, Duilio, 150, 197n7
colonialism: in Allied military guidebooks, 19–20; fascism and, 29; Hayes on, 63–64; legacy of, 7–8; literary treatment of, 10, 12, 13, 14, 105; Malaparte's critique of, 126–128. *See also* Franco-Moroccan *goumiers*
contact zones, 12, 97, 105, 131, 167n1, 194n47
Cumberbatch, Benedict, 147

D'Annunzio, Gabriele, 66, 89
Dante Alighieri, writings of: conversion in, 133–134, 152; *Divina Commedia*, ix, x, 53; narrative structure of, 155, 158–159, 161; *The Gallery* comparison to, 13; *Naples '44* comparison to, 14; *Paradiso*, 134; *Purgatorio*, 4
D'Aquino, Maria Luisa, 153, 210n13. See also *Quel giorno trent'anni fa*
Days of Glory (Bouchareb), 150
defascistization, 48–49, 52
De Filippo, Eduardo, 150, 169n55, 196–197n7
De Marco, Paolo, 141, 204n4, 207n73
Depaola, Stephanie, 7, 199n40, 201n69, 202n72, 208n86
de Sica, Vittorio, 125
destination Italy, 17–41; about, 4, 5, 17–20, 171nn2–3; culture and industries of, 17, 30–31, 30–32f,

Index | 233

33–34, 35f, 36–37; as false Italy, 8–9, 20–24, 25, 27–28, 40–41, 172n16; language recommendations for, 21, 25–26, 37–40, 39f, 173n42; literary treatment of, 59, 62–63; as Oriental, 139–140, 144; redemption of, 19–20, 24–25, 27–30, 34–37, 40, 172nn18,21; souvenirs, 17, 18, 21, 40, 173n31; as transnational space, 105; women as, 58–59, 62–64, 65; women in, 22, 26–27, 28, 31–33, 68

diaries: autofictional narratives as, 12–13, 14; by Italian women, 153–154, 209n1, 210n13 (see also *Quel giorno trent'anni fa*)

Diggins, John P., 177n5, 179n36, 192n8

dragnets and mass medical exams, for prostitutes, 6, 44, 45f, 58–61, 120, 143–144, 169n43

Dunkirk (Nolan), 150

Eight Jews (Debenedetti), 68
Ellwood, David, 1, 5, 6, 84
Emberton, Carole, 3
The End of It (Goodman), 201n77
Enloe, Cynthia, 7, 19, 130
Evans, Julian, 133

Fabbri, Lorenzo, 46
fallen Italy. See Italy-as-whore
false Italy, in Allied military guidebooks, 8–9, 20–24, 25, 27–28, 40–41, 172n16
fascism: colonial aggressions of, 29; defascistization and, 49; Malaparte and, 112–113; military guidebooks on, 24–25, 27–28, 34–36; racist rhetoric of, 70, 71, 86–87, 118, 123; redemption from sin of, x, 2, 3, 8, 9–11 (see also Italy-as-whore); resistance movement against (see *Resistenza*); *romanzi rosa* tainted by, 67; Rome, as birthplace of, 47; as scapegoat in Allied military guides, 17, 20, 21, 24–25, 27–30, 34–36
Fenoglio, Beppe, 183n18
feminist movement: on female wartime experiences, 6–7, 155; on *romanzi rosa*, 11

financial transactions, x, 2, 5–6, 21, 156. See also Italian prostitutes

Fosse Ardeatine massacre: about, 10, 45, 179n45; cinematic treatment of, 50; literary treatment of, 9–10, 46, 51, 70–72

France: Allied military guidebooks on, 22–23, 32; colonialism legacy of, 7–8

Franco-Moroccan *goumiers*, 123–131; about, 14, 123–125, 201n77, 201n87; hand cannibalism scene, 126–131, 127f, 149; and homosexuality, 130, 146; mass rape by *goumiers*, 14, 145–146, 154, 201n69; as shorthand for indiscriminate violence, 7, 149–150

Freccero, John, 133, 158–159

friendship, redemption through, 11, 85–90, 191nn156–157. See also *Sposare lo straniero* (Peverelli)

Fuller, Margaret, 4

Fussell, Paul, 92, 194n50

Gallagher, Tag, 46
Galleria Umberto I: description of, 13, 92–93; as porous space, 94, 95–96; postwar, 108–110; as transnational space, 105, 106–110; womblike nature of, 103, 104

The Gallery (Burns), 91–110; about, 13, 91–93, 193n29; critical interpretations of, 91–92, 192n8, 195n69; Galleria as transnational space in, 105, 106–110; homosexuality in, 93, 96; *Naples '44* comparison to, 14, 132, 133, 135–136; narrative arc of, 12–13, 93–94, 95, 98–105, 107, 193nn29,31, 194nn48,50; porosity and, 94–98, 101–103, 106–108; queer redemption in, 13, 93–94, 96–97, 98–105, 110, 135

"The Gallery" (Marvell), 193n29
Garofalo, Anna, 120, 182n101
Gatt-Rutter, John, 194n50, 205n11
gender dynamics. See Allied-Italian encounters, gender dynamics of
Generale della Rovere (Rossellini), 72
Germany: Allied military guidebooks on, 24, 32, 32f, 33, 39f; Italy's betrayal of, 3, 4–5; occupation by, 1,

Germany (*continued*)
3, 10–11, 153–154 (see also *La lunga notte*; Naples; Rome, "liberated")
Gershovich, Moshe, 7, 124, 201n69
Giorni di gloria (Visconti), 50
Girgus, Sam B., 2
The Girl on the Via Flaminia (Hayes), 58–65; about, 47, 58–63, 178n26, 181n79; adaptations of, 68, 178n26, 181n79, 182n101; Hayes on, 62–64; Italian women as destination Italy in, 58–59, 62–64, 65
global humanism, 95, 97, 104–110
Glynn, Ruth, 15, 94, 97, 113, 167n1, 194n47, 196–197n7
Gobetti, Piero, 112
Gonzalez, Vernadette, 4, 19
"good Italians" (*italiani brava gente*), myth of, 9, 11, 63, 69, 105
Gordon, Robert, 10, 183n18
goumiers. See Franco-Moroccan *goumiers*
Gramsci, Antonio, 197n17
Guide to the Occupation of Enemy Territory—Italy (GOETI) (1943): about, 8, 17–20, 171n8, 174n50; on false Italy, 8–9, 20–24, 25, 27–28, 40–41; on foreign language use, 21, 37; invader-tourist juxtaposition in, 19–21, 172n16; on prostitution, 22–23
Guillaume, Augustine, 112, 126, 128

happy endings: melodramatic ending for *La lunga notte*, 74–78; melodramatic ending for *Sposare lo straniero*, 80–83, 85, 87–89; as *romanzi rosa* characteristic, 11, 64, 69, 183n8
Hayes, Alfred: about, 42–43; on destination Italy, 62–64, 65, 105; as *Paisà* collaborator, 10, 178n20. See also *All Thy Conquests*; *The Girl on the Via Flaminia*; "Italy—Enchantress of Writers"
Hegarty, Marilyn, 7
Heller, Joseph, 148
Hersey, John, 62, 169n55, 177–178n19, 192n8
Hipkins, Danielle, 44, 46, 170n63, 178n20, 184n23, 187n82, 190n141

History (Morante), 73
Hofmann, Paul, 178n34
Holiday (magazine), Burns's travel articles in, 108–110, 109*f*, 196n110
Holocaust: cinematic treatment of, 72; Italian involvement in, 69, 70; literary treatment of, 10, 11, 69–74, 84, 90, 183–184n18. See also anti-Semitism; Fosse Ardeatine massacre
The Holocaust in Italian Culture (Gordon), 183n18
homosexuality: cinematic representation of, 104, 170n67; literary representation of, 93, 96, 102, 146, 200n46
Hoover, Herbert, 2–3
Hotel Excelsior, in Rome, 6
Hughes, H. Stuart, 40–41

Il re di Poggioreale (Coletti), 150
Inside Rome with the Germans (Mary Saint Luke), 153–154, 209n1
Iovino, Serenella, 94
Italian immigrants. See Italian war bride narratives
Italian language: Allied military guidebooks on, 21, 25–26, 37–40, 39*f*, 173n42; as language of passion, 89; as "language of the moment," 101–102
Italian partisans, 3–4, 10, 29, 185n3; in *La lunga notte* 67, 68, 69–78, 80, 84; in *Paisà* 43, 50, 57–58, 65. See also Fosse Ardeatine massacre; *Resistenza*
Italian prostitutes: Allied military guidebooks on, 22, 26–27; epidemic of, 49; in Galleria Umberto I, 106; literary treatment of, 10, 14; mass medical exams for, 6, 44, 45*f*, 58–61, 120, 143–144, 169n43; in Naples, x, 5–6, 115–123, 141–142, 169n39; politicalization of, 22–23; wedding applications and, 136–137
Italian war bride narratives: about, 11, 14, 175n70; *The Gallery* as contrast to, 93, 192n15; media coverage of, 68, 184n22; nonfictional accounts, 184n19; redemption in, 81–83, 85–

90; suicides in, 79, 88, 191n48. See also *Sposare lo straniero*
Italian women: Allied military guidebooks on, 22, 26–27, 28, 31–33, 174n68, 175n70; as beyond redemption, 61–62, 63; as blame for Italy moral decay, 49–50; as "borderline spaces," 68–69 (see also *La lunga notte*; *Sposare lo straniero*); depiction of, 5–7; in destination Italy, 22, 26–27, 28, 31–33; as destination Italy, 58–59, 62–64, 65; feminist movement, 6–7; literary treatment of, 11, 14, 116–117, 170n63 (see also "borderline" texts); in *Resistenza*, 6–7; *romanzi rosa* as damaging to, 67; storytelling as redemption for, 85–90; as symbolic bearers of nations, 4–5, 11–12 (see also Italy-as-whore); wartime experiences of, 6–7, 32–33, 84, 153–155 (see also *Quel giorno trent'anni fa*)
Italy as whore: in Allied military guidebooks, 8–9, 20, 21–24, 25, 27–30, 172n18; in *All Thy Conquests*, 53–55, 65; fascism and, x, 2–3, 8, 9–11; gendering redemption and, 4–8, 106–107; in *The Girl on the Via Flaminia*, 58, 59–62, 65; in *La pelle*, 116–117; in *Paisà*, 55–58, 61–62, 86; redemption of, 4–5, 8–9, 64 (see also destination Italy)
"Italy—Enchantress of Writers" (Hayes), 62–64, 65, 105

Julius Caesar (Shakespeare), 50

Kadish, Mortimer, 125
Kaputt (Malaparte), 111–112, 114, 122, 126, 140, 183n18, 197n18
Karl, Frederick Robert, 194n50
Kundera, Milan, 113, 197n18

La Capria, Raffaele, 14–15, 128, 132, 171n75, 192n8, 203n102, 206n26
La ciociara (Moravia), 125
Lacis, Asja, 93, 94, 97, 139, 193n27
La lunga notte (Peverelli), 69–78; anti-Semitism in, 69, 72–73, 90; as "borderline" text, 11, 69, 73–74, 75, 78, 184n23; Holocaust narrative in, 69, 70, 72, 73, 183–184n18; lack of critical interpretation of, 69; melodramatic happy ending of, 69, 74–78; *Paisà* comparison to, 78; redemption in, 81–82; *Resistenza* in, 70–73, 74–75, 84, 183–84n18; as *romanzi rosa*, 67–70; sexualized encounters in, 72–73, 86; *vite romanzesche* (novel-like lives) quality of, 73–74
Lambiase, Sergio, 12, 125, 204n4
Landolfi, Tommaso, 125
language. See Italian language
La peau (French translation by Novella), 119
La pelle (Malaparte), 111–131; about, 111–115; adaptions of, 125, 127f, 148, 149, 150, 150f, 196–197n17, 198n25; critical interpretations, 113–114, 197nn17,18; *goumiers* depicted in, 125–131, 146; historical context of, 9, 12–13, 114–115, 117, 120, 123–126, 129–131, 198n25; *Naples '44* comparison to, 133, 140–146; *Paisà* comparison to, 122; sexualized interracial encounters in, 115–123
La storia (Morante), 73
Lejeune, Philippe, 205n9
Leopardi, Giacomo, 4, 59–60, 61, 136
Le quattro giornate di Napoli (Loy), 150
Life Magazine: on Carretta lynching, 48, 179n36; on liberation of Rome, 47; on *Paisà*, 55; on war brides, 68
Lilly, Robert, 7
Linklater, Eric, 124–125, 170n55
Litvak, Anatole, 178n26
The Long Night (Peverelli). See *La lunga notte*
Los Angeles Times, *Naples '44* film adaption review in, 147
Lowry, Robert, 170n55
Loy, Nanni, 150
Lucamante, Stefania, 73
Lyautey, Pierre, 112, 126, 204n104

Maghraoui, Driss, 7, 124, 201n71
Malaparte, Curzio, 112–113, 198n21. See also *Kaputt*; *La pelle*
Mann, Klaus, 43

Marcus, Millicent, 43, 98, 125
marriages, x, 11, 13. *See also All Thy Conquests*; *The Girl on the Via Flaminia*; Italian war bride narratives; *Paisà*; *Quel giorno trent'anni fa*; *Sposare lo straniero*
Marry the Foreigner (Peverelli). *See Sposare lo straniero*
Marshall, Samuel Lyman Atwood, 18, 171n8
Marshall Plan, 9, 27
Marvell, Andrew, 193n29
Mary Saint Luke (nun), 153–154, 209n1
mass medical exams, for prostitutes, 6, 44, 45*f*, 58–61, 120, 143–144, 169n43, 182n101
mass rape, 14, 145–146, 154, 201nn69,71
Matthews, Herbert, 47–49, 52–53, 178n34, 179n37, 180n66
McClintock, Anne, 4
McCormick, Anne O'Hare, 47–49, 52–53
medical exams, for prostitutes, 6, 44, 45*f*, 58–61, 120, 143–144, 169n43, 182n101
melodrama: defined, 65, 69; in film adaptation of *La pelle*, 125; in *La lunga notte*, 74–78; in *La storia*, 73; in "Rome" episode of *Paisà*, 43, 44, 46, 50, 57, 61, 65, 71, 151; in *Sposare lo straniero*, 80–83, 85, 87–89
men. *See* African American soldiers; buffalo soldiers; Franco-Moroccan *goumiers*; homosexuality; U.S. Fifth Army
Meneghello, Luigi, 184n18
Michi, Maria, 44, 55, 151*f*, 181n81
Mikula, Maja, 185n35
military guidebooks. *See* Allied military guidebooks
Minghelli, Giuliana, 44, 50, 179n45
mixed-race children, 12, 79, 88, 122, 130
Monte Cassino, Battle of, 114, 123
The Moon Is Down (Steinbeck), translations of, 67, 183n13
Morante, Elsa, 73
Moravia, Alberto, 125
Morocco, 98–99, 108. *See also* Franco-Moroccan *goumiers*

Moussorgsky, Modest Petrovich, 193n29
Mumford, Lewis, 178n34
Murch, Walter, 113, 198n21
Mussolini, Benito: deposition of, 1, 5; execution of, 114; foreshadowing death of, 53; military guidebooks on, 20, 23, 29–30, 34–36, 41
myths: about, 2, 3, 8–9; of colonialism, 128; gender myths of fascism, 11, 67; of "good Italians," 11, 63, 69, 105; of liberation and occupation, 10, 41, 44, 62, 71–72; of mass rape, 123–124; in military guidebooks, 17–20, 28, 36–37. *See also* "good Italians" (*italiani brava gente*), myth of

Naples: "liberation" of, 1–2, 167n7; literary treatment of, 12–15, 90 (see also *The Gallery*; *La pelle*; *Naples '44*); porosity of, 94–98, 106–108; post-armistice allegory of, 12, 14, 90, 112 (see also *La pelle*); post-armistice description of, 5–6, 12, 90, 112, 140–141, 153, 156; postwar description of, 108–110; pre-armistice description of, 111–112; prewar description of, 93, 94, 112, 139; prostitution in, x, 5–6, 115–116, 141–142, 169n39
"Naples" (Benjamin & Lacis), 93, 94, 139
Naples '44 (Lewis), 132–152; about, 132–135; adaptions of, 132–133, 135, 146, 147–151, 148–149*f*, 151*f*, 197n7, 205n6; conversion in, 133–140; critical interpretations of, 133; *The Gallery* comparison to, 14, 132, 133, 135–136; as historical source, 133, 141–146, 204n4, 205nn6,9; *La pelle* comparison to, 133, 140–146; narrative structure of, 12–13; plot of, 14; *Quel giorno trent'anni fa* comparison to, 155; rape scenes in, 125
Napoli Milionaria! (De Filippo), 150, 169n55
Nazzaro, Gian Battista, 204n4
neorealism: about, 10, 11; in Italian cinema, 43, 65; *Paisà* and, 44, 46, 65; Peverelli's novels as contrast to, 68–

Index | 237

69, 89–90; *romanzi rosa* comparison to, 65, 67, 70, 73
New York Review of Books: on *The Gallery*, 91–92; *Kaputt* republication by, 197n18
New York Times: on accuracy of *La pelle*, 141; *All Thy Conquests* review in, 177n5; on armistice, 2–3; "Italy—Enchantress of Writers" (Hayes), 62–64, 65, 105; on Italy's war declaration on Germany, 3; on military guidebooks, 174n50; *Naples '44* film adaption review in, 147; *Naples '44* review, 132; Rome's liberation coverage in, 1–2; on war brides, 184n22
Nichols, Mike, 148
Nolan, Christopher, 150
North Africa. *See* Algiers; Casablanca
northern Italians: Allied military guidebooks on, 33, 34, 40; self-redemption of Italy by, 3–4
Norton, Charles Eliot, 4, 134
Not so Wild a Dream (Sevareid), 6
Novella, René, 119

occupation: Allied governments' differing approaches to, 1–3, 5; Allied military guidebooks on, 17–19 (see also *Guide to the Occupation of Enemy Territory—Italy*); defined, 2; by Germany, 1, 3, 10–11, 153–154 (see also *La lunga notte*); myth of, 10, 41, 44, 62, 71–72; as redemptive, 3. *See also* Naples; Rome, "liberated"
October 16, 1943 (Debenedetti), 68
Operation Husky: about, 1, 8, 18. *See also Guide to the Occupation of Enemy Territory—Italy*
Origo, Iris, 153–154, 158, 159, 202n87, 209n2

Paisà (Rossellini): about, 42–43, 44; *All Thy Conquests* comparison to, 42–43, 44–47, 54; Caretta lynching omission from, 10, 45–46, 50, 53; critical interpretations of, 43–44, 46, 89; episodic structure of, 43–44, 61–62, 65, 178n20; flashback use in, 44, 45*f*, 177n14; Fosse Ardeatine massacre omission from, 71; *The Girl on the Via Flaminia* comparison to, 61–62; interracial encounters in, 199n36, 199n39; Italy as whore, 86; *La lunga notte* comparison to, 78; *La pelle* comparison to, 122; marketing strategy for, 55, 181n81; *Naples '44* film adaption with clips from, 151, 151*f*; prostitution in, 55–58, 65; reception of, 89; *Resistenza* in, 50, 57–58. *See also* Fosse Ardeatine massacre
Patierno, Francesco, 132–133, 135, 146, 147–151, 148–149*f*, 151*f*, 197n17
Peverelli, Luciana: about, 64, 65, 67–68; critique of, 66–67. *See also La lunga notte*; *Sposare lo straniero*
Pickering Iazzi, Robin, 67
Pictures at an Exhibition (Moussorgsky), 193n29
Pirro, Ugo, 179n45
Pocket Guide to France (1951), 32
Pocket Guide to Germany (1944), 24
Pocket Guide to Germany (1956), 32, 32*f*
Pocket Guide to Germany (1965), 33
Pocket Guide to Germany (1982), 39*f*
Pocket Guide to Greece (1966), 34
Pocket Guide to Italy (1952–87), 27–41; about, 8–9, 19, 20, 172n24, 175n75; cover of, 29*f*, 35*f*, 38*f*; on culture and industries of Italy, 30–31, 30–32*f*, 33–34, 35*f*, 36–37; on fascism, 27–28, 34–36; on Italian women, 28, 31–33; repression of militarism in, 28–30, 34–36, 63–64
Pocket Guide to Turkey (1981), 39*f*
Point of Honor (Kadish), 125
Ponzani, Michela, 7
porosity, of Naples, 94–98, 106–108
Porzio, Maria, 7, 175n70
Pratt, Mary Louise, 97, 194n47
Private Angelo (Linklater), 124–125, 170n55
prostitution. *See* Italian prostitutes; Italy-as-whore

queer redemption: narrative arc of, 13, 93–94, 98–105, 110, 135; transnation-

queer redemption (*continued*)
alism and, 13, 96–97, 104–105, 135, 171n73. See also *The Gallery*
Quel giorno trent'anni fa (D'Aquino), 153–161; about, 9, 152, 154–155; financial transactions in, 156; on liberation of Naples, 12, 153–154, 155–157, 160; *Naples '44* comparison to, 155; on rebirth, 154, 155–156, 158–161; self-characterizations in, 157–159, 212n42

Racconto d'autunno (Landolfi), 125
race dynamics: about, x, xi, 7–8; Allied-Italian encounters as, 125; literary treatment of, 14, 117–118; of sexual encounters, 12, 118–123, 130–131
rapes: Allied-Italian encounters compared to, x; literary treatment of, 10, 14, 84, 144–145; mass rape by *goumiers*, 14, 145–146, 154, 201nn69,71
realism, of *romanzi rosa alla Peverelli*, 68, 89
rebirth: of American soldiers, 13, 91, 136; in destination Italy, 19; of destination Italy, 6; of Italian women, 76–77, 81; in *Paisà*, 57, 65; of Rome, 74, 76–77; through writing diary entries, 15, 154, 155–156, 158–161
redemption: about, 2–4; armistice as, 1, 2–3, 167n2, 168n24; defined, 2–3, 8; from fascism, 2, 3, 8, 9–11 (*see also* Italy-as-whore); gendering, 4–8 (*see also* destination Italy; Italian prostitutes; Italy-as-whore); paradigm of, 14–15 (*see also Naples '44*); personal narrative of, 15 (*see also Quel giorno trent'anni fa*); queer, 13 (*see also The Gallery*; queer redemption); in romance novels, 11 (*see also La lunga notte*; marriage; *romanzi rosa*; *Sposare lo straniero*); Rome's "liberation" and, 9–10 (*see also All Thy Conquests*; *Paisà*; Rome, "liberated"); through porosity, 94–95, 96, 101–103; through tourism, 8–9 (*see also* Allied military guidebooks; destination Italy); of unresolved traumas, 9–10, 13–14 (*see also* colonialism; Fosse Ardeatine massacre; Holocaust; *La pelle*; mass rape; *Naples '44*; slavery legacy)
Regis, Pamela, 183n8
Resistenza (Resistance): cinematic treatment of, 50; literary treatment of, 70–73, 74–75, 84, 183–184n18; as "return to history," 67; self-redemption of Italy through, 2–4; women's role in, 6–7, 155, 184n18
Ricottini, Maria, 49
Ripa di Meana, Fulvia, 184n18
Roberts, Mary Louise, 7, 117
Rogin, Michael P., 179n45
Roma città aperta (Rossellini), 10, 43–44, 50, 70, 104, 179n45, 183n11, 184n18
romanzi rosa (romance novels): about, 11, 64, 65, 181n3; assumptions about, 67–68; happy endings in, 11, 64, 69, 183n8; melodramatic happy endings in, 74–78, 80–83, 85, 87–89; redemption through female storytelling in, 85–90. See also *La lunga notte*; *Sposare lo straniero*
Rome, "liberated," 42–65; about, 1–2, 10, 167n7; cinematic treatment of, 10–12 (*see also Paisà*; *Roma città aperta*); drama of, 50–53; literary treatment of, 10–12, 67–68 (*see also All Thy Conquests*; *The Girl on the Via Flaminia*; *La lunga notte*; *Sposare lo straniero*); media coverage of, 47–50; prostitution in, 5, 6, 55–58; redemption for, 42–45, 46, 50, 53–55, 61–62, 70–71, 74, 76–78; religious rebirth envisioned for, 154; women as exchangeable in, 58–61
"Rome" episode, in *Paisà*. See *Paisà*
Rossellini, Roberto, 43. See also *Generale della Rovere*; *Paisà*; *Roma città aperta*
Russo, John, 4, 206n19

Saint Paul, 134, 135–140
Schoonover, Karl, 46, 71, 181n81
Sciascia, Leonardo, 171n10

Scrivener, Jane. *See* Mary Saint Luke (nun)
Serra, Ilaria, 68
Sevareid, Eric, 6
sexualized figures and sexual encounters: about, x, 4, 169–170n55, 170n67; in *All Thy Conquests*, 53–55; and colonialism, 12; destination Italy as, 64; in *La lunga notte*, 76–78; in *La pelle*, 118–123; in *Paisà*, 55–58; queer redemption through, 93–94, 96–97, 98–105, 135; race dynamics and, 12, 118–123, 130–131, 170n66; in *Sposare lo straniero*, 78–79; women as bearers of national symbolism, 4–5, 11–12 (*see also* Italy-as-whore)
Shakespeare, William, 50
The Sicilian Specialist (Lewis), 125
Sicily: Allied military guidebooks on, 20–24, 27; description of, 20–21; invasion of, 1, 17, 18, 27
Skin (Malaparte). *See La pelle*
Slant, *Naples '44* film adaption review in, 148
slavery legacy: about, 3, 7–8, 105, 180n66; literary treatment of, 10, 14, 105, 199n39
Smith, Derek, 148, 208–209n96
Soldier's Guide to France (1944), 22–23
Soldier's Guide to Italy (September 1943), 8, 20, 24–27, 37, 174n51
Soldier's Guide to Naples (1944), 112
Soldier's Guide to Sicily (British issued), 18, 26, 171n10, 175n85
southern Italians, 4, 33, 34, 40, 175n85. *See also* Naples; Sicily
Sposare lo straniero (Peverelli): about, 11, 67–70, 83–84; anti Semitism in, 88, 90; as "borderline" space to investigate Italian identity, 11, 69, 79–80, 87–88; Holocaust in, 84; marketing strategy for, 79; melodramatic happy ending of, 69, 80–83, 85, 87–89; redemption in, 81–83, 85–90, 191nn156–157; as *romanzi rosa*, 67–70; sexual encounters in, 78–79, 84–85, 86–87, 170n63
Steinbeck, John, 67, 183n13

Suckert, Edda Ronchi, 197n17
Suckert, Kurt Erich. *See* Malaparte, Curzio
survivor narratives, 73–74

Tanzi, Cornelia, 49–50
Teresa (Zinnemann), 68
That Day Thirty Years Ago (D'Aquino). *See Quel giorno trent'anni fa*
Thompson, Luke Y., 148
Togliatti, Palmiro, 180n66
tourists and tourism. *See* destination Italy
transnationalism: about, 12–13, 14; Galleria as transnational space, 106–110; porosity of Naples and, 94–98, 106–108; queer redemption through, 13, 96–97, 104–105, 135, 171n73; war brides narrative as example of, 86–88, 90
traumas, unresolved, 9–10, 13–14. *See also* colonialism; Fosse Ardeatine massacre; Holocaust; *La pelle*; mass rape; *Naples '44*; slavery legacy

U.S. Fifth Army, 47
U.S. government: colonialism and, 13; guidebooks on Italy (*see* Allied military guidebooks; destination Italy); Italian foreign policy, 1–4, 5, 10, 19; prostitution report for, 5–6; slavery legacy and, 3, 7–8, 47, 53, 105; on soldier–civilian sexual encounters, 7

Vance, William, 179n36
Variety, *Naples '44* film adaption review in, 147
Varricchio, Mario, 93, 184nn19,22, 191nn148,157
venereal diseases: Allied military guidebooks on, 22, 26–27; literary treatment of, 58, 116–117, 120; mass medical exams for, 6, 44, 45f, 58–61, 120, 143–144, 169n43
via Rasella, 70, 71, 185n35
Viganò, Renata, 184n18
Village Voice, *Naples '44* film adaption review in, 148
Vincent, Jonathan, 101–102

Vine, David, 36–37
virgin-whore, 114–115, 118–123, 131, 142, 143–144
Visconti, Luchino, 50
vite romanzesche (novel-like lives), 73–74
Vittorini, Elio, 183n18

war-as-hell allegory, ix–x
War in Val d'Orcia (Origo), 153–154
The Wedding Officer (Capella), 205n6
Weissberg, Jay, 147
whores. *See* Italian prostitutes; Italy-as-whore
Wiblin, Ian, 106, 193nn27,31
Williams, Brackette F., 121
Within the Labyrinth (Lewis), 125, 138, 170n56, 208n83

women. *See* feminist movement; Italian prostitutes; Italian war bride narratives; Italian women
World War II Italy: about, 1–4, 29–30; English literary representations of, ix–xi (*see also* Allied military guidebooks; *All Thy Conquests*; *The Gallery*; *The Girl on the Via Flaminia*; *Naples '44*); Italian literary representations of, ix–xi (see also *La lunga notte*; *La pelle*; *Quel giorno trent'anni fa*; *Sposare lo straniero*); Italian cinematic representations of, ix–xi (see also *Paisà*)

Zeiger, Susan, 81

Marisa Escolar is Assistant Professor of Italian in the Department of Romance Studies at University of North Carolina, Chapel Hill.

WORLD WAR II: THE GLOBAL, HUMAN, AND ETHICAL DIMENSION
G. Kurt Piehler, series editor

Lawrence Cane, David E. Cane, Judy Barrett Litoff, and David C. Smith, eds., *Fighting Fascism in Europe: The World War II Letters of an American Veteran of the Spanish Civil War*

Angelo M. Spinelli and Lewis H. Carlson, *Life behind Barbed Wire: The Secret World War II Photographs of Prisoner of War Angelo M. Spinelli*

Don Whitehead and John B. Romeiser, *"Beachhead Don": Reporting the War from the European Theater, 1942–1945*

Scott H. Bennett, ed., *Army GI, Pacifist CO: The World War II Letters of Frank and Albert Dietrich*

Alexander Jefferson with Lewis H. Carlson, *Red Tail Captured, Red Tail Free: Memoirs of a Tuskegee Airman and POW*

Jonathan G. Utley, *Going to War with Japan, 1937–1941*

Grant K. Goodman, *America's Japan: The First Year, 1945–1946*

Patricia Kollander with John O'Sullivan, *"I Must Be a Part of This War": One Man's Fight against Hitler and Nazism*

Judy Barrett Litoff, *An American Heroine in the French Resistance: The Diary and Memoir of Virginia d'Albert-Lake*

Thomas R. Christofferson and Michael S. Christofferson, *France during World War II: From Defeat to Liberation*

Don Whitehead, *Combat Reporter: Don Whitehead's World War II Diary and Memoirs*, edited by John B. Romeiser

James M. Gavin, *The General and His Daughter: The Wartime Letters of General James M. Gavin to His Daughter Barbara*, edited by Barbara Gavin Fauntleroy et al.

Carol Adele Kelly, ed., *Voices of My Comrades: America's Reserve Officers Remember World War II*, Foreword by Senators Ted Stevens and Daniel K. Inouye

John J. Toffey IV, *Jack Toffey's War: A Son's Memoir*

Lt. General James V. Edmundson, *Letters to Lee: From Pearl Harbor to the War's Final Mission*, edited by Dr. Celia Edmundson

John K. Stutterheim, *The Diary of Prisoner 17326: A Boy's Life in a Japanese Labor Camp*, Foreword by Mark Parillo

G. Kurt Piehler and Sidney Pash, eds., *The United States and the Second World War: New Perspectives on Diplomacy, War, and the Home Front*

Susan E. Wiant, *Between the Bylines: A Father's Legacy,* Foreword by Walter Cronkite

Deborah S. Cornelius, *Hungary in World War II: Caught in the Cauldron*

Gilya Gerda Schmidt, *Süssen Is Now Free of Jews: World War II, The Holocaust, and Rural Judaism*

Emanuel Rota, *A Pact with Vichy: Angelo Tasca from Italian Socialism to French Collaboration*

Panteleymon Anastasakis, *The Church of Greece under Axis Occupation*

Louise DeSalvo, *Chasing Ghosts: A Memoir of a Father, Gone to War*

Alexander Jefferson with Lewis H. Carlson, *Red Tail Captured, Red Tail Free: Memoirs of a Tuskegee Airman and POW, Revised Edition*

Kent Puckett, *War Pictures: Cinema, Violence, and Style in Britain, 1939–1945*

Marisa Escolar, *Allied Encounters: The Gendered Redemption of World War II Italy*

www.ingramcontent.com/pod-product-compliance
Lightning Source LLC
Chambersburg PA
CBHW030438300426
44112CB00009B/1061